Fourth Edition

Early
Childhood
Education

Fourth Edition

Early Childhood Education

Developmental/Experiential Teaching and Learning

Barbara Day

University of North Carolina
Chapel Hill

Merrill, an imprint of
Macmillan College Publishing Company
New York

Maxwell Macmillan Canada
Toronto

Maxwell Macmillan International
New York   Oxford   Singapore   Sydney

Editor: Linda Sullivan
Production Supervisor: WordCrafters Editorial Services, Inc.
Production Manager: Aliza Greenblatt
Text Designer: Linda Zuk
Cover Designer: Curtis Towe Designs
Photo Researcher: Anne Vega
Illustrations: Academy ArtWorks

This book was set in Palatino by Americomp,
and printed and bound by Book Press.
The cover was printed by Phoenix Color Corp.

Macmillan College Publishing Company
866 Third Avenue, New York, New York 10022

Macmillan College Publishing Company is part of the Maxwell Communication Group
of Companies.

Maxwell Macmillan Canada, Inc.
1200 Eglinton Avenue East, Suite 200
Don Mills, Ontario M3C 3N1

Library of Congress Cataloging-in-Publication Data
Day, Barbara (date)
    Early childhood education: developmental/experiential teaching
and learning / Barbara Day. — 4th ed.
        p.   cm.
    Includes bibliographical references (p.   ) and index.
    ISBN 0-02-327923-0
    1. Open plan schools—United States.   2. Creative activities and
seat work.   3. Early childhood education—United States—Curricula.
I. Title.
LB1029.06D39   1994
372.21—dc20
                                                          93-37977
                                                          CIP

Printing: 2   3   4   5   6   7   Year: 8   9   0

To our Daughter Susan,
who brings us pride, love, and happiness
and helps us live our lives with a deep inner joy and peace;

and

To our Godchildren: Billy, Beth, David, Andrew, Vince, John, Rachel, and Barbara
who celebrate life with us
and help us enjoy the many good things our world has to offer;

and

To our first God-grandchild, Anderson,
a very special little person who enriches us all;

and

To the many young children everywhere,
especially two wonderful nephews, Jennings and Matthew,
whose lives are made fuller by caring teachers
who know and practice developmentally appropriate
teaching and learning.

Preface

Early Childhood Education: Developmental/Experiential Teaching and Learning, fourth edition, is designed to help early childhood teachers, administrators, and curriculum specialists provide a developmentally appropriate learning environment for young children ages 4 to 8. Such a learning environment is based on the following principles:

- Appropriate curriculum stimulates learning in all developmental areas: physical, social, emotional and intellectual.
- Learning experiences are designed to support individual differences in ability, interest, development, background, and learning style.
- Learning experiences provide children with the opportunity to actively manipulate and explore materials. Hands-on learning strategies emphasize the acquisition of higher-order critical thinking skills as opposed to drill and rote memorization.
- Curriculum is designed to provide children with choices of many concrete and relevant learning experiences. If learning is relevant for children, they are more likely to persist with a task and are more motivated to learn.
- Learning opportunities are presented predominantly in learning centers, where children work individually, and in small groups as opposed to whole-group instruction.
- Learning is viewed as integrated, and opportunities to develop math, science, and literacy skills can occur simultaneously rather than in discrete segmented lessons. Units of study and topic work are used to present related and integrated curriculum. (NAEYC, 1990)

Designing, organizing, and managing a developmentally appropriate learning environment for young children is a complex task, one that requires careful planning and organization of both the curriculum and the classroom environment. Effective curriculum organization consists of:

1. A variety of learning centers containing experiential activities that accommodate children's individual developmental levels and learning styles

2. Skills groups that are used for direct instruction in specific curriculum areas

3. Integrated approaches (i.e., units of study, thematic approaches, extended interest areas) that incorporate curriculum content across many subject areas to make learning meaningful and useful within the broad context of the child's world.

Systematic organization and management structure the environment to facilitate learning within such a curriculum. Color coding, contracts, and social-behavioral discipline methods are three effective organization and management techniques. Color coding learning centers and the materials, books, and activities within them creates order in a complex environment by enabling children to independently identify, work with, and replace materials. Contracts, written plans for each child's day, enable teachers to individualize learning experiences and plan a balanced program. Contracts also enable children to stay on task independently and to develop initiative and responsibility in carrying out assignments and selecting free-choice activities. Finally, effective social-behavioral classroom management techniques help minimize discipline problems and develop children's self-responsibility and control.

Three characteristics of developmentally appropriate learning environments—active, involvement, experience-based learning, and individualization—are essential for effective learning. Children learn by doing, and therefore the curriculum is structured to promote their active participation. Learning centers provide a variety of experiences through which children can actively seek and discover knowledge about themselves, build on previous learning, and stimulate new learning and experiences. Teachers structure and guide the learning process based on their knowledge of the abilities and background of each child. Because children have unique developmental needs, learning styles, and interests, teachers tailor the learning process to fit each child. In a developmentally appropriate learning environment, where caring teachers systematically plan and organize individualized learning experiences, each child can be creative and discover the many joys that learning has to offer.

Many historical precedents lend credibility to this developmental/experiential approach. The European educator Pestalozzi (1746–1827) proposed that the young child learns best through activity and sense perception. Pestalozzi's learning through discovery approach influenced Froebel (1782–1852), the "father of the kindergarten," who proposed that the curriculum reflect the interests, impulses, and capacities of the specific group of children involved. Froebel observed that play is the child's main vehicle for learning, and he further proposed that a curriculum for young children be based on the child's natural desire to play and discover. Experiential learning values and utilizes play as a natural process of discovery. Maria Montessori (1870–1952), Italian physician and educator, stressed the use of a prepared environment to meet children's need to order and organize their world. Montessori recommended and used active involvement of children in the learning process, multi-age grouping, and self-correcting materials, all features that have been incorporated in the developmentally appropriate classroom.

John Dewey (1859–1952), a major figure in the progressive education movement, advocated many of the same principles associated with developmental/experiential learning. The expression of individual pupil interest, learning through experience, and the acquisition of skills necessary for success in everyday life are but a few of the principles that Dewey found necessary for a sound learning experience. These principles, along with those expressed by Pestalozzi, Froebel, Montessori, and Piaget, validate the concept of experiential learning. It is not merely another education fad or a flash-in-the-pan approach; rather, it is an approach based on traditional philosophies relating to the education of young children. And it works!

An early childhood learning environment should be a comfortable, colorful place where children and adults can live together in a happy and relaxed atmosphere. This environment can be designed for large complexes where teachers work together in teams, or it may be designed for self-contained developmental classrooms. The inside area should be carpeted, if possible, and large enough to allow for fluidity of movement and also to provide space for large- and small-group activities and individual activities. The space should be flexible enough to provide small areas for special tutoring or quiet, individual, or small-group activities. There should be many windows, and there should be easy access to the outdoors, which is a vital part of the total learning environment.

Learning centers or areas provide the core of an early childhood learning environment; this book discusses eleven such centers. The discussion of each learning center includes: environmental resources, materials (commercial and teacher-made), objectives, and suggested activities. The suggestions for each center are a sample of appropriate activities, and are not intended to be all-inclusive. Basic books and other resource materials will continue to be part of the total program.

The possibilities for centers are limitless. Centers should contain self-correcting activities at various levels of difficulty that require a minimum of teacher direction. An attractive center invites investigation and provides opportunities for children to learn through exploration. Some centers may be prepared by the teacher to accomplish a specific objective. Others may be an eclectic arrangement of interesting items where children find their own purposes. Still other centers may be assembled spontaneously to meet the particular interest of the moment.

An important element of this environment is its flexibility. Activities flow from one area to another, and every possibility for optimal use of space is explored. There may, of course, be physical limitations, depending on the design of the structure; but whenever possible, the flow should include the outdoors, halls, a parent room or space where parents are involved with children, and perhaps a cooking area. Learning centers and areas should be well planned to allow ease of movement and accessibility.

The organization of the learning areas changes with changing needs. Often the curriculum is evolving, rather that prescriptive. Choice is provided, depending on the needs and interests of each child. Children demonstrate responsibility as they move from center to center and complete the assignments. Children and adults are caring and sensitive to each other, and there is an atmosphere of trust and structured freedom.

How might developmental/experiential early childhood learning environments appear to an observer? Imagine yourself visiting an environment like this one for the first time. You have heard of an open learning environment such as the one you are about to visit, but somehow you feel that it will be different from the verbal descriptions. You finally reach the building, and you are impressed by what you see:

Outside the K–1 multiage classroom is a busy patio with children engaged in a variety of activities. Two children are building a log cabin with a kit of large linking boards. Next to them, two more children are creating their own rolling toy with a giant set of plastic nuts, bolts, wheels, and tools. At the sand and water tables, children are pouring, mixing, and molding. An "interstate highway" winds its way around and through the tables and tools as two "highway engineers" construct a roadway with bridges, cars, and trucks. Bubbles float through the air, drifting over from children at a small picnic table equipped with soap solution and wands. One meditative child rides a rocking seesaw alone, while on another seesaw, a girl and a boy rock higher and higher. On the waterway "canals," boats float in the sun waiting for the next ship's "captain" to come along. A small basket holding balls and jump ropes attracts the attention of a small boy.

Inside, the classroom hums with energy, yet the noise level remains low. Small cubbies filled with games, books, and materials divide the large room into child-sized nooks and spaces. Colorful bulletin boards display children's drawings, stories, and projects. Children move purposefully from place to place as they finish one activity and start another. In one corner, children are balancing blocks, feathers, sponges and crayons on a scale. Beside them, four children are engaged in a cooperative sorting activity. First, they determine the criteria for their groupings. Will the arrangement be based on size, shape, color, or kind? The tub full of attribute blocks lends itself to a variety of arrangements. The children reach an agreement; the groups will be sorted first by shape and then rearranged by color.

In the writing corner, the teacher assistant reads a poem, "Mommies" by Nikki Giovanni, to a six-year-old girl. The child then starts her own "Mommy" poem: "Mommies make you eat spinach and carrots. But I like them anyway!" She adds a picture of her own Mommy to the page.

Next to her, a five-year-old boy is cutting and pasting a silhouette of Abraham Lincoln. The assistant moves over to him and writes as he dictates, "Abraham Lincoln was a famous president." On the floor, three other five-year-olds make up their own fairy tale by arranging picture cards.

Two small cars whiz past as experiments with inclined planes take place in the science center. In the block corner, another log cabin is taking shape as its two builders discuss whether or not Abe Lincoln needed a chimney to go along with his fireplace.

At an easel, a rainbow of red, green, and pink valentines appears beneath the brush of a little boy. At the nearby table, a variety of heart designs are taking shape in the hands of several young artists.

Puzzles and board games occupy some children, while inside a wooded structure, one child reads a book of riddles to a large stuffed rabbit. The classroom teacher chats with two children serving plastic cupcakes, scrambled eggs, and ice cream to the stuffed animals and dolls in the dramatic playcorner. "Is this brunch?" she asks, adding a brief definition of the term. The children giggle with delight and invite another friend in for "brunch."

The teacher moves around the room, collecting a small number of children for math skills work. She settles down with them on the floor in an area of the room reserved for group work. The children create equivalent and nonequivalent sets using a colorful collection of small toys. Then they try drawing their own equivalent sets.

A group of children now gathers with the teacher in the work/study area and begins a language/reading skills group. These first graders plan an oral game using consonant blends and complete reading assignments from a variety of books. Each child then adds a picture and story page to his or her booklet on famous African Americans. Today's emphasis is on African-American inventors and scientists. Astronauts begin to appear along with illustrations of huge ice cream sundaes in honor of Alfred Cralle, the inventor of the ice cream scoop.

Another small group is organized, ready to begin a whole language activity with a "big book." Today's selection, *Clifford, the Big Red Dog*, is greeted with excitement as a stuffed version of Clifford participates in the reading of the story.

In another corner cubbies are filled with reference books. One child uses the playground page in the Sesame Street Word Book to identify a variety of simple machines such as the slide, the seesaw, and the swing. Yet another child has the *Afro-Bets Book of Black Heroes* open to the page on Mary McLeod Bethune, known for establishing her own school. This child is meticulously designing her own schoolroom on drawing paper.

The lights blink in the classroom and the children respond to this signal to clean up. Materials are returned to shelves, papers put in folders, crayons and pencils sorted and put away. A few children keep working, clearly intent on adding the final touches to their projects. Children retrieve folders from small boxes placed in each center. They get out their contracts and check off completed tasks. Rainbows of color-coded charts hang in each learning center. Center "helpers" double-check the clean-up job completed by their peers. Within five minutes, the entire class has gathered in the homebase circle area and is enjoying a brief appearance by Mr. Elephant, a thoroughly grouchy and hungry puppet. Mr. Elephant reminds everyone that it is, indeed, lunch time.

Lunch is followed by story time, singing, and share time. While the children listen to *An African Tale, Mufaro's Beautiful Daughters*, a parent volunteer is setting up a special presentation. Using an egg beater and cookie cutters, both designed by African-American inventors, she will engage the children in cooking and eating no-bake peanut butter fudge. Recipes are given to each child so that they may try this treat at home. They will also have the opportunity to enjoy the benefits of the ice cream scoop—as a gallon of lime sherbet is scheduled to be divided equally.

The children then return to either learning centers or small groups until the Spanish teacher arrives for a twenty-minute session with everyone. After a final *adios* from Carlos, the children are ready for a brief rest time. Some children find a cozy spot and read quietly. Others lie down to rest; some take a short nap. Meanwhile, the teacher quietly calls each child to a sunny corner of the room, and together they look over the contract, the work in the child's folder, and any other projects the child wants to share. They talk about the day's experiences and plan for tomorrow. After rest and conferences, it's time for outdoor play. Today, the parachute is out and excited cries greet the ups and downs of the chute as children try to avoid being draped in its folds. (Day, 1992)

What is this experience about? What does it tell you about this classroom? It is an experiential learning environment to be sure, but what does it mean? In essence, it is a rich, developmentally appropriate learning environment where children are surrounded with the artifacts of reading, writing, and mathematics. They are constructing their own understanding of letters, words, and numbers through a variety of interesting learning activities based on each child's natural abilities, interests, and enthusiasm for learning. Skilled teachers carefully observe the children and offer appropriate challenges. The wealth of materials and experiences are carefully organized and children are encouraged to be independent, to follow directions, to be self-motivated, to explore, to inquire, and to discover. Of utmost importance is the joy of learning that these children are experiencing.

This fourth edition includes all curriculum areas designed around learning centers, complete with objectives, materials, activities, and experiences for children and a theoretical overview for each.

Major emphasis is given to organizing and managing a developmentally appropriate learning environment for young children. This includes guiding the behavior of all children, including those with exceptional needs. Curriculum organizational components and classroom management components are presented in detail. Curriculum area chapters are:

- Communication: The Language Arts
- The Fine Arts
- Home Living and Creative Dramatics
- Investigation in Science and Mathematics
- The Social Studies: A Mulicultural Emphasis
- Sand and Water Play
- Blocks
- Woodworking
- Movement

- Outdoor Play
- Early Childhood Classroom Designs

The practical nature of this text extends into two areas of great importance today that were not presented in previous editions.

- emphasis on authentic/alternative assessment; and
- technology for young children

Additionally, there are two new chapters emphasizing historical, philosophical, and sociological perspectives in early childhood education and developmental/experiential learning.

This book is intended to aid you in helping young children find joy and challenge through a variety of developmentally appropriate learning activities.

Acknowledgments

We extend special recognition and many thanks to the teachers and administrative staffs of the Frank Porter Graham Child Development Center; University of North Carolina, Chapel Hill; the Jeffreys Grove School; Wake County School System, Raleigh, North Carolina; and the Elizabeth Seawell Elementary School, the Glenwood Elementary School, the Estes Hills Elementary School; Chapel Hill-Carrboro City Schools, Chapel Hill, North Carolina, the Montessori Day School, North Carolina; the Overton Pre-School; Carolina Friends School, Chapel Hill, North Carolina; the Duke School for Children, Durham, North Carolina; Kiddlington Infant School, Oxford, England; the Eno Valley Elementary School, Durham County Schools, Durham, North Carolina; Hickory Grove Elementary School, Charlotte-Mecklenburg Schools, Charlotte, North Carolina; Demonstration Classroom, the University of North Carolina at Chapel Hill; Creswell Elementary School, Creswell, North Carolina; North End Elementary School, Roxboro, North Carolina; and Havelock Elementary School, Havelock, North Carolina, for their cooperation and support in allowing most of the photographs in this book to be taken in their classrooms and learning centers; to *The Chapel Hill News*, and photographer David Surowiecki for his photograph; and to the faculty and staff of New Hope Elementary School.

Thanks also to graduate students in early childhood education and colleagues including Karen Castor, Anetta Davenport, Kay Drake, Knox Efland, Corinne Farmer, Anne Hauser, Camille Lore, Jessica Persinger, Kim Powell, Melanie Price, Marki Pringle, Heather Rice, Elizabeth Russell, Torrey Templeton, Sabrina Tyndall, Connie Weil, Nancy Whitaker, and Yolanda Woodhouse.

A special debt of gratitude is extended to Dave Peloff at the University of North Carolina, Chapel Hill, for his tireless dedication and invaluable contributions in the production of this book. Thanks also to Barbara Smith and Janine Castro, graphic artists, for the excellent illustrations throughout this book.

We appreciate the helpful comments and suggestions of the following reviewers: Rebecca Bailey, University of Central Florida; Michael E. Knight, Kean College of New Jersey; Ruth McBride, Colorado State University; Lorraine Shanoski, Bloomsburg University; Patricia Waters, Towson State University; and Tim Wilson, University of Central Arkansas.

Brief Contents

Contents

Developmentally Appropriate Learning

Overview: Developmental/Experiential Learning

Young children grow, develop, and learn at different rates. Some 5-year-old children are ready to grasp a pencil firmly and begin letter formation, while other children of the same age have difficulty maintaining any hold on a pencil. Fine-motor skills and other physical competencies vary according to each child's developmental level. Cognitive, social, and emotional capabilities vary as well. For example, one child might cling desperately to her mother before the onset of school, while another child joyously bounces through the door without a backward glance. What challenges do early childhood educators face with such a diverse population?

First and foremost, early childhood educators attend to the *whole* child: the child's physical, social, emotional, and cognitive development. A definition of developmentally appropriate practice for children from birth to age 8 by The National Association for the Education of Young Children (NAEYC) identifies two dimensions of developmentally appropriate practice (Bredekamp, 1987):

1. Age appropriateness. A predictable sequence of growth and development characterizes young children, and developmentally appropriate learning environments attend to what we know about how young children grow, develop, and learn.
2. Individual appropriateness. Developmentally appropriate practice affirms that each child is unique, with individual differences. Appropriate learning environments not only recognize this uniqueness, but also reflect individual differences in the curriculum and experiential learning experiences offered to each child.

In the Association for Supervision and Curriculum Development's, *A Resource Guide to Public School Early Childhood Programs* (Day, 1988a), administrators and teachers are challenged to take the broadest possible long-term perspective in defining and addressing programming challenges—the most important challenge being to focus on the individual needs of young children. Schools must have the resources and opportunities they need to provide children with the following:

Children grow and develop at different rates and those rates are often unrelated to chronological age—so say these five-year-olds.

- A comfortable, safe, and stable environment every day, year round, for all of the hours that parents are at work.
- Consistent and nurturing care and education.
- The opportunity to be physically active.
- Opportunities to explore and meaningfully interact with the world around them.
- Opportunities to interact with, learn from, and be appreciated by other children.
- Stimulation and support to develop cognitively, socially, emotionally, and physically in their own time and in their own ways.

In addition to the NAEYC and the Association for Supervision and Curriculum Development (ASCD), the National Association of Elementary School Principals (NAESP) has offered guidelines and tenets for states, school districts, boards of education, principals, parents, and concerned citizens interested in the establishment and conduct of a high-quality educational program for young children. Related to developmentally appropriate teaching and learning, NAESP suggests that above all "the curriculum responds to the different learning and developmental needs of young children" (1990, p. 31). Based on both firsthand, day-to-day experience and extensive research into how young children learn, the following principles are taken as fundamental:

1. Throughout the preschool years and into the primary grades, the curriculum should be presented in an integrated format rather than in 10- or 20-minute segments for each content area. Toward that end it should be planned around themes, with the themes being developed through learning centers in which the children are free to plan and select activities to support their individual learning experience.
2. Children in preschool through primary grades should be engaged in active—rather than passive—learning activities. The curriculum must be seen as more than a program purchased from a publisher.
3. Spontaneous play, either alone or with other children, is a natural way for young children to learn to deal with one another and to understand their environment. Play should be valued and included in the program plan.
4. Because children come to school with different knowledge, concepts, and experiences, it is important that new learning be connected to something that is known and relevant (NAESP, 1990).

In summary, the young child learns differently from the older child, and this difference is not only acknowledged, but informs the educator about appropriate learning environments for the young child. Knowledge of child development forms the cornerstone of any high-quality early childhood education program (Bredekamp, 1987).

The Developing Child

Piaget's theory of cognitive development (Piaget, 1950; Piaget & Inhelder, 1969) forms the foundation for developmentally appropriate practice. According to Piaget, children's cognitive development evolves in a series of stages. For children 2 to 7 years old, the preoperational stage of development links their learning to direct interaction with their environment. Children in this stage are eager learners, constantly exploring, manipulating, and experimenting with the environment in order to learn more about it (Day, 1992a).

Preoperational children share a set of unique characteristics as learners. Since young children learn by doing, developmentally appropriate practice calls for concrete, real, and relevant learning activities (Bredekamp, 1987). Active learning that allows children to explore, inquire, and discover is important.

Learning that promotes interaction with adults and peers facilitates the emotional and social development of the young child. Egocentrism characterizes young children, and this inability to see a situation from another person's view changes with social interactions. As children form friendship ties with significant others, they begin to comprehend and appreciate another's viewpoint. Additionally, young children engage in egocentric speech, which Piaget (1950) considered a useful tool for them to make sense of their world. Egocentric speech reflects a child's inner dialogue and is verbalized by the learner. It often occurs during play, and as the child grows it becomes a silent, inner dialogue. Finally, young children are unable to consider more than one aspect of a situation at a time. This inability to "decenter" was first noted by Piaget. Children cannot be taught how to decenter. Rather, they gradually develop this ability through their interaction with the environment.

Play, according to Piaget (1950), is an ideal vehicle for developmental/experiential learning. Through play, young children solve problems and acquire enriched meaning for language and ideas, while expressing and meeting their emotional needs. They try out new roles and activities with confidence and success. Large- and small-motor skills develop as children freely move about during play. More sophisticated social skills result as they interact with peers and adults (Bredekamp, 1982).

Play is the hallmark of creativity. Piaget explains that children's ideas are the cumulative integration of what they know with the new material that they are learning (Drake & Sher, 1992). Play promotes this ongoing process. Play presents opportunities for children to identify problems and then create their own problem-solving strategies. Their skills of evaluation and synthesis develop as they use their imagination and toy with ideas (Mayesky, Neuman, & Wiodkowski, 1985).

Education during the preoperational stage of development must match the developmental and experiential needs of the young learner. In the Piagetian view, when children reach the ages of 7 to 9 the preoperational stage of development gradually gives way to concrete operational thought. Then children begin to have the capacity to think about and solve problems in their heads. Although still rooted in concrete experiences, they are better equipped to use words and symbols for problem solving (Day, 1992a). Yet, while children remain in the preoperational stage, their ability to master the tasks of this stage is best promoted by active learning environments.

The contributions of Piaget, as well as the other early childhood educators discussed in Chapter 1, pave the way for developmentally appropriate practice. Pioneers in the education of young children articulated the unique needs of the young child. During the last decade, the National Association for the Education of Young Children and the Association for Supervision and Curriculum Development have issued policy statements clarifying developmentally appropriate practice for young children.

Practical Implications for the Learning Environment

Learning environments that demonstrate developmental and experiential compatibility with the unique needs of young children share three characteristics: (1) They promote active involvement, (2) they are individualized, and (3) they are child centered (Day, 1992a).

1. Young children learn by doing. They learn through exploration and discovery, using all of their senses. The optimum learning environment promotes active participation and provides many opportunities for children to see, feel, hear, smell, taste, and touch.

2. The unique, individual needs of children are recognized. Differences among young children are evident, and these differences guide instruction. Developmental levels, learning styles, family backgrounds, and children's interests are among the factors that help formulate the learning environment.

3. A child-centered approach that focuses on children's total development, supporting cognitive, social, affective, and physical growth, best serves the young child. Developmentally appropriate practice (Bredekamp, 1987) characterizes this child-centered focus.

Teacher's Role

The role of the teacher in a developmental/experiential learning environment is that of facilitator. The teacher carefully sets up the learning environment and creates a positive atmosphere in the classroom. The teacher expresses joy in learning and models curiosity. The teacher becomes an explorer to learn along with the children, and learning is seen as a common enterprise.

The teacher provides feedback to the children that is specific and descriptive, but not evaluative. Encouraging children to take ownership of their own learning helps them motivate themselves and places the locus of control within the child. An emphasis on success, with an acceptance of errors as a natural part of the learning process, gives children confidence to try without fearing failure.

Several strategies help teachers promote an experiential learning environment where children feel free to explore and investigate readily. Trostle and Yawkey (1981) developed the following seven strategies for teachers whose goal is to foster play and creativity in their classroom (Day, 1988b):

1. **Physical cues.** Teachers permit children to use the objects they want to use. Teachers provide and help children find materials that are interesting, useful, and safe.

2. **Playfulness.** When teachers act out creative roles, children will soon model the process. For example, when teachers express enthusiasm about a science phenomenon, the children will begin to emulate the excitement and express curiosity.

3. **Exploration.** Teachers provide time for children to explore new objects and materials before using them in creative thinking.

4. **Oral Cues.** Teachers use "idea sparkers" to expand creativity. For example, the teacher asks a child playing with a doll how he might show the doll walking to the store to buy bread.

5. **Descriptions.** Teachers elaborate on what the children have already said and make it more visually descriptive.

6. **Modifying objects.** Teachers remove objects that have lost their creative appeal and change them to make them more interesting.

7. **Adding objects.** During children's role playing, teachers provide additional relevant objects that the children may assimilate into their creative play.

positive feedback - building self-esteem

The teacher as a facilitator carefully monitors the learning environment while giving the children space to play alone, with peers, or within their imaginary worlds. Hovering over children decreases their spontaneity and creativity. In contrast, a teacher who is appropriately attentive recognizes the "teachable moment" and may ask a provocative question or offer an alternative problem-solving technique to help children expand their thinking processes. The teacher's rigorous work in preparing the learning environment makes optimum developmental/experiential learning possible.

The following characteristics of learning environments best provide developmentally appropriate and experiential learning opportunities.

The Developmental/Experiential Learning Environment

To evaluate whether or not they are providing an optimum developmental/experiential learning environment, teachers should ask themselves the following questions. (For a complete checklist, see Day, 1988b, Chapter 13).

- Do you focus on the *total* child, the child's cognitive, affective, physical, and social development?

- Is your curriculum organized around the developmental needs, learning styles, and needs of each child, rather than around a time schedule, a curriculum guide, or textbooks?
- Do you encourage active participation of each child and foster observation, exploration, and expressive activities through writing and artwork?
- Do you focus more on the process of learning than the content of learning? Are you more concerned with *how* the curriculum is taught than *what* is taught? (Day & Drake, 1983, 1991)

Learning environments that are developmentally appropriate promote the active experience of learning. Just as important as teacher behavior and special teaching strategies is the general environment in which learning occurs. If a safe and stimulating environment is provided that fosters creativity, then children will naturally learn.

Naturally inquisitive, children venture out, relate to the environment, and learn that the environment reacts to them. Their perceptions of the positive or negative reactions to their probings determine the likelihood of future investigations and their understanding of the limits within that environment. Limits channel children's energies and help them make sense of how the world operates. The teacher's task is to construct a learning environment that welcomes exploration and has meaningful and necessary limits, rather than arbitrary limits that inhibit creativity.

An appropriate setting has several environmental characteristics. Maxim (1985) has listed the following environmental conditions that stimulate creativity among children:

1. Time limits are removed from activities in which children are deeply involved.
2. A free, open atmosphere is established where open expression is encouraged.
3. The children are allowed to share ideas and to stimulate one another's thinking.
4. Conditions producing stress and anxiety are removed from the environment.

The structural framework recommended for a developmental/experiential learning environment consists of a variety of learning centers with materials and activities that engage children's unique developmental abilities and interests. The organizational and management techniques suggested—color coding, contracts, and behavioral-social management techniques—give children the support, security, and confidence to learn effectively and creatively.

Developmentally appropriate practice is best implemented in learning environments that foster continuity among early childhood educators and the children they teach. Teachers best meet the needs of young children if they are well acquainted with the children's cognitive, affective, and physical needs. Hence, when serving young children, familiarity is essential. Since children grow, develop, and learn every day, they require a teacher who observes them carefully and then uses those observations to provide an optimum learning environment for each child.

To ensure retention of high-quality infant and preschool caregivers, teachers must be given adequate salaries with accompanying benefits. Unfortunately, staff retention has been and will continue to be a challenge for providers of care for young children.

For elementary-age children, The National Association of State Boards of Education (NASBE) recommends that elementary schools establish early childhood units to more effectively group children ages 4 to 8 (Schultz, 1988). Early childhood units allow for continuity. Teacher teams and mentor teachers stay with a multiage grouping of young children throughout their early primary years. Most elementary schools group children by their birthdates, with the assumption that age is a major determinant of intellectual, social, and motor readiness. Multiage grouping offers an alternative structure for children to build skills in an interactive, developmentally appropriate context (Webb, 1992).

Children who are provided with a developmental/experiential learning environment are more apt to draw upon their innate creativity than those who do not have access to such an environment. Concrete materials and activities in learning centers stimulate and foster children's natural desire to explore and learn about themselves and the world around them.

The benefits of a setting that is developmentally appropriate are immeasurable for the children and teachers involved. Children want to try new ideas and experiences, and they will express themselves freely (Mayesky et al., 1985). In an environment that values and enhances the development of their individuality and their potential for creative thinking and learning new skills, children will feel good about themselves and will fully experience the joy of seeking and finding many solutions to life's challenges. Teachers will experience the joy of developing closer relationships (and having fewer discipline problems) with children, appreciating the uniqueness and individuality of each child, and helping children realize their full creative potential.

Chapter 1

Early Childhood Education: A Historical Perspective

Early childhood education has a rich history. Its roots began with the dawn of humankind. When societies expend time, energy, and resources caring for children, this expenditure involves education. *Education*, which derives from the Latin *educare*, literally means "to lead out." Educators of young children share a long tradition of caring for and drawing out children's innate gifts. Nurturing and enhancing the creative potential of each child especially interests early childhood educators.

Throughout history, differing views of young children have shaped educational practices. In ancient times, the young child was often considered as property with few rights. In recent times, the well-being of the young child has been increasingly recognized and fostered.

An understanding of the unique heritage of early childhood education provides insights about how the past informs present policies and practices and instills a sense of commitment to young children and to the profession. Today's early childhood educators can gain clarity regarding future directions by drawing upon the pioneer work of earlier educators whose legacy they share.

Ancient Greece to the Renaissance

In ancient times, young children were neither respected nor nurtured. On occasion, Greek and Roman parents practiced infanticide, favoring the survival of firstborn and male children (Lay-Dopyera & Dopyera, 1993). The schools of ancient Greece, initiated by Socrates, Plato, and Aristotle, catered to male children from wealthy families. Formal schooling for all other children was nonexistent. Instead, education for young children revolved around rituals in which they learned their respective societal roles. This was most often done through dances, storytelling, ceremonies, and apprenticeships.

Ancient people viewed children as miniature adults who differed only in quantitative ways. Children were seen as smaller, weaker, and less intelligent versions of adults. Works of art from the period bear witness to this fact, depicting children as undersized adults.

Cruel and harsh handling often accompanied this misunderstanding of children. During medieval times (the 5th through the 13th centuries), most children were put to work soon after they reached 7 years of age. Farm work, mining, and later factory work took children away from their homes and any available schooling.

The Renaissance (late 1300s and early 1400s) and Reformation (14th through 16th centuries) gradually brought about a more universal view of education. The Medieval Church made schooling available for students from common backgrounds. Reading, writing, and arithmetic instruction became the norm, although schooling was riveted on the agenda of the Church.

The turn of the 16th century ushered in exciting times for the Western world. Prominent leaders emerged in education, and they introduced a new understanding of the young child. Today's education of young children derives from the thought and work of the men and women who pioneered new ways of seeing how children think, learn, and create.

European Educators

During the early 1600s, John Amos Comenius (1592–1670), a Czech educator, laid the foundation for later educators. He believed in the natural development of children and encouraged teachers to observe and work within this natural order. In 1658, he wrote and illustrated the first picture book for children, called *Orbis Pictus* (*The World of Pictures*).

Following along Comenius's emphasis on the natural order, Jean Jacques Rousseau (1712–1778) recognized the natural goodness of children. Rousseau, a native of Geneva, was a social philosopher and writer. In his classic book *Emile*, he described how a fictional child, Emile, would be raised in a natural island environment. Rousseau wrote of the futility of imposing an adult perspective on children. He contended that education serves children best when it recognizes their innate goodness and follows their unique interests and activities. Today's child-centered education owes its inception to Rousseau and his early writings on children's innate wisdom.

Johann Heinrick Pestalozzi (1746–1827), a Swiss educator, also believed in the natural goodness of children. Pestalozzi stressed the development of the senses, as well as the teaching of basic skills. Pestalozzi's educational theories were based on *Anschauung*, a German word that means "perception" or "observation." He felt that all true knowledge comes from observing objects, people, and moral situations. Hence, learning by actively using the senses was an important cornerstone for Pestalozzi.

Pestalozzi encouraged teaching children in groups and allowing children to work with one another. A caring, home-like environment was esteemed, since Pestalozzi recognized the importance of a nurturing home. His writings, *How*

Gertrude Teaches Her Children (1801) and *Book for Mothers* (1803), explained to caregivers how to put his thought into practice. He not only wrote about education, but also opened an Education Institute in Bergdorf, Switzerland, where he offered teacher preparation and influenced students from all over Europe. One such student was Froebel.

A German born educator, Friedrich Wilhelm Froebel (1782–1852) is considered "the father of the kindergarten." He coined the term *kindergarten*, which in German means "children's garden." Like a garden, he believed children should be nourished and cared for. Play was an important component in his kindergarten. He created the first educational toys, or "gifts," as he called them, and fostered their use in children's play. He also incorporated the use of fingerplays. Like Pestalozzi, Froebel started a teacher-training program.

Another German educator, Rudolf Steiner (1861–1925), born in Austria, founded the Waldorfian approach to education. Commissioned by a German industrialist, Steiner set out to design a school that would promote a peaceful, just society. His first school opened in Germany in 1919. Its inclusivity was novel for its time; it educated all socioeconomic classes and genders. Today, over 400 Waldorfian schools make this the most common approach to private schooling in the United States and abroad.

Maria Montessori (1870–1952), the first Italian woman trained as a medical doctor, worked among poor children in the slums of Rome. There she identified the importance of proper care for young children. In 1907, she opened a preschool, Casa dei Bambini (Children's House), where she designed the materials and teaching procedures. Her work soon spread throughout Europe and the United States. Today's Montessori schools are tributes to her name and principles.

Montessori placed great emphasis on having a prepared environment. She believed that children pass through "sensitive periods" during which their curiosity propels them to acquire particular knowledge and skills. Hence, the environment is crucial to promoting the proper setting for learning to take place. She affirmed early educational emphases on the importance of sensory development. To this end, most of her educational materials were tactile, to challenge the senses as well as the mind.

Jean Piaget (1896–1980), a Swiss psychologist, formulated a theory of intellectual development based on his academic work and parenting experience with his three children. Piaget's work deepened the understanding of young children and confirmed many assumptions of the early educators who came before him. For these reasons, the profession of early childhood education is forever indebted to him.

Piaget's theory (1950) posits that children progress through four stages of learning: the sensorimotor stage (birth to age 2); the preoperational stage (2–7 years); concrete operations (7–11); and formal operations (11–15). According to this "constructivist" view, children *construct* knowledge through their experiences with concrete objects and through social interactions.

Learning is an *active* process. For Piaget, children learn by doing. Play serves as an ideal vehicle for learning to take place. As an intrinsic motivator, play helps children perceive learning as fun, achieve a sense of mastery, and discover truths on their own. The teacher acts as a facilitator by setting up conditions for learning to occur and then by fostering children's innate curiosity.

America's Legacy in Early Childhood Education

In Colonial America, education served primarily religious purposes. The early Puritan leaders wanted children to attain literacy in order to read the Bible. In some towns, the same person served as minister and teacher, and classes often were held in the community church.

Eventually, communities built one-room schoolhouses and hired one teacher to teach children across a wide range of ages. Learning conditions were harsh, with buildings inadequately heated. Often, children had to walk long distances to attend school. Instruction focused on rote learning and memorization of facts. Discipline was unreasonably shameful and often physically cruel.

As in European countries, education in the forming American Union was segregated along gender, socioeconomic, and racial lines. For example, education for white male children was valued, whereas the education of females and children from minority groups was considered less important. During the years of African-American enslavement, education was virtually nonexistent for African-Americans (Gordon & Browne, 1993). After the Civil War, private and public schools opened but remained segregated by race. Finally, by 1954, a unanimous decree by the U.S. Supreme Court ruled that segregation of African-American and white students in public education was unconstitutional (Brodinsky, 1976).

U.S. Educators

In 1779, Thomas Jefferson introduced a document titled *A Bill for the More General Diffusion of Knowledge* to the state of Virginia. Jefferson proposed that universal education be made available to all free children at the expense of the state. His plan proposed a 3-year elementary education emphasizing basic skills for both genders. Although this bill was not passed in Virginia, it inspired future leaders in education (Brodinsky, 1976).

One such leader, Horace Mann (1796–1859), is considered the father of public education in the United States. As secretary of the Massachusetts State Board of Education, Mann lobbied for a compulsory education law. In 1852, Massachusetts enacted the first law, with other states following suit. Mann's insistent belief that "free education is the birthright of every American child" bore fruit when illiteracy rates in the United States quickly fell to a level lower than that of any other industrial nation.

In 1855, the first American kindergarten opened in Watertown, Wisconsin. Its originator, Margaretha Schurz, studied with Froebel, and she conducted the kindergarten entirely in German. The first English-speaking kindergarten was opened in Boston by Elizabeth Peabody (1804–1894) in 1860. This private kindergarten was soon followed by the first public kindergarten, located in St. Louis. Susan Blow (1843–1916) was chosen to organize a classroom in 1873, and her success led to the establishment of more than 50 public kindergartens in St. Louis.

The crowning victory of kindergarten proponents occurred at the 1876 Centennial Exposition in Philadelphia, where a model kindergarten drew crowds of spectators. Children were seen creating, playing, and working together, rather than sitting in rows reciting and memorizing tasks. The innovative demonstration spurred the spread of kindergartens throughout the United States.

Both Stanley Hall (1844–1924) and his student, Arnold Gesell (1880–1961) initiated the scientific study of the development of young children. Hall, an educator and psychologist, anecdotally recorded developmental stages of children. His interests led him to apply the results of his investigations to teaching.

Gesell, a psychologist inspired by his mentor Hall, began to systemically observe and analyze child development. He found that children's behavior follows developmental patterns. His research laid the foundation for other developmental works, the more popular among them authored by Benjamin Spock and Terry Brazelton.

John Dewey's (1858–1952) famous dictum, "learning by doing," influenced the Progressive Movement in U.S. education. As a professor of philosophy who once taught school in his native Vermont, he sensed that there were better ways to prepare children to live responsibly. For Dewey, the goal of education is to help children to live cooperatively. Education, he believed, is a "process of living," and schools should be a microcosm of society. To this end, according to Dewey, schools should focus on real-life skills and be child centered.

The nursery school movement in the United States began in New York City in 1919 with the Bank Street College of Education. Lucy Sprague Mitchell (1878–1967), one of the pioneers in implementing Dewey's Progressive Movement for young children, blended theory with practice and opened a nursery school connected with Bank Street's laboratory school. Soon after, Abigail Eliot, who had worked with the McMillan sisters in England, where the nursery school movement began, became director of a school and training center for early childhood educators in Boston.

Early Childhood Education in the 20th Century

The momentum for early childhood programs grew during World War II when nearly one-third of American women worked in war-related jobs. Through the Lanham Act (1940), federal legislation provided funds to set up schools for the care of young children. After the war, funding for the child care centers ceased, and the Lanham Act war nurseries were dismantled. Women were encouraged to return to the home, while men received priority for employment outside the home (Roopnarine & Johnson, 1993).

In 1957, when the Russians launched their first missile, Sputnik, the United States reviewed its educational edge. Montessori preschools reappeared. The Progressive Movement gained recognition, and the open classroom became more common.

In 1965, as part of the nation's "War on Poverty," Project Head Start was funded to counteract the effects of poverty among children. Head Start is a preschool program that targets low-income children from 3 to 5 years of age. Presently, Head Start reaches 400,000 children each year; many more children living in poverty have needs going unmet (Slavin, Karwait, & Madden, 1989). Research on Head Start confirms that it is a cost-effective, successful program to help combat poverty. Every $1 spent in high-quality preschool programs saves $6 in costs for subsequent public assistance, crime, and special education.

Longitudinal studies confirm Head Start's academic achievements. Children participating in Head Start have higher literacy rates than other children from low socioeconomic backgrounds. They are more likely to secure employment and seek postsecondary schooling than their counterparts who are not enrolled in Head Start. In 1991, Head Start served about one in four eligible children (Guy, 1991).

High-quality child care remains a dire need in the United States. Changing societal patterns have created more demand for early education of young children. By the year 2000, 7 in 10 preschool children will have mothers who work outside the home (Children's Defense Fund, 1990). Private, church, and synagogue-related centers typically have more requests than they can fulfill. This great demand, also felt by Head Start, is sure to increase in the future.

Despite the fact that it is an emerging political issue, adequate funding for affordable, high-quality child care lacks federal and state initiatives. Moreover, there is much diversity among centers in the quality of care. Typically, teachers of young children receive exceptionally low pay and few benefits. Retaining consistent staff members is a continuing challenge for centers that have limited resources (Child Care Employee Project, 1989).

Two child advocate associations strive to professionalize the field of early childhood education. The Child Development Association (CDA) began in 1973, and the NAEYC grew to 77,000 members in 1991. NAEYC instituted the National Academy for Early Childhood Accreditation (NAECA), which helps early childhood programs conduct self-improvement studies to receive recognition for quality. In 7 years, nearly 1,800 programs have been accredited by the Academy (Roopnarine & Johnson, 1993).

NAEYC has developed a position statement on developmentally appropriate practice (Bredekamp, 1987). The statement defines appropriate practice for infants; toddlers (about 1–3 years); 3-year-olds; 4- and 5-year-olds; and primary grade children (5–8 years). This comprehensive statement draws from child development theory and research compiled through the years.

An optimum creative learning environment draws upon the seven intelligences, according to Howard Gardner (1983), a contemporary developmental psychologist. These intelligences are linguistic, mathematico-logical, musical, spatial, kinesthetic, interpersonal, and intrapersonal. Gardner believes in the importance of careful observation of young children by parents and teachers, allowing children to reveal their intellectual potential naturally (Goleman, Kaufman, & Ray, 1992).

Creative learning settings not only provide optimum learning opportunities for children to develop their curiosity and creativity, but also give teachers wonderful opportunities to observe children as they work and play. Developmentally appropriate settings are becoming increasingly important as educators develop and implement "authentic" assessment. Measurement-driven instruction that stresses rote learning and isolated skills is being replaced by instruction that recognizes the diverse developmental capabilities of children. The cultural heritage and innate gifts of each child are more likely to be identified and drawn out in learning environments that employ developmentally appropriate curriculum, teaching, and assessment (Bracey, 1987).

Pioneers in the education of young children have demonstrated the value of fostering creative learning settings. When the rich tradition of early childhood education is acknowledged, teachers of young children more readily contribute to the well-being of the children they serve. With careful observation and reflection, educators build upon this tradition of caring for and nurturing young children and pave the way for future educators. The challenge remains to hone the craft of providing the best creative learning setting possible to draw out the innate qualities of every child.

Guiding Child Behavior and Organizing and Managing the Learning Environment

Prosocial behaviors are most likely to appear in children who live in a nurturing environment, where understanding and caring are modeled, where responsibility is expected, and where inductive reasoning is used . . . [where] adults help children see the consequences of their behavior on other people through logic and reasoning.

E. Essa, Introduction to Early Childhood Education, 1992

Developmentally appropriate guidance of children's behavior focuses on helping them develop a positive self-concept; a sense of responsibility, motivation, self-control, dignity, and respect for each other; the ability to cooperate with others; and problem-solving skills. Positive discipline, control theory, and child guidance are discipline methods that have the attributes that make up a meaningful discipline program.

Positive Discipline

Efforts have been made by many professionals—educators and psychologists included—to abolish traditionally negative notions of discipline by suggesting alternative methods of guiding child behavior. The positive discipline approach (Nelsen, 1987) is one such alternative. Placed on a continuum with strict forms of discipline at one end and total lenience on the other, positive discipline falls somewhere in the middle. This method of disciplining offers children choices that are bounded by fair limits. Together, the child and the teacher decide on the best course of action to pursue in the instance of inappropriate behavior. Often this involves deciding on an alternate way of handling the problem situation, as well as an opportunity to practice the new behavior. Having had an influence on the way discipline will affect him or her, the child will be more likely to accept the alternate behavior and adopt it in future situations.

Positive discipline is also concerned with social contributions that children can make. Teachers who use positive discipline must encourage the children to help others as much as they can and to do things for their peers as well as for their families and elders. Children are not merely told what to do and how to do it. They are part of the effort to come up with ways they can help, and they have opportunities to practice their ideas; thus, they understand why it is important to become a contributing member of society.

In addition, Nelsen (1987) has emphasized the significance of the feelings of belonging and love in children's lives, both at home and in school. This does not mean that the teacher has to show open love and affection for every child all of the time. However, just letting them know that their input is appreciated ("I really appreciate your helping me take down the bulletin board." "What a great idea!") and acknowledging their accomplishments ("I can tell you put a lot of effort into your drawing." "Wow! Look at the improvement you've made between your last two assignments") signify to the students that someone cares. This awareness of children as individuals can also be communicated through nonverbal means such as eye contact, a pat on the shoulder, proximity to their bodies, and smiling. It is the teacher's responsibility to point out children's strengths, rather than their weaknesses.

Control Theory

Another method of discipline, control theory, forms a foundation on which to base a successful discipline program. This theory does not explain control in the traditional manner. According to Glasser (1990), children cannot be controlled by adults. It is useless to make students do what they do not want to do, because they will not gain any meaning from something they feel they were forced to do. One way to reduce children's feelings of frustration and boredom is to make learning tasks relevant to them. This can be done by assessing their interests and using them to plan learning activities and by relating what is going on in the classroom to relevant events in the outside world.

Another way to alleviate students' feeling of helplessness is to empower them to begin to accept responsibility for their own behavior, rather than coercing them. In order to become less of a coercive teacher, or what Glasser (1990, p. 31) calls a "boss manager," and more of a noncoercive teacher, or "lead manager," the teacher must take the following five steps:

1. Make school work developmentally appropriate and related to the children's interests.

2. Demonstrate your expectations and gather input from the children as a better means to the end result.

3. Ask the children to look over their own work to see whether they have done the best they can do.
4. Act primarily as a facilitator and guide.
5. Figure out a viable solution with the children if a problem should occur.

Control theory is based on the assumption that people strive to control their behavior throughout their lives in order to satisfy their five basic needs—survival, love, power, freedom, and fun. Children often choose to do only those things that satisfy one or all of these basic needs. Teachers must try to understand these needs as they exist in each child so they can guide children in ways that will lead them to more self-controlled behaviors. From birth on, all children recognize the need to struggle in order to survive, but they also need to feel love and a sense of belonging. Teachers convey love and belonging through simple and consistent gestures and verbal expressions. The child's need for power and success can be broken down into three levels:

1. The need to feel that someone who is respected is listening to what the child says. Otherwise, attention may be gained in antisocial ways.
2. The need to be assured that what the child says matters (e.g., "You're right!").
3. The need to have others say, at times, that their way may not be the best and the child's may be better. (This level is not necessary, but it is nice to have.)

There is also a need for a certain amount of freedom and independence, although children acknowledge and accept the need for a rule system. The final basic need, for fun, is satisfied when the needs for love, power, and freedom are met. Glasser (1990) insists that all of these needs can and should be met in schools.

Child Guidance

According to proponents of the child guidance approach who also believe in positive discipline, the intent of disciplining children should be to help them establish self-control and develop a high self-concept. Children should be guided toward more appropriate and constructive behaviors. Gartrell (1987) has proposed taking the following seven steps to a firmly established child guidance approach:

1. Use preventive techniques. *example: rearange room*   *example take toy away*
2. Seek to understand the individual child.
3. Strive to understand the situation.

4. Develop a solution orientation approach to problems.
5. Respond clearly in problem situations.
6. Reconcile the situation.
7. Recognize your humanness.

Use Preventive Techniques

- Make sure the children are active learners so boredom does not occur.
- Reinforce all positive behavior; do not always call attention to negative behavior.
- Act as a professional and be willing to try a variety of discipline measures.
- Form close relationships with children to cheer them on during the good times and offer support during the rough times.
- Provide extra orientation time for explaining classroom rules, routines, and procedures for those who need it.
- If children seem bored, change the activities.
- Make sure children are not left waiting with nothing to do during transitions.
- Involve restless children first in activities.
- Use aides or parents to help with children who are easily distracted.

Seek to Understand the Individual Child

- Take into account the ages of the children; sharing and taking turns are difficult for 3 to 7 year olds.
- Consider the needs of the children; children meet their needs in different ways.
- Be aware of family situations; family crises affect the way children learn.
- Be familiar with the three levels of mistaken behavior:

The experimentation level: Children will try out different pronunciations of a word trying to come up with the correct one. If the word is a "bad" word, encourage the children to practice alternative words that are acceptable at school.

The social habit level: Children learn a certain behavior and use it because they think it is suitable. Teach the children appropriate behaviors to substitute for inappropriate behaviors. Do not punish them.

The deep emotional needs level: Children who are distressed about many aspects of their lives may respond in an exaggerated and angry way to different and, perhaps, minor situations. Try to understand the source of their anger.

Strive to Understand the Situation

- If a problematic incident has occurred, do not jump to conclusions; try to gain as much information as possible by asking a series of questions regarding the nature of the situation (e.g., whether or not it was an accident; whether the children can solve the problem themselves or need the teacher's assistance).
- When dealing with a group, do not single out one child, but deal with the general situation. Instead of saying "There you go again, Jenny, splashing water from the water table all over the floor," say "Let's all use the water table gently so the water doesn't go over the edge."

Develop a Solution Orientation Approach to Problems

- Avoid just telling the children what *not* to do. Offer them a practical and workable solution so that the next time a problem arises they will know how to handle it.
- Let children handle minor problems on their own to increase their problem-solving skills.

Respond Clearly in Problem Situations

- Adjust the degree of authority, according to the severity of the problem.
- Ensure the children's freedom of choice and responsibility.
- If the use of words does not work and a threat of physical harm is imminent, provide children with a cooling off time by removing them from the problem situation (i.e., timeout). Removal should not be out of the room or for long periods of time.
- Restrain children, if necessary, by using a gentle but firm bear hug until they calm down and the problem can be discussed and understood.

Reconcile the Situation

- If the use of restraint or removal is necessary, reconcile the situation as soon as possible.
- Discuss the situation after everyone involved has calmed down and the children have returned to the group.
- Allow the children to talk about the situation from their perspective.
- Focus the discussion primarily on facts, not on inferences.
- Allow the children to return to the group in one of several ways: when they feel ready, after a previously set timer goes off, or with some adult encouragement.

- Avoid forcing children to say they are sorry; they need time to think things through.

Discipline Problems

Even with the implementation of straightforward disciplining measures, discipline problems will occur. The following are examples of common problems and suggestions for their remediation (Clewett, 1988):

1. *Using inappropriate language.* Teach the children alternative words to replace the inappropriate ones.
2. *Name calling.* Tell the children the child being teased would like to be called by his or her appropriate name.
3. *Speaking when the adult is speaking during group time.* Remind the children that it is the adult's turn to speak and they will have their chance. Do not forget to be consistent and give the children an opportunity to speak.
4. *Ignoring clean-up.* Give everyone his or her own job to do and offer to help.
5. *Using loud voices.* Tell the children you cannot hear when they are speaking too loudly because it hurts your ears.
6. *Playing in the bathroom.* Let the children know that playing is not appropriate in the bathroom, but guide them to areas where it is appropriate.
7. *Leaving the room without permission.* Ask the children to let you know where they are going ahead of time.
8. *Abusing materials.* Demonstrate the proper way to handle materials and channel the children's abusive behavior into more constructive outlets—for example, from spreading glue all over their desks to gluing pictures onto a piece of paper.
9. *Engaging in continued disruptions or temper tantrums.* Remove disruptive children from the situation, but stay with them until they cool down.

Children with Special Needs

Children with behavior difficulties are often the victims of abuse or neglect and therefore require special attention from teachers. While all children can benefit from greater self-esteem, the abused or neglected child desperately needs to be given opportunities to develop a sense of self-worth. By developing a personal relationship with and understanding of a troubled child, the teacher can play a vital role in instilling self-confidence.

One of the greatest challenges for early childhood teachers is dealing with an abused or neglected child. The key is to identify the possible existence of abuse or neglect and to take an active interest in a child's social and educational development. Recognizing the special needs of these children is the first step in instilling in them the self-confidence that is vital for their survival in an abusive environment.

Two major categories of problem behaviors are commonly found in abused or neglected children: aggressive behavior and shy or withdrawn behavior. Different approaches should be used with each.

Aggressive Behavior

Balancing the overall need to have a safe, inviting learning environment and the individual needs of an aggressive child is a challenge for an early childhood teacher. Many abused and neglected children have learned by example to be aggressive, and they are often venting anger and frustration that cannot be expressed safely at home. The teacher should not immediately reject the aggressive child or rely on punishment and negative reinforcement to change the unsuitable behavior. Rather, the teacher should act calmly but firmly to end the incident without assigning blame. This should be followed by an attempt to identify the source of the child's frustration or anger. Some general guidelines for dealing with aggressive behavior are as follows:

1. Under no circumstances should the aggressive behavior be acceptable. All children should know clearly stated rules that say children are not allowed to hurt others and that such behavior will not be permitted.
2. Aggressive actions should not be ignored in the hope they will "go away," because this gives the child the subtle message that the behavior is condoned by the adult.
3. Prevention is the best cure. Alertness to the precursors of violent activity, particularly with troubled children, can allow the teacher to intervene before aggressive action takes place.
4. Focus attention on acceptable behaviors. Some children may simply need more positive reinforcement for cooperative, nonaggressive behaviors whereas others may need help identifying and learning alternatives to aggression and violence.
5. Aggressive children should be given attention for appropriate social behaviors as well as being given non-behavior-specific positive messages of acceptance and caring.
6. Environmental factors that contribute to aggressive behavior should be minimized. For instance, being crowded, rushed, or not given enough time for physical movement may contribute to frustration and anger in children. (Essa, 1992, pp. 528–530)

Shy and Withdrawn Behavior

The greatest danger in the case of children who are shy and withdrawn due to abuse and neglect is that their behavior will not be perceived as a problem because it does not disrupt the normal activities of the classroom. Children of this nature are often so quiet and timid that they are inadvertently ignored by their classmates and teacher. The lack of attention afforded shy and withdrawn children can lead to a reinforcement of their feelings of isolation and low self-esteem.

Teachers can significantly help shy children to become more involved by providing a reassuring, positive environment while gradually introducing them to small-group activities. To begin with, the teacher can pair the shy child with an easygoing, nonaggressive classmate for a cooperative, noncompetitive activity. The exercise should be designed to give the shy child specific opportunities to experience success, and the teacher should positively reinforce those successes whenever they are observed. Once the achievements of the shy child have been recognized and reinforced, a third child can be added to the group for similar activities. Eventually, the child can be included in larger groups as his or her self-confidence increases. However, shy or withdrawn children should not be put under pressure to participate in activities that cause them extreme stress (e.g., speaking in a group or acting in a role play activity).

The Learning Environment

In addition to the different methods of disciplining children, the environment in which learning takes place can itself minimize behavior problems. In order to make the most out of a learning experience, the teacher must (a) provide a structured and consistent schedule that is balanced between quiet and more lively activities; (b) divide the class into small groups whenever necessary; (c) arrange the physical environment so it promotes free but structured movement; and (d) organize developmentally appropriate learning centers that reflect the variety of interests held by the children (Clewett, 1988). This type of environment can be achieved once the teacher is aware of what the developmentally appropriate practices are for the students.

Developmental Assumptions and Goals

An effective early childhood program encompasses all of the developmental assumptions made about children in the particular age group concerned and works toward achieving all of the developmentally appropriate goals associated with these assumptions. These assumptions and goals then form the basis for designing an environment, teaching strategies, and activities that are attuned to young children's developmental levels and learning styles.

Developmental Assumptions

The work of Swiss psychologist Jean Piaget (1896–1980) provides comprehensive insight into the development of young children. Piaget's theory has been supported in concept and practice by such early child development leaders as Pestalozzi, Montessori, Froebel, and Dewey, as well as by modern researchers and practitioners. Current professional standards articulated by the NAEYC cite the application of child development knowledge as the primary determinant of the quality of early education programs (NAEYC, 1986b). The following paragraphs present a brief summary of Piaget's observations on development and learning in young children.

According to Piaget (1950), children from approximately 2 to 7 years of age are in the preoperational stage of development. Children at this stage are eager to learn and are constantly exploring, manipulating, and experimenting with the environment in order to learn more about it. They are rapidly acquiring language, and they yearn to learn and use new words. This stage spans a wide range of ages and unique abilities, and each child develops at his or her own rate in the cognitive-intellectual, psychosocial, and physical-motor domains.

In the cognitive-intellectual domain, children are just beginning to develop the ability to reason and to represent what they see with symbols such as words. However, they still tend to focus on one aspect of an object or situation and have difficulty distinguishing between perception and reality. Further development of their cognitive abilities is enhanced by concrete experiences that allow them to reflect on what is happening during these experiences, rather than being "taught" abstract rules.

In the area of psychosocial development, Piaget (1950) observed that children at the beginning of the preoperational stage tend to maintain their egocentrism, as well as the necessity to satisfy their own needs. They have a difficult time sharing and understanding that everything does not revolve around them (Morrison, 1988). However, toward the end of this stage, children become less egocentric and gradually learn to understand the viewpoints of others. Because of their development away from a self-centered base, encouragement and esteem-building help to strengthen children's self-images and gains in learning. Young children need and respond to praise, smiles, encouragement, and any positive acknowledgement of a job well done. Preoperational children also need many opportunities to listen to others, talk with others about their experiences, and respond to others and ask questions of their own (Morrison). If they are provided with opportunities to do all of these things, children's development away from egocentrism will be reinforced.

The physical-motor development of preoperational children is dominated by their gross motor skills. These children need to interact with large objects that can be manipulated easily. After numerous occasions of practicing these skills, children can gradually move onto smaller objects as their manipulative ability becomes increasingly fine tuned. In order to maintain their gross motor abilities, however, they need to exercise their large-muscle groups by running, jumping, climbing, pulling, and pushing.

According to Piaget (1950), an effective medium for combining the three areas of development, is play. As young children develop, they tend to progress from solitary, observational kinds of play to more active, cooperative forms of play. Through play they solve problems, acquire enriched meaning for language and ideas, creatively express and meet emotional needs, experiment with new roles, develop social relationships and skills, exercise and develop muscles, and generally explore and make sense of the world around them (Read, Gardner, & Mahler, 1987).

The High/Scope Curriculum Comparison Project (Schweinhart, Weikart, & Larner, 1986; Weikart, Epstein, Schweinhart, & Bond, 1978) supports the application of Piaget's (1950) child development theory in the early childhood curriculum. This project was a 15-year evaluation comparing the short- and long-term effects of three types of preschool programs for children identified as being at risk: a traditional child-centered nursery school, the open-framework High/Scope model, and a direct instruction program. The programs differed in two ways: the number of child- versus teacher-initiated activities, and the focus on narrower academic versus broader social goals.

The traditional nursery school focused on child-initiated free-play activities, with the teacher playing a supportive but noninterfering role. This program also included experiential learning and had broad social goals. In the High/Scope program, the teachers and children planned and initiated activities together. The teachers also organized the environment around interest-based learning centers to promote active learning. This program focused on the social, physical, and cognitive aspects of development. In the direct instruction program, the teacher initiated closely prescribed interaction sequences, with students playing a responsive role. This program was primarily concerned with the children's acquiring clearly defined academic skills.

Research findings indicated that children in all three programs achieved and maintained significant gains in their IQ scores and academic progress. However, the High/Scope program and the traditional nursery school, where participants were engaged in child-initiated activities, reported that their participants exhibited more positive social behavior patterns by age 15 than participants in the teacher-centered direct instruction program. Specifically, both the High/Scope and traditional nursery school participants committed half as many acts of delinquency, became more involved in sports and extracurricular activities, and believed that they were more highly regarded by their families. Schweinhart (1986) has suggested that the difference may be attributed to the fact that the traditional nursery school and High/Scope program had explicit social goals for the children, promoted greater self-responsibility and initiative by giving children some control over their activities, and addressed the total needs and interests of the children instead of focusing narrowly on a particular academic performance.

Based on Piaget's (1950) child development theory and the results of the High/Scope Curriculum Comparison Project, developmental assumptions can be drawn. These assumptions support a creative and developmentally appropriate approach to early childhood education that encourages active exploration, experimentation, and inquiry within an open and carefully structured environment. The assumptions are as follows:

1. Children develop at different rates that are often unrelated to chronological age.

2. Children are naturally inclined to follow their interests.

3. Children learn best when they play an active part in their own learning.

4. Children's cognitive-intellectual, psychosocial, and physical-motor development are enhanced through play.

5. A warm, open, and active environment fosters social development.

6. An abundance of concrete and sensory learning materials provides a rich atmosphere for optimal learning.

7. A creative and active approach involving learning centers stimulates and motivates children to learn.

8. In a learning atmosphere based on trust and structured freedom, children are encouraged to use their own initiative and be self-reliant.

9. Children have unique learning styles (i.e., auditory, visual, tactile, etc.), personalities, interests, and abilities.

10. Programs that are geared toward the total child are the most successful.

Early Childhood Program Goals

Several goals for early childhood programs can be derived from the foregoing 10 developmental assumptions. These goals are embedded in the provisions that should be made for each child within such a program, such as (a) activities based on the children's interests and at varying levels of difficulty; (b) many opportunities to engage in play; (c) teachers who are open and accept individual differences and adjust their teaching styles accordingly; (d) materials that encourage manipulation; (e) an environment arranged in interesting learning centers for each subject area; and (f) a schedule that allows simultaneous activity within learning centers to occur throughout the day.

In addition to the previously stated goals and assumptions, which form a developmental basis for a high-quality early childhood program, the NAECP has outlined 10 components of group programs for young children, which are included in the Academy's *Criteria for High Quality Early Childhood Programs* (NAEYC, 1986a). These components are as follows:

1. Interactions between children and staff provide opportunities for children to develop an understanding of self and others and are characterized by warmth, personal respect, individuality, positive support, and responsiveness. Staff facilitate interactions among children to provide opportunities for development of social skills and intellectual growth.

2. The curriculum encourages children to become actively involved in the learning process, to experience a variety of developmentally appropriate activities and materials, and to pursue their own interests in the context of life in the community and the world.

3. Parents are well informed about and welcome as observers of and contributors to the program.

4. The program is staffed by adults who understand child development and recognize and provide for children's needs.

5. The program is administered efficiently and effectively, with attention to the needs and desires of children, parents, and staff.

6. The program is sufficiently staffed to meet the needs of and promote the physical, social, emotional, and cognitive development of children.

7. The indoor and outdoor physical environment fosters optimal growth and development through exploration and learning opportunities.

8. The health and safety of children and adults are protected and enhanced.

9. The nutritional needs of children and adults are met in a manner that is consistent with their overall physical, social, emotional, and cognitive development.

10. Systematic assessment and evaluation of the effectiveness of the program in meeting its goals for children, parents, and staff are conducted to ensure that high-quality care and education are being provided.

Learning Centers

The learning center approach is based on the 10 developmental assumptions listed above and is designed to achieve all of the goals associated with these assumptions. Learning centers are designated areas in the classroom that contain a variety of learning activities and materials drawn from the classroom's basic skills program and from the themes and units being pursued. These centers are also designed to teach specific concepts to children. They may be created by the teacher alone, the students and teacher together, or the students alone. The centers allow the children to manipulate objects, engage in role playing and conversation with each other, and learn at their own pace. Learning centers can be adapted to a variety of learning styles, levels of maturity, and differences in experiential background (Day & Drake, 1986).

Activities within the centers may be required of all students, assigned to only some students, or entirely optional. Although the environment is appropriately structured, children act relatively independently when moving from center to center. Contracts serve as a guide to tell children which center they should go to and what they should do when they get there. Contracts also allow children to *choose* which center to go to as well as which activity to do within that center during a part of each day. Centers offer children the opportunity to become self-motivated and responsible learners.

The rationale for the learning center approach is simple and straightforward. It consists of the following three premises:

1. A good early childhood program must focus on clearly defined goals and objectives. A developmental program with learning centers meets this criterion. Learning centers provide a succession of carefully directed and structured experiences that promote the development of academic, communication, and social skills; a positive self-concept, independence, and the ability to make choices; and values such as respecting, helping, and understanding others.

2. Learning centers respond to the demand for early childhood programs that accommodate individual developmental levels and needs by offering a variety of experiences through which children can develop at their own rates.

3. Learning centers capitalize on children's natural curiosity, desire to learn, and active style of learning by providing for experimentation, inquiry, and discovery. Centers make learning attractive and meaningful, while teaching practical skills and basic concepts. Children also have the freedom to choose and initiate activities based on their own interests.

With this rationale in mind, teachers can modify their classrooms to accommodate the learning center approach. To begin with, teachers need to assess realistically the number of learning centers and the amount of materials they can manage in the centers. This number may be low at first, but gradually, as they feel more comfortable with the approach, they can add additional centers and materials. Teachers should start with centers in which the children need the least amount of teacher direction. The purpose of each center must be clear. Directions for travel from center to center, entering and exiting each center, and using the materials in the centers should be explicitly stated before the children use the centers. Eventually the children will become independent and able learners as they become accustomed to their new and enjoyable responsibility of choosing a center. Their choice is based on a nonrestrictive, individualized schedule and availability of space. (This may be marked by clothespins, which represent the number of children allowed in each center and are taken by the children as they enter the center.) Children choose activities based on their level of difficulty and discuss their accomplishments and progress with the teacher during conference times.

Examples of possible learning centers to include in a developmentally appropriate classroom are shown in Figure 2-1 and described in the following sections.

Blocks Center

Blocks provide children with an opportunity for enhancement of concepts in each area of the curriculum by allowing the children to work independently or with others in manipulating the blocks. In their work with blocks, children

Color-coded clothespins serve as tickets that allow children to enter a center. Susan chooses a science clothespin, slips it on, and wears it while working in the science center.

discover spatial relationships, balance, and their ability to create things. They also develop their hand-eye coordination and their large and small muscle groups.

Materials in a blocks center include large-, medium-, and small-sized blocks; blocks of different shapes such as triangles, arcs, and squares; and accessories such as carpet squares, puppets, dried beans, and fabric scraps for building and decorating. Blocks centers that have a variety of materials can contribute greatly to children's creativity and use of imagination.

Language Arts Center

The ability to communicate effectively through reading, writing, speaking, and listening is crucial to children's development. Children must be given every available opportunity to use and practice these skills. Language arts centers should promote the child's ability to think creatively, critically, and logically.

A variety of learning centers can be designed to promote development of language arts skills. Examples include a books center, which may have magazines, newspapers, stories, and resource books; a writing center, which may

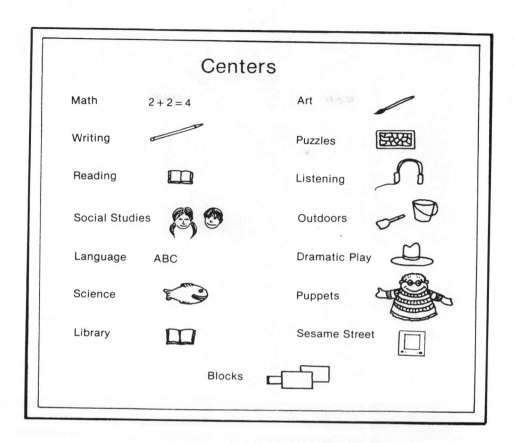

Centers

Math	2 + 2 = 4	Art	
Writing		Puzzles	
Reading		Listening	
Social Studies		Outdoors	
Language	ABC	Dramatic Play	
Science		Puppets	
Library		Sesame Street	
		Blocks	

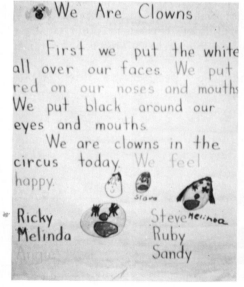

We Are Clowns

    First we put the white all over our faces. We put red on our noses and mouths. We put black around our eyes and mouths.
    We are clowns in the circus today. We feel happy.

Ricky
Melinda

Steve Melinda
Ruby
Sandy

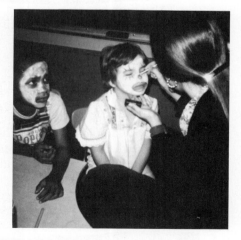

Figure 2-1 Examples of symbols for learning for learning centers (*top*). In the writing center (*bottom left*), we do many fun things. After painting our faces (*bottom right*), we dictated a language experience story about what we did.

We can use the record player with earphones all by ourselves.

have word boxes, different kinds of paper, pencils and crayons, and pictures; and a listening center, which may have record players and tapes, filmstrips, a television set, and earphones.

Fine Arts Centers

Fine arts centers include both music and art centers. These centers help children develop aesthetic appreciation and expressive skills and enhance their perceptual, language, gross and fine motor, social, and emotional development.

The music center includes instruments such as drums, xylophones, and guitars; activities such as singing, listening, marching, and composing; and materials such as paper, books, pictures, and tapes. The music center must be strategically placed and carefully monitored by the teacher in order to minimize disruptions caused by instruments.

The art center includes different kinds of paper, scissors, rulers, tape, pencils, paints and paintbrushes, chalk, food coloring, clay, charcoal, sponges, foil, and toothpicks. "Beautiful junk" such as coffee cans, cloth scraps, lace, felt, and jewelry should also be in the art center.

Art and music activities can be combined. For example, the children can make their own instruments and musical storybooks.

Home Living and Creative Dramatics Center

The home living and creative dramatics center allows children to play (their primary mode of learning) in a natural and secure setting. Children involved in play are interacting socially while practicing problem-solving and cooperation skills. This setting is ideal for teachers to observe their students and gain insight

Today we've moved one art center table outside onto the patio.

into the children's background and developmental needs. This center also provides opportunities for children to engage in cooking and stitchery activities, which promote small-muscle development, hand-eye coordination, and knowledge of good nutrition.

The home living and creative dramatics center may contain child-sized furniture and appliances; dress-up clothing; a full-length mirror; sewing equipment; and cooking materials such as pots, pans, and aprons. This center should also include props for creating a variety of settings, such as a store, a post office, or a hospital.

Science and Mathematics Investigation Centers

Science and mathematics investigation centers are geared toward satisfying the children's natural sense of curiosity. Children are constantly observing, classifying, and making inferences about their experiences. Teachers should take advantage of their students' curiosity and develop centers that will encourage manipulation and exploration of interesting materials. These centers incorporate activities relating to the scientific processes of observation, classification, measurement, computation, experimentation, and prediction that provide the framework for development of basic mathematics and science concepts and skills.

The science center contains tuning forks, wood, bottles, candles, levers, screws, mirrors, tape measures, egg timers, magazines, microscopes, and chart and graph paper. Natural objects included in the center are flowers, rocks, leaves, water, and soil, which may be kept in an indoor or outdoor garden. Teachers may also wish to further children's development of responsibility by

We're having a "make-believe" party in the home living and creative dramatics center. Problem-solving and cooperation skills are being tested as we
make hats, bake the cake, and make the decorations.

having a "living things" center with small animals such as rabbits or guinea pigs
that can be observed and cared for by the students.

The math center includes dominoes, attribute blocks, play money, compasses, Cuisenaire rods, number lines, button collections, and scales.

Movement

Although movement activities occur in an open space rather than within the
confines of a learning center, movement is a central part of any early childhood
program and should be introduced along with the core learning centers. Children are born with the need to move and to express their feelings. A movement
education program can easily be incorporated into the daily schedule. Children
involved in such a program learn to express themselves creatively, gain positive
self-images, acquire knowledge of how their bodies move, and develop motor
skills. A movement education program, like all other aspects of a developmentally appropriate program, must allow the children to perform movements that
are on their developmental level. The children will first learn more general body
movements and then progress to more complex combined movements and cooperative movements with other children.

An effective movement program requires a large open area, the availability of partners, a tambourine, and some type of audio equipment such as a tape player and tapes. Other resources include objects for manipulation such as balls, hoops, and ropes. Examples of movement activities are balancing, crawling, running, skipping, and body rolls.

Outdoor Play

As with indoor learning center materials, outdoor play equipment such as sliding boards, swings, wading pools, and jungle gyms should suit the developmental needs of the children. Playing outdoors gives children a chance to escape the confines of the classroom into an environment where nature prevails and there are sunshine, birds, and trees. Children are encouraged to bring "inside" learning activities outside in order to experience them in a different setting.

Activities children engage in outdoors include jumping rope, playing kickball, studying flowers, and building forts. The sky is the limit on children's imaginations when they can interact with the outside world.

Social Studies Centers

The social studies program helps prepare young children to become contributing members of their classroom, school, community, and society. Through critical

These swings suit the developmental needs of the five-year-old just fine.

This four-year-old likes to play with "real" continent maps in the
Social Studies center. She also likes to make her own. Mrs. Beamer
taught the class a continent song, too.

thinking and problem-solving skills, children develop knowledge of facts, concepts, and generalizations.

Social studies centers may be based on the need for rules and laws, community and career awareness, understanding the justice system, different people and places, and the need for civic responsibility. In conjunction with center
activities, general classroom discussions and activities (e.g., small-group
problem-solving tasks, formulating classroom rules, setting up and running a
pretend store or bank, mock elections) are arranged.

Materials included in the social studies center are activity kits, globes and
maps, reference books, biographies, records, posters, telephones, slide projec-
tors, envelopes and stamps, and works of art.

Sand and Water Play Centers

Sand and water play centers provide children with the means to get back to
nature. Activities within these centers are fun and self-motivating. Children
thrive on the sensory experiences they gain from playing with sand and water.
Many opportunities exist for the advancement of mathematics (measuring),
language and communication (dramatic play), and science (experiments with
sand and water) skills. Children are also using their small and large muscle
groups by digging, building, and measuring while they play.

Sand and water play activities include holding boat races and floating and
sinking experiments with a variety of objects, making letters in the sand, and
planting and watering seeds. Materials for the centers include measuring spoons
and cups, plastic dishes, weights, sponges, liquid soap, plastic eyedroppers,
and shovels.

Woodworking Center

Although this center has received some criticism for safety hazards, if it is monitored properly and children are taught how to use it responsibly, it is a tremendous asset to the learning program. Most children have always wanted the chance to use their own tools, and the sense of accomplishment that comes with creating something that is their own. They want to use their hands to learn about the creative process and to feel the different textures of the materials with which they will be working. In addition to these tactile experiences, woodworking provides an emotional release for children, allows them to apply their problem-solving skills, and develops their hand-eye coordination.

Some basic woodworking operations include hammering, gluing, fastening with screws, drilling, and sawing. Projects that involve these operations include making birdhouses, trucks and cars, puzzles, buildings, and people and animal figures. Materials for a woodworking center include wood, toothpicks, cardboard, pencils, scissors, glue, sandpaper, paint and paintbrushes, magnets, and bandages. To obtain some of these materials, it is helpful to establish com-

Safety is emphasized in the woodworking center. We use real tools and parents come to help.

munication and rapport with local hardware stores, paint stores, and lumber companies.

Arrangement of Learning Centers

The arrangement of learning centers has a tremendous influence on the activities and attitudes of the students. Centers are generally separated by the furniture included in them (e.g., bookshelves). Choosing the appropriate materials and furniture arrangement and making the room attractive are important in providing a stimulating and motivating environment in which children can learn. The arrangement of learning centers must take traffic patterns, transitioning, and the center's purpose into account.

Each center's purpose is different. Some centers are geared toward more active group activities whereas others are designed for quieter and more independent activities. The quieter centers, such as the reading and writing centers, should be placed away from the noisier centers, such as the blocks and music centers.

In addition, the furniture placed within the centers must be given careful consideration. For example, dramatic play and blocks centers require more open floor space than do math and writing centers, where tables are essential. Furniture should include low bookshelves, portable chalkboards, low cabinets or

Appropriate materials and arrangement of furniture were very important considerations in planning this learning environment for young children.

This raised platform encourages and invites children to write their own books, share them with others, and stretch out in comfortable positions.

tables, and, for the reading center, child-sized chairs or beanbags (Morrow, 1989).

All centers should be inviting and make children feel secure. To help facilitate recognition, the centers should be labeled at the children's eye level and assigned a particular color (Day & Drake, 1986). If all of the previously mentioned steps are taken when arranging learning centers, an efficient, attractive, comfortable, and self-guiding environment should emerge.

Effectiveness of Learning Centers

Learning centers are effective because they

- Encompass the learning of the total child.
- Enhance children's cognitive-intellectual, psychosocial, and physical-motor development.
- Utilize lead management (Glasser, 1990), with the teacher acting as facilitator.
- Promote independence, responsibility, and self-motivation by offering an environment in which structured freedom is inherent in the design.
- Help to minimize discipline problems by maintaining active interest in materials and activities that are relevant and are geared to the children's interests.
- Operate based on the 10 developmental assumptions described previously, and are, thus, developmentally appropriate.

Learning centers also make use of the all-important developmental and learning activity of play. Young children's self-concept is associated with play. In fact, children view themselves as successful or unsuccessful in terms of how well they play (Marshall, 1989). When children were asked by Marshall how others could describe them (for example, in written observations), they often responded in terms of physical activities in which they felt they performed well (e.g., "I'm good at kickball").

In learning centers, children are not grouped by ability or expected to conform to the abilities of the rest of the children, two practices that can have detrimental effects on their self-concept. Instead, in a learning center environment children's autonomy and unique levels of development are supported and encouraged. Children in a learning center, when compared to children in a teacher-controlled classroom, exhibit higher levels of motivation and self-worth. Research has shown that children who do not develop positive self-concepts at a young age are at risk for problems later in life, such as dropping out of school and juvenile delinquency (Asher, Renshaw, & Hymel, 1982; Cauley & Tyler, 1989; Parker & Asher, 1987).

Children learn concepts by manipulating objects and actively exploring their environment (Kamii & Williams, 1986). With the learning center approach, children are continuously provided with opportunities for manipulation and for indoor and outdoor exploration. These experiences enable them to interact with each other and act independently in a cognitively, socially, and physically rich environment.

Research by Dunn and Dunn (1987) reinforced the importance of teaching children in a manner that will correspond to their individual styles of learning. They asserted that the best environment for individualized learning is an environment that is both flexible and varied. Students need to be able to work alone or in groups; have consistent yet adaptable schedules; have visual, audio, and tactile experiences; and learn at their own pace.

Based on this and other research and the earlier discussion of child development, the conditions for effective learning center usage can be stated as follows:

1. Development and implementation of an effective management system that is clearly understood by the teacher and the children.

2. Teacher's knowledge of each student's ability, achievement level, prior experiences, maturity level, and learning style, and use of this knowledge in planning goals and objectives for the program.

3. Attractive, well-planned, and well-organized centers.

4. Centers that provide an abundance of self-correcting materials at a variety of levels.

5. Instruction of children in proper and effective use of center materials and equipment.

6. Individual and group planning, guidance, and evaluation of activities.

7. Children's understanding of the purpose of and expectations for effec-

tive use of materials in centers, including responsibility for maintaining simple records of their activities.

8. Integration of skills and concepts within and between centers to ensure relevancy. (Day & Drake, 1986)

Management Techniques

An effective classroom management system's main function is to enable both teachers and students to accomplish their learning goals comfortably and securely. A good management system establishes a firm but flexible structure that encourages creativity. This structure frees teachers to focus on planning, facilitating, evaluating, and supporting individualized learning and frees children to learn securely and independently. Structure also allows children to satisfy their basic needs for survival, love, power, fun, and freedom and to learn according to their own learning styles and interests.

The two major components of an effective classroom management system are color coding and contracts. These management methods are to be used in conjunction with the different types of discipline discussed previously.

Color Coding

Color coding, the first component of classroom management, is intended to provide children with an efficient and independent way of moving between learning centers and completing activities within the centers. When specific colors and symbols are assigned to centers, books, games, and task cards, children who have not mastered their reading skills are able to locate and use the things they need.

At the entrance to each learning center is a chart that depicts the name of the center, the center's color and symbol, and colored clothespins that represent the number of children permitted in the center at one time (Figure 2-2). For example, for the reading center, the chart, the book symbol, and the clothespins are all light blue. The children must attach the clothespins to their clothing when they enter the center and replace them on the chart when they leave the center.

Color coding of games and activities is accomplished by cutting various shapes such as triangles, squares, and circles from different-colored contact paper and placing these stickers onto the games and activities. To promote organization, corresponding stickers are also put on the shelves where the activities belong (Figure 2-3). For example, if a student were assigned a green circle activity, he or she would go to the shelf marked with a green circle and choose an activity.

Color coding can also be used to indicate level of difficulty. By matching different colors with different levels of difficulty the teacher is able to individualize all tasks and activities. For example, the least difficult activities might be labeled with yellow stickers, the moderate activities with red stickers, and the most difficult with green stickers (Day & Drake, 1983).

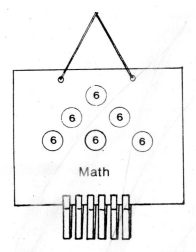
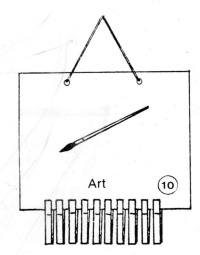

Figure 2-2   Learning center charts

Color coding teaches children to become responsible for the care and organization of materials. Children can function independently and easily within this system.

Contracts

Contracts are used to control classroom traffic and to provide a learning program that is tailored to meet the children's individual needs. Contracts provide structure by establishing the number of visits children make to each center during the week, as well as the variety of centers they visit. Each contract includes daily

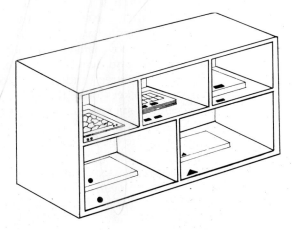

Figure 2-3   Shelves color coded with stickers

evaluations, which measure children's progress and serve as a "report card" to be brought home at the end of each day. These daily evaluations, which are completed in meetings between children and the teacher (or a teacher aide if one is available), are used to review, provide feedback, update records, and plan future activities. They are essential to the success of the contract system.

Contracts also let children work at their own pace within each center and throughout the day. The contracts reflect the children's schedules and may be divided between time with the teacher, time on independent activities planned by the teacher, and time doing activities in the centers of their choice. Children can follow their own interests during free-choice time and are held accountable for the completion of their contracts every day. The contracts may also be designed for small-group use; their flexibility is as broad as the range of creativity of the children and teachers who use them. Contracts may cover one to several days' activities and/or subject areas and may involve a few steps, pictorial diagrams, and color coding or just simple written directions.

Day and Drake (1983) have described four levels of contracts, which progress on a continuum from young children and/or nonreaders to readers at the third- and fourth-grade level.

Stage 1 Contracts

Stage 1 contracts are simple picture contracts (see Figure 2-4). The teacher or the child color-codes the contract by using crayon to underline the name of the center with the same color as the center's clothespin chart. For example, the art

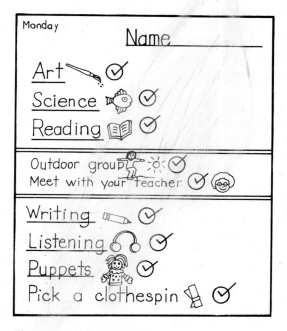

Figure 2-4   Stage 1 contract

clothespins and chart are dark blue; whenever art appears on the contract, it is underlined in dark blue. Children have two clues to help them use their contracts: (1) They read the center symbol, a paintbrush, as "art"; and (2) they match the dark blue underlining on their contracts to the dark blue clothespin chart that hangs beside the art center. After completing the art activity, the children check off "art" on their contracts and refer to the contracts to move to another center. At the end of a contract, the phrase "Pick a clothespin" indicates that the child can select a free-choice center.

Stage 2 Contracts

Some children will use only clothespins, or only picture contracts, for a longer time than others do. When children can follow a picture contract successfully, they are ready to begin Stage 2. This contract level adds some required center activities as well as a minimal amount of reading. The required activities give the children responsibility for specific tasks. This structure helps children develop independent work habits and also reinforces teacher-designated skills. To follow a Stage 2 contract, the child needs to recognize the center symbols, match shapes, and read three color-words. These contracts are easily used by children with limited reading and writing skills.

Children using Stage 1 and 2 contracts can begin to work in centers independent of the teacher. Contracts can also begin to cover a longer period of the day. The children can copy their assigned tasks from the board, or the teacher can fill in the contracts for them. The standardized coding system used on the contracts (e.g., "Do the activity," "Play the red triangle game") provides a format that allows the same series of contracts to be used over and over again.

Rather than spending time each afternoon designing contracts with specific tasks such as "Look up Benjamin Franklin" or "Do the magnet experiment" written on them, the teacher has a standard contract form for each day of the week (Figure 2-5).

Stage 3 Contracts

Stage 3 contracts (Figure 2-6), require more proficient reading and writing skills. Children fill these contracts out for themselves by copying assigned tasks from the chalkboard. Then they select free choices from a chart that lists the available centers, selecting one free-choice center from each side of the center's chart. The chart is designed so that the child must select one center from the more difficult or cognitively oriented centers and one from the psychomotor/creative areas.

Stage 4 Contracts

Stage 4 contracts require children to keep written diaries of their activities. Children write in specifics about what they completed in the science center, what their creative story was about, and so forth (Figure 2-7).

All contract formats should be easily understood and manageable for the children. Teachers must orient children to the use of the contracts and the materials involved so the children can work confidently and efficiently with them. Individual personalized folders that hold the children's contracts and

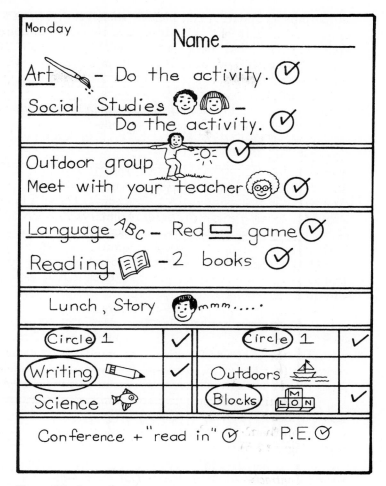

Figure 2-5   Stage 2 contract

pencils help them organize their work and maintain a record of their progress.

Contracts are planned to vary the centers required so that each center is visited two or three times a week. Sample contracts for Monday through Friday illustrate this program (Figure 2-8).

Results of Research on Learning Centers and Contracts

Research indicates that classrooms using learning centers and the contract system of management promote on-task behavior. Day and Drake (1986) found that children in classrooms that featured eight or more all-day learning centers were multiaged (5- and 6-year-old children grouped together) and used contracts had on-task behavior rates of 92%. Consequently, these children received 120 more

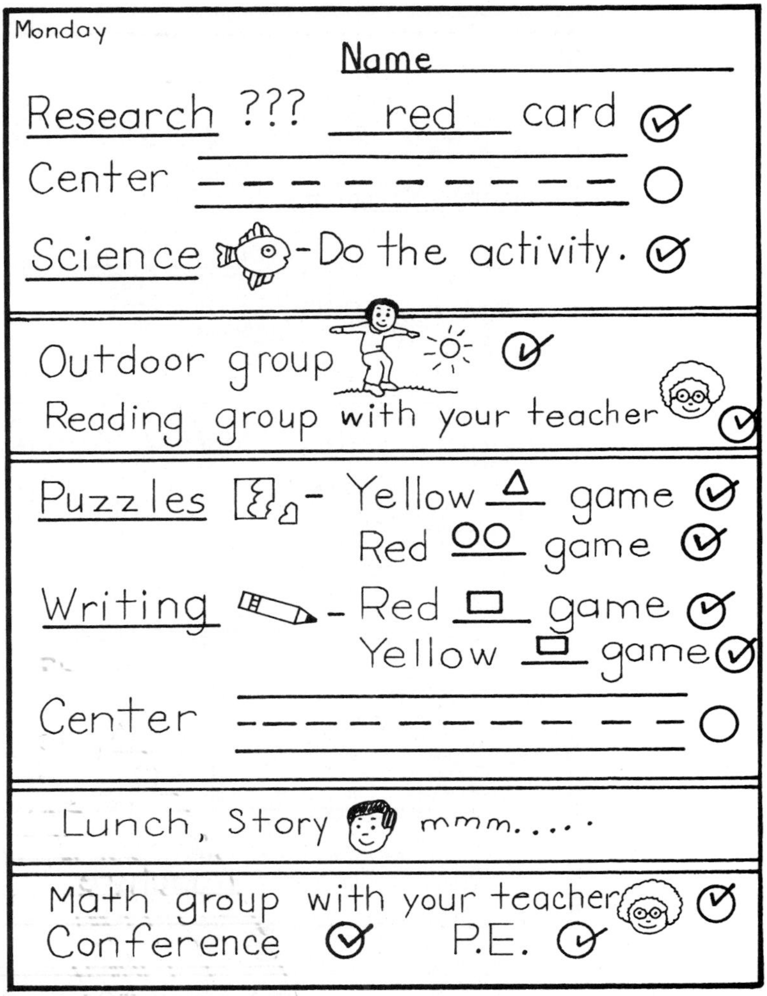

Figure 2-6 Stage 3 contract

hours of schooling (20 more school days) during the school year than children whose classrooms were operating without learning centers and contracts. The on-task behavior in other classes ranged from 79% to 81%.

This study also investigated the relationship between various types of early childhood classroom environments and the on-task behavior rates generated by the children in each program. For this purpose, the classroom environment was defined in terms of the number of simultaneous activity segments operating at any one time (Day & Drake, 1986). Eighteen kindergarten and first grade classrooms were observed and then categorized into the following five different organizational patterns.

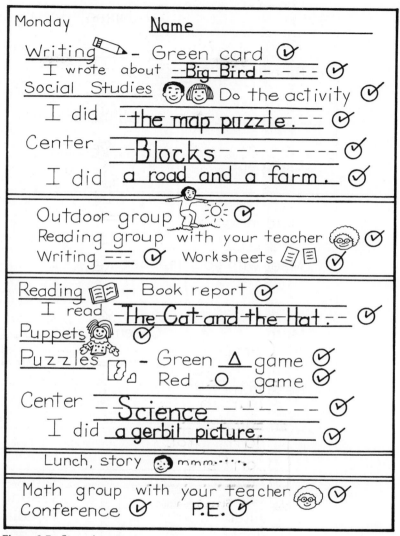

Figure 2-7   Stage 4 contract

Type 1. Six-year-old children in classrooms that operated for most of the school day with only one or two simultaneous activity segments.

Type 2. Five-year-old children in classrooms that operated multiple activity segments (including eight or more learning centers) for the first hour of the school day, then operated only one or two simultaneous activities for the rest of the school day.

Type 3. Six-year-old children in classrooms that operated multiple activity segments during the morning. The afternoon included only one or two simultaneous activity segments.

S-Mon.   Name _____

☐ Blocks

☐ Science   Do the activity.

☐ Language   Yellow _____game
                       Red _____game

☐ Outdoor group

☐ Meet with your teacher

☐ Math   123   Green _____game
                Red _____game

☐ Research   ?   Yellow card

☐ Dramatic Play

Circle 2			Circle 2		
Games			Writing		
Outdoors			Reading		
Blocks			Listening		

Lunch, story

☐ UNC - TV

☐ Meet with your afternoon group

Figure 2-8   Sample contracts

S- Tues.   Name _____

☐ You and Me   Do the activity

☐ Art   Circle 1

☐ Listening

☐ Games   Red _____game
                                                 Yellow _____game

☐ Reading   3 books

☐ Outdoor group

Circle 1		Circle 1	
Math **123**		Dramatic Play	
Science		Language A B C	

Lunch, story

☐ Library   ☐ Art

☐ Music   ☐ P.E.

Figure 2-8   (*continued*)

S- Wed.	Name _____

☐ Writing   ✏️   Big card   yellow worksheet

☐ Reading   📖   3 books

☐ Puppets

☐ Blocks

☐ Outdoor group

☐ Meet with you teacher

☐ Science   Do the activity.
Read 2 books

☐ Outdoors - Circle 1

Sand   Water   Tools   Easel

Circle 2		Circle 2	
Math	2 + 2 = 4	Listening	
Language	A B C	You and Me	
Research	???	Dramatic Play	

Lunch, story

☐ UNC - TV   ☐ Meet with your afternoon group

Conference   ☐ "Read-In"   ☐ P.E.

Figure 2-8 (*continued*)

S- Thur.   Name _____

☐ Class Meeting   [?]   Special activities in   🐟

☐ Meet with your teacher   😊

☐ You and Me   Do the activity.   👧👧
                       Read 2 books.

☐ Games   Yellow _____game
                 Red _____game.
☐ Writing   Yellow _____game.
                 Red _____game.

☐ Library   📖   Get a new book

☐ Language   ⟨ABC⟩   Yellow _____game.
                      Red _____game.

☐ Outdoor group   ⛵

Circle 1		Circle 1	
Math 678		Dramatic Play 🎩	
Reading 📖		Outdoors ～	

😊 ⌣⌣⌣   Lunch, story   📖

☐ UNC - TV   ▢

☐ Meet with your afternoon group

Figure 2-8   (*continued*)

S- Fri.   Name _____

☐ Writing   Yellow worksheet

☐ Math 123   Yellow _____ game

☐ Meet with your teacher.

☐ Art   Do the activity or use the

☐ Outdoor group

☐ Library   ☐ Dramatic Play

☐ Listening   ☐ Puppets

Circle 2		Circle 2		
You and Me		Reading		
Research ? ? ?		Blocks		
Language A B C		Games		

Lunch, story

☐ UNC - TV

☐ Meet with your afternoon group

Figure 2-8   (*continued*)

TABLE 2-1   Percentage of On-Task Behavior by Classroom Type

Type	Activities	Time	Contract	On-Task Behavior (%)
1	1–2	—	no	79
2	multiple	1 hr/day	no	79
3	multiple	½ day	no	78
4	multiple	all day	no	81
5A	multiple	all day	yes	85
5B	multiple	all day	yes	87
5C	multiple	all day	yes	92

Type 4. Five-year-old children in classrooms that had multiple activity segments operating all day.

Type 5. Five- and six-year-old children in classrooms that operated multiple activity segments all day and used written contracts as a management technique.

Children in Type 5 classrooms were grouped in 5-year-old kindergarten programs (Type 5a), 6-year-old first grade programs (Type 5b), and multiaged 5- and 6-year-old programs (Type 5c). Table 2-1 shows the on-task behavior rates generated by each type of classroom.

Types 1, 2, and 3, which had either limited or no simultaneous activity, had similar on-task behavior rates of approximately 78%. A small positive change in on-task behavior rates was produced by Type 4 classrooms, which operated multiple activity segments for the entire day (82%).

However, pronounced changes in on-task behavior rates were observed in the Type 5 classrooms, which combined the all-day use of multiple activity segments with the use of written contracts. This situation generated on-task behavior rates as high as 92%.

Tables 2-2 and 2-3 illustrate higher on-task behavior rates for 5- and 6-year-old children working in learning centers rather than doing seatwork activities. These results suggest the need for a variety of experiences within an early childhood classroom.

TABLE 2-2   Percentage of On-Task Bahavior for 5-Year-Olds

Activity	On-Task Behavior (%)	Activity	On-Task Behavior (%)
Music	100	Science	80
Listening	93	Research	75
Housekeeping	81	Study Area	78
Water	100	Writing	75
Sensory/Motor	88	Reading	29
Outside	98	Cooking	72
Math	84		

TABLE 2-3   Percentage of On-Task Behavior for 6-Year-Olds

Activity	On-Task Behavior (%)	Activity	On-Task Behavior (%)
Math	100	Outside	100
Reading	93	Sand	91
Science	89	Listening	86
Writing	85	Cooking	82
Sensory/Motor	100	Study	78
Art	97	Housekeeping	60
Blocks	88		

An interesting example of the interaction between the developmental readiness of children for an activity and the on-task behavior rates generated by that activity was observed in the reading centers studied. In these centers, 5-year-olds had on-task behavior rates of 29% and 6-year-olds had on-task rates of 93%. Clearly, the reading centers were not designed for 5-year-old children, who are typically nonreaders. The implications of these findings are that reading centers need to be organized with stimuli other than print in order to engage more 5-year-old children in the activities. For example, books in the center should be accompanied by a tape recording.

In conclusion, a complex early childhood environment featuring learning centers in conjunction with effective management techniques can achieve higher rates of on-task behavior than a less complex early childhood classroom relying on large- and small-group instruction and seatwork assignments.

Parent Involvement

The ultimate success of any early childhood program involves the children's parents as classroom volunteers, tutors, field trip monitors, and fundraisers. Parents can also become active members of school committees and policy review boards. If parents also make use of the schools to enhance their own education in and awareness of child development, they can be of great service to the schools, the community, and their own children. Parents are their children's most influential teacher.

Parents who are directly involved in their children's education also tend to become advocates of the classroom program. Certain aspects of the program (e.g., discipline) will carry over into the home, providing consistent correlation between the school and home environment. Parent involvement also provides teachers with insight into their students' personalities and ways of doing things.

In order to encourage active parent involvement, teachers must be willing to give parents a certain amount of responsibility and plan what the parents will do during their time in school. Parent involvement is also promoted if teachers are willing to go to the parents' homes at times, rather than always expecting parents to come to the school. Although teachers cannot expect all parents to become full participants in their child's education, they must not neglect the opportunity to provide all parents with a chance to become involved.

To establish a comprehensive parent involvement program, a well-planned orientation session should be organized. The teacher and parent volunteers can notify other parents about the session. The session should include statements about the school's and the teacher's philosophy, the classroom's learning goals

---

Parent Involvement Activities

1. **Home Visitations:** Home visitation can serve as an integral part of the home-school partnership. This visitation might include the teacher's visiting the homes of each child in the class as well as having other school system staff members such as the home-school coordinator assist with home visits. The initial teacher visits should occur early in the year, with at least one additional visit to each home later in the year. Additional visits should be encouraged.

2. **Communication with Parents:** Regular communication with parents of children in the class should be maintained. Each family should receive some communication at least twice each week from the classroom staff. This communication may be either written (student contracts, newsletters, notes), or personal (face to face, telephone). Parent conferences should take place on a regular basis (preferably two times per year as a minimum).

3. **Parent Participation:** Parents with children in the class should be actively involved in the classroom learning environment. To the extent possible, this would involve parents' spending time in the classroom on a volunteer basis. Teachers should work with parents to define the responsibilities that parents will have in the classroom (e.g., working with children, preparing supplies.)

4. **Site-Based Management Committee/Parent Advisory Group:** Each school or center should have a parent advisory group to provide input to policy formation, suggestions for operation of the classroom, and evaluation of the ongoing program. This group should meet on a regular basis throughout the year. Some schools have chosen to combine the parent advisory group with the site-based management committee.

5. **Family Education Program:** Each school or center should have a systematic family education program that serves as a regular source of information for families on child development, nutrition, health and safety, and other areas of interest to the families participating in the program. Information provided should be geared to the cultures and education levels of the families being served.

6. **Resource Center:** Each school or program should operate a resource center to loan educational toys, materials, and small equipment to parents, day care, and preschool programs in the community and teachers in the school or center. The center should have as a goal the enrichment of programs serving pre-kindergarten children throughout the community.

7. **Program Administration:** Vital to the success of the program is active participation of the program administration in each of the areas described above. The administrator sets the tone for the school and is a vital part of the team of teachers, parents, and resource persons.

* Adapted from Families and School Committee of the Pre-Kindergarten Task Force for Program Development, North Carolina Dept. of Public Instruction, Raleigh.

and objectives, the school and classroom rules, classroom management techniques, the responsibilities of the parents, and a survey of parent abilities and interests (Morrison, 1988).

Parent-teacher conferences are the most common way to gain parent involvement, but they are not the only way. Many parents have their first contact with their child's teacher through these conferences. Follow-up conferences conducted at a later date show parents that teachers really care about their children and also present an opportunity to encourage further parent involvement (Morrison, 1988).

Conclusion

Optimum learning occurs in an environment that includes a comprehensive discipline program, developmentally appropriate learning centers, effective management techniques, and a high degree of parent involvement.

The teacher's attitude of acceptance toward his or her students is crucial to their psychological well-being. Children constantly strive to attract the attention of their teacher. If the teacher's attention and subsequent responses are usually negative, the children feel demeaned and humiliated and may stop trying altogether. However, if the teacher responds positively to the students and asks for their opinions, the students will continue to strive to achieve in order to please the teacher. If problems arise, an effective teacher takes the time to guide children toward more appropriate and socially acceptable behaviors.

In addition to positively reacting to and promoting understanding of behavior, the teacher must embrace students' individual differences and adapt the learning environment and activities to their different learning styles and levels of development. For these activities to maintain the children's attention, they have to be relevant to their interests. It is essential, then, to have an environment in which the teacher and the children shape their learning together—an environment in which the children can grow intellectually, socially, emotionally, and physically. Learning centers provide this type of environment.

Learning centers are built around children's interests and are designed to allow children to work at their own pace. The centers and the activities within the centers are color coded, a type of classroom management technique that promotes independence and responsibility. The activities within the center are color coded to reflect their level of difficulty. Children using contracts, another management technique, have an individualized schedule that may be based on color codes or reading. Younger children can simply match the color on their contract to the corresponding center and find the developmentally appropriate activity specified on their contract.

In order to maintain a completely successful learning program, parent involvement in their children's education is critical. By participating more frequently in school and classroom activities and planning, parents gain insight into what goes on in their child's life outside of the home, and children appreciate the additional interest their parents show in their education.

Chapter 3

Evaluating, Assessing, and Recording Developmentally Appropriate Learning

Student evaluation is basic to student growth. It demands careful, thoughtful attention. Yet what typically passes for student evaluation, what fills the public discourse, is an overarching model of assessment, built around a host of standardized tests, that doesn't get particularly close to student learning and doesn't provide teachers with much information of consequence. It is in most settings a wasteful effort that guarantees too many students a limited education and does little to increase public confidence in the schools.

V. Perrone, Expanding Student Instruction

Evaluation is an integral part of the educational process. Effective teachers continually monitor and assess students' needs and progress, appraising academic, social, and physical growth and planning individualized programs to support that growth. Effective teachers realize the importance of understanding where their students are so they can plan a program that is developmentally appropriate for each child. In addition, teachers assess their own strengths and weaknesses and are sensitive to the effectiveness of their interactions with students. Evaluation is a continual process that consciously or unconsciously guides instructional decisions for the teacher who is concerned with maintaining a developmentally appropriate program.

Evaluation, as defined by NAEYC, is the systematic analysis of program-related data that can be used to understand how a program delivers services or what the consequences of its services are for the participants (NAEYC, 1988). Often evaluation is confused with assessment, which is the process of observing, recording, and otherwise documenting the work children do and how they do it, as a basis for educational decisions affecting those children (NAEYC,

1988). Stated simply, assessment is the actual collection of data, and evaluation is the process of making a judgment about the information uncovered.

Traditional Methods of Assessment

There are numerous ways in which to assess students' progress in an educational program. For various reasons, the most popular method in today's schools is the use of standardized tests. They provide an easy method for comparing one student to another within the same class or in another state. Thus, parents can compare their children, teachers can compare the achievement of their classes, principals can discuss the improvement in their schools, superintendents are able to refer to the production in their districts, and newspapers can hold the states accountable to the public for the quality of education in the schools. The National Commission on Testing and Public Policy (NCTPP, 1990) found that schools relied on standardized tests to make important decisions about children's entry into and exit from kindergarten, promotion from grade to grade, and placement in remedial programs.

Children's educational experiences are being determined by their scores because they may be labeled, placed in certain tracks, or unnecessarily retained (Gullo, 1991). Standardized tests influence not only these decisions, but also institutional and instructional goals and teacher performance (Madaus & Tan, 1993). Perhaps even more important, because test scores are used to measure a school's worth, standardized tests are driving the curriculum in schools nationwide.

Unfortunately, society is placing a great deal of emphasis on this assessment tool, which may be inappropriate for many reasons. Standardized tests give a distorted view of learning, narrow curriculum and teacher performance, and often are not developmentally appropriate for use with young children.

When assessment takes the form of standardized tests, the perception of children's efforts is reduced to how many questions they have answered correctly on a given day. Depending on this "snapshot" of a child to assess his or her progress does not come close to truly assessing the child's learning and does not provide much information of consequence to help the teacher judge how to best meet the child's needs (Perrone, 1991). Percentile scores cannot tell teachers and parents all they need to know about their children, because test scores offer no insight into the thought processes of students. Instead of assessing what they *understand*, standardized tests test them for what they *know* (Zessoules & Gardner, 1991). In this way, learning is viewed solely as correct or incorrect answers.

There is more to the learning process than performing well on standardized tests, but in many classrooms, high test scores have become the goal, instead of information gained from an assessment tool. Research has shown that when multiple-choice, norm-referenced, and criterion-referenced standardized tests are used as the major assessment methods to evaluate students' performance, both instruction and curriculum are narrowed (Feuer & Fulton, 1993). Teachers spend precious instructional time preparing students especially for these tests, which may contain whole groups of information not included in their schools' curriculums. Teachers are placed in the difficult position of choosing between teaching what they know will be on the test and how to take the test, and teaching what they believe to be important for the children. Often, teachers sacrifice more meaningful intellectual engagements in order to help students develop the necessary skills for drill, seatwork, and ditto sheets (Madaus & Tan, 1993).

Most disturbing is the extent to which educators depend on these tests even though they are often developmentally inappropriate for young children. The NCTPP believes that children aged 4 and 5 are too young for testing and would benefit more from exploratory play (Hymes, 1991). Children's level of development must be taken into consideration because it determines how they will respond to assessment methods. If a method is not appropriate, it may actually interfere with the ability of the child to exhibit a skill the child does in fact have. For example, in assessing a kindergarten child's skill in color recognition, if the teacher asks the child to answer by filling in bubbles, the child may lack the fine-motor skills necessary to pencil in the answers, and thus be unable to exhibit the skill (Gullo, 1991).

Authentic Assessment Methods

The NAEYC agrees that standardized tests are not the best way to evaluate the progress of children. It recommends assessment practices that are more developmentally appropriate:

- Progress should be assessed by teacher observation and recording of information, with the results being used to plan further instruction.
- Progress should be reported to parents in narrative form, preferably in conference.
- No letter or numerical grades should be given during the primary years.
- No child should be retained, but [should] progress through the curriculum at [his or her] individual pace. (NAEYC, 1988, p. 72)

The Southern Association on Children Under Six (SACUS) also encourages a ban on mass use of standardized tests for children who are 8 years of age and under because these children are not developmentally ready for such tests. SACUS suggests the following five criteria for appropriate assessment:

- Assessment must be valid and related to the goals and objectives of the educational program.
- Assessment should encompass the whole child, relating the child's physical, social, emotional, and mental development.
- Assessment should involve repeated observations to help teachers find patterns of behavior on which to base decisions.
- Assessment should be continuous in that each child must be compared to his/her own development—not an average.

- Assessment must involve a variety of methods in order to provide more complete information. (Grace & Shores, 1992, p. xi)

These criteria suggest the use of alternative methods of assessment that are more appropriate, more valid, and more helpful to teachers making decisions about their students' needs. Proponents of alternative assessment argue that learning can be better assessed using methods that examine students' actual performance on significant, relevant tasks (Herman, Aschbacher, & Winters, 1992). These various methods of assessment, which are considered to be more developmentally appropriate, are known as *authentic assessment,* and they are viewed as more closely related to what students actually know, understand, and can perform in the classroom. Because authentic assessment allows teachers to develop a more genuine picture of their students, the assessment appears stronger. "Powerful assessment measures should reveal more than what students know. . . . Powerful assessment must also capture how those new understandings metamorphose. In this way, assessment serves as evidence of students' evolving strengths and weaknesses" (Zessoules & Gardner, 1991, p. 47). Some characteristics of authentic assessment are outlined as follows by the Northwest Regional Educational Laboratory:

1. measures multiple dimensions of child's development
2. implemented as an ongoing process
3. generates data which is useful for instructional purposes
4. takes place in a natural setting
5. provides information to share with parents
6. is free from cultural or gender bias
7. takes advantage of a variety of child's natural response modes (Faddis, 1991, p. 32)

Authentic assessment is effective because it is performance oriented, it assists teachers in instructional decision making, it is longitudinal, and it is individualized. It involves a variety of methods that are child oriented, highlighting student work and performance as core data (Chittenden, 1991). The key to developing a truly effective assessment program is to employ a number of different types of assessment tools, using a variety of techniques, in order to gather a great deal of information about the child. Chittenden has offered a framework representing three different strands of measure: tests, observation, and performance samples.

Tests

Although the use of standardized tests should be limited, other test-type assessments could be a part of an assessment program. Early childhood developmental screening provides an overall picture of students' development in key areas and helps to identify children who may need further in-depth screening or remediation. The Early Prevention of School Failure is a testing program designed to achieve early identification of students aged 4 to 6 years who are at risk and to provide remediation for their developmental learning disabilities. A less formal type of testing might be a teacher-made test designed to evaluate a student's mastery of a given skill. For young children, the testing portion of an assessment program should remain at a minimum.

Observation

Continuous observation is the second component of a framework for assessment, and it may be the most critical and significant, potentially providing the richest source of information. Teachers discover children's strengths and weaknesses—not only in skill development, but also in thinking processes—through simple, informal observation on a daily basis. However, observational data are the most elusive to record (Chittenden, 1991). Observation can range from formal to informal, using various techniques of observing and recording data such as the following:

rating forms	narrative descriptions
checklists	journals
anecdotes	group conversation
photography	videotaping
contracts	children's observation

Formal techniques include scripting, transcribing, and analyzing; informal techniques include noting, checking off, and discussing. Both can yield significant results as they apply to making decisions about children and assessing their needs. All observation methods require interaction with students: talking to them, observing their behavior, recording and synthesizing. Particularly noteworthy methods of observation are checklists, contracts, and teacher records.

There are numerous checklists available for quickly recognizing characteristics that are changing as a result of a child's development and growth. Teachers with a great deal of experience with children and their needs often develop their own lists to keep up with student progress. In his *Work Sampling System* (a performance assessment system that combines checklists, portfolios, and summary reports), Meisels (1992) provides developmental checklists for teachers of students ranging from age 3 to third grade. The checklists provide an opportunity for teachers to document progress three times a year in seven categories of performance and behavior: personal and social development; language and literacy; mathematical thinking; scientific thinking; social and cultural awareness; art and music; and physical development.

The advantages of using a behavioral/developmental checklist (see Figure 3-1) far outweigh the time and effort required to use one:

1. Checklists focus on developmental changes so [the teacher] can more easily identify progress.

SEMINOLE SPRINGS ELEMENTARY SCHOOL

PRIMARY EXPERIENCE PROGRAM

DEVELOPMENTAL CHECKLISTS

Child's Name:_____ School Year:_____

Teacher:_____ Child's Age: 5 6 7 8

Language Arts

The language development checklists include the areas of listening, oral language, reading and writing. These checklists allow us to follow the child's development. The checklist information is based upon the teacher's professional observations.

	Aug-Oct	Oct-Dec	Jan-Mar	Mar-Jun
	/_/_/	/_/_/	/_/_/	/_/_/
I. Listening				
1. Listening Behavior				
A. Listens while the teacher is talking/reading	____	____	____	____
B. Listens while another child is talking/reading	____	____	____	____
C. Listens to various media (audio tapes, film, etc.)	____	____	____	____
2. Listening Comprehension				
A. Follows instructions	____	____	____	____
B. Responds meaningfully to literature	____	____	____	____
C. Responds meaningfully in conversation	____	____	____	____
II. Oral Language	/_/_/	/_/_/	/_/_/	/_/_/
1. Appropriate Speaking Behavior				
A. Talks in small group situations	____	____	____	____
B. Talks to large groups	____	____	____	____
C. Relates personal experiences	____	____	____	____
D. Volunteers/shares information	____	____	____	____
E. Asks questions	____	____	____	____
F. Adjusts volume of voice for size of group	____	____	____	____

Key to Indicators

Each developmental area is marked to correspond with the Primary Experience report. They will be marked as <u>RED</u> for readiness, <u>DEV</u> for developing, and <u>IND</u> for independent.

Each skill area will be represented by the letters <u>N</u> for Never, <u>S</u> for Sometimes, and <u>U</u> for Usually.

Figure 3-1 A behavioral/developmental checklist

	Aug-Oct	Oct-Dec	Jan-Mar	Mar-Jun
III. Knowledge About Books	/_/_/	/_/_/	/_/_/	/_/_/
A. Understands that books contain meaning	___	___	___	___
B. Holds books right side up	___	___	___	___
C. Knows where a story starts	___	___	___	___
D. Knows how to turn pages	___	___	___	___
E. Recognizes: ___words; ___letters; ___spaces	___	___	___	___
IV. Reading Attitudes	/_/_/	/_/_/	/_/_/	/_/_/
A. Talks about books	___	___	___	___
B. Voluntarily spends time in the book center	___	___	___	___
C. Enjoys the school library	___	___	___	___
D. Enjoys listening to literature read aloud	___	___	___	___
E. Participates in shared reading	___	___	___	___
V. Reading Development Checklist				
1. The Beginning Reader	/_/_/	/_/_/	/_/_/	/_/_/
A. Enjoys listening to literature	___	___	___	___
B. Voluntarily chooses to look at books	___	___	___	___
C. Uses literature as a basis for dramatic play or illustrations	___	___	___	___
D. Has favorite stories and wants to hear them repeatedly	___	___	___	___
E. Relates experiences	___	___	___	___
F. Can relate a sequence of events	___	___	___	___
G. Understands some print and common words	___	___	___	___
H. Wants to see his or her words written down	___	___	___	___
I. Imitates reading by attempting to match memory of story to words	___	___	___	___
J. Follows a line of print in enlarged text	___	___	___	___
K. Realizes that print has meaning	___	___	___	___
L. Understands directionality of print (left/right and top/bottom)	___	___	___	___
M. Identifies the names of most le ters	___	___	___	___
N. Makes meaningful predictions	___	___	___	___
O. Attempts to write	___	___	___	___

Figure 3-1 *(continued)*

	Aug-Oct	Oct-Dec	Jan-Mar	Mar-Jun
2. The Developing Reader	/_/_/	/_/_/	/_/_/	/_/_/
A. Understands the concept of a word	___	___	___	___
B. Recognizes some rhyming words, blends, word endings, etc.	___	___	___	___
C. Sometimes points at text while reading	___	___	___	___
D. Reads some printed materials independently	___	___	___	___
E. Has store of sight words for reading and writing	___	___	___	___
F. Uses all the cueing systems	___	___	___	___
G. Makes meaningful substitutions when reading	___	___	___	___
H. Comprehends what has been read; can retell a story	___	___	___	___
3. The Independent Reader	/_/_/	/_/_/	/_/_/	/_/_/
A. Reads silently but sometimes reads aloud when text is difficult	___	___	___	___
B. Makes predictions about words (uses all three cueing systems)	___	___	___	___
C. Self-corrects when reading doesn't make sense	___	___	___	___
D. Comprehends at different levels (literal, interpretive, critical)	___	___	___	___
E. Adjusts silent reading rate to material and purpose	___	___	___	___
F. Invented spellings are approaching standard spellings	___	___	___	___
VI. Reading Comprehension	/_/_/	/_/_/	/_/_/	/_/_/
A. Applies higher level thinking and reasoning skills	___	___	___	___
B. Expects what is read to make sense and self-corrects when meaning is lost	___	___	___	___
C. Uses prior knowledge to construct meaning	___	___	___	___
D. Adequately retells the story demonstrating an awareness of characters, setting and plot	___	___	___	___
E. Discusses or demonstrates understanding of key concepts in informational texts	___	___	___	___
F. Distinguishes between reality and fantasy	___	___	___	___
G. Distinguishes between fact and opinion	___	___	___	___
H. Identifies problem and solution	___	___	___	___
I. Identifies cause and effect	___	___	___	___
J. Interprets information through summarizing and drawing conclusions	___	___	___	___

Figure 3-1   *(continued)*

	Aug-Oct /_/_/	Oct-Dec /_/_/	Jan-Mar /_/_/	Mar-Jun /_/_/

VII. Strategies for Word Identification

Readers use three cueing systems to unlock words. They ask: Does the word make sense in the sentence? Does the word fit in the structure of the sentence? and What sound do the letters make? The effective reader uses all of these cues at the same time.

A. Reads on to the end of the sentence ____ ____ ____ ____

B. Starts sentence again and rereads ____ ____ ____ ____

C. Uses initial letter or letter clusters as
a cue and then predicts ____ ____ ____ ____

D. Uses pictorial cues ____ ____ ____ ____

E. Asks a friend ____ ____ ____ ____

F. Skips the word ____ ____ ____ ____

G. Substitutes another meaningful word ____ ____ ____ ____

H. Other appropriate strategies ____ ____ ____ ____

VIII. Writing Developmental Checklist

	/_/_/	/_/_/	/_/_/	/_/_/

A. Voluntarily chooses to write ____ ____ ____ ____

B. Creates stories through dramatic play,
painting, etc.

C. Draws a series of sequenced pictures
to tell a story ____ ____ ____ ____

D. Asks to have dictated words written down ____ ____ ____ ____

E. Contributes to group compositions ____ ____ ____ ____

F. Prints a few letters ____ ____ ____ ____

G. Prints strings of random letters ____ ____ ____ ____

H. Prints meaningful groups of two or more words ____ ____ ____ ____

I. Uses simple sentences ____ ____ ____ ____

J. Writes a sequenced piece with two or
more sentences ____ ____ ____ ____

K. Writes a story with two or more paragraphs ____ ____ ____ ____

L. Uses invented spelling ____ ____ ____ ____

M. Applies spelling skills to written word ____ ____ ____ ____

N. Uses punctuation correctly ____ ____ ____ ____

IX. Spelling Developmental Checklist

	/_/_/	/_/_/	/_/_/	/_/_/

A. Uses random letters to represent sounds ____ ____ ____ ____

B. Uses initial consonants to represent whole words ____ ____ ____ ____

C. Uses initial and final consonants for
each word ____ ____ ____ ____

D. Uses initial, final and medial consonants
for each word ____ ____ ____ ____

E. Uses vowels as place-holders (vowels incorrect
but in correct positions) ____ ____ ____ ____

F. Approximates standard spelling ____ ____ ____ ____

Figure 3-1   *(continued)*

Mathematics

The mathematics developmental checklists include the areas of sorting, patterning, addition, subtraction, measurement, time, money, geometry, and interpretation of graphs, charts and tables. The information on these checklists is based on formal and informal testing and the teacher's professional judgment.

I. Sorting
   A. _____Sorts a collection of objects
   B. _____Resorts a collection of objects
   C. _____Identifies sorting rule

II. Patterning
   A. _____Identifies and extends a pattern
   B. _____Creates a pattern
   C. _____Records a pattern on paper

III. Numeration
   A. Counts numbers to: ___10; ___20; ___100; ___1000
   B. Reads numbers to: ___10; ___20; ___100; ___1000
   C. Writes numbers to: ___10; ___20; ___100; ___1000
   D. Count by: 10's to ____; 5's to ____; 2's to ____
   E. Reads and writes number names to ten _____
   F. Matches quantity to numerals _____
   G. Identifies numerals as: ___largest; ___smallest; ___more; ___less
   H. Can sequence numbers presented out of order___
    I. Can write numerals that come ___before; ___after; or ___between any given
       number to: ___10; ___50; ___100; ___1000
   J. Recognize s ___ odd and ___ even numbers
   K. States the place value of digits in;___1's; ___10's; ___100's; ___1000's
   L. Can write numerals from an expanded form (i.e., 100+50+3=153)
   M. Understands and uses the symbols ___<; ___>; ___= with numerals
       to ___10; ___100; ___1000
   N. Identifies ordinal positions of numbers to ___10; ___100; and ___1000

Figure 3-1 (*continued*)

IV. Addition and Subtraction
A. Dependent on manipulatives to solve problems____
B. Not dependent on manipulatives for problem solving____

Addition:
C. ___Uses horizontal notation and ___vertical position
D. ___One-digit numbers; ___two-digit numbers; ___three- or more-digit numbers
E. ___Without regrouping or ___with regrouping
F. Basic facts through: ___10; ___20
G. ___Column addition
H. Solves word problems
I. ___Money problems

Subtraction:
A. ___Uses horizontal notation and ___vertical notation
B. ___One-digit numbers; ___two-digit numbers; ___three- or more-digit numbers
C. ___Without regrouping or ___with regrouping
D. Basic facts through ___10; ___20
E. ___Solves word problems
F. ___Money problems

V. Fractions
A. Uses ___"whole" and ___ "one half" in relation to objects
B. Identifies ___one half; ___one third; ___one fourth of a given shape or region
C. Divides a real object or picture of a real object into: ___halves; ___thirds; and ___fourths
D. Identifies functions and parts of a fraction
E. Separates a set of no more than 12 objects into: ___halves; ___thirds; ___fourths; or ___smaller fractions
F. Reads fractions in ___words and ___numerical form
G. Writes fractions in ___words and ___numerical form

Figure 3-1   (*continued*)

VI. Measurement

Time

A. Identifies clock as a measurement of time____

B. Writes numerals 1 through 12 on a clock face____

C. Can identify ___hour; ___minute; and ___second hands on the clock

D. Reads time in ___whole; ___half; ___quarter hour; ___five minute intervals

E. States ___days of the week and ___months of the year in order

Linear

A. Measures length using ___objects; ___inches; ___centimeters; ___feet; ___ yards

Weight

A. Identifies ___ounces; ___pounds; ___grams; ___kilograms as units of weight

B. Uses a scale to weigh ___objects and ___self

Volume

A. Identifies ___cups; ___pints; ___quarts; ___half gallons; ___gallons; and ___liters
    as liquid measures

VII. Money

A. Identifies ___penny; ___nickel; ___dime; ___quarter; ___half dollar; ___dollar

B. Matches coins with their values

C. Determines the value of a set of coins equaling no more than ___5 cents;
    ___10 cents; ___25 cents; ___50 cents; ___$1; ___more than $1

D. Uses decimal notation to write value of money over $1___

VIII. Geometry

A. Can identify ___circle; ___rectangle; ___square; and ___triangle

B. Matches objects with same shape ___

C. Identifies the number of sides in ___a rectangle; ___triangle; and ___square

IX. Interpretation of Graphs, Charts and Tables

A. Reads a ___bar graph and ___table

B. Constructs a ___bar graph and ___table

Figure 3-1   *(continued)*

Social/Emotional

This section reports where the child is in his/ her social and emotional development. It is not a report of behavior problems. Teacher's professional judgment is used to identify developmental stages.

I. Adult-Child Relationships

    A. ___Dependent on adults for security needs

    B. ___Attends to task with limited adult attention

    C. ___Little or no dependency on adults for meeting needs and maintaining behavior

    D. ___Follows classroom rules with few reminders

II. Child-Child Relationships

    A. Most frequently prefers to play and work ___alone; ___near others; ___cooperatively with other children

    B. Enjoys the company of ___same age peers; ___younger children; ___older children

    C. ___Shares

    D. ___Shows concern for classmates' feelings and predicaments

    E. ___Respects others belongings

III. Attitude Toward Learning

    A. ___Attempts new tasks with little self doubt

    B. ___Occasionally chooses learning tasks during recreation (i.e., reading during free time, etc.)

    C. ___Cooperates with group learning tasks

    D. ___Self-starter

IV. Teacher Comments

V. Suggestions for Mom and Dad

Figure 3-1 (*continued*)

2. There is a closer match between curriculum goals and assessment outcome, so the information is more relevant and helpful to the teacher.
3. Checklists provide concrete and systematic means to modify instruction.
4. Checklists allow for more individualized assessment.
5. They provide multiple opportunities for the child to demonstrate competence.
6. They do not interrupt the daily routine.
7. Checklists provide concrete information to parents. (Meisels & Steele, 1991, p. 2)

Contracts

Contracts are another form of individual assessment related to observation. They provide a written plan and record of each student's daily activities and progress. They are an excellent and efficient means of monitoring performance, because the children themselves can check off completed activities and evaluate how well they did. Along with self-correcting materials, contracts give children a clear idea of their own progress. Teachers check children's progress as work occurs, and they meet with each child daily to review the day's work. Relevant completed work is stapled to the contract for children to take home so that parents can also monitor progress.

During the daily conferences, teachers can evaluate overall problems and progress and plan the next day's contract accordingly. In this way, teachers can assign activities at an appropriate difficulty level, and they can ensure a balanced program. It is important for teachers to be realistic about the amount of work included in the contract and to allow flexibility for exploration and new experiences.

Contracts occur along a continuum. First there is the teacher-made, teacher-assigned contract in which the student has little or no input. This type is used more frequently in traditional classrooms and puts little responsibility for planning in the hands of students. The second type is the teacher-made, student-assigned contract, which contains content in an area the student has selected. This might be an area of weakness or an area of particular interest to the student. Teachers can use several different types of contracts and should include some student-assigned activities. The level of contracting depends on the student's reading ability and ability to be self-responsible. (See sample contract in Chapter 2.)

Recordkeeping

Engaging in discussions with children, noting their behavior, and recording their achievements, as well as documenting their strengths and weaknesses, are all a part of the observational record. Some teachers keep journals or logs to make anecdotal records that help them note the progressive nature of the child's development. Records should indicate general behavior patterns as well as academic achievements. Pleasant or disturbing family occurrences, illnesses, accidents, and highlights at school should all be noted, as these may be important in assessing the child's overall development. These records indicate the social interaction and emotional development to which the child's academic learning is related. Figure 3-2 shows two summative reports as examples of recordkeeping.

Over all, observational methods involve recordkeeping and accurate and detailed reports of the individual child's developmental levels and what he or she is doing. Recordkeeping should be an informal, simple process, with records being easy to keep and easy to read. Two important ideas about observation are worth noting. First, the best format of observation is to use the methods with which the teacher feels most comfortable. He or she should use a variety of techniques, but should be allowed to choose which methods will comprise the observation portion of the assessment program in his or her class. Second, observation should not be treated as a separate entity from teaching and learning. Conversely, it should be integrated into the instructional day as a part of the program (Chittenden, 1991).

Portfolios

The third and final component of a framework for assessment is the inclusion of performance samples, or what is more commonly referred to as *portfolios*. As a tool for assessment, portfolios, or groupings of students' work, focus on what students can do and have done. When teachers collect samples of students' work over a period of time and work with students to review and revise their work, both teachers and students become aware of strengths and weaknesses, and teachers can easily devise a more individualized program to meet each child's needs.

There are many different types of portfolios and many ways to manage the use of portfolio assessment in the classroom. When designing a portfolio program, it is important to establish not only the purpose of maintaining the portfolio, but also the standards by which the portfolio will be evaluated (Grace & Shores, 1992). In order to establish the content of a portfolio, the teacher must consider what it will be used for and by whom. It could be a working portfolio for the student, which contains all the projects and work the student is presently working on, including art projects, math papers, a list of books the child has read, and so forth. Or, it could be a permanent folder exhibiting final, polished projects the teacher and student have chosen to become a part of the student's record. Often, this permanent portfolio also contains testing and observational data that have been collected throughout the year. The portfolio may include work from one subject for one teacher, or it may be part of a school-wide system used to replace report cards. Depending on the instructional purposes of particular classrooms, schools, and districts, the specific contents of portfolios will vary. The following outline suggests how to organize a portfolio for preschool and primary grade children:

Art Activities (Fine Motor Development)

- Drawings of events, persons, and animals. The child might dictate to a classroom volunteer, or the child might write his or her own explanations.

**NEW HOPE ELEMENTARY SCHOOL
NARRATIVE REPORT
PHYSICAL MOVEMENT EXPERIENCES**

For the period covering September 3, 199X to October 31, 199X

Student's Name: _____

Teacher's Name: _____

K–1
The children have explored general and personal space, qualities of movement, and the distinction between locomotor and nonlocomotor movement using the medium of geography and more specifically the Hawaiian islands. The islands represent personal space, and the ocean represents general space. We explored the contrast between tense and fluid movements via the exploration of volcanic activity, lava flow, and their role in the formation of land masses. We created a dance sequence reflecting the volcanic process, using the movements of exploding, floating, and freezing.

The children have also created an original rain dance, after exploring traditional Native American rain dances. The children generated the movements for our dance by analyzing the elements of rain (clouds, drops, puddles, lightning, and thunder).

The children have also explored levels of movement through the consideration of oceans. We explored the rising and falling of waves, the ebb and flow of the tides, and the swirling of whirlpools. We also explored some of the ways people live off the oceans by "casing" body parts and "reeling" them back in.

Parent's Signature: _____

Figure 3-2 Summative reports

**NEW HOPE ELEMENTARY SCHOOL
NARRATIVE REPORT**

ADDITIONAL EXPERIENCE _____

For the period covering November 4, 199X to January 17, 199X

Student's Name: _____

Teacher's Name: _____

The primary focus of reading this second quarter has been the study of drama as a form of literature. A social studies unit on interdependence was also integrated as the children planned and performed a stage production of the traditional folktale "Stone Soup." Sharing and cooperation, the underlying theme in "Stone Soup," became the focal point of our classroom as each child took an active part in the planning and presentation of the play. During our study of "Stone Soup," the children experienced the opportunity to:

- Develop basic drama vocabulary and techniques.
- Work together as well as appreciate individual contributions.
- Study and memorize a script.
- Help design costumes, sets, and invitations for a play.
- Learn to focus and concentrate.
- Gain satisfaction from rehearsing and presenting drama to a live audience.

We also discussed the origin of folktales and the various renditions of the same story. We read two other versions of "Stone Soup" for comparison and contrast.

Parent's Signature: _____

Figure 3-2 (*continued*)

- Photos of unusual block constructions or projects, labeled and dated.
- Collages and other examples of the child's use of various media.
- Samples of the child's manuscript printing. (The appearance and placement of the letters on the page are evaluated in the context of a developmental continuum.)

Movement (Gross Motor Development)

- Notes recorded by the teacher or videotapes of the child's movement activities in the class or on the playground, which reflects the child's developing skills.
- Notes, photographs, videotapes and anecdotal records that demonstrate the child's skills and progress in music activities and fingerplays.
- Notes from teacher interviews with the child about his or her favorite active games at school.

Math and Science Activities (Concept Development)

- Photographs of the child measuring or counting specific ingredients as part of a cooking activity.
- Charts on which the child has recorded the planting, care, watering schedule, periods of sunlight, and so forth, of plants in the classroom or on the school grounds.
- Work samples demonstrating the child's understanding of number concepts.
- Work samples, teacher notes, and taped pupil interviews illustrating, in a progressive fashion, the child's understanding of mathematical concepts.
- Photographs and data gathered from checklists and taped pupil interviews that document the child's conceptual understanding, exploring, hypothesizing, and problem-solving. A checklist the child completes, in which she or he guesses which object will float prior to putting the objects in the water and then notes which items actually do float, is an example of data that demonstrate the child's conceptual understanding, hypothesizing, and observational skills.

Language and Literacy

- Tape recordings of a child re-reading stories she or he "wrote" or dictated to a parent, teacher, or classroom volunteer.
- Examples of the child's journal entries.

- Copies of signs or labels the child constructed.
- A log of book titles actually read by the child or read to the child by a teacher, parent, or other adult.
- Copies of stories, poems, or songs the child wrote or dictated.
- Taped pupil interviews that reveal the child's increase, over time, in vocabulary and skill in use of the language.

Personal and Social Development

- Teacher notes and anecdotal records that document interactions between the child and his or her peers. Such interactions can indicate the child's ability to make choices, solve problems, and cooperate with others.
- Teacher notes, anecdotal records, and video recordings documenting events that occurred on field trips. Such incidents may illustrate the child's social awareness.
- Chart of the child's choices of activities during a particular week or month.
- Notes from teacher-parent conferences. (Meisels & Steele, 1991)

Figures 3-3 through 3-11 show various ways to organize a portfolio, as well as examples of the types of checklists and other forms a teacher might wish to include.

Many teachers find that it is helpful to have both a working and a permanent portfolio in the classroom. Students add daily to their working portfolios, and as projects are completed, or at given conference times, teachers and students choose the work to add to the permanent portfolios. Dates should always be included on student work placed in a portfolio, and the teacher should check its contents regularly to be sure that all areas of the curriculum are being documented at regular intervals throughout the year. In order for the assessment to be valid, it must show long-term development and growth.

Using Authentic Assessment in Parent Conferences _____

Portfolios provide a built-in system for planning parent conferences. By looking at concrete examples of a child's work—not by discussing the abstract concept of a child's development and needs—the parents will be able to see and more easily understand the type of progress their child is making. A child's accomplishment should always be compared to his or her earlier accomplishments. A portfolio should never be used to compare a child to an average or to another child. It is helpful if the teacher reviews strengths and weaknesses as noted in the portfolio (work samples, observational methods, or test results) and provides written suggestions for the parents (Grady, 1992).

SOUTH BRUNSWICK TOWNSHIP PUBLIC SCHOOLS*

The committee on assessment has affirmed the purposes of maintaining a portfolio for every child who enters our program until he or she completes the second grade. First, we hope to help teachers, specialists, and parents describe the child and his or her program without using standardized tests as the primary source of data. Second, the portfolio allows every teacher to document progress for every child, providing data to support and inform decisions about daily teaching and about class placement. In short, the portfolio gives substance to our contention that we take children wherever they are when they enter our program and move them forward as they become competent readers and writers.

The following list sets forth the directions for the use of the portfolio.

1. On the front of the portfolio is a "Table of Contents" covering all three years.

2. Materials from each grade level should be kept in a manila folder that is clearly marked for each grade level.

3. The teacher's assessment kit includes all forms. There are many options for teachers.

   A. There are checklists available to attach to children's work samples. If you fill out a checklist, staple it to the work sample and put a second asterisk on the table of contents.

   B. There are observations forms that are to be used for children who are having difficulty. If you decide to add an observation sheet, indicate so by putting an asterisk in the "other" column.

   C. There are alternative forms for taking a reading sample.

4. At least once a year, each teacher will have a portfolio conference with his or her administrator or the Director of Instruction to review progress, clarify directions, and talk about children who are having difficulty.

The following list sets forth the contents of the portfolio:

1. **Self-Portraits**
What:	A picture drawn to the prompt: "Draw a picture of yourself." The picture could be drawn on the front and back of the manila folders that mark each grade level.
When:	At the beginning and end of each school year.

* Member: Association for Supervision and Curriculum Development, Early Childhood Consortium, 1988–1993, Dr. Barbara Day, Chair.

Figure 3-3 Sample of a school district's portfolio contents

2. **Interview with the Child**
   What: The interview can take several forms, depending on the level of the child. Several interview forms are included. The teacher should select the term that is most appropriate for that child.
   When: Each child should be interviewed at the beginning of each year. When you observe major changes in the behavior of the child, another interview might be in order.

3. **Interview with the Parent**
   What: The questionnaire found in the teacher's assessment kit should go home to parents before conference time. Discussion of the questionnaire and other related information about the child's literacy behavior should occur at the conference and notes recorded on the questionnaire form.
   When: Form goes home before fall conferences.

4. **Concepts About Print Test**
   What: Student test paper.
   When: At the beginning and end of kindergarten. If child is having difficulty, repeat the test as needed.

5. **Word Awareness Writing Activity (WAWA)**
   What: Student paper marked with a score. Directions for this activity are in the assessment kit.
   When: At the end of kindergarten.
   At the beginning and end of grade 1.
   If child is having difficulty, repeat the activity as needed.
   (Optional word list is provided.)

6. **Reading Sample**
   What: Include a reading sample showing strategies the child is using to deal with print and a short analysis of the results.
   See directions for taking a reading sample. Teachers may attach a descriptive checklist (included in the teacher's portfolio) if more information about the child is needed.
   When: At least twice a year, until the child is using self-correcting strategies and reading fluently.

7. **Writing Sample**
   What: An example of free writing done by the student. It should be unedited by the teacher, but the teacher can translate the child's

Figure 3-3 (*continued*)

words if they cannot be read easily. Teachers should attach a descriptive checklist (found in teacher's portfolio) if more information about the child is needed.

When: At the beginning and end of every year.

8. **Class Record Form**
   What: A class record form which asks you to review accumulated knowledge about your students. If you answer "no" to any questions or if you do not have enough accumulated knowledge to answer at all, you should fill out an auxiliary checklist about that child. If you err, it would be better to err by including too much data than not enough.
   When: A class list should be completed in fall and spring.

9. **Sight Word List**
   What: A list of the most frequently used words in *The Wright Group* Big Book Series.
   When: As appropriate.

10. **Story Retelling**
    What: Story Retelling is written, oral, and/or pictorial retelling of a story read to the child or read by the child.
    When: Three times every year.

Figure 3-3   *(continued)*

SOUTH BRUNSWICK BOARD OF EDUCATION*

School _____

Teacher's Name _____

	Pre K	Beg K	Mid K	End K	Beg 1	Mid 1	End 1	Beg 2	Mid 2	End 2
1. Self Portraits	*	*		*	*		*	*		*
2. Interview with the Child		*			*			*		
3. Interview with the Parent	*	*			*			*		
4. Concept about Print Test		*		*						
5. Word Awareness Writing Activity (WAWA)				*	*		*			
6. Sight Word List				*	*	*	*			
7. Reading Sample				*	*	*		*	*	
8. Writing Sample		*		*	*		*	*		*
9. Class Record			*			*			*	
10. Story Retelling	*	*	*	*	*	*	*	*	*	*
11. Optional Forms										

* Member: Association for supervision and Curriculum Development, Early Childhood Consortium, 1988–1993, Dr. Barbara Day, Chair

Figure 3-4 Language arts checklist

DEVELOPMENT OF CHILDREN'S STRATEGIES
FOR MAKING SENSE OF PRINT*

O–N/A

1 EARLY EMERGENT
Displays an awareness of some conventions of writing, such as front/back of books, distinctions between print and pictures. Sees the construction of meaning from text as "magical" or exterior to the print. While the child may be interested in the contents of books, there is as yet little apparent attention to turning written marks into language. Is beginning to notice environmental print.

2 ADVANCED EMERGENT
Engages in pretend reading and writing. Uses reading-like ways that clearly approximate book language. Demonstrates a sense of the story being "read," using picture clues and recall of story line. May draw upon predictable language patterns in anticipating (and recalling) the story. Attempts to use letters in writing, sometimes in random or scribble fashion.

3 EARLY BEGINNING READER
Attempts to "really read." Indicates beginning sense of one-to-one correspondence and concept of word. Predicts actively in new material, using syntax and story line. Small, stable sight vocabulary is becoming established. Evidence of initial awareness of beginning and ending sounds, especially in invented spelling.

4 ADVANCED BEGINNING READER
Starts to draw on major cue systems; self-corrects or identifies words through use of letter-sound patterns, sense of story, or syntax. Reading may be laborious, especially with new material requiring considerable effort and some support. Writing and spelling reveal awareness of letter patterns and conventions of writing such as capitalization and full stops.

5 EARLY INDEPENDENT READER
Handles familiar material on own, but still needs some support with unfamiliar material. Figures out words and self-corrects by drawing on a combination of letter-sound relationships, word structure, story line, and syntax. Strategies of re-reading or of guessing from larger chunks of text are becoming well established. Has a large, stable sight vocabulary. Conventions of writing are understood.

6 ADVANCED INDEPENDENT READER
Reads independently, using multiple strategies flexibly. Monitors and self-corrects for meaning. Can read and understand most material when the content is appropriate. Conventions of writing and spelling are—for the most part—under control.

* Rating scale developed by South Brunswick teachers and Educational Testing Service staff—January, 1991.

Figure 3-5 Rating scale for reading, K–2

**NEW HOPE ELEMENTARY SCHOOL
PARENT QUESTIONNAIRE**

Directions: Please answer the following questions. If you need additional space, use the back of the page. Return this form to your child's homeroom teacher by _____.

1. What are your child's special interests (games, books, hobbies, toys, TV programs, etc.)?

2. Does anyone read aloud to your child? If so, how often?

3. Does your child have a special time to complete homework or projects?

4. Do you have concerns or questions regarding your child's development and/or academic growth? If so, what?

5. Does your child have access to any of the following: TV, VCR, computer, camera, radio, tape player?

6. What makes your child happy?

7. What upsets or angers your child?

8. Is there any other information that you would like to share with us which would help us better serve your child?

Child's Name: _____   Date: _____

Parent's Signature: _____

Figure 3-6   Parent interview form or questionnaire

CHILD'S READING INTERVIEW

Name: _____   Age: _____   Date: _____

1. When you are reading and come to something you don't know, what do you do?

   Do you ever do anything else?

2. Who is a good reader you know?

3. What makes _____ a good reader?

4. Do you think _____ ever comes to something she/he doesn't know?

5. "Yes" When _____ does come to something she/he doesn't know, what do you think he/she does?

   "No" Suppose _____ comes to something she/he doesn't know. What do you think she/he would do?

6. If you knew someone was having trouble reading how would you help that person?

7. What would your teacher do to help that person?

8. How did you learn to read?

9. What would you like to do better as a reader?

10. Do you think you are a good reader? Why?

Figure 3-7

STUDENT'S NAME _____

CODES: N = Not at this time   S = Sometimes   M = Most of the time

WRITING OBSERVATION

	Pre K	Beg K	Mid K	End K	Beg 1	Mid 1	End 1	Beg 2	Mid 2	End 2
DATE										
Attitude Chooses to write										
Sustains concentration										
Integrates writing into activities										
Reads writing to others										
Wants to display writing										
Picture/Print Relationship Draws only (may dictate)										
Draws picture, then writes										
Writes, then draws										
Editing Can recognize some errors (spacing, punctuation, capitals, etc.)										
Can correct some errors										

Figure 3-8 Writing checklist

STUDENT'S NAME _____

CODES: N = Not at this time   S = Sometimes   M = Most of the time

READING OBSERVATION

	Pre K	Beg K	Mid K	End K	Beg 1	Mid 1	End 1	Beg 2	Mid 2	End 2
DATE										
Reading Attitude Chooses to read										
Sustains interest										
Selects appropriate books										
Shares reading experience with others										
Shared Book Experience (Group) Listens attentively										
Joins in when able										
Responds to questions, texts, and pictures										
Comprehension Makes connections from own experience to what is read										
Makes predictions about text										
Gives reason for liking or disliking the book										

Figure 3-9   Reading checklist

STUDENT'S NAME _____

CODES: N = Not at this time   S = Sometimes   M = Most of the time

ORAL LANGUAGE CHECKLIST

	Pre K	Beg K	Mid K	End K	Beg 1	Mid 1	End 1	Beg 2	Mid 2	End 2
DATE										
Speech Skills Uses Appropriate Volume										
Articulates Clearly										
Settings Talks to Teachers										
Talks to Peers										
Talks in Small Group Situations										
Talks in Large Group Situations										
Uses of Languages Asks for Help From Peers										
Asks for Help From Adults										
Asks Questions										
Initiates Conversations										
Takes Turns Speaking										
Relates Personal Experiences										
Responds Relevantly to Topic										
Expresses Point of View										
Expresses Feelings										
CAN RETELL A SEQUENCE OF EVENTS FROM EXPERIENCE										

Figure 3-10   Oral language checklist

KINDERGARTEN REPORTING FORMAT
LINCOLNWOOD SCHOOL DISTRICT*

Name _____

Birthdate _____

Parent Name _____

B-day ☐

Address ☐

Phone # ☐

Child Knows:

School/Year _____

Teacher _____

READING (Tested Objectives)

☐ 1001 Apply Concepts of Print

☐ 1002 Identify Upper/Lower Case Letters

☐ 1003 Identify (use) Consonants

☐ 1004 Reconstruct Sequence of Events

ORAL/WRITTEN COMMUNICATION (Tested Objectives)

☐ 2001 Tell Own Full Name

☐ 2002 Tell Phone Number

☐ 2003 Dictate Thoughts

☐ 2004 Hold Pencil/Crayon Correctly

☐ 2005 Write First Name

☐ 2006 Demonstrate Knowledge of Alphabetical Order

READING (Tested Objectives)

1001 Apply Concepts of Print (4/4 needed for mastery)

☐ beginning point ☐ turning pages ☐ left to right ☐ top to bottom

1002 Names Letters

Upper Case (23/26 for mastery)

☐ I	☐ S	☐ E	☐ Y	☐ J	☐ V	☐ Q
☐ U	☐ A	☐ C	☐ K	☐ F	☐ O	☐ T
☐ L	☐ R	☐ D	☐ B	☐ W	☐ G	☐ H
☐ P	☐ N	☐ M	☐ X	☐ Z		

Lower Case (23/26 for mastery)

☐ b	☐ n	☐ w	☐ i	☐ p	☐ c	☐ h
☐ q	☐ r	☐ v	☐ s	☐ m	☐ z	☐ t
☐ g	☐ k	☐ f	☐ y	☐ d	☐ j	☐ x
☐ a	☐ e	☐ i	☐ o	☐ u		

1003 Knows Consonant Sounds (17/21 for mastery)

☐ b	☐ n	☐ w	☐ i	☐ p	☐ c	☐ h
☐ q	☐ r	☐ v	☐ s	☐ m	☐ z	☐ t
☐ g	☐ k	☐ f	☐ y	☐ d	☐ j	☐ x

Figure 3-11

* Member: Association for Supervision and Curriculum Development, Early Childhood Consortium, 1988–1993, Dr. Barbara Day, Chair

MATHEMATICS (Tested Objectives)

Number Sense/Numeration

☐ 2. Demonstrate ability to count by 1's to 20:

| 1 | 2 | 3 | 4 | 5 | 6 | 7 | 8 | 9 | 10 | 11 | 12 | 13 | 14 | 15 | 16 | 17 | 18 | 19 | 20 |

☐ 3. Demonstrate one to one correspondence 0 – 10.

☐ 5. Form sets with numerals 0 – 10

☐ 6. Identify Ordinal numbers first–fifth. ☐ First ☐ Second ☐ Third ☐ Fourth ☐ Fifth

☐ 7. Read cardinal numerals 0 – 20; write cardinal numerals 1 – 10.

Read

| 1 | 2 | 3 | 4 | 5 | 6 | 7 | 8 | 9 | 10 | 11 | 12 | 13 | 14 | 15 | 16 | 17 | 18 | 19 | 20 |

| 1 | 2 | 3 | 4 | 5 | 6 | 7 | 8 | 9 | 10 |

Write

☐ 10. Compare/order 0 – 10.   ☐ 11. Identify coins: ☐ Penny ☐ Nickel ☐ Dime

Patterning

☐ 17. Identify/compare/contrast special pattern characteristics of a relationship: **Color/Shape/Size**

Algebra/Relationships

☐ 24. Identify/Compare whole numbers 0 – 10 (more/less) with/without manipulatives.

Geometry

☐ 27. Identify positions in a picture/object:
      ☐ Above/Below   ☐ Inside/Outside   ☐ Over/Under   ☐ Left/right

☐ 28. Identify/Sort/Classify plane shapes with or without manipulatives.

☐ ● ☐ ■ ☐ ▬ ☐ ▲ ☐ ◆ ☐ ⬮

☐ 29. Compare basic shapes for similarities/differences:

Time Measurement

☐ 37. Identify days in the week, yesterday, today, tomorrow.

Operation/Computation – Whole Numbers

☐ 39. Construct sets (one more/less) through 5.

☐ 41. Solve oral problems in story context with manipulatives.

Figure 3-11   *(continued)*

REQUIRED PORTFOLIO DATA:

Oral/Written Communication: **2003 Dictated Thoughts**

     2005 Write First Name

Mathematics: **Write Numerals 0 - 10**

     Construct sets (more/less) through five.

4 drawings/dictated writings/child written SAMPLES (October, January, March, May)

<u>Observations</u>

Figure 3-11   (*continued*)

NARRATIVE   (Optional)

_____

Parent's Signature
Fall Conference

_____

Parent's Signature
Spring Conference

Figure 3-11   (*continued*)

If organized effectively and evaluated appropriately, portfolios can represent the full range of assessment. By including a multimethod approach, teachers gain a clear picture of students' growth and development. Portfolios involve the students actively so that they develop a real interest and become motivated to perform well, thus encouraging high self-esteem (Tierney, Carter, & Desai, 1991). Equally beneficial is the close relationship between instruction and the assessment of learning that develops when portfolios are used. Because the organization of a portfolio allows for the inclusion of observational methods and testing results, it is an ideal package in which to hold the entire framework of a strong assessment program.

Assessment of the Learning Environment

Equally as important as assessment of children's growth and development is assessment of the learning environment to ensure that developmentally appropriate learning can take place. A good starting point for evaluation is to take a broad look at all major aspects of the learning environment: teacher-child relationships, the teaching/learning process, curriculum organization, materials and equipment, the physical environment, and the outdoor environment.

Teachers should assess the quality of each major component of the learning environment and target specific areas for improvement. In addition to this overall evaluation, teachers must also assess the effectiveness of the learning environment in terms of its impact on children's behavior and engagement in learning. Developmental classrooms are complex, fluid settings that encompass diverse developmental and learning goals and involve a wide range of individual and group activities. In order to assess the effects of this multifaceted environment accurately, teachers must observe and analyze many variables.

The Wasik-Day Open and Traditional Learning Environment and Children's Classroom Behavior Instrument (Day & Drake, 1983) provides an effective mechanism for correlating student behavior with a number of environmental variables. Designed for use in early childhood through sixth grade classrooms, this instrument provides a specific classroom behavior scale for measuring the effects of six variables: place, group leader, number in group, movement, academic behavior, and communication. The observer using the Wasik-Day Instrument collects data on a specific child for 10 consecutive 1-minute intervals, checking the appropriate box for each variable at the end of each minute. An example of a completed Wasik-Day Instrument is shown in Figure 3-12. Definitions of each category on the instrument and instructions for tabulating behaviors are as follows:

Time. Record hour and minute at the beginning of each 10-minute recording session. Note any changes that cause a break in a consecutive 10-minute recording. If a break occurs, go to a new 10-minute set.

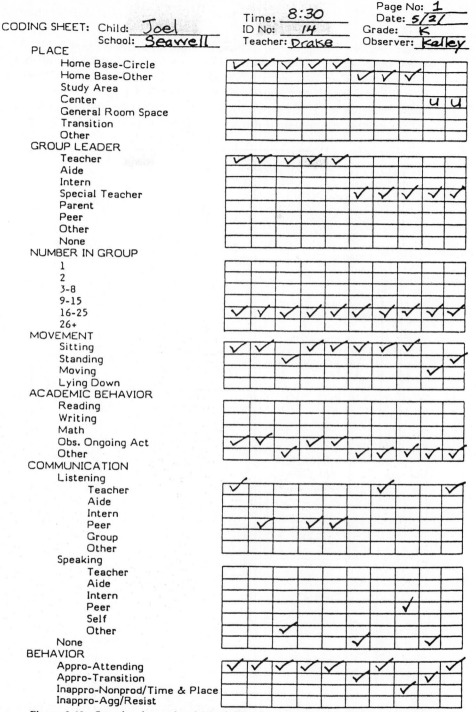

CODING SHEET: Child: Joel   Time: 8:30   Page No: 1

School: Seawell   ID No: 14   Date: 5/21

Teacher: Drake   Grade: K   Observer: Kelley

Figure 3-12 Sample of completed Wasik-Day Open and Traditional Learning Environments and Children's Classroom Behavior Instrument

Source: Day and Drake(1983).

Place. Prepare a map of the room and label all areas (Figure 3-13).

Home base—circle. Code when the child is in home base for circle activities. Examples of these activities are morning scheduling arrangements, listening to a story, or observing a flannelboard activity.

Home base—other. Code when the home base area is used for all other activities (for instance, when the music teacher, parent, or teacher aide uses the

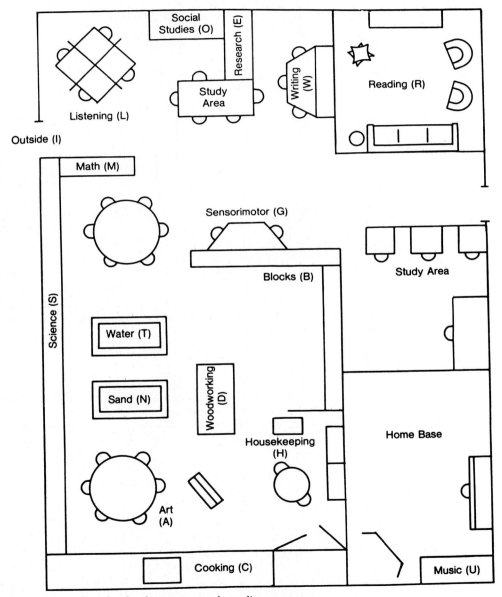

Figure 3-13   Sample of a classroom map for coding purposes.

home base for other activity). Also code if one or more children are using the home base as a study area.

Study area. Code when specifically designated areas are used for completing individually assigned work.

Center. Code when the child is in a learning center. Denote the center by the following code: A-Art, B-Blocks, G-Sensorimotor, H-Housekeeping, M-Math, U-Music, R-Reading, E-Research, S-Science, O-Social Studies, D-Woodworking, W-Writing, L-Listening, C-Cooking, T-Water, N-Sand, I-Outside, X-Other.

General room space. Includes all space not specifically designated by one of the other categories. These areas should be denoted by shaded areas on the map.

Transition. Code when a child is moving from one area to another, changing activities, gathering materials for work, or cleaning up. Child may be in one of the designated areas.

Other. Code if an area is not covered and describe the setting on the back of the code sheet.

Group Leader. Code the individual who is explicitly the leader of the ongoing activity in which the child is involved. The leader does not need to be physically near at all times. If the teacher is in a one-to-one relationship with the child, code the teacher as the leader. If children are together with no designated leader and one child becomes the leader, code group leader as peer. Codes: Teacher, Aide, Intern, Special Teacher, Parent, Peer, Other, and None.

Number in Group. Code the number of children in the group in which the child is involved. For example, count all children sitting on the floor in a common area listening to a story. If the child is sitting at a table with other children, count the total number of children at that table. Do not include adults.

Movement

Sitting. Code sitting behavior regardless of whether the child is sitting on a chair, floor, table, or other structure.

Standing. Code standing regardless of where the child is standing.

Moving. Code when locomotion is involved. Do not code fidgeting as moving.

Lying down. Code when the child is in a prone position, regardless of the classroom activity.

Academic Behavior

Reading. Code when the child has all appearances of reading (looking at pages in books, periodically turning pages). Book must have words.

Writing. Code when the child is using a pencil, crayon, or other writing instrument to print or write letters or words. If the child is reading and writing, code as reading when no writing is being done.

Math. Code if the activity is math and the child is involved with the activity. Code even if the child is reading or writing math problems.

Observing ongoing activity. Code when an activity is being explained or demonstrated or when some topic is being presented and the children are supposed to be listening. Activity must be appropriate for the classroom.

Other. All other academic or appropriate classroom behavior not specified above, including art, music, science, social studies, and clean-up time.

Communication

Listening. Code as listening when the child appears to be attentive to the person who is speaking. Subcategories are teacher, aide, intern, peer, or other.

Speaking. Code the individual to whom the target child is speaking. If the child is talking out loud or singing and has not directed this toward anyone, code as the subcategory self. The subcategories are teacher, aide, intern, peer, self, or other.

Note. Code when the child is neither listening nor speaking.

Appropriateness of Behavior

Appropriate-attending. Code the time a child is behaving appropriately and the overt behavior suggests active involvement in learning activities. This includes productive independent activity such as reading, writing, painting, constructing, or working with a teaching device; assertive work such as asking for help or support; contributing information and ideas; cooperative behavior such as talking to or working with peers; and appropriate dependent activity such as answering direct questions and carrying out requests.

Appropriate-transition. Examples of a child's behavior that are classified appropriate but not as attending include arranging materials for work, waiting for help from a teacher, sitting quietly in a chair but showing no overt productive behavior, and sitting while a teacher presents material but not responding to it.

Inappropriate-nonproductive or inappropriate time or place. Code as nonproductive behavior looking around and engaging in repetitive physical movements such as rocking in a chair, swaying back and forth, fidgeting, or aimless wandering. For inappropriate for time and place, code all appropriate behaviors performed outside the time limits or in an inappropriate setting. Examples are continuing with one activity when it is time for another to begin, not being in the appropriate place while carrying out work, speaking out of turn, and interrupting another person.

Inappropriate-aggressive or resistive, attention-getting. For aggressive or resistive behaviors, code direct attack on a child or teacher, grabbing, pushing, hitting, kicking, name calling, destroying property, and physically or verbally resisting instructions or directions. For attention getting, code activities that result in and are being maintained by social attention. Examples would be bothering or annoying others, criticizing, making noise, loud talking, clowning, excessive hand raising, temper tantrums, and excessive requests for assistance.

Before using the Wasik-Day Instrument, observers should be trained in a basic time sampling procedure using the instrument and a stopwatch. For individuals familiar with classroom settings, 6 to 8 hours has been sufficient training time. Observers should first learn the categories on the instrument and the layout of the room from a coded map. They should then practice coding data from both videotapes and actual observations of children in classroom settings. Observers should familiarize themselves with a new classroom for at least 30 minutes prior to collecting data.

When observing over a long period of time, observers should take breaks after every 20 minutes of recording. In addition to recording observations on the instrument, observers should complete a Daily Schedule Sheet as shown in Figure 3-14. This sheet provides important information on time, activity, and place that may be necessary to interpret the data on the Wasik-Day Instrument. Observers do not record data during children's rest time, lunch, outside play, and other times when children are outside the classroom.

Before an observer codes data for research or evaluation purposes, overall instrument agreement of 85% or higher on ratings of five different children should be obtained with a second observer. Both observers collect 10 minutes of data for each comparison. In each comparison, the percentage of total instrument-observer agreement can be calculated as follows:

1. Count the total number of actual observer agreements across all categories.

2. Divide the total number of actual agreements by the total number of possible agreements. (In a 10-minute observation, 70 is the total number of possible agreements: 7 categories × 10 minutes = 70 possible agreements).

3. Multiply the result by 100 to obtain the percentage of total instrument-observer agreement.

For example, if two observers had 63 agreements in a 10-minute observation, the total instrument-observer agreement would be (63 ÷ 70) × 100 = 90%.

In addition to calculating total instrument-observer agreement, the percentage of agreement on each of the seven categories should also be calculated. This calculation is the same as above, except that the total number of possible agreements in each category is 10 (1 category × 10 1-minute intervals). Training should continue until observer agreement on each category is 90% or higher.

Figure 3-14 illustrates one 10-minute observation of a child named Joel. During the first 5 minutes, Joel was primarily sitting in a large group at home base, observing the on-going activity, and behaving appropriately. During the second 5 minutes, Joel made a transition to the music center. Another teacher took over as group leader in the home base area, and shortly afterwards Joel

A Completed Daily Schedule Sheet:

School _Seawell_   Classroom _#7_

Child _Joel_   Grade _K_

Observer _Kelly_   Date _May 2_

Summary of Daily Schedule

Time	Activity / Place	Comments
8:30	Circle	
8:35 - 9:10	Special teacher (Music)	
9:10 - 9:30	Circle	
9:30 - 10:40	Centers	
10:40 - 11:35	Lunch	
11:35 - 11:41	Circle	
11:41 - 12:34	Outside	
12:34 - 12:37	Transition	
12:37 - 12:57	TV	
12:57 - 1:18	Outside Skill Group (never happened before)	
1:18 - 2:11	Centers	
1:37 - 1:58	Helping other child - did his work for him	
1:49 - 1:50	Bathroom	
2:11 -	Recess and home	

Figure 3-14 Sample of a completed daily schedule.

moved to the music center, remaining in a large-group setting. There was one instance of inappropriate speech with a peer during this time.

Data such as this from the Wasik-Day Instrument can be used for many purposes. Observations of many children can be analyzed over time to determine the overall impact on classroom behavior of different group sizes, learning centers, activities, and leaders (teachers, aides, parents, student teachers, and interns). In addition, many observations of one child can be analyzed to determine the influence of the same variables on individuals and to assess changes in an individual child's behavior over time.

Another rating scale that is used to evaluate the environment of a developmentally appropriate classroom is the **Early Childhood Environment Rating Scale,** developed at the Frank Porter Graham Child Development Center at the University of North Carolina at Chapel Hill (Harms, Clifford, & Cryer, 1980). This scale consists of 37 items that are rated on a scale of 1 (inadequate quality) to 7 (excellent quality). The developers consider that the environment containing the basic indicators of good early childhood education would receive a rating of 5 (good), but it would take extra characteristics for an item to receive a rating of excellent. The scale may be used in day care facilities, Head Start programs, parent cooperative preschools, private preschool programs, play groups, church-related preschools, and kindergarten programs.

Raters are given descriptions of factors to look for in an environment, and then they rate the classroom in question according to the standards given. The 37 items are grouped into areas, including the following:

Personal Care Routines

1. Greeting/departing
2. Meals/snacks
3. Nap/rest
4. Diapering/toileting
5. Personal grooming

Furnishing and Display

6. For routine care
7. For learning activities
8. For relaxation and comfort
9. For room arrangement
10. Child-related display

Language-Reasoning Experiences

11. Understanding of language
12. Using language
13. Using learning concepts
14. Informal use of language

Fine and Gross Motor Activities

15. Perceptual/fine motor
16. Supervision: Fine motor activities
17. Space for gross motor
18. Gross motor equipment
19. Scheduled time for gross motor activities
20. Supervision: Gross motor activities

Creative Activities

21. Art
22. Music/movement
23. Blocks
24. Sand/water

25. Dramatic play
26. Schedule
27. Supervision: Creative activities

Social Development

28. Space to be alone
29. Free play
30. Group time

31. Cultural awareness
32. Tone
33. Provisions for exceptional children

Adult Needs

34. Adult personal area
35. Opportunities for professional growth

36. Adult meeting area
37. Provisions for parents

Conclusion

Authentic assessment is integral to early childhood environments that are good for children; authentic assessment is implicit in the goals and criteria outlined by the NAEYC. It is clear that if a teacher is practicing developmentally appropriate practices in the classroom, the students' progress should be appraised by developmentally appropriate assessment methods (Zessoules & Gardner, 1991). Standardized tests may reveal interesting statistics and trends, but they do nothing to help children learn (Grady, 1992). It is imperative that teachers use authentic assessment methods in order to provide the best possible instruction for children.

Part Two

Curriculum, Integrated Learning, and Learning Centers

Chapter 4

Communication: The Language Arts

Language Arts in the Elementary School

Much of a young child's life depends on the ability to communicate in an effective manner. Communication spans all content fields. For this reason, language arts is a foundation for success in school programs and life in general, opening the doors to well-developed oral and written communications. Language arts consists of a series of interrelated thinking and code-breaking processes: listening, speaking, reading, and writing. Pappas, Keifer, and Levstik (1990) have developed a model that clearly illustrates these processes and their relationship to one another (Figure 4-1).

Processes that incorporate the language arts should be taught in a manner that is real and relevant to the child. "Language learning is easy when it's whole, real, and relevant; when it makes sense and is functional; when it's encountered in the context of its use; when the learner chooses to use it" (K. Goodman, cited in Krogh, 1990). Students' enjoyment of reading and their understanding of reading strategies occur within the integrated language arts (Templeton, 1991). According to the International Reading Association, language learning should incorporate the following:

- Learning activities that build upon functions, uses, and strategies of reading and writing that prevail in the children's home background.
- Opportunities for children to use written language for a wide variety of purposes, audiences, and situations.

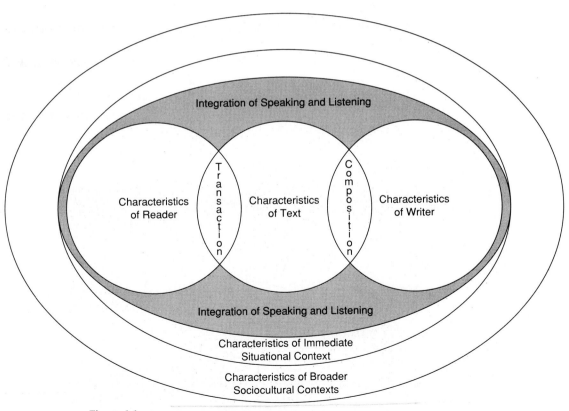

Figure 4.1

- A view of reading and writing as a process that progresses at each child's individual rate (Krogh, 1990).

According to the NAEYC (1986), a literacy program should be developmentally appropriate to each child's abilities and interests. Because development is highly individualized, it is common for children to perform at different levels of skill in reading, writing, and comprehension. Therefore, they should be given opportunities to see how useful writing is before they are given instruction in letter names, sounds, and word identification. Meaningful experiences using the child's own language help foster the connection between print and speech. Such experiences include dictating children's stories; using class charts and graphs; and experimenting with writing by drawing, copying, and using inventive spelling.

Meaningful experiences help children to develop a positive sense of self-worth (Rogers & Zimmerman, 1990). Students' feelings about themselves directly correlate with their success in the language arts. A correlated language arts program should integrate the teaching of reading, writing, speaking, and listening while emphasizing information skills, critical thinking, and creativity. Such a program will accomplish the following goals:

1. The students will gain an understanding of how language develops and functions.
2. The students will become independent readers, writers, speakers, and listeners.
3. The students will learn to use language creatively.
4. The students will develop an appreciation of the aesthetic powers of the written and spoken word.

5. The students will experience the joy and pleasure of reading, writing, speaking, and listening (Rogers & Zimmerman, 1990).

Children also need concrete, hands-on activities with oral language and listening to instill the relationship between speaking and writing, and writing and reading (Heller, 1991). However, to achieve maximum benefits, these activities must involve a variety of methods and materials and relate to all areas of curriculum. Listening experiences can actively involve children in constructing meaning from speech and preparing them to read and write. Subsequently, children experiment with using letters for which they have derived a sound correspondence (Lay-Dopyera & Dopyera, 1993). Out of this arises the concept of inventive spelling.

When children have opportunities to write freely, they experiment with the spelling of words and try to apply the rules they know. Spelling is developmental and progresses through stages when children participate in a program in which writing is a high priority. According to Lay-Dopyera and Dopyera, children begin to write by stringing letters together so that they resemble words. They know that they must use a variety of letters—not too many and not too few. Later, spelling progresses to being based on sound. As children experiment with writing, they produce words that make sense to them and that they can "read." Often, some of the letters in the words are correct, illustrating that the children have made the letter-sound association. Experimenting with invented spelling should be encouraged to help children progress through the developmental spelling stages.

Reading

Reading is an active, constructive, social-meaning-making process that consists of a range of transactions with a variety of texts. Children are actively involved in monitoring and evaluating their own reading—constantly thinking critically and creatively (Pappas et al., 1990). The overall goal of reading is to give children a foundation for lifelong literacy.

A reader experiences several transactions within the text, from emotional to self-reflective. The reader initially identifies with the text emotionally through empathy or by using mental and sensory images. As the text progresses, the reader links the text with prior experiences or with other ideas within the text. At this point, the reader is experiencing a *connective transaction*.

Throughout the text, the reader exhibits descriptive and analytic tendencies. These are initiated when the reader notices various features of the text. Furthermore, the reader interacts interpretively and elaboratively with the text. A child engages in these types of interactions whenever he or she does the following:

1. Constructs meaning by using reasoning or problem-solving strategies.
2. Hypothesizes by making predictions.

Susan is a good leader. She is helping us learn the words to "The Miss Polly Song."

3. Explores the text through inferences.
4. Revises or adds to the text.
5. Ponders over any incongruities and discrepancies within the text.

Finally, the reader becomes involved in self-reflection with the text. This is the ultimate transaction, for it is the one in which the reader notices and monitors his or her own processes during reading. Transactions such as these foster children's skill in taking control of their reading processes questioning the authority of texts, and reading critically and creatively (Pappas et al., 1990).

A print-rich environment can provide children with a multitude of meaningful experiences that will allow them to enjoy the many contributions that literature can make to the classroom. Literature has benefits that enhance such areas as motor development, affective development, social development, and cognitive development for the child (Lay-Dopyera & Dopyera, 1993). These benefits evolve from the following:

- Imitation of movements and activities heard in stories.
- Depiction of what is acceptable and admirable or undesirable and deplorable by models in the stories.
- Exposure to contrasting experiences and feelings by characters within the stories.
- Experience with a rich set of perspectives for thinking about their own feelings and behaviors in social relations.
- Incorporation of various types of educational areas such as classification, number, seriation, causality, space and time concepts, and spoken and written language (Lay-Dopyera & Dopyera, 1993).

Multiple experiences with print and books develop children's literacy and support their efforts to attempt the various discoveries that evolve from a print-rich environment. These discoveries are facilitated by daily exposure to reading, writing, speaking, and listening.

Approaches to Reading Instruction

There are many ways in which children can learn and refine the process of reading and the strategies involved in making reading successful. Students must come to understand that the content of reading and the reading strategies developed are meaningful and applicable in a broader context (Templeton, 1991). An integrated language arts program incorporates many approaches that can be used in teaching reading such as the directed reading and thinking approach, the language experience approach, conferencing, and the basal reader approach. Any of the approaches to teaching reading described here can be effective if used in the proper setting and matched to each child's needs and interests. Ultimately, to meet the needs of all children, teachers must provide activities that integrate and develop speaking, listening, reading, and writing skills.

Directed Reading and Thinking

The directed reading and thinking approach (DRTA) teaches in such a way that students will develop the necessary background knowledge that underlies reading as well as the knowledge of how to apply appropriate reading strategies. The purposes for reading are set by the group through predictions about the reading. The method of interaction is a group discussion in which the teacher serves as a facilitator. During the group interaction, the children are encouraged to think and contribute often, supporting and refuting the predictions made.

Language Experience

The language experience approach (LEA) is a popular method of reading instruction. It is a marvelous way of integrating children's language and background knowledge with beginning reading and writing. This approach draws upon the language and experiences of the children and provides a natural way for children to come to understand the features and functions of written language (Templeton, 1991). As a child speaks, the teacher writes down *exactly* what is said. The child develops an understanding of the idea that print is talk written down and that it can be read. Such an individualized approach uses the student's interest and personal involvement in a creative and personal way. This approach can greatly benefit students from culturally disadvantaged backgrounds.

Reading Conferences

Reading conferences are another effective way to provide direct instruction for individual students. The teacher's focus is not only on developing students' reading knowledge and strategies, but also on elaborating and refining their thinking (Templeton, 1991). Conferences allow for informal evaluations of each child's progress through sharing, questioning, oral reading, planning, and recording. These conferencing techniques enable the teacher to respond immediately to where students are in their reading, what they think about it, and what they need help with.

Basal Readers

The basal reader approach is still used in many school systems. This approach, which involves the use of a graded set of reading books, provides a systematic program that organizes skills and vocabulary in a developmental and sequential manner. Basal programs usually provide an introduction to new vocabulary, a purpose for reading, an opportunity to read silently and orally if desired, questions for comprehension development, and practice with specific skills. Disadvantages include a vocabulary that is not based on the vocabulary and experiences of the child, little or no child input, little student–student interaction, and little room for individualization.

Reading Materials

Commercially published trade books (fact and fiction)
    Stories of the country, seasons, and nature
    Stories of other countries
    Realistic animal stories
    Fanciful animal stories
    Modern fanciful stories
    Folk and fairy tales
    Nursery rhymes
    Poetry
Big books
    Child made
    Commercially published
    Group authored
Child-made resource books
    Shape books
    Minibooks
    Accordion books
Reference books
    Children's encyclopedias
    Science library

Newspapers
> Class
> Local
> City (current)

Magazines (popular as well as children's)
Catalogs
Group-authored chart stories
Group-authored informational charts
Child- and group-authored messages
> Notes
> Cards
> Invitations
> Announcements
> Letters

Posted directions
> Classroom rules
> Use of centers
> Recipes
> Activities' directions

Charts
> Color
> Numbers
> Alphabet

Lists
> Words-We-Know list
> Songs-We-Know list
> Favorite Books list
> Lunch menu

Schedules
> Daily schedule
> Calendar
> Classroom helpers

Labels
> Location of centers
> Objects in the classroom
> Containers for personal belongings
> Mailboxes
> Coatracks
> Captioned drawings
> Contents of cupboard

Talk-starter picture cards
Puppets
Flannelboard with flannel objects, labels, letters, story characters
Magnetic board, letters
Lotto games
Matching picture and letter games

Parquetry blocks, designs
Puzzles (variety of topics and number of pieces)
Spelling and reading games
Crossword puzzles
Tapes: blank, teacher made, and commercially prepared

Reading Objectives

1. To develop an understanding of the relationship between oral language and written symbols.
2. To foster success and satisfaction in beginning reading.
3. To develop a basic sight vocabulary.
4. To develop word-attack skills, picture and context clues, structural analysis.
5. To further develop comprehension and interpretive skills and to read for meaning.
6. To develop the ability to read silently.
7. To develop the ability to read orally with proper expression.
8. To develop a desire to read for achievement, pleasure, information, and understanding.
9. To encourage independent reading and thinking, for information and recreation.
10. To apply skills in other content areas through reading.

I love to play word games all by myself with my teacher—and on the floor, too!

Environmental Resources

One to two tables and two to four chairs
Small table with typewriter
Low shelves used also as a divider
Rocking chair, easy chairs, couch
Carpet, rug, or carpet squares
Pillows or floor cushions
Book rack
Open storage for records and tapes
Carrels for individual use
Electrical outlets

Materials for K–2 Children in Language Arts

Tape recorder, earphones
Paper: lined and unlined, white and colored
Sentence strips
Blackboard
Pencils
Markers
Crayons
Paints
Brushes
Various scrap materials that can be used for book covers
Manipulative letters: wood, sandpaper, pipecleaner, plastic, cardboard
Cans labeled with a letter each: small cans with small letters, large cans with
        capital letters in another color
Pictures of farm animals
Pictures of wild animals
Pictures of vegetables
Pictures of fruits
Pictures of birds
Pictures of flowers
Various other pictures of different groups of things and places
Series of pictures (for putting in correct sequence)
Dramatic play equipment
Dress-up clothes
Props
Furniture
Films
Cards with words on them
Many cards for children to write their own words on
Groups of cards with rhyming words (self-correcting, with the other word on
        the back)
Groups of cards with rhyming pictures (self-correcting)
ABC Bingo game

Groups of pictures with one different for visual discrimination
Tiles with letters on each
Play and real telephones
Mirror (full child body length)

Suggested Reading Readiness Activities

Auditory Discrimination
For the following activities, the objective is auditory discrimination. The children work with environmental sounds and speech sounds.

Snail Sounds. Make a game board in the shape of a snail. Give each child a copy of the same game board. Clap your hands and have the children move that number of spaces. All of the children will finish together at the center of the snail.

Musical Sounds. Show the children three to six different rhythm instruments and let them play the instruments to hear how each one sounds. Review the names of the instruments and check the children's comprehension of the names by asking them to hand you certain instruments. Hide the instruments (behind a screen, box, or table) and play one instrument at a time. Have the children guess the name of the instrument or find the similar instrument from a display of duplicate instruments. The latter is easier for children who are having trouble remembering the names.

Fill in the Blank. Say three distinct words to a child and then repeat two of the words. Invite the child to try to remember and repeat the word you left out. In the beginning, always leave out the last word. Next, leave out the first word. Finally, advance to leaving out the middle word. The most advanced version is to leave out words in random order.

Following Directions. Give each child a yard of yarn and have the children follow these directions:

- Make a circle on the floor with your string.
- Walk around your circle.
- Jump inside your circle.
- Put one foot outside your circle.
- Make your circle into a triangle.
- Sit inside your triangle . . . and so on.

Matching Art. Name a letter sound and have the children draw objects that begin with the same sound. Continue with a variety of letter sounds and then review the pictures and their sounds.

What Was That? Have the child observe and listen to the sounds that five chosen objects make when they are dropped on the floor. (Make sure you choose unbreakable objects!) Ask the child to turn around while someone else drops one of the objects. The child guesses which object was dropped.

What's Shaking? Have the child shake a variety of covered containers with one small object in each. (Possible containers are milk cartons, toilet paper tubes, or paper towel tubes covered with contact paper.) Place similar objects on a tray that is visible to the child. By listening to the sound and looking at the objects on the tray, the child tries to guess what is inside. Materials that can be included are pennies, paper clips, rice, flour, bells, beans, and macaroni.

Sound Alike. Place in front of the child three objects, two of which begin with the same sound. You or the child say the name of each object, and the child picks up the two objects that have the same beginning sound. An example of a possible set is *book, ball,* and *apple.*

Elevator. Provide at least four examples of these two types of sounds: high sounds (bell or drinking glass with a spoon) and low sounds (drum or table to tap). Play the noisemakers and ask the child to imitate the sounds while pretending to be an elevator. The child stands up for high sounds and squats on the ground for low sounds.

Musical Response. Sing a question with a definite tune to the child. (A good tune to use is "Mary Had a Little Lamb.") The child answers back using the same tune.

Sound Tracks. Give the children track boards that are alike. Clap your hands and ask the children to move that number of spaces. All should finish together.

What's What? Make a tape recording of familiar indoor and outdoor sounds. Some examples are a bell ringing, a teacher talking, lawn mowers running, dogs barking, microwave beeping, and telephone ringing. Ask the children to name or draw the sounds they hear.

Guess Who? Make a tape recording of each child's voice during a group sing-a-long or discussion. The children try to identify the voices they hear.

Sequencing
For the following activities, the objective is to sequence events correctly.

Story Sequence. Separate the pages of a short paperback copy of a book that the child has read several times either alone or with you. Make sure you cut off the page numbers. Paste these pages on pieces of posterboard of equal width and length. Have the child read each page and place them in the correct order so that the story makes sense.

Map Board. Draw a map of your school. Let the child number the order of pictures of events that happened to him or her that day at school.

Variation. Let two or three children compare their maps and see what they did that is similar or different.

Before and After. Cut out or draw pictures of real-life events. Show these pictures to a child one at a time. Have the child describe and/or draw what happened *before* the occurrence in the picture. Next, have the child do the same thing for what could happen *after.*

Variation. Later, place the child's pictures and the original pictures in random order. Have a child put the pictures in the correct order.

Comic Sequence. Make up sequencing cards from comic strips. Have the child examine the story cards and arrange them in the correct order from left to right. A star on each holder or piece of paper indicates which is the starting point. Allow the child to tell his or her own interpretation of the sequences. This interpretation can also be tape recorded for future listening practice.

What's Wrong with This Picture? Draw several sequences of events on 4- × 12-inch pieces of posterboard. Tell the child that there are three pictures on each card, but they might not be in the right order. The child takes the numbers provided (numbers 1, 2, and 3 cut from red posterboard) and places them on the pictures in the correct order.

Integration. In science and social studies, a variety of occurrences have an order that can be reinforced through sequence cards. Two science examples are the growth of a flower from a seed and the order of the planets from the sun. Social studies examples include what happens when there is a fire and what to do during a tornado drill. Make four laminated pictures of events that would happen during one of these occurrences. Have the child put the cards in the proper order. You can number the back of each picture as to its place in the event so that the activity is self-correcting.

Cartoon Mania. Glue cartoon strips to posterboard and cut the segments apart. The child reads each segment and places them in order so that the story makes sense.

Visual Discrimination
For the following activities, the objective is visual discrimination.

Going Home. This is a flannelboard activity. Design and cut out a bird nest and four birds (each smaller in size than the next and each of a different color). Place the bird nest on the flannelboard and the bird cutouts at random distances on one side of the nest. Have the children look at the board and tell which bird is closest to the nest. Guide the children in explaining why the selected bird is closest. Continue the activity with three birds on one side of the nest and one bird on the other side.

Little Rugs. Make little wallpaper squares. A child spreads out the squares and attempts to place matching "rugs" on top of each other. The rugs differ in color, pattern, and texture. Identical shapes on the back indicate correct matches.

Go Fish. Prepare a chart that looks like water and write some selected words on the chart. Design place cards shaped like fish that have the same words on them. Attach a paper clip to each fish. Put the fish cards in a box or bowl, and give the child a fishing rod with a magnet on the end of the string. The child "fishes" for a card and then places the fish in the water on the word that matches.

Lotto. Make a card for each child and divide it into 9 to 12 squares, with a different letter in each square. Then make a set of small cards to fit over the squares. Make three for each letter. Players take turns drawing cards and matching them to letters on their big card. The player who fills his or her card first wins.

Sizing Up the Matter. Cut out or draw pictures of similar items that differ in sizes. Spread them out in random order on a table or on the floor. The child finds two items of the same kind and identifies the differences in sizes. For example, "One is a short flower and one is a tall flower."

Pattern Perception. On paper or on a miniwhiteboard, make a simple pattern such as ##—#. Ask the child to copy the pattern at least two times. Then write another pattern for the child to copy, such as A1B2C3. Discuss the pattern with the child while he or she continues it; for example, A1B2C3D4E5. Later, challenge the child to make more difficult patterns, such as AAaaA, BBbbB, CCccC, DDddD, or EEeeE.

Stare at the items in the toy chest. Look away. See how many you can name without looking back.

Missing Objects. Make a collection of several objects. Display these objects. Then put them in a bag, shake it, and take the objects out again. Leave one object in the bag. The child guesses what object is left in the bag.

Silhouettes. Make a silhouette of each child and have the children guess who it is. To make the silhouettes, tape white paper on the wall and use a film projector light. Have the child stand about 1 foot from the wall, facing sideways. Trace the child's head. Cut it out carefully and mount it on black paper. These make nice gifts.

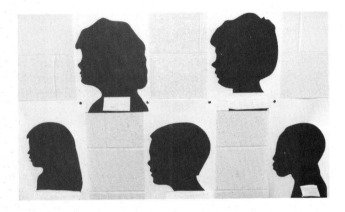

Alphabet Recognition
For the following activities, the objective is to recognize the letters of the alphabet.

Umbrella Game. Using posterboard or tagboard, draw a large umbrella with capital letters on it. Out of another sheet of tagboard, cut out raindrops with lowercase letters on them. Have the children match these raindrops to the letters on the umbrella.

ABC Concentration. Make two sets of letter cards for all of the letters of the alphabet. You will have 52 cards in all. Place the cards face down and have the children alternate turning over two cards at a time. If they make a match, the player can keep the cards and continue playing until he or she can no longer make a match. The game continues until all the matches have been made.

ABC Bingo. Make individual cards with six letters of the alphabet on each card. Give each child a card and six chips or scraps of paper to cover any letter called. Call out the letter of the alphabet and/or hold up a large card with the lowercase letter on it, and have the children cover the letter if it appears on their card.

Alphabet Puzzles. Using posterboard or tagboard, cut large rectangular cards. Put a capital letter on one side and a lowercase letter on the other. Cut it down the middle. Mix the pieces and then have the child match the puzzle pieces. Reinforce this activity with computer games.

Cherry Tree. Cut out a tree design using tagboard or posterboard and print the uppercase alphabet on the tree. On small pieces of red tagboard, cut out circles (for cherries) and print the lowercase alphabet on them. The child takes the cherries and matches the letter on each cherry with its capital letter on the tree.

Footprints. Make a colorful set of footprints. Left feet have uppercase alphabet letters; right feet, lowercase. The children arrange them in order across the room or in circles.

Alphabet Worm. On heavy paper, draw a worm with a body of 26 connecting circles, all containing capital letters. On a separate sheet, draw and cut out matching circles, all containing lowercase letters. The children match the letters.

We like to help each other play alphabet games on the computer.

Sandpaper Solutions. Trace and cut letters from sandpaper and paste the letters onto another sheet of paper (one sheet per letter). With eyes closed, the child traces the letter with his or her finger and guesses what the letter is.

Sandbox Writing. Fill a shallow box with sand. (An alternative to sand is salt over black construction paper.) The child practices making letters by using a finger to write in the sand. When finished, the child produces a "clean slate" by wiping away the letters and mixing up the sand.

Alphabet Train. Make train cars from milk cartons covered in contact paper, each with a letter on the side. After arranging them in alphabetical order, have the children remove objects from the locomotive and place them in the correct car.

Alphabet Fish. Using orange construction paper, cut out many small fish, each containing letters (both upper- and lowercase). Glue a paper clip on each one. A child uses a magnetic fishing pole and tries to identify the letters on each fish caught. Each child is provided with a paper "fishbowl" (which he or she may draw) and may glue on the fish that were recognized.

Hang It Up. Take a piece of tagboard and write the child's name at the bottom. At the top, put a hole above each letter of the child's name and place a brad fastener in the hole. Design letter strips with the letters of the child's name at the bottom and a hole at the top. The child matches the letter strips with the letters in his or her name. Assist the child in identifying the letters as they are matched. Hang each letter with the brad fastener in the proper hole on the tagboard.

Alphabet Land. Make a game board and set of alphabet playing cards. A player moves along by picking a card, saying the letter, and placing a marker on that letter. The child then returns the card to the bottom of the deck. The first one to reach Alphabet Land is the winner.

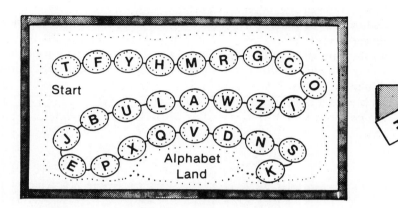

Suggested Phonetic Analysis Activities

Beginning and Ending Consonant Sounds
For the following activities, the objective is to recognize beginning sounds.

Collages. Find large sheets of paper and write a consonant at the top of each. The children find words or pictures in magazines or newspapers that begin with these letters. After they cut them out, they glue them on to make collages. The children can write their names on or beside their pictures.
 Variation. Each collage poster can be cut into the actual letter represented. These letters can then be used as a display alphabet for the classroom.

Sea Search. The child looks at laminated magazine pictures of beach scenes and circles the objects in the pictures that begin with *s*. Some examples are sand, sun, sky, seashell, shovel, shells, and surf.

A Tisket, a Tasket. Tape a letter (both upper- and lowercase) on the side of a basket. The child takes the basket around the room and hunts for small objects that begin with the sound of that letter.

Refrigerator Magic. Provide a metal cookie sheet and magnetic refrigerator letters. Give the child only the letters that you want him or her to work with (use a variety of letters each time you use this activity). Ask the child to spell a word that is part of a word family such as *day.* Then ask the child to change one letter and make the word *may.* Do the same thing for other words in the family such as *lay, hay, say, Jay, pay, ray,* and *way.* This game can be used with a variety of word families.

Post Office. Each child gets a large envelope with a consonant printed on the front side. The children take turns being the mail carrier. The mail carrier gets a bag full of pictures and pulls a picture out of the bag. Then he or she tries to find the person with the envelope whose letter matches the initial consonant sound.

Flannelboard Activity. The child puts a letter card at the top of the flannelboard and puts all the picture cards on the board, along with the "Yes" and "No" cards. The child puts a "Yes" card under the picture if it begins with the letter at the top and a "No" card under the picture if it does not begin with that letter.

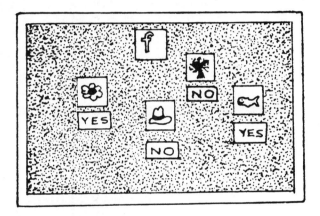

Tic Tac Toe. One player gets five Xs (cut out of posterboard), and the other player gets five Os. In order to place an X or an O on a section, the child must name the letter and an object that begins with that letter.

Feely Bag. This can be an individual or small-group activity. Fill a bag with objects and have the student reach into the bag and pull out an object. Then have the child name the object and the consonant heard at the beginning of the word.
Variation. Let the child guess what an object is before taking a look at it.

Circle Fun. Cut circles into puzzles. Put a picture of an object on one half and the letter the word begins with on the other half. Mix all of the puzzle halves together and allow the children to match pictures with their initial consonant sounds.

Snake. Make a playing board out of posterboard. Players "snake" their way to the finish line, giving a word beginning with whatever letter they landed upon.

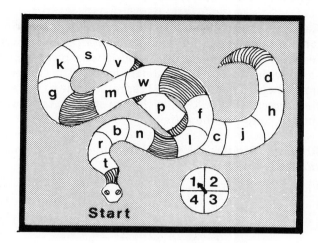

Word Animal. Make an animal out of tagboard. Leave slots to slide a strip of consonant letters, blends, or digraphs through to make sensible words (or nonsense words).

Copy Cat. Read a short story to the child, periodically pausing to repeat a word. Then invite the child to repeat the word with you and tell what it means. You can repeat the sentence and give clues if necessary. Say the sentence again, and substitute the meaning for the word.

Variation. Have the child select a word that he or she hears as you read and invite you to tell what the word means. Have the child repeat the sentence containing the selected word.

Cassette Match. Record words that are familiar to the students on a cassette tape. Remember to leave enough of a pause between words for the child to respond to the activity. Make cards with pictures representing each word and cards with a variety of consonant letters. The student listens to the word on the tape, chooses the picture that represents the word, and matches the picture with the correct letter. Allow the child to stop the tape periodically if he or she needs time to complete the activity.

Rhyming Riddles. Have children identify beginning sounds by figuring out riddles such as the following:

I am thinking of a word that begins with *m* and rhymes with *cat*.
I am thinking of a word that begins with *s* and rhymes with *ring*.
I am thinking of a word that begins with *h* and rhymes with *chair*.

Freddy Fish. Make and laminate large fish on which to display children's pictures of things with initial *F* sounds. This activity can be adapted to any initial consonant sound, such as "Danny Duck" or "Kathy Kangaroo." Try to use the names of children in the class if possible.

Letter Wheel. Make a large wheel from tagboard, divide it into sections, and write an initial consonant in each section. Then make a smaller wheel, divide it into corresponding sections, and put a picture or drawing in each section. Attach the smaller wheel to the larger wheel so that the two are movable and can be manipulated by the child. The child moves the wheels to match the initial consonants with their corresponding pictures. The child then says what word each picture represents and the letter the word begins with.

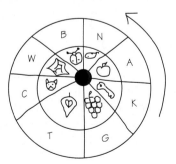

Drag Race. You will need a piece of tagboard with a design of a race track on it, a pair of dice, and four toy cars for markers. Divide the track into sections and place a consonant letter in each section. The child rolls the dice and moves his or her car that number of spaces. To remain on the space, the child names the letter and one word that begins with that letter. If the player cannot supply a word, he or she goes back one space.

Variation. This game can be played by four people playing in pairs. This will encourage cooperative learning.

Drive-U-Nuts. Make cards with four pictures on each. The children must arrange them so that any sides touching must have matching initial sounds. With each match, have the child name the initial sound that matched. Challenge the children by making only one possible solution for all of the cards to be matched.

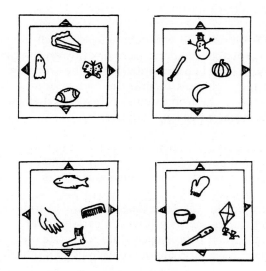

Consonant Sound Books. Provide "books" representing 21 consonants. The children cut pictures from magazines that begin with the same sound as the consonant on each book. The children may want to make their own consonant sound book and either draw or glue in pictures.

Concentration. Make 1- × 1-inch posterboard cards and paste or draw pictures on half of them. On the other half, write the initial consonant letters of the names of the objects on the picture cards. Turn all of the cards face down. Have the children turn over two cards at a time and try to make a match. Whenever a match is made, the player gets another turn.

Pizza Party Pictures. Glue pictures of words that begin with consonants to a cardboard pizza tray. Write the consonants on clothespins. Have the child clip the clothespin beside the picture of the word beginning with that letter.

Variation. You can follow up the activity by graphing how many words you found for each letter. Ask questions like the following:

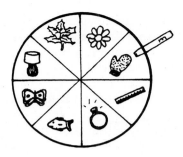

Which letter had the most words?
Which letter had the least words?

Sort-a-Sound. You will need a 3- × 5-inch file box, unruled index cards, and a set of alphabet dividers. Glue or draw on the cards pictures of objects that start with the initial consonants. Write the word on the back of the card. Have the child file each card behind the correct letter. (This also reinforces alphabetical order.) The children can make the cards themselves. (The same box can be used when initial vowels are studied.)

Initial Sounds Puppets. Let each child make a puppet that represents the initial consonant sound in his or her name. Later, you can use these puppets to practice and reinforce many consonant letters.

Nature Walk. Take the class for a walk outdoors. Have the children look at or collect things that begin with a certain letter.
      Variation. Allow each child to dictate one sentence about an item found on the nature walk. Write down each child's sentence exactly the way it was stated for a complete language experience story about the nature walk.

Treasure Hunt. Hide 10 to 20 small picture cards for each initial consonant being practiced. Give each team a letter, and tell the players that they must look for cards picturing objects that begin with that letter. The first team to find all of its cards wins.

The Guessing Game. Show the class a variety of objects and review the name and initial consonant sound of each object. Blindfolded students identify various objects and name the beginning sounds. The students can touch the objects and listen to the objects if they make a sound, but they cannot peek.

Hot Potato. Say a word and toss a ball to a student in the class. The child must say a word beginning with the same sound and then toss the ball back to you. Continue the game with all of the children in random order.

Twister. Design a mat by attaching red, yellow, blue, and green laminated construction paper on the floor. Then design a spinner with the same four colors on it, as well as an initial consonant on each section. The child spins the spinner and lands on a section. In order to place a hand or a foot on the corresponding color, the child must name a word that begins with the letter on which the spinner stopped.

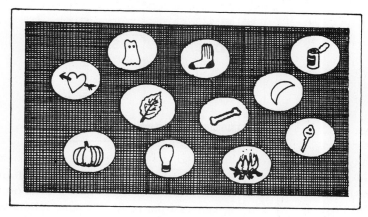
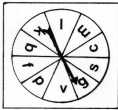

Name It. Say a child's name and have children name other objects in the room that begin with the same sound.

I Spy. "I spy something that begins like *ball.*" The children guess what the object is. Children can also make up "I spy" sentences.

For the following activities, the objective is to identify ending sounds.

Wall Mural. Divide a large piece of paper mounted on the wall (or a bulletin board) into squares. Write a letter in each square. Have the children draw or paste pictures that have the same ending sound as the letter.

Leaves on a Tree. Draw several trees, with an ending sound on the trunk of each. Make several leaves with various pictures. The child places the leaf picture on the tree that has that ending sound.

For the following activities, the objective is to identify beginning and ending sounds.

Art Matchup. Laminate a full-size sheet of posterboard with the design shown here. Have the child draw or cut out pictures and paste them on small pieces of construction paper. The catch is that the pictures must be of objects that begin with each particular letter. Later use the same laminated sheet of posterboard to have children draw or find pictures whose ending sounds match the ones on the sheet.

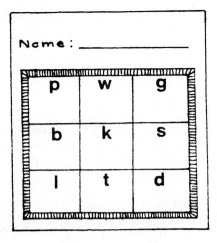

Window Magic. Design and cut out a school from posterboard and print the lowercase consonant letters in the windows. Make game cards on 1- × 1-inch pieces of posterboard. On the game cards, print the same letters (both upper- and lowercase) on one side and glue or draw pictures that begin with that consonant on the other side. Place the small cards next to the school with the picture side facing up. Each child draws a picture card, says the name of the picture, and says the sound the picture begins with. Then the child places the picture card on the letter window that matches the sound the picture begins with. After all of the windows are covered, the child can turn the cards over to see whether he or she is right.

Consonant Lotto. Divide a game board into nine sections. Write a consonant in each section and make a picture card for each section as a beginning consonant and an ending consonant. Have the children look at the pictures and decide on their beginning consonant or ending consonant sound. (Decide which sound to work with before the activity starts). The children then match the pictures to the nine sections.

Mix and Match. Make a chart with consonant letters and attach hooks under the letters. Hang pictures randomly on the hooks. Have the child sort the pictures

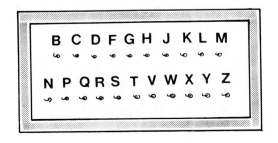

according to their beginning or ending sounds (but do not do both at the same time) and put them in their correct place.

Picture Houses. Make a house for each consonant letter. Either make picture cards for each house or let the children cut out pictures from magazines. Have the children place the pictures in slots of the correct house according to beginning or ending sounds.

Initial and/or Final Consonant Sound Bingo. Make a variety of Bingo-style cards. Cut clear, simple pictures from magazines or old workbooks. As these are held up, each player places a marker on the matching letter. The usual Bingo rules apply.

Checkers. Place letters on a checkerboard or design your own game board. To move a game piece, the player must say a word that either begins or ends with the letter on which he or she lands.

Sort the Objects. Using 21 cans representing the 21 consonant sounds, have the child sort objects according to the beginning or ending sound.

Auto-Matic. Make cars, wheels, and cards as illustrated. The child places a picture card on the door of the car and looks for wheels with the corresponding beginning and ending sounds.

Consonant Blends and Digraphs
For the following activities, the objective is to identify blends and digraphs.

Letter Addition. Write several words on a chart that can be changed to an initial blend by adding one letter. Some examples are sets such as the following:

ran, ray, rip, read, ride
park, pace, pat, peck
lap, lag, lip, lick

Have the children work in pairs to figure out what letter can be added to change each word.

Blends Race. Make a track game out of tagboard. Fill it in with blends and write the directions on the game board.

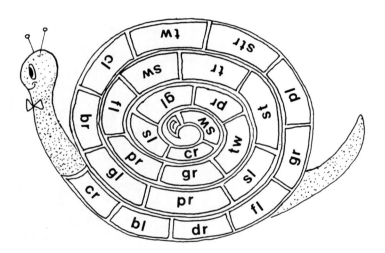

1. Spin the spinner.
2. Move that number of spaces.
3. If you can say a word with that blend, you may stay. If you cannot, go back to the space where you were.
4. The first player to arrive in the middle is the winner.

Digraph Action. Write on a sheet of chartpaper as many action words as you can that begin with digraphs. Some examples are *breathe, cry, crawl, fly, drive, grab, skip, slip, sleep, smile, step, stand still,* and *twist.* Walk around the room and whisper an action word into each child's ear, but tell the child to keep it a secret. Then each child acts out his or her word while the rest of the class tries to guess what the word is.

Blend Action. On a sheet of chartpaper, write as many action words as you can that begin with blends. Some examples are *cheer, chat, chomp, shake, shiver, think, whisper,* and *whistle.* Follow the same procedure as in "Digraph Action" and whisper a word into each child's ear. Let each child act out the word while the rest of the class tries to guess what the word is.

The Disappearing Dandelion. The child blows off the seed feathers from the dandelion seed puff by saying words that begin with the *wh* sound, such as *why, when, where,* and *whisper.* The child is challenged to say enough words to blow off all the seed feathers from the stem.

Blend Wheel. Make one large circle and one small circle. Print blends on the small circle and word endings on large circle. After laminating them, pin the circles together in the center with a brad. By turning the circle, new words are made.

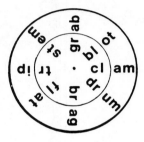

Digraph Concentration. Make a set of cards with pictures and digraphs written on them. The player places cards face down and tries to match each card.

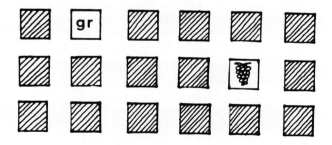

Digraph Twisters. From a large piece of paper, read aloud several tongue twisters with digraphs, for example, "Whitney whistled while Whitey whispered." Then cover the digraphs with small pieces of paper and have the children decide which letters are missing. The paper can be removed to make the activity self-correcting.

Variation. Allow the children to make and illustrate their own tongue twisters.

Blend Twisters. Along with the children, design several tongue twisters with blends beginning each word. Write the tongue twisters on a chart that the children can refer to. Some examples are:

Brandon's brother Brad brought brown bread for breakfast.
Frank fried French fries for friendly Fred.

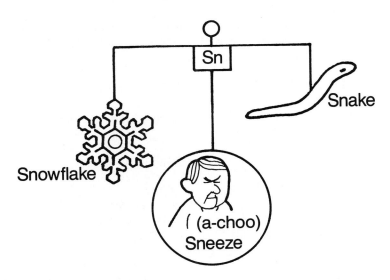

Gather the children into groups of two and have them play whisper races. A pair of children chooses one of the tongue twisters that the class made. The two children try to see who can say the tongue twister the fastest.

Mobiles. Have the children make mobiles of pictures that have the same consonant blends and digraphs.

Distinguishing Vowels and Recognizing Rhyming Words
For the following activities the objectives are to distinguish vowels and recognize rhyming words.

Body Parts. Give each child pictures of two feet, a head, a hand, and a knee. Write on chartpaper in random order all of the words that rhyme with the four picture words. Call out a word and have each child hold up the picture that rhymes with the word. As a group, repeat the word for reinforcement.

Vowel Cutout. Give the child a vowel letter made from construction paper and several magazines. Have the child cut out pictures with that vowel sound and glue them into the letter.

Rhyming Word Connection. Write on four cards familiar words that rhyme with words the children are not likely to be familiar with. Write four sentences on sentence strips that include the rhyming words that the children are not familiar with. Read each sentence to a child and stop before you reach the rhyming word you would like decoded. The child finds the card that rhymes with the left out word, says the word on the card, and then says the word that was not read with the sentence.

Variation. You can "think aloud" the strategy by saying, "If *m-a-p* is *map*, then *l-a-p* must be *lap*."

Vowel Clowns. Make five clowns using the different vowels for their noses. The child chooses from a stack of short vowel "hats" the hat that each clown will wear.

Peek-A-Boo. Write on posterboard or chartpaper two-line poems such as the following:

> Mr. Baker will you make
> A very yummy birthday cake?

> The sun will come and shine on me,
> My friend, my dog, and every tree.

Make a cover for the second rhyming word (i.e., *cake* and *tree*). Let the child read or listen to the poem and guess the hidden word. The child can look under the cover to see whether he or she is right.

Rhyme Time. Make a track on a game board. Players roll a number cube and move around the track saying a word that rhymes with the one on which they land.

Rhyming Time. Make a track as shown, using between 10 and 25 footsteps. Write the directions in the game board.

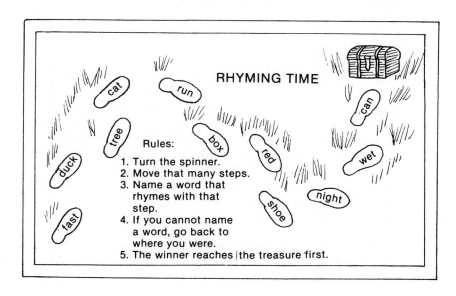

RHYMING TIME

Rules:
1. Turn the spinner.
2. Move that many steps.
3. Name a word that rhymes with that step.
4. If you cannot name a word, go back to where you were.
5. The winner reaches the treasure first.

Oscar Octopus. Draw a large octopus. Have the children draw and cut out things beginning with the *o* sound. Have them glue their cutouts onto Oscar's arms. Variations can be made using other short vowel characters: Adam Ant, Eddie Egghead, and so on.

Rhyme Time Concentration. Make a set of 20 rhyming-word picture cards. The players place cards face down and pick two at a time for each turn, trying to pick two cards that rhyme. The player with the most matches is the winner. Cards are made self-correcting by writing the numbers on the back.

 Rhyming Words Hat. The children pull the strip through the hat, as shown, as they make and say the rhyming words.

House of Rhyme. Make several large houses. Have the children place the rhyming words (printed on doors and windows) on the appropriate house.

Rhyming Clowns. Make a bulletin board display of several clowns holding balloons. Have the children place words that rhyme on the balloons.

Suggested Structural Analysis Activities

For the following activities, the objective is to identify contractions and be able to identify the words making up the contractions.Contraction Line.

Make 30 cards; divide each by a diagonal line. On the left side of the diagonal, write two words that can be made into a contraction in black. On the right side, write a contraction in red. The students deal all the cards but one. This one is placed on the table, and the students take turns trying to match contractions and contraction words (like dominos). The first one to use all cards is the winner.

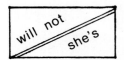   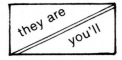

Contraction Flowers. On a big board, outline a flower with lots of petals. Write contractions inside the outlined petals. Now make petals with the two words from which the contractions are made. The student should place each petal inside the correct outlined petal.

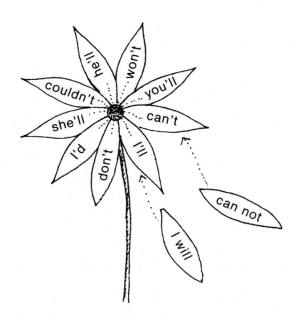

Corresponding Clothespins. Make a long board listing contractions. Take twice as many clothespins as you have words and make 1- × ½-inch covers for them. Write the words that make up the contractions on the covers and glue these to the clothespins. The student clips the proper clothespins to the board. The board can be self-correcting on the back by means of color, letter, or number coding.

Snoopy makes learning contractions easy for us.

Snoopy Game. Draw Snoopy dogs and label them with contractions. Label each doghouse with the words that make up the contraction. The child places Snoopy on the appropriate doghouse.

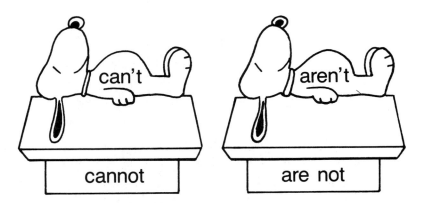

Recognizing Root Words, Suffixes, and Prefixes
The objective for the following activities is to recognize root words, suffixes, and prefixes.

Prefix or Suffix Wheels. These laminated tagboard wheels have removable centers on which are printed common root words. The child inserts a center (attached to a brad), turns the wheel, and reads the words made. The wheel has either prefixes or suffixes. All combinations make a word. The child can then write the word, determine its meaning, and write it in a sentence. (Inflected endings may also be used.)

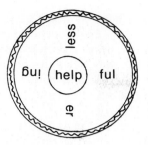

Root Word Sort. Make a 28- × 14-inch pocket folder. Write root words on the pockets. Make cards to fit in the pockets with words on them that have prefixes and suffixes added. Have the students "file" the cards in the correct pockets. They must pronounce the root word each time. (Prefix and suffix folders can be made and the same cards used.) An answer-key card can be attached to the back of the folder.

Word Pyramid. This can be a team competition or an individual activity. Given a root word, the team or person must build a "word pyramid" on the board or on paper, adding prefixes, suffixes, and so on. If it is a team activity, the team with the largest pyramid wins. A flannelboard can be used with blue felt root words, pink felt prefixes, and yellow felt suffixes.

Batters Up. This game is made on a piece of cardboard. Draw a baseball diamond. On first base, make a pocket with root words; on second base, a pocket of prefixes; and on third, a pocket of suffixes. Players choose a root word. If they can add a prefix, they get a double and go to second base. If they can add a suffix, they get a triple and go to third base. If they can add both a prefix and suffix, they score a home run. The player with the most home runs is the winner.

"Rooty" the Bug. Rooty has three parts. His head is a prefix, his body is a suffix, and his thorax is the root word. The folder has three pockets containing prefixes, suffixes, and root words. Students see (and draw) all the Rooty bugs that they can make.

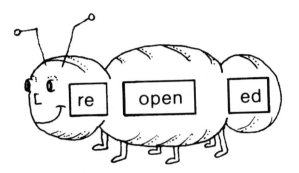

Forming Plurals
For the following activities, the objective is to form plurals.

The Plural Clown. Cut out or draw a clown with three pockets. On each pocket, write a singular or plural word (depending on degree of difficulty) that forms its plural in a different way (*s, es, ies*). Print the singular of these words on tagboard squares. Have the students read a word and make it plural by placing it in the correct pocket. (Answers may be color coded.)

Foldover Endings. Write root words on the front of flashcards, and write the appropriate plural ending (or other inflected ending) on the back of the cards. When a card is folded, the ending should be properly positioned at the end of the root word. By manipulating these cards, the student can *see* how plurals (or other endings) are added. The student should guess at the ending, fold over the flap, read the word, and write it in a sentence.

Recognizing Compound Words
For the following activities, the objective is to recognize compound words.

Compound Mania. Cut four 8- × 8-inch and four 4 × 4-inch pieces of posterboard into octagon shapes (cut off the corners). Place the small octagons in the center of the large ones and outline the small ones with a pen. Copy compound words on the two pieces, with half of each compound on the large octagon and the other half on the small octagon. The child takes the large cards, which contain the last half of the eight compound words, and places them face up. He or she then takes one of the small octagons, which contains the first half of the eight compound words, and places it on the center of the large card. Do the words make sense? If not, the student turns the small card or places it on another large card until all eight compound words are formed.

Help the Rabbit Find Its Tail. A rabbit, word cards, and word tails can be made with tagboard and laminated. Several possible answers can be placed on the backs of the word cards and word tails. The student puts together the rabbit and tails to make compound words.

Compound Word Wheel. This can be made with laminated tagboard. Clothespins are made to match with a word on the tagboard, thereby making it a compound word. (The same sort of wheels can be made for antonyms, synonyms, and homonyms.)

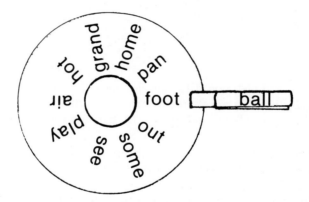

Compound Word Puzzle. Write compound words on cards and cut down the middle of each card. The children then fit the pieces together.

Spinning Wheels. Draw a car and write several words on the wheels. Attach a circle (with a wedge cut out) to the wheels. The child turns the wheels to make compound words.

Comprehension

The development of reading comprehension is complex, and it is influenced by the total reading program. Other influences include the child's personality, motivation, and habits, as well as background experiences. Comprehension can be enhanced through activities that integrate more than one area of reading. The areas in comprehension include:

1. Following directions
2. Multiple meanings
3. Context and picture clues
4. Classification
5. Sentence structure
6. Pronoun antecedents
7. Recall of sequence
8. Recall of details
9. Main idea
10. Summarization
11. Characterization
12. Comparisons, associations, relationships
13. Inferences
14. Predictions
15. Generalizations, conclusions
16. Judgments, analysis

These skills should be developed as a whole within the context of a reading selection. Comprehension can be practiced through questioning, cloze procedures, re-telling, and other activities involved in the process of gaining meaning from print.

Suggested Integration Activities

Sharing. Allow the children to read to the class their favorite stories that they wrote in their journals. Introduce the concept of "author" and explain pride through authorship.

Labeling. Label artwork and stories that will be displayed or published for others to read. The children will begin to relate the names of their classmates to the work of those classmates. Throughout the year, children "read" the titles and authors of various works.

Look! Look! Make a book that dedicates each page to a child in the class. The book allows for repetitive language by having similar sentences on each page. Each page reads, "Look! Look! I can see [insert child's name] looking at me." On each page, glue a photograph of a child. As children "read" the book, they will become familiar with the names of their classmates and experience the joy of reading at the same time.

Speaking

Oral language is an important facet of the school curriculum. Educators realize the importance of personal expression and communication in furthering the educational process. The more children who are allowed to talk and are encouraged to express themselves, the better their concept and vocabulary development, articulation, and consequently, their reading and thinking skills will be.

Children need many experiences and activities to involve them in hands-on exploration of their environment. A dominant goal is to enrich and expand their knowledge and understanding of their world and to enable them to express themselves effectively.

Children bring to school a basic competency in oral language. By age 6, a child has acquired most of the adult patterns of speech. The role of the teacher is to provide an array of experiences that will move the children beyond basic competency to a more masterful fluency. Demonstrating interest in what children say will increase their oral fluency. Young children enjoy talking with the teacher, with other children, and in small-group situations. Oral language can be developed through puppetry, creative play, drama, formal and informal conversation, choral speaking, and oral reading. Literature is also an important stimulus for oral language. Critical and creative thinking can be well developed and expressed by children through oral language activities.

Speaking Objectives

1. To communicate with others.
2. To develop powers of expression.
3. To acquire better speech patterns.
4. To expand vocabularies.
5. To share experiences with others.
6. To use speech as a tool to adjust to social situations.
7. To contribute information to the class.
8. To begin to participate in group planning.
9. To discuss problems together and arrive at solutions that represent the best thinking of the group.
10. To develop new and clarifying concepts and relate to past experiences.
11. To help plan, carry out, and evaluate activities within the children's level of maturity.
12. To take advantage of opportunities for developing language through a variety of experiences.
13. To express thoughts and feelings.
14. To become more expressive through dramatic play.
15. To make friends with others.

Sharing their water-color books is fun for all of the children and rewarding for Matthew and Jennings.

16. To communicate in an organized way.
17. To participate in group discussions.

Suggested Speaking Activities

Creative Expression Center. Set up many centers for creative play—with a doll house, sand and water, materials for housekeeping and dressing up, and trains and trucks.

Explanation Activity. Encourage older children to help explain things to younger children—through art activities, words, and activity cards.

Teacher Reading. Model speech patterns for the children. Read good literature to expose them to varied language models. Always encourage discussion of the stories.

Teacher Listening. Listen to the children explain their errors in vocabulary, or give them correct vocabulary words. Help them to clarify and make their speech more accurate.

Displays. Present interesting objects, displays, or animals for the children to talk about to increase their ability to communicate with others.

Free Conversation. Allow the students to talk freely among themselves. Always take the time to talk with children individually.

Teacher-Student Storytelling. Begin telling a story. Go around a small group, having each child add something to the story and one child end it.

Sequencing Cards. Use sequencing cards (with pictures on them) that, when put together in the proper order, will form a story. Have the children play with these cards, put them in the proper order, and tell the teacher or a friend what story they form.

Wordless Books. Use wordless books—books with good illustrations, but no writing, to help the children expand their vocabularies. Have one child tell another his or her version of the story.

Games. Ask the children to bring in their favorite games and teach their friends how to play them to help them learn how to share experiences with others.

New Vocabulary. Introduce new vocabulary words that convey action by having the children act the words out.

Dramatizations. Ask the children to dramatize stories, events, or their responses to certain situations. This may also be done with puppets and a puppet stage.

Pictures. Bring in pictures—copies of good works of art—that the children can describe, tell stories about, and discuss their reactions to. They can do this among themselves or with the teacher.

Telephones. Allow the children to play with telephones and toy microphones to practice using speech as a tool of communication.

Audiovisual Aids. Use records, tapes, films, and slides to extend vocabulary and provide opportunities for discussion.

used troll + school bus

Finger Plays. Use finger plays to help the children to develop language concepts such as order, number, left, right, up, and down and gain practice in speaking.

Poetry. Encourage the children to express their thoughts and feelings by dramatizing poetry. One child may dramatize a poem while another child reads it. All forms of creative dramatics, freely improvised and carried out by the children themselves, are excellent for spontaneity and freedom of expression.

"Feely Box." Use a "feely box" to develop a vocabulary of descriptive words. The child reaches into a box containing different objects, selects one, and feels it without looking. The child describes the object to other children without telling them what it is.

Filmstrip Stories. Select a filmstrip that does not have words written in. Have the children make up a story about the filmstrip to develop their powers of expression.

Field Trips and Class Activities. After field trips and class activities, ask the children to tell about the experience. Write the account in story form on a chart. Have the children read the story back.

Stories. Have the children discuss solutions together and arrive at the best solution after reading a story to them. Before reading the conclusion, ask the children to tell what they think the outcome will be.

Riddles. Set aside a time for each child to bring a riddle to read to the group to practice oral skills while contributing information to the class.

Interviews. Have one child interview another child. They should ask for information about each other; for example, ''Tell me about your favorite pet,'' or ''What is your favorite thing to do?'' These interviews could be tape recorded. They will help the child develop the ability to communicate with others and use speech as a tool in social situations.

Mrs. Davenport introduces a new book to a small group of children.

Listening

Developing listening skills is an important part of language arts. It is through listening that a child first becomes aware of language and begins to imitate sounds. Listening is the identification of oral symbols that, combined with background experiences, produce meaning. Listening implies attention and responsive thought, be it casual or critical. It requires effort on the part of the listener. As a result, children need to be taught *how* to listen and how to think about what they have heard. A child's listening vocabulary far surpasses his or her speaking, reading, or writing vocabularies. Through listening, children can learn concepts and ideas that are otherwise unavailable to them.

Structure the classroom to promote listening. Model good listening habits to the children by *being* a good listener. Some purpose for listening should be stated.

Children with short listening spans need to lengthen them gradually through opportunities to listen to a variety of things that are based on their own experiences at first and on the experiences of others later. This involves a broadening of the child's own experiences through participation in many concrete situations that the child can see as well as hear. Children should learn to listen, understand, and respond to many different situations.

Viewing and Listening Equipment

Language Master 101 and other language experience machines
Record player and records
Tape recorder and tapes (regular and/or cassette)
Videotape recorder and tapes
Slide, flimstrip, and picture viewers and filmstrips
Slide projector and slides
Earphones (8 to 12 separate or 2 sets of 6), jacks
Film projector and film
Screen
Overhead projector, transparencies (blank and prepared)
TV, radio, walkie-talkie
Programmed materials
Filmstrips with coordinating records
Camera and film
Two-way telephone

Listening Objectives

1. To learn how to follow directions.
2. To gain information.
3. To be able to carry out activities.

4. To enjoy stories and poems.

5. To share pleasing experiences with others.

6. To increase vocabulary.

7. To improve sentence patterns.

8. To acquire imitative ways of enunciating and inflecting.

9. To respond to physical stimuli.

10. To listen critically.

11. To listen appreciatively.

12. To recall information.

Suggested Listening Activities

Concealed Sounds. Have the children play games in which objects that make sounds are hidden by one child and the other children try to identify the objects.

Musical Notes. Play notes on the piano to determine whether the children can tell half steps from whole steps. Also, determine whether they can tell high notes from low notes on the piano or other musical instruments.

Reading. Read high-quality stories, rhymes, and poems to the children often for their enjoyment.

During total group time, Mrs. Drake reads a story about bunnies to the children. Good listening skills are very much in evidence here.

Listening Games. Teach the children finger plays, songs, and poems, to which they must naturally listen carefully to learn. This will help them learn to imitate correct enunciation and follow directions.

Music Composition. Have the children compare various pieces of music or songs, noting tempo, rhythm, pitch, tone, and so on.

Poetry Reading. Read poems to the children. Have them give their reactions, tell what mood the poem put them in, and what it meant to them.

Poetry Discussion: Comparisons. Have the children compare poems on the same subject, such as winter or spring, discussing how each poem makes its point and describes its subject.

Poetry Discussion: Contrasts. Have the children contrast poems that are different, such as one that is happy and another that is sad.

Music Recordings. Play recordings of music and songs of various moods and types. Use the radio for special broadcasts or to find out about the weather or news.

Listening to Sounds. Encourage children who are nearby to pay attention to particular environmental sounds, some of which are very soft and others of which are a little louder, such as the rain, wind, a goldfish or tadpole, a church bell, a bird, a wasp.

Tape Recordings. Tape record some common sounds and have the children identify them—the sound of an electric mixer, a car door slamming, running water, brushing teeth.

Listening-Memory Game. Play a game that taps both listening skills and memory; for example, "I took a trip to Zanzibar." The first child might say, "I took a trip to Zanzibar and I took along my toothbrush." The next child might say, "I took a trip to Zanzibar and I took along my toothbrush and comb." And so it would go, as many objects would be added to the list, and each child would have to remember them all and add one more. This game can be played well with small groups of children and will help them follow sequence and recall information.

Traveling Game. Do "a traveling tale," similar to the example given in the listening-memory game, in which one child begins a story and every other child adds something in turn. Each child must listen in order to figure out what he or she will add.

Listening to Silence. Have the children listen next to a wall, a floor, or a window to determine whether they can hear anything or tell what is going on.

Listening to Quiet. Have the children listen when they are all quiet to determine whether they can still distinguish noises and sounds.

Listening to Tapes. Have the children listen to tapes of stories, teacher made or commercial, to develop their language skills. Let them make tapes of their own voices and the voices of other children so that they can play them back and listen.

Identifying Voices. Tape the voices of many different children. Play back the tapes and have the children identify the voices.

"Who Is Talking?" Select five or six children to stand somewhere in the classroom. Have the other children turn their backs to them. Touch one student and have him or her say something. The others try to guess who is talking. The one who guesses correctly trades places with the one who was talking.

Poetry and Singing. Introduce young children to poetry through singing. Through songs, children can respond to the rhythm of poetry.

A Sound Walk. Take the children for a walk outside or perhaps inside the building. When they return, see how many different sounds they remember hearing.

Listening with Art. Give each student a 9- × 12-inch piece of construction paper and a 2- × 12-inch strip. Demonstrate as you ask the children to fold their paper in half lengthwise, and in half lengthwise again. Line up the edges of the paper. Keep the papers folded and ask the children to fold the paper in half widthwise, and in half widthwise again. When the children unfold their papers, there should be 16 boxes. Have them turn the paper so that the long side is at the top, and draw lines with a crayon as shown:

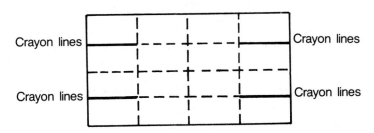

Tell the children to cut slits along the crayon lines. Then ask the children to bend the paper along the lines between the slits, overlap the corners, and glue the corners in place. When all four corners are glued, they glue on the basket handle. This basket can be used for many special occasions. The students will enjoy decorating the basket. This activity helps children learn to follow directions.

Poetry. Read a poem to the children. Then read the poem again, omitting some of the rhyming words. Ask the children to supply the missing words.

Writing

For the past 20 years, researchers, teachers, and parents have learned much about how young children learn to write. There are seven developmental stages through which most young children progress in writing: (1) they use processes similar to those they use to acquire oral language; (2) they engage in pseudowriting practices; (3) they learn basic principles for recording language in graphic form; (4) they use invented spellings; (5) they learn to compose in writing; (6) they learn to write in more than one mode; and (7) they learn to improve the quality of their writing by composing within social contexts. (Palmer, 1992, p. 80)

[handwritten: faulswriting ←]

[handwritten: Spelling the way it sounds]

Writing is a means of expression in language. It includes the formation of letters and the skill of composing. The child's emotional, physical, and intellectual development is reflected by the ability to write. Small-motor development and hand-eye coordination are involved in the ability to write. The functional skills of writing include handwriting, spelling, punctuation, and capitalization. These skills are learned best in meaningful and practical situations.

Before a child can write meaningfully, the child must have a good foundation in oral language. A verbal atmosphere in which the child is talked to and things are explained, along with exposure to firsthand experiences such as going to the zoo or the circus, develop this language ability. A literate environment in which books and newspapers are read and reading is valued and enjoyed also contributes greatly to promoting writing skills. Children witness the relationship between oral and written language when they see and hear others deriving meaning from written language.

Creative writing emphasizes thought rather than form. There are three basic stages of writing in the primary grades: precomposing, composing, and rewriting. In the precomposing stage, children brainstorm ideas that are relevant to them and that they can write about. In the composing stage, children actually write and draw, using their own natural language. In the revising stage, children, with the help of the teacher, proofread and revise or add to their writing. Care should be taken to maintain a child's enthusiasm for writing by emphasizing the positive aspects of a picture or a piece.

The teacher should create an environment that encourages writing. A writing center where materials are openly available to illustrate, write, and assemble stories into a book can be beneficial. Lots of small-motor activities and frequent opportunities for creative writing are essential in the language arts curriculum. Practice and repetition are necessary for progress to be made. Beginning writers need pleasant, relaxing activities and encouragement from the teacher. Children should begin to appreciate the beauty of language and how they can use it to express their feelings. Various experiences with oral language, good literature,

and concrete observations, along with the chance to express themselves freely in an independent, open atmosphere, help children develop thoughtful, original writing.

Writing Materials

Paper: lined, plain white paper, construction paper, chart paper, index cards, tracing paper, wallpaper scraps, wrapping paper scraps

Pencils, crayons, watercolors, colored markers, scissors, paper clips, yarn, brass fasteners, glue, stapler, staple remover, cardboard for book covers, correction fluid, and other materials necessary for making books

Pictionaries, dictionaries, and a high-frequency word list

Picture file, story-starter file (mounted pictures for writing about titles, stories, and words)

Photographs (current snapshots of children and activities)

Used magazines

Books with blank pages and open-ended titles

Chalkboard, white and colored chalk

Mailbox

Book jackets

Word boxes

Writing Objectives

1. To write with a purpose.
2. To write in complete sentences when appropriate.
3. To use correct punctuation and capitalization.
4. To spell words well enough to be understood, according to developed skills.
5. To write legibly and neatly.
6. To sequence ideas clearly.
7. To choose appropriate words. (*describe object*)
8. To write in a variety of forms.
9. To write for others to read.
10. To evaluate one's own handwriting.

Suggested Writing Activities

Handwriting

Letters. The child can feel, trace, and compare manuscript and cursive letters. Letters can be made by the teacher and/or children out of felt, sandpaper, wood, masonite, or clay with letter cookie cutters. Children use these letters to feel, trace with their fingers, trace around with a pencil or crayon, stack for visual discrimination, compare upper- and lowercase, and compare cursive and manuscript writing. Rubber letter stamps with stamp pads in different colors are also fun.

Shaving Cream. Pile some shaving cream on each desk and allow the children to practice writing letters with their fingers. When they are finished, wipe off the desks with a damp sponge.

Autograph Book. Put an autograph book in the writing center. The class collects autographs of the class members, who write in their very best handwriting to practice writing neatly and legibly.

Sand Box. Have children who are just learning to write practice forming their letters in sand. Salt may also be used. Line the bottom of a shoebox lid with black paper, and fill it with 3 tablespoons of salt or sand.

Secret Code for Numbers. Give the children a secret code where certain numbers stand for letters. Give them a message and let them try to figure it out. Then have them write the message in their best handwriting.

Poem Booklets. To provide practice in writing neatly and legibly, have the children copy poems in their poem booklets. Have them illustrate the poem according to what they think the poem is about. A decorated cover completes the booklet.

Mystery Sheet. Give the children a sheet of paper on which the letters have been written in alphabetical order, with some left out of the sequence. The children fill in the missing letters in their best handwriting.

Riddle Box. Have the children write riddles in their best handwriting. Place these riddles in a box to be shared with the group later. They can also be compiled into a class riddle book.

Silly Sentences. Write sentences on the board with errors in letter size, spacing, heights, and form. Discuss and have the students write the sentences correctly—to "correct" *your* sentences as they learn to evaluate handwriting and correct for error.

Word Lists. Place charts on display throughout the room on which children can list words in their best handwriting. Topics may include vocabulary words learned from science or social studies units.

Telephone Book. Make a collection of the names and telephone numbers of the children. Have the children make a telephone book and write their names and numbers in their best handwriting. This is also good practice for alphabetical order.

Self-Evaluation. After the children have examined their own handwriting, have them point out two strengths, such as writing on the line and closing circles; then have them point out one weakness that they can work toward improving.

Alphabet Fish. Write letters on cut-out fish. Attach a paper clip to each one. Make a fishing pole out of a yardstick, string, and a magnet. Players "fish," pull out a fish, and reproduce the letter on the fish on their paper or on the chalkboard before they can keep the fish.

Bingo. To learn to recognize cursive letters, have the children play Bingo with Bingo cards of cursive upper- and lowercase letters. The first to get a row of letters up, down, or across is the next caller.

Secret Code for Letters. Students can create their own alphabets by creating a code for letters. Have the children write messages to leave in the language arts center. The students who come to the center next can try to figure out the messages. An example of such an activity is "Sentence Scramble."

Color-Coded Manuscript Cards. Make a set of cards that show the formation of letters by steps. Use a different color for each stroke. Make cards for all letters.

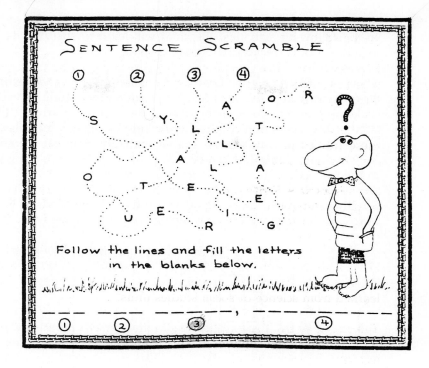

Start each letter formation with a green stroke ("Go") and end with a red stroke ("Stop"). These cards may be placed in the center or used for individual practice.

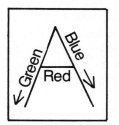
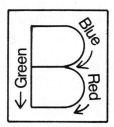
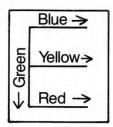

Practice Writing Cards. Cut tagboard to fit a duplicating machine and make a stencil of handwriting lines. Run the paper through the machine one sheet at a time. Place squares containing an upper- and lowercase letter and pictures of objects with the initial sound of the letter on each card. Use colored markers to show the formation of letters using arrows and numbers. Laminate the cards. Have the children use erasable pens to practice writing the letters. You can also put basic vocabulary words on back of the cards for the children to practice writing.

Spelling

In the following activities, the child will learn to spell words and develop an awareness of correct and incorrect spelling.

Stand to Spell. Construct large letters of the alphabet and distribute them to the class or group. The leader calls out a word, and the students with the letters that make up the word come to the front of the group and arrange themselves in the right order. The group checks the spelling. The leader may also call out another word using the same letters, so that the students must rearrange themselves. For variety, a clothesline can be strung up and the cards hung with clothespins in the correct order.

Spelling Squares. Ask the child to write as many words as possible using the letters in the squares. Use of a dictionary is encouraged.

	Two-letter words	Three-letter words	Four-letter words	Longer words
c t u o m a g r p s e i				

Anagrams. Using the letters of a given word, have the children rearrange them to form new words (map–pam, door–odor).

Word Groups. Have the child identify the patterns in word groups, such as fat, cat, mat, and add on to the groups. Word group charts can be displayed throughout the room and added to as students discover more words that belong in the groups.

Rhyming Words. Have the children write a word that rhymes with selected spelling words.

Word Search. From the selected spelling words, make a word search. Have the children visually discriminate and circle the spelling words. This can be done as a group activity or an individual activity.

"Tap and Say." Place letters randomly on the floor, a piece of paper, or a chalkboard. The players point to or tap letters to spell words. "Phonics Hopscotch" may be played by hopping to letters in the correct order.

Displayed Word Lists. Using a large wall space, alphabetize words that the students may need to use often. As the year progresses, the number of words on the wall will grow and the children will use the word lists as a reference for spelling high-frequency words.

Spelling Contract. Have the children write spelling words on a piece of paper. Each child is to find a friend or an adult to call out the words for him or her to spell. The person who calls out the words signs the contract. Each child should have five people sign the contract before test time.

Anagrams. Have the children help make four sets of 1-inch-square alphabet cards. Put them in a box. Players put all the cards face down and draw five. They then try to form words with their letters in crossword puzzle style, scoring one point for each letter used. A new card is drawn for each one used. The player with the most points after all cards are used or time is up wins.

Sign In. Have a sign-in attendance or job chart for each day even if it is not yet legible. The children will sense the purpose for their writing no matter what their ability is.

Spelling Booklet. Young children can make a spelling booklet with a page for each letter. On these pages, the children write the words that they can spell on the correct initial letter page. They can readily see their progress this way, and so can their parents.

Dictionaries. Older children can make dictionaries on subjects of interest. Pronunciation, syllabication, and spelling of the word with different endings may be included.

Letters. Make letters to be manipulated into words and sentences out of felt, sandpaper, or construction paper. Rubber letter stamps can also be used.

Crossword Puzzles. Crossword puzzles are good for reinforcing spelling, and they help stop tendencies to juggle letters. They are self-correcting, and children can work alone or as partners to pool their knowledge.

Hangman. This popular children's game reinforces spelling. Players try to guess a word letter by letter before the "man is hung."

Ghost. Ghost is a game in which players continue to add letters to a word without being the one who brings the word to an end. Affixes of all kinds can be used as long as it is a real word.

Scrabble.® Games such as Scrabble are great for spelling practice. Games can be made with tagboard letters and a game board. Many new words are learned, and the dictionary is used often.

Track Games. Track games can be made in which the child must spell the called-out word correctly before he or she can move on. Children enjoy the competition, and correct spelling is encouraged.

Creative Writing

In the following activities, the child will develop prewriting and composition skills. In general, provide as many experiences, visitors, and class trips to museums, factories, and parks as possible to allow for meaningful language and concept development. Always encourage lively discussion among the children concerning what they expect to learn and what they have learned. From use of oral language and the discussion of many ideas will come the fluency and thought content necessary for writing.

Reading. Choose a familiar subject such as animals, family, friends, trips, and nature and read selections from children's books. Have the children write on that particular subject, integrating their own experiences with what they have heard.

Description. Bring interesting objects to class, such as gourds, Indian corn, and magazine pictures that the children can examine for color, shape, and texture to develop concepts and vocabulary.

Perception. Encourage the children to write not only about their own perceptions of objects (how objects make them feel) but also about how they feel about events, situations, persons, and seasons.

Collections. Have the children bring to school collections of objects that represent the qualities of a particular season. Encourage them to make a display of all the objects brought. Expressions of their own feelings and thoughts, and perhaps poems, will result.

Class Books. Using a common theme, have each child contribute a page with an illustration and a short sentence to a class book. Possible themes include sea animals, holidays, and favorite parts of a story.

Musical Thoughts. After listening to and thinking about a musical selection such as Tchaikovsky's *Nutcracker Suite* or Prokofiev's *Peter and the Wolf,* have the children express their thoughts about it, either through drawing a picture or writing down words. This can be adapted easily to whole-class instruction or to language-center use with headphones. The child's own thoughts and language make this a meaningful experience.

Making Booklets. Use *comic strips* and either erase the wording for creative writing or leave it for reading pleasure. Or make books in *particular shapes*: "What Is Round?" "If I Were a Monster." Or *compose books* in which all children have an opportunity to write "My Favorite TV Show," "Our Family on Vacation," and so on.

Case Stories. Make a briefcase out of poster paper and fill it with small "cases," each with a title for a mystery story.

My fifth-grade "big buddy" comes to read with me every week. He is a special friend.

It's Magic. Make a large poster with a picture of a magic potion or a geni. The children "break the spell" by writing a story. Examples are "Help! I've Been Turned into a Toad!" and "Save Me! I'm Inside a Teapot!"

New Ending. The children can either illustrate or write a new ending to an unfinished story. Tape record a story, leaving out its culminating events, and allow the students to listen with headphones until the reading has stopped. Next, the students turn off the recorder and finish their own version of the story. This activity allows students to use their own language and work at their own ability level.

Message in a Bottle. Have the children write messages to "send," in a jar or bottle. Other children can take out previous messages to read then replace them in the bottles.

Class Vote. Have the students write their votes on ballots. Votes are usually limited to one word, such as someone's name for Citizen of the Month or class president, or a simple "yes" or "no" in response to a question.

Independent Reading. Encourage independent reading by providing time daily to do so. Help select and recommend good books to the learners.

Reading and Writing Buddies. Pair up younger students with older ones. An older class can adopt a younger one within the same school. Each child has a buddy to read to him or her and copy down story dictation to accompany illustrations. The younger children look up to their buddies while the older students gain a sense of responsibility by setting a positive example.

Role Play. Children can have a lot of fun playing waiter and waitress. Provide paper and pencils, along with an apron, to take "orders" from customers. The children can also make up shopping lists and mark off items as they "shop."

Class-Made Alphabet Book. Use several alphabet trade books as examples to make your own class book. Have each child choose a letter to draw and illustrate (some may get two letters, some may share a letter). Find two objects that begin with that letter to draw on the same page. Bind all of the pages in order, and display the book in the class all year long.

Language Buddies. Pair the children with a class of upper-elementary-level students to translate and practice language skills. After showing many examples of invented, or preconventional, spelling of younger students, the upper-elementary students can act as assistant editors and translators. More students are able to have their dictated stories transcribed this way, and they are excited about writing for an older audience.

Letter to an Author. After reading an interesting story, ask the children what they would like to ask the author. Questions can be about the story or personal ones about the author. As children put forth questions and comments, copy them down on chartpaper for all to see. Send the final composed letter to the author or the author's publisher. Many authors respond!

Story Cubes. The children can illustrate their own stories or illustrate the sequence of a story they have heard or read by using a story cube. Prepare a sheet

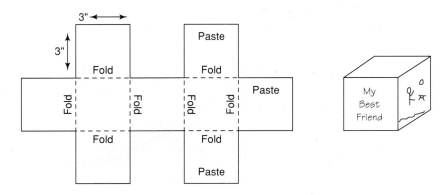

of white construction paper with the block pattern, with squares approximately 3 inches × 3 inches, for students to cut out (see illustration). Students draw and color scenes on each block face, with one face each for the child's name, the title of the story, and the author. Fold on the dotted lines, paste the sides together, and share it with the class.

Poems. Select poems for illustration and copying, or give the children ideas for poems of their own.

Mailbox. Place a mailbox in or out of the classroom to encourage children to communicate in writing. Notes, invitations, thank-yous, get-well notes, and so on can go through this channel. Mail can be sent through a classroom mail carrier.

Make a Story. Write a story on sentence strips. Mix them up and clip them together. The students arrange the strips in order.

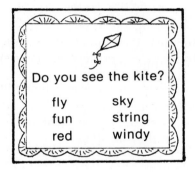

Picture Files. Fill a box with mounted pictures on tagboard. Select pictures that are appealing to children. On some cards, include story starters and vocabulary words relevant to the pictures (see illustration). Leave others with only pictures.

Word Web. This helps to combine the whole class's prior knowledge to associate words with a particular concept. Write the concept on the board and ask the children for words to describe the concept or words that fit into that category.

Sequels. When a favorite story comes to an end with no sequel, children can write their own. It does not have to be a sequel to a book; it can be a sequel to a television show or movie. Share the sequel with the original author. Many times authors respond.

Excuses, Excuses. Have children write their own notes for absences or tardies. Of course the parents will have to cosign.

Morning Message. As students watch, write a short message on the chalkboard. While pointing to each word, read the message aloud. This helps to convey the concept of reading from left to right and that print represents words that can be spoken.

Puppet Shows. Have the children create the dialog for puppet shows. This provides excellent opportunities to practice writing skills.

Newspaper. Organize the children into small groups to take turns reporting the day's events. The "Editor of the Day" might use the typewriter to make the final copy.

Photos. Take Polaroid® photos of the children's current experiences to stimulate them to verbalize and discuss the sequence of events and perhaps to write about the events.

Sequence Cards. Mount sequence cards on tagboard and laminate them. Have the children arrange the sequence cards in the correct order and write a story about the events.

Shape Booklets. Cut writing paper into shapes—animals, flowers, clothing, and others. Have the students write sentences or stories about the shapes. They can add a cover that they illustrate.

Kinds of Sentences. Show the children a picture and ask them to write questions about it. Using other pictures or the same picture, ask them to write statements and exclamatory sentences.

"Things to Do." Make a "Things to Do" file that involves writing. The children may add their own ideas. The following are some suggested ideas:

1. Look out the window and find three things that are moving. Describe them.
2. Draw a picture of three animals. Write about the one you like best.
3. Look at the aquarium. Write about what it would be like to be a fish.

What Kind of Sentence? Use cardboard covered in colorful contact paper. Staple four library card holders or envelopes on the cardboard, three holders that represent different kinds of sentence and the fourth holder containing a variety of sentences. A child or small group of children may sort the sentences into the correct holder.

All-Around Stories. The students start a story line and pass it to the next student in a group to add some more sentences. Continue until all writers have written at least once and the story is completed. A timer can be set for the duration of each writer's turn. When the timer goes off, the story is passed clockwise to the next person. Children really enjoy hearing stories to which they have all contributed.

Story Dictation. Make the connection between oral speech and written language through story dictation. Write down the children's words exactly; they can be accompanied by an illustration. Have the children "reread" the story.

Writing. Have the children write about how they perceive an object in the environment (an anthill, a kitchen stove, or the school cafeteria). Have them observe color, shape, and texture and describe the object through the way it is observed using the five different senses.

Program Writing. To simulate computer commands that involve discrete steps, have the children follow recipe cards with pictures, then write down the steps involved in performing a complete task such as brushing teeth, making a paper hat, or making a peanut butter and jelly sandwich. Be careful not to leave out any steps.

Punctuation and Capitalization

Punctuation Paradise. This is a game for teaching punctuation. Make a game board and use the following rules:

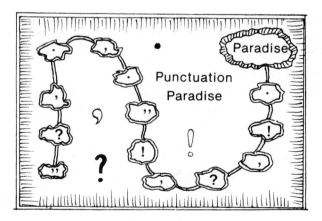

1. Each player places a marker on the board.
2. Roll the die and move the correct number of spaces. Give a sentence that contains the punctuation.
3. Continue until a player reaches "Paradise."

Tic-Tac-Toe. Have the students play as you would normally, but give a sentence and use the mark of punctuation, rather than the usual *X* or *O*.

?	,	"
.	!	?
,	"	.

Sentence Scramble. Prepare several sentences without punctuation marks at the end on sentence strips. Cut the sentences apart. Prepare cards with appropriate punctuation marks. Scramble the words in each sentence. Display the mixed-up sentence on a flannelboard, pocket chart, or some other means of display. Ask the children to unscramble the sentence and select one of the punctuation marks on the cards to be used at the end of the sentence.

The Case of the Missing Punctuation. After class instruction or a minilesson on punctuation, have the children insert periods, question marks, exclamation marks, and commas where needed in a piece of writing. To make this activity more relevant to the students, use their writing samples, removing punctuation and the students' names beforehand. This activity can be used for capitalization also.

Alphabet Center

An alternative way to teach a language arts skill is by setting up a center in the classroom for that particular skill. The following drawing is a sample Alphabet Center.

Suggested Alphabet-Related Activities

Feed-Me Poster. Draw a hungry lion on tagboard or heavy posterboard. At the corner, fasten a milk carton using brads. On the milk carton, place a card for a letter sound that is being studied (clip it on so that letters may be changed). In an envelope attached to the back, place several picture cards; some of these cards begin with the letter sound on the milk carton and some do not. The children must "feed" the lion the letter cards that begin with the specified sound.

Match the Letter Cards. Make a set of cards containing all the upper- and lowercase letters that are to be matched with yarn. Have the children match the letters.

Letter-Shaped Books. Construct book covers and cut paper to fit them so that the outline of the book represents the shape of a letter of the alphabet. Have the children cut from magazines and newspapers all kinds of examples of that letter in printed form. Paste the examples in the books.

First-Sound Sorting Boxes. Make three boxes, each designated with one letter. Objects are to be sorted according to their initial sounds (e.g., *n*: notebook, needle, nine, necklace, nuts, nail). Letters in boxes can be changed according to what is being studied. Have the children sort the objects into the boxes, matching the initial sound of each object with the appropriate letter.

Sets of Alphabet Cards. Make two sets of capital letters and two sets of lowercase letters. Have children match capital to capital, lowercase to lowercase, and capital to lowercase. The sets may be made from any type of paper.

Shoestring Chart (for use with alphabet cards and beginning sound pictures). Construct a chart with small pockets that can hold the letter and picture cards, which are interchangeable. Use shoestrings to match the cards across the board. Post an envelope on the back to hold all the cards until they are needed.

Letter Boxes. Cover half-pint milk cartons (tops removed) with contact paper. Use tagboard alphabet strips for sorting into these boxes. Have the child sort the letter cards into the boxes with the matching letters. The box can be used for upper- and lowercase letters. Paper clip letters onto boxes so that they can be changed.

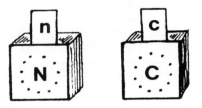

Beginning Letter Sound Picture Cards. On colorful tagboard, paste several pictures beginning with letter sounds that the children have studied. A set of alphabet squares goes along with this game. Have the children place these letter squares on the board covering the pictures that begin with their sounds.

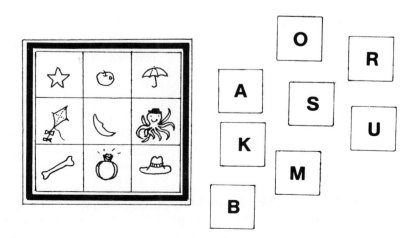

Octopus Match. Construct a game board on which the arms of an octopus serve as holders for cards that are to be matched. What is matched depends upon the learning skills that are being taught at that particular time. As a first step, the child may match letters that are the same, then upper- and lowercase letters, and finally letters and pictures that begin with that letter. Cards are matched with yarn.

Phonics Arrow Game. Cut squares of tagboard. On each square, print a letter, affix a tagboard arrow, and paste up three pictures at the bottom of the square, only one of which begins with the letter sound being studied. Have a child take the phonics card and look at the letter whose sound he or she is to listen for. Then have the child name the pictures at the bottom of the card and find the picture desired. Have the child turn the arrow to the picture whose beginning sound matches the letter at the top of the card. When finished, the child turns the arrow back to the top of the card.

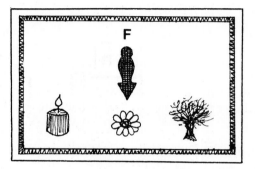

Phonics Boards. Construct nine 18- × 24-inch tagboards. Each board should present three beginning letter sounds accompanied by approximately 10 pictures for each sound. Ring the pictures that begin with the same sound with plastic rings or plastic bracelets. The child says the name of each object and rings the ones that begin with a particular sound.

Variation. Construct a board containing 3 letters with 10 pictures pasted on it for each letter. Have the child decide which letter to work with and circle it with a ring. Then have the child circle the 10 pictures that begin with that sound using a ring for each picture.

Alphabet Train. Make a train of 26 cars from half-pint milk cartons. Each car stands for a letter of the alphabet. Put two or more objects beginning with each sound of the alphabet inside the train cars (for example, Aa = apple, alligator, Dd = doll, duck). Have the child take each object and sort into the proper alphabet car according to its beginning sound.

Mystery Fill Box. Cut in the side of a large ice cream container. Attach the upper part of a child's sock to this so that the child can reach through the sock into the opening. The child will try to feel and guess the object beginning with a certain letter sound. The top of the carton can be removed to reveal whether the child is correct.

The "B" Barn. Using different letters on the barn, have the children cut out pictures beginning with those letters.

Other Alphabet-Related Activities

Block-Building Task Cards. Have the children choose various letter task cards that instruct them to build something that begins with the letter sound shown. The children then draw the construction.

Spatter Painting. Have available letter stencils, wire screen, newspapers, an old toothbrush, construction paper, and tempera paint. Have the children place letters on light-colored construction paper. Using thin tempera paint, spray paint through the screen with the toothbrush.

Placemats. Have the children make letter designs on placemats using construction paper or other suitable materials. The placemats may be used in the housekeeping corner or taken home to parents.

Paintings. At the painting easel, have each child paint a picture onto a letter-shaped piece of paper, perhaps something that begins with the letter shown on the paper.

Potato Printing. You will need a large potato, a paring knife, construction paper, and tempera paint. Cut the potato in half. On the flat side, the child marks a letter shape. Cut around the shape. Pour a small amount of paint into a jar lid. The child dips the design into the paint and prints it on construction paper.

Tube Prints. You will need a piece of old inner tube, a block of wood, white glue, scissors, tempera paint, a shallow pan, and newsprint. Make a letter on the paper. Repeat the shape on a piece of inner tube. Cut it out. Imprint the shape on a piece of wood about the same size as the shape. Allow it to dry. Place the stamp in a shallow pan containing tempera. Gently press the printer on the paper you are printing.

Letter Stamps. Supply a set of letter stamps and printing ink for the children to print with (commercial materials).

Clay or Play-Dough. Let the children use these materials to fashion letters. Have a set of alphabet letters nearby for reference.

Fingerpaint Alphabet Letters. Show the children how they can make letter designs when fingerpainting. Encourage large strokes with fingers and fists. Repetition of some letters will make an interesting design.

Sponge Print Letters. Have the child use a small sponge held by a clothespin to dip into various colors of tempera paint placed in a muffin tin or half-pint milk cartons. The child transfers the sponge print to paper.

Hole-Punch Letters. Use small sheets of light cardboard, oaktag, and so on. Have the child make a letter (for example, by tracing wooden letters). The child can then punch holes around the shape of the letter with a hole puncher.

Letter Cards. Make a set of cards, each listing several letters. Have the child choose a card, find some junk that begins with the letters selected, and arrange the junk onto a collage.

Letter Mosaics. On light cardboard, draw letter outlines. The children make decorative letters by gluing on seeds, torn paper, cereal, beans, and so forth.

Sew on Burlap. Trace letters on burlap and have the children follow the pattern with a needle and yarn.

Yarn Letters. Have the children use yarn or string to make letters that can be pasted onto construction paper.

Letter Collage. Using letter stencils, have the children trace the letters they choose onto construction paper (or fabrics). Then have them cut out the letters and put them onto a background material to make a collage.

Letter Feel. Place small wooden or plastic letters in a pillowcase or small sack. Have the children take turns feeling one letter at a time and trying to guess which letter they feel. The ones who can write their letters may write their guesses down.

Evaluation and Assessment

Some uses of assessment are:

1. To diagnose needs and plan further instruction and experiences.
2. To see progress during certain time periods.

3. To build confidence in students by helping them determine their strengths and progress made.
4. To communicate with parents, specialists, and so on.
5. To evaluate the teacher's *own* teaching goals, objectives, environment, techniques, and materials.

Methods of evaluation and assessment in the language arts include the following:

1. Teacher observation, individual conferences, and anecdotal records.
2. Evaluation of nonverbal, individual classwork.
3. Self-evaluation by the student. ← Did you get 5 ants on your log ⌐
example
4. Teacher-made tests, oral tests, performance tests, skill tests, checklists, and standardized tests. everyone color red on your sheet today.
5. Evaluation through verbal activities.
6. Parent conferences.

There are many ways in which to evaluate progress in the language arts. Evaluation is positive and continuous, and students are evaluated in terms of their individual abilities and progress. It helps the teacher to determine what the student *can* and *does* do with regard to skills and concepts, attitudes, and habits. Evaluation can be of a survey, formative, diagnostic, or summative nature. Errors are not used *against* the children but are used *for* them in future planning and in cooperation between teacher and student.

Chapter 5

The Fine Arts

Art and music have been termed "the creative arts." They offer innumerable opportunities to express individuality and imagination. Being creative, feeling creative, and experiencing creativity are all enjoyable, and learning is more fun in classrooms where the process of creative thinking is recognized and understood by both teachers and children. Incorporating creative thinking into all areas of the curriculum contributes to a positive attitude toward learning. As a teacher once commented, "I used to think that if children were having *too* much fun they couldn't be learning. Now I understand how they are learning in a more effective way."

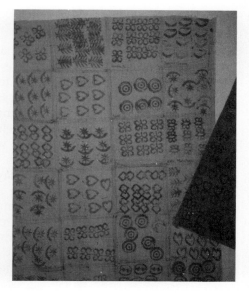

Experientially based early childhood curricula are congruent with a play and problem-solving approach. From this perspective, observing the *process* of play and exploration, understanding how the structure of an activity influences the potential for creative thinking, and viewing play and exploration as parts of the lifelong process of creative thinking are critical components of teaching.

Not only should the school be a beautiful place where children feel free to express themselves, it should also be adapted to the child's point of view. Child-sized tables and supplies are a must, and artwork must also be hung at a child's eye level. The children's own work should be displayed prominently so they will do their best and be proud of the end results. This has been realized perhaps to its fullest extent by the teachers in the British infant schools. Stories and illustrations by the children are usually double-mounted and displayed attractively in the classrooms, hallways, or other areas of the school. No matter how modest or elaborate the product, the children take great pride in their work. Much attention is given to each example, and the children are eager to start the next project.

A developmentally appropriate arts education program focuses on the needs and interests of children, with the ultimate goal being to foster an understanding of and involvement in the arts and to convey an appreciation of children's individual expressions. Good teachers cultivate the self-expression of *all* children, rather than singling out the "best" and "prettiest" of the creations as "successful." Conveying the attitude that each child's art is in some way unique teaches a valuable lesson as the children learn to enjoy and respect ideas and visual representations that are different from their own. This acceptance of differences in each other's art can be the beginning of a much broader acceptance of differences in such areas as culture, race, and creed.

Fostering Creativity

Playful teachers have a natural advantage in facilitating creativity in their classrooms, because they are more likely to play *with* children. Likewise, playful teachers are more likely to observe children's play from a childlike perspective. They actively search for situations in which they can be role models for exploration, divergent thinking, problem finding, and problem solving—in other words, for creativity itself. There is a natural correlation between playfulness and creativity. Teachers who are aware of these traits are more likely to enter into children's play with no preformulated expectations, thus providing a relaxed, evaluation-free play environment.

There are teaching methods that foster the development of creativity in early childhood classrooms. There is, however, no recipe or formula for making these methods work effectively. The "creative curriculum" is really an attitude that begins with the teacher's own ability to interpret curriculum and recognize and capitalize on creative behavior. The following are some suggestions to help optimize creative potential in young children:

- Incorporate and adapt to the children's interests and ideas.
- Provide a variety of materials for exploration and play.
- Help the children focus on their own special talents or strengths.
- Allow the children time to think about and develop their own ideas.
- Accept unusual ideas and responses from the children. Show them that their ideas have value. Encourage them to be proud of their own ideas, as well as each other's.
- Suspend judgment and evaluation of the children's attempts at creative thinking.
- Encourage the children to guide and evaluate their own work.
- Avoid competition.
- Facilitate the creative process by stopping to observe; then respond (do not react) in elaborate ways, asking open-ended questions, providing resources, participating without predetermined expectations in the children's activities.
- Show the children that you *value creativity* (the children's as well as your own)!

The Learning Environment

The child's environment has an important role in providing early learning opportunities. Every place where children work or play is a living and learning environment. Play helps children develop physically, mentally, and socially. Children need a place where they can spread out projects to work at their own pace. The optimal living and learning environment is therefore one that fosters exploration and creativity while providing opportunities to build motor, cognitive, and social skills. Much has been written about the learning characteristics of children, and most authorities agree that children learn best from manipulating objects in their environment and experimenting with processes. They benefit from exposure to a wide variety of materials coupled with an activity schedule that encourages development, maintenance, and mastery of skills. The teacher's task is to arrange and equip a living and learning environment that is conducive to successful childhood nurturing experiences. This involves selecting materials that are appealing and stimulating and planning activities that provide opportunities for children to work on important developmental skills and abilities.

Curriculum Materials

As an early childhood educator, you will need to develop curriculum materials in a variety of subjects and categories. Be sure to include objects (both actual and representational) as well as pictures that vary with respect to size, background, and color. Children must have concrete learning experiences before they can begin to process abstract information. Therefore, the use of objects is important when working with young children. Furthermore, children love to handle small items and are usually more motivated to participate with hands-on curricula than when only pictures are presented. Gather familiar as well as novel items, and remember that sufficient quantity and range of difficulty within each unit will ensure effectiveness with children of different ages and abilities. As you gather items for instructional units, take advantage of materials available at thrift stores and garage sales. Broaden your shopping habits to include craft shops, pet supply departments, and hardware stores. Organize these resource materials for easy access and keep your sets of materials intact to eliminate the need to gather them over and over again.

High-interest materials spark exploration and play. Novel materials seem to naturally bring out children's curious and questioning dispositions. Safe industry by-products or leftovers may be excellent sources of such materials, as well as working examples of recycling. One company donated a box of 3- × 3-inch flat plastic squares that became the genesis of many activities. Another teacher had access to discarded mat board from a local frame shop. These were used in a variety of activities, from making raised relief maps, to constructing buildings for a mock community, to standing in as makeshift easels. A computer manufacturer donated thousands of loose computer keys to a first grade classroom. These small plastic squares with letters, numbers, and symbols on them were the center of many creative activities throughout the year.

In every group of children there always seems to be one or two who are "into everything"—the trees on the playground, the discarded boxes in the hallway, and the custodian's closet full of large buckets and wide dustmops. All of these everyday objects are seen as materials to be examined most carefully. One teacher canvassed garage sales to purchase broken household appliances (old toasters, tape recorders, etc.) and then, after removing the electrical cords, provided space in the classroom for children to use screwdrivers and pliers to take them apart (without, of course, intending to have them put back together in the correct order). Thus, finding materials is only half of the battle; recognizing the potential in a variety of unstructured materials takes a keen eye. Early childhood educators have always been accused of being scavengers—a compliment when interpreted in light of the relationship of novel materials to creativity!

Activities

Many of the commercially available activities come with all parts necessary for individual or shared creative play, and they are appealing to a fairly broad cross section of age and ability groupings. Other experience centers can be developed by gathering both new and used items from various sources. Some of these teacher-made pretend activities are more effective in setting the stage for communication than their commercial counterparts. Children like to actively take part in developing their own learning environment, and they acquire an important sense of ownership by helping to complete special projects at school. Family participation is encouraged by asking parents to assist their child in gathering items needed for special activities or new learning and experience centers. This can be accomplished readily by sending home a simple note similar to the examples shown in Figure 5-1.

Examples of color, pattern, texture, line, space, contrast, shape, and rhythm as experienced through art, movement, dance, music, and creative drama should confirm the concept that all the arts are interrelated in the lives of growing children. These aesthetic elements apply in some distinctive form to all of the creative arts.

When young children first engage in airplane play, for example, they pre-

Dear Mom,
 In Ms. Bailey's class we will be studying the color PURPLE! Please send one or two PURPLE items to school with me on Wednesday.
  Thank you,
  Sarah

Dear parent,
 In class we'll be creating ice sculptures starting this Tuesday, for two weeks. Please send as many containers (different sizes and shapes) as possible with your child each day.
  Thanks a bunch!
  Ms. Bailey

Figure 5-1. Sample requests for materials

tend to be the airplane, zooming around the room, dipping their extended wings, curving into a two-point landing before taking off again to their own cascading sounds of "Varoom . . . Varoom. . . ." Movement, sound, and drama, expressed in line, form, and contrast, are integrated into one dramatic whole. Such spontaneous play can provide the basis for greater freedom in fingerpainting or preschematic painting or even scribbling by the very young child.

In addition to providing materials for sensory and perceptual awareness, teachers of young children support them as they begin to make associations. Children develop important understandings when they make the associations that when clay is too hard, it needs more water; when there is too much water in the playdough, it becomes too sticky; the bigger drums make a deeper sound than the smaller ones; and on an autoharp, the shorter strings have a higher pitch than the longer ones. Teachers purposefully facilitate such observations. Eventually, children learn to cluster these associations together, and they begin to reach for generalizations.

Art activities that encourage children to explore various media and processes are most likely to encourage creativity and heightened language development. Experimenting with the properties of watercolors and brushes, watching the colors run together and blend, is far more valuable than making a watercolor "picture." Even second and third graders can become frustrated in their attempts to make this medium cooperate with their increasing desire to approximate reality in their artwork. To ease this dissatisfaction with their artistic abilities, they could, for example, create a striking bulletin board using their watercolor washes as the soft mosaic background against a foreground of black abstract designs that they cut out while listening to classical music. What might children perceive about paint? It glides; it drags; it blobs; it spills; it spreads magically on wet paper and in water; it can be made lighter, darker, more intense, less intense; it can mix to make new colors; and it can swallow up all the colors to make that special shade of brown known as "yucky!"

Consider the following materials but focus on the actual *processes* when planning art activities: pastels, clay, scratch boards, resists, temperas, collages, sculpture, printing inkblots, charcoal and erasers, and watercolor markers.

Recipes

Salt Paint

⅓ cup salt
¼ tsp. food coloring

Spread in pan to dry.

Sand Paint

½ cup sand (washed, dried, and sifted)
1 tbsp. powdered tempera

Fingerpaint

Liquid starch may be used in combination with powdered paint for color. Add 1 tbsp. glycerin as a preservative and store in an airtight container. (Glycerin can be bought readily at the drugstore and makes an excellent preservative for all types of paints.)

Soap Bubbles

wire coathanger   4 drops corn syrup
1 tbsp. liquid detergent   dish
2 tbsp. water

Pour 4 drops of corn syrup into the dish and carefully add the water and detergent. Mix gently. Bend the coathanger hook to make a loop.

Great Stuff

½ cup cornstarch   1 cup salt
¼ cup cold water   ½ cup water

Mix ½ cup cornstarch and ¼ cup water. Stir 1 cup salt into ½ cup water and heat. Pour heated mixture into cornstarch mixture. Mix thoroughly. (Small objects take 2–3 days to dry.)

Playdough

1 cup flour   ½ cup salt
1 cup water   2 tbsp. vanilla
1 tbsp. oil   food coloring
1 tbsp. alum

Mix dry ingredients. Add oil and water. Cook over medium heat until like mashed potatoes. Remove from heat. Add vanilla and color. Divide into balls. Work in color. Store in tightly covered container.

Playdough (*uncooked*)

4 cups flour mixed with
1 cup salt

Add powdered tempera paint coloring to this mixture.
Add water until the mixture is soft and workable, but not sticky.
Store in an airtight container.

To add color to any of these recipes with the least mess, place the clay in a strong plastic bag. Drop in approximately three to four drops of food coloring or two teaspoons of tempera per cup of clay. Knead the color into the mixture by squeezing the bag until the color is evenly distributed.

A successful project from *Mudpies to Magnets* is making "rainbow stew." Mix ⅓ cup sugar, 1 cup cornstarch, and 4 cups cold water. Cook until thick and divide into three bowls. Add a generous amount of red, blue, and yellow food coloring to the bowls. You want the colors to be bright. Ask the children which colors they want in their individual bags. Then place about 3 tablespoons of each color they have requested into a heavy-duty sealable bag. Roll the bags to push the air out and then seal and tape them closed with duct tape. The children knead, squish, and manipulate the different-colored balls into every possible color combination, creating their own rainbow stew.

Rainbow stew, as suggested in *Mudpies to Magnets:* kneading, squishing, and manipulating different-colored balls into many color combinations.

Clay

Clay is a versatile, inexpensive material that has high appeal. Children enjoy manipulating clay and experimenting with its plastic properties. It is a texturally pleasing and responsive medium that has many uses in the art curriculum.

Suggested Activities

Explore

1. Obtain a ball of clay or playdough.
2. Experiment with the clay by twisting, pulling, pressing, etc.
3. Make a three-dimensional object.

Fossil Print

1. Roll out a ball of clay until it is about ¼ inch thick. (Use a rolling pin or round can.)
2. Press the ribbed side of a shell into the clay.
3. Let the print dry.
   Variation: Put dried weeds on waxed paper. Press clay into weeds.

High-Relief Sculpture

1. Roll out a ball of clay until it is about ½ inch thick.
2. Make a circle as large around as a dinner plate.
3. Crumple a piece of newspaper into a ball.
4. Center the clay slab on top of the ball.
5. The center represents your face.
6. Create facial detail by imprinting and adding on pieces of clay.
7. Let it dry.

Clay Slab Shapes

1. Roll out a piece of clay until it is about ¼ inch thick.
2. Use cookie cutters or a dull knife to cut out shapes.
3. Create texture by imprinting and adding clay.

4. Allow to dry.
5. Paint it with tempera if desired.

Clay Beads

1. Roll bits of clay into ¼ inch balls.
2. Pierce each ball through the center using a needle or opened paper clip.
3. Allow it to dry.
4. Decorate it with colored markers or tempera.
5. Use the clay beads with paper beads (see Thanksgiving project), colored pasta, or dyed seeds to make a Native American necklace.

In this classroom we do art projects every day. We can select our own materials.

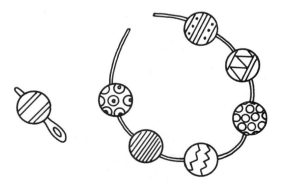

There are lots of "brushes" in nature—just take a walk outside and find them. Collect dried grasses and flowers, feathery wheat stalks, straw, thin pine branches, and twigs. Later, use thin wire, colored pipe cleaners, or twine to bind the natural brush materials together or to attach them to a twig handle for stability. Continuing with the Native American motif, a variety of bright paint colors can also be made from ordinary foodstuffs.

The Basic Elements of Art

Color

As has been true for many years, although children manipulate color according to their stage of development, experimenting with color is a pleasurable experience for most children regardless of their expertise. An understanding of the contribution color makes to any composition helps children improve their own use of color. Pleasing results in design and composition depend on color harmony (Paine, 1949).

The world of color affects us on many levels. The ability to use color to express ourselves can be very satisfying. Children may be introduced to the joyful world of color gradually, through watercolor painting. The transparency and fluidity of the medium allow the children to participate in the initial creating of the forms.

The delight they experience in the gesture and the movement of the brush across the page motivates young children to begin to paint. By watching the teacher demonstrate, they learn how to dip the paintbrush into the water, squeeze it, dip it into the paint, and move it across the page. At this stage, the teacher generally does not draw forms, but simply lets the colors flow freely. The emphasis is on the process. Only gradually do children become conscious of the actual colors, delighting in the designs and patterns that arise. As they become older, more form is brought into the process.

Suggested Activities

Explore

1. Use blue and yellow tempera.
2. Fold a piece of newsprint in half.
3. On one half put a spoonful of blue.
4. On the other half put a spoonful of yellow.
5. Refold.
6. Rub hard across the newsprint.
7. Use circular motions.
8. Open and unfold the newsprint.
9. You should have created a new color.
   Variation: Use any combination of primary colors.

Color Collage

1. Decide on a color theme.
2. Cut out pictures that are that color from magazines.
3. Find natural objects that are that color.
4. Glue the pictures and objects to construction paper.

Color Walk

1. Get a paper bag.
2. Go outside and collect objects of many colors.
3. Discuss your collection with your classmates.

In the Waldorf preschool, the children watercolor with only the three primary colors (red, yellow, and blue), so that the colors can be experienced in their purest expression. They are introduced one at a time. To begin with, young children are satisfied to work with just one color and will fill the whole page up with different tones of that color. When a second color is finally introduced, the children are fascinated to watch the "red fairy play with the blue fairy." By the end of the year, all three colors will be "playing" together, creating ever more imaginative possibilities.

The type of materials used is important. The watercolors must be of high quality, so that they remain transparent and can mix clearly with other colors. The paper must be of heavy, sturdy grade, because young children use active brush strokes. The brush, too, must be durable and wieldy. Brushes about 1 inch wide with natural bristles give the best results.

Crayons

Crayons are an excellent and commonly used tool for elementary school children. Each child should have many opportunities to explore the use of crayons.

Suggested Activities

Rainbows

1. Get a piece of newsprint.
2. Experiment with using the flat side of a crayon to make broad strokes.
3. Practice.
4. Get a sheet of white drawing paper.
5. Use the flat sides of crayons to make a rainbow.

Crayon Texture

1. Draw with crayon on a piece of precut sandpaper.
2. Cover the sandpaper with white paper.

Crayons are an excellent and commonly used tool for young children. Each child should have many opportunities to explore the use of crayons.

3. Ask the teacher to press this with a warm iron.
4. Two pictures will result.
5. Use glue to mount both pictures on construction paper.

Chalk

Chalk is a popular drawing material that offers many possibilities for expression. To develop their ability to effectively use chalk, children will:

1. explore the different ways to use chalk to create lines, texture, and shades.
2. experiment with blending colors of chalk.
3. use chalk with other media.
4. observe how others have used chalk as a tool for expression.

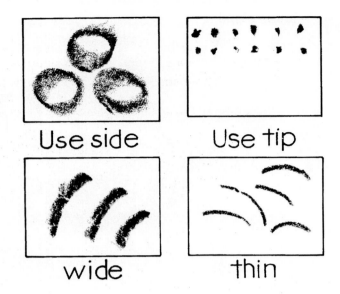

Tempera

Tempera is another commonly used art medium for young children. Children can use tempera to paint, print, wash, and so forth.

Suggested Activities

Explore

1. Get a piece of newsprint.
2. Use tempera and a variety of brushes.
3. For brushes, include pine branches, Q-tips, scouring pads, bones, feathers, etc.
4. Experiment with making different kinds of lines.

Accidental Design

1. Fold a piece of construction paper in half.
2. Spoon a blob of tempera on one half.
3. Refold the paper.
4. Rub your hand over the paper.
5. Open it up.
6. Name the shape you have made.

Blown Painting

1. Get a piece of construction paper.
2. At one end put a spoonful of runny tempera.
3. Blow through a straw to make the tempera flow in many directions.

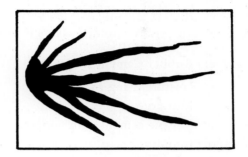

Rain Painting

1. Sprinkle 2 or 3 different colors of dry tempera on construction paper.
2. Set the paper outside in the rain.
3. Watch the rain do the painting.

Tempera Prints

1. Line a tray with a paper towel or a sponge.
2. Pour in thick tempera paint.
3. Arrange an assortment of beautiful junk (bolts, nuts, spools, etc.).
4. Dip an object in tempera.
5. Print with the object on newsprint.
6. Experiment with different objects.
7. Get a piece of construction paper.
8. Create an overall design by printing with beautiful junk.

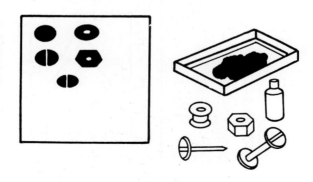

Tempera Painting

1. Get a piece of newsprint.
2. Explore using brushes of different textures and widths.
3. Hold the brushes at different angles to see what effect this has on your mark.
4. Get a piece of construction paper.
5. Use different brushes and colors to create a picture of yourself.

Tempera Rubber Cement Resist

1. Paint a picture using rubber cement.
2. Allow it to dry.
3. Paint over the cement with tempera.
4. Allow it to dry.
5. Use an eraser to remove the rubber cement.

Tempera Stencil

1. Fold a piece of waxed paper or construction paper into a rectangle.
2. Cut out pieces along the fold.
3. Open and flatten the paper.
4. Tape the cut paper to another piece of construction paper.
5. Make a pouncer by wrapping several cotton balls in a small piece of cotton cloth and closing it with a rubber band. (See the discussion of pouncing that follows.)
6. Pour tempera into a tray lined with sponge or paper towel.
7. Dip the pouncer into the tempera.

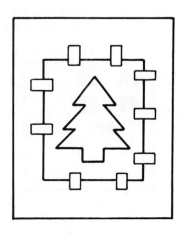

8. Remove excess paint by printing first on newsprint.
9. Lightly pounce the color over the stencil.
10. Remove the stencil.

Pouncing

This process would fit nicely into kindergarten or first grade if used in its simplest form. It can be used by older children for advanced techniques.

1. Touch the pouncer in the paint first, then on folded newspaper to unload excess paint and spread it evenly over the surface of the tool.
2. Lightly pounce the color over the pattern in the stencil.

More than one color may be used if each is used lightly. Pulverized chalk or dry tempera may be used in place of the paint, except that a rubbing motion may be necessary with the pouncer.

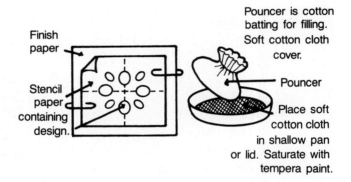

Murals

Murals are large pictures. The average classroom mural is from 4 to 8 feet long. Younger children do not view a mural activity as a cooperative adventure. However, by the third grade, children can plan and work together on a mural. It should be emphasized to the students that, whatever the chosen topic, several students should be able to work on it.

Texture

The three-dimensional quality of a surface is called *texture*. It may be an intrinsic factor or one that is artificially created. Texture is used and created in many ways in art.

To develop their awareness of texture as a basic element of art, children will:

1. experience, recognize, and describe textures.
2. create textures by using a wide variety of materials.
3. use a variety of textures.
4. observe the textures of natural and man-made objects.

5. observe how others have created and simulated texture in their compositions.

Suggested Activities

Texture Walk

1. Get a piece of newsprint and some crayons. (Chubbies are recommended.)
2. Collect objects inside and outside the classroom for texture rubbing.
3. Cover the object with newsprint.
4. Rub hard over the surface with the side of a crayon.
5. Discuss your rubbings with classmates.

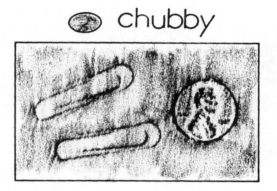

Fluffy Pictures

1. Decide on an animal or shape to make. (Suggestions are lambs, clouds, ducks, or chicks.)
2. Use cotton balls.
3. Color the balls if desired by shaking them in a bag with a little dry tempera.
4. Glue the balls to construction paper.
5. Add detail with crayons and colored markers.

Frosty Picture

Caution: Epsom salts are poisonous.

1. Get a piece of blue construction paper.
2. Use crayon to draw a "snowy day" picture.

3. Paint over this with an Epsom salt mixture (4 oz. Epsom salts dissolved in 1 pint hot water).

4. Crystals will appear on the surface.

Snakes

1. Get a white paper plate.
2. Color both sides with crayon.
3. Cut each plate around and around in a spiral.
4. Draw an eye on one end.

Native American Tepees

1. Cut paper bags into triangles.
2. Use crayons to decorate each triangle with Native American symbols.
3. Arrange various size teepees on construction paper.
4. Glue them.
5. Create a background of a Native American village with crayon.

Sand Painting

1. Paint a picture with white glue.
2. Use a brush or Q-tip to apply the glue.
3. Sprinkle the glue with colored sand.

Tray Art

1. Draw designs in a tray filled with flour, salt, cornmeal, or sand.
2. Use your fingers and other objects.

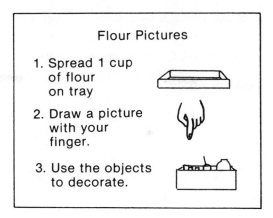

Weaving

Weaving allows children to work with many textures and colors and to develop the concept of over and under in the process. With teacher assistance, children can make simple looms from paper, cardboard, onion sacks, and other materials.

Suggested Activities

Paper Looms

1. Fold a piece of 12″ × 18″ construction paper in half.
2. Beginning on the fold, make cuts.
3. Stop 2 inches from the top.

Cardboard Looms

1. Measure and draw a line across the top and bottom of a piece of cardboard about ½ inch from the edge.
2. Cut an uneven number of slits from the edge to the line at about ½ inch intervals.
3. Cut the top and bottom.
4. Begin warping by pulling string through the first slit at the top of the loom.
5. Tape string to the back of the loom.
6. Carry string across the front of the loom to the first slit at the bottom of the loom.

7. Go behind the tab created by the first and second slits.

8. Carry string across the front of the loom to the second slit at the top.

9. Repeat until all slits are used. Tape the string to the back of the loom.

Yarn Weaving

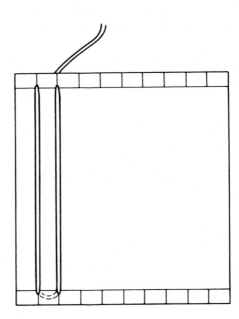

1. Make a cardboard loom.

2. Use yarn for the warp and weft.

3. Weave the yarn.

4. Tie the yarn ends together in back.

5. Slip the woven piece off the loom.

6. Insert a dowel and use your weaving as a wall hanging.
   Variation: Weave in dried grasses and other natural materials.

Magazine Photo

1. Make a paper loom.

2. Cut a large photograph from a magazine.

3. Cut a strip from the photograph.

4. Use the strip to weave. (The strip is the weft.)

5. To avoid confusion, weave each strip before cutting the next.

6. Cut the strips in succession.
   Note: Use magazines printed on high-quality paper (*National Geographic,* for example).

Lofts

Enclosures for classroom lofts can be made out of farmer's cloth, a smooth but heavy wire. By tying long ribbons, lace, and strips of material to the top hole in the "fencing," children can weave the entire loft. It does not matter if they skip holes or weave in a continuous direction. They help each other by poking and pulling the material through the holes. Fences outside that are already existing or specifically created for activities such as this can also be woven with reeds, grasses, and other natural materials.

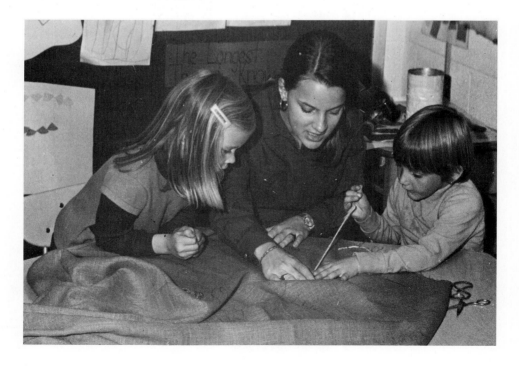

Sculpture

Sculpture is the creation of three-dimensional objects by taking from, adding to, or assembling materials (Lansing & Richards, 1981). It is yet another vehicle for the expression and communication of ideas.

Suggested Activities

Animals

Totem Pole

Eskimo Mask

1. Get a white paper plate for the center.
2. Use crayon and scraps to make your face on the plate.
3. Glue 5 Popsicle sticks to the back of the plate.
4. Allow the sticks to project around the edge of the plate.

5. Decide on 5 things you would like to be better at doing. (This is a lucky mask.)

6. Use paper scraps to make a symbol for each of these 5 things.

7. Glue each symbol to the end of one of the Popsicle sticks.

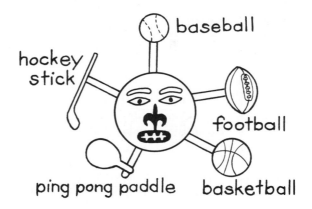

Boxes

Cardboard boxes of all shapes and sizes are wonderful for creating free-standing sculptures. Children can tape them together and paint them; the boxes become hospitals, fire trucks, and whole communities, even dragons and "boxasaurs."

The "ceiling" of a large cardboard box can serve as a type of Michelangelo-type painting surface. Tables also have "ceilings"; they and the bottoms of classroom lofts can have big sheets of paper stapled or taped to them to create the same fun experience of painting like the masters. One child painting on the "ceiling" always attracts five or six other children. They talk endlessly about how they could paint their bedrooms, and when they cannot quite reach, they discuss alternatives. Group activities like this are much more than just fun; they also help the children learn how to work cooperatively and relate to each other socially.

Easels

Easels are a necessity in any elementary art program. They allow the children to move about while they are painting and to really get the rhythm and feel of the experience. Easels also make it possible for children to step back and look at their own work objectively. Easels that can be attached to a wall are perhaps the best option for very young children, because they cannot be kicked or tripped over. Outdoor easels are also a wonderful idea, allowing children more freedom to spray or splatter paint. Easels made out of Plexiglas are creative tools for interaction among children, because the children can see each other as they paint.

Newspaper Sculpture

To make a newspaper sculpture, begin by rolling the newspapers, at least three rolls per child, preferably more if possible. Tape the rolls and have the children shape the newspaper rolls as they choose. Have lots of masking tape ready and start attaching the rolls to one another, and then to the floor, the ceiling, a piece of cardboard, or even a wall. The result will be a free-form sculpture of impressive magnitude. The class may add to the sculpture over a period of days. They can paint it or decorate it with sticky dots, string, ribbons, glue and glitter, or whatever they can think of. Newspaper sculpture succeeds with a wide range of ages. One benefit of this project is that children are placed in a situation requiring negotiation and group planning without even realizing it.

Line

Children can be encouraged to see lines as they exist in nature and as they occur in deliberate patterns and forms. "Take a walk with a line" is the encouragement that artist Paul Klee offered his students (cited in Moore, 1968).

Lines have direction and destination; they create rhythm and movement. They are one of the basic elements of art.

To develop their ability to see and use line within a composition, children will:

1. describe lines as wide, thin, zigzag, crooked, etc.
2. use lines to create a sense of movement.

3. use lines to create overall patterns.
4. observe how others have used the line element within their compositions.
5. observe lines as they occur in nature.

Suggested Activities

String Print Line Design

1. Wrap string randomly around a block of wood.
2. Paint the string with tempera.
3. Press the painted side against a sheet of newsprint.
4. Repeat until the design is completed.

Design Lines

1. Make brushes by notching the ends of strips of cardboard.
2. Dip the tips of these brushes into tempera.
3. Touch or drag the brush across a sheet of construction paper.
4. Repeat until the design is completed.

Abstract Line Design

1. Scribble with a black crayon on construction paper.
2. Make big scribbles and thick, dark lines.
3. Do not let the scribbles touch the edges.
4. Color each space with crayon.
5. Cut around the scribble.
6. Glue it onto construction paper.

Spiderweb Catch

1. Locate a spiderweb.
2. Sprinkle it with talcum powder.
3. Carefully lift it onto a piece of black construction paper.
4. Ask the teacher to spray the web with a fixative.

Printing

Printing is another way of creating art that can extend children's array of artistic devices.

Suggested Activities

Fingerprints

1. Get a sheet of newsprint.
2. Press one of your fingers onto a stamp pad or onto a tray filled with thickened tempera.
3. Press your finger onto the newsprint.
4. Experiment by making prints with all different parts of the hand (fingertips, knuckles, palm, etc.).
5. Add details with colored markers and crayons.

Monoprints

1. Apply fingerpaint to a washable surface.
2. Use your fingers, Q-tips, and brush tips to draw a picture.
3. Cover the picture with fingerpaint paper (shiny side down).
4. Rub over the paper.
5. Remove the paper.
6. Your picture has been printed on the paper.
   Note: A plastic cutting board makes a good washable surface.

Styrofoam Prints

1. Get a Styrofoam tray.
2. Draw a picture using permanent colored markers.
3. These markers will dissolve the foam.
4. Use a brush or a sponge to apply a thin layer of tempera to the surface of the tray.
5. Place a piece of construction paper over the tempera.
6. Rub the paper.

Vegetable/Fruit Prints

1. Use any variety of halved and quartered fruits or vegetables.
2. Select one and press the cut surface into a tray of tempera.
3. Press it onto newsprint.
4. Experiment.
5. Create different shapes and designs.
6. Get a piece of construction paper.
7. Print an overall pattern or design on the paper.

Shape

Shape is important to the composition of design and a necessary tool for visual expression of ideas. An understanding of shapes and their function in design is important in children's artistic development.

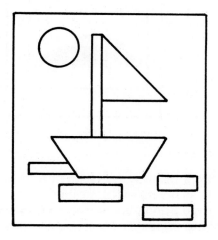

Suggested Activities

Shape Pictures

1. Cut out a collection of geometric shapes. (The teacher may precut these.)
2. Arrange the shapes on construction paper to form a design.
3. Glue the shapes to the paper.

Sponge Pictures

1. Use sponges that are precut into geometric shapes.
2. Dip the sponges in tempera.
3. Print by pressing each sponge onto construction paper.
4. Fill the paper with your design.

Magazine Hunt

1. Select a shape as a theme.
2. Look in magazines.
3. Cut out pictures of that shape.
4. Arrange the pictures on construction paper.
5. Glue them to the paper.
   Variation: Outline the shapes with black crayon.

Collage

Collages are a fun way for children to express ideas. The word *collage* comes from the French verb *coller*, meaning to stick. Collages are created by sticking pieces of paper, cloth, and/or other materials to a background. They are useful for improving the child's sense of pattern, color, and texture.

Suggested Activities

Nature Collage

1. Collect assorted natural materials (seeds, pods, twigs, leaves, etc.).
2. Arrange them on heavy cardboard or tagboard.
3. Glue the materials with white glue.

Face Collage

1. Get a small paper plate.
2. Use beautiful junk to create a face on the plate.
3. Glue it with white glue.

Seed Collage

1. Press a ball of great stuff or playdough into a plastic lid.
2. Arrange seeds and beans on top of the playdough.
3. Press seeds into the playdough.
4. Allow it to dry.

"I" Collage

1. Cut a big capital "I" from butcher block paper. (The teacher may precut this.)
2. Fill it with pictures, drawings, and words that represent things you can do.

Patchwork Collage

1. Divide a piece of cardboard into several rectangular spaces using a pencil and ruler.

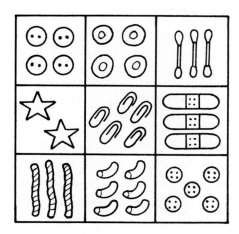

2. Fill each rectangle with one type of beautiful junk.

3. Glue it with white glue.

Tissue Paper Collage

1. Lay a piece of plastic wrap on a 9″ × 12″ piece of newsprint.

2. Paint the plastic with a mixture of ½ glue to ½ water.

3. Tear tissue paper into irregular shapes.

4. Lay the tissue paper on the glue-covered wrap.

5. Overlap the tissue paper until the entire piece of wrap is covered.

6. Allow it to dry overnight.

7. Peel the wrap from the tissue paper.

8. Hang the finished product in the window.

Space Relationships

In a well-constructed composition, the proportions are balanced and varied. Equal importance is placed on used and unused space (Paine, 1949). All elements relate to one another to create a harmonious design.

An understanding of these concepts is basic to children's artistic development. The better their grasp of these ideas, the more flexible their responses.

To develop their awareness of space relationships, children will:

1. explore the concept of negative space.

2. experiment with ways to create large and small spaces.

3. develop concepts of over/under, inside/outside, near/far, etc.

4. use these concepts in solving "creative" problems.

5. observe how others have manipulated space relationships in their compositions.

Suggested Activities

Negative/Positive Pictures

1. Get a piece of 9″ × 12″ construction paper and a 6″ × 9″ piece of fadeless paper. (Fadeless is preferred because it has a white back.)
2. Select contrasting colors.
3. Cut into the smaller piece on the long edge.
4. Go in and out on the same edge.
5. Do not cut through the other edges.
6. Match the negative to the positive in the center of the construction paper.
7. Glue them together.
   Variation: Cut a smaller piece of paper in half. Place the two halves together and cut them. Arrange them accordingly.

Expanded Geometric Shapes

1. Select a geometric shape from precut shapes.
2. Cut the shape apart in parallel sections.
3. Select a piece of construction paper in a contrasting color.
4. Arrange the sections in order on the construction paper.
5. Leave space between the sections.
6. Glue them.

Pizza

1. Get a cardboard circle.
2. Cut out pizza toppings from scrap paper.
3. Mix dry red tempera with liquid starch.
4. Brush the tempera onto the cardboard circle.
5. Put on the toppings.
6. Sprinkle the top with cornmeal "cheese."

Overlapping Paper Picture

1. Decide on a theme (Suggestions are city buildings, cars on a street, crowds of people, etc.).
2. Cut objects out of scrap paper.

3. Arrange the objects so that they overlap to create a realistic design.

4. Glue them to construction paper.

Developmentally Appropriate Practices in Art Education

> The visual arts education curriculum has a scope and sequence that accommodates children's interests, skills, and capabilities based on goals and objectives that are developmentally appropriate. The curriculum includes a balance of creating art, perceptual activities, and responsive activities designed to enhance the cognitive, affective, and motor development of all children. (Colbert & Taunton, 1992, p. 2)

In 1992, the National Art Education Association (NAEA) issued a briefing paper, *Developmentally Appropriate Practices for the Visual Arts Education of Young Children.* The following three major themes found in high-quality art education programs were given: (1) Children need many opportunities to create art; (2) children need many opportunities to look at and talk about art; and (3) children need to become aware of art in their everyday lives. In addition, an overview of the key aspects of art education programs outlining "appropriate" and "inappropriate" behavior as related to each of these areas was suggested as summarized in Table 5–1.

Music

Music is a natural and pleasurable part of children's lives and the world around them. Children hear the music of nature in the concert of cicadas on a summer evening, the purring of a kitten, the rush of wind before a storm, and the crash of waves against the shore. Children make music from birth onward. There is music in the cooing and babbling of infants, the spontaneous singing and dancing of young children, and the rhythm and chant of school children jumping rope. Music offers many vehicles for expression and a diverse range of responses.

Music may be planned as an exploration of sounds to acquire knowledge and skills leading to playful experimentation of instruments and rhythms, melodies, and lyrics.

A unique feature of music is that it is available to anyone at any time. We intellectually capture and retain our music experiences. When we conceptualize music, we "hear" it. Because we can "hear" sounds intellectually, we can create music in our minds.

Through acculturation, children acquire varying degrees of musical competencies between infancy and the middle school years. These competencies (musical intelligence) tend to be of an intuitive nature and, lacking a planned, structured spiral curricular musical program, remain as such without much appreciable maturation even into adulthood (MMCP, 1970). To accomplish the goals and objectives of music education, a multifaceted instruction program should be structured that will help each child learn to:

TABLE 5-1 Key Aspects of Art Education Programs

Program Component	Inappropriate Practice	Appropriate Practice
Curriculum	* Curriculum lacks developed goals and objectives. * Goal of teacher is to display children's work that is "pretty" * Lessons are based primarily on the teacher's interests and background. * No attempt is made to follow up lessons with another that builds on what was learned.	* Goal is to encourage children's development and their involvement in and understanding of the visual arts. * Teachers convey an appreciation of children's individual expressions and nurture individual styles. * The choice of lessons and activities is based on children's interests, and the major concepts and skills are used in subsequent lessons and built upon throughout the curriculum.
Choice of Art Materials	* Teachers use materials not intended for children that hinder their expressions and require much help from the teacher	* Teachers use materials that can be easily manipulated, are safe, and meet the needs of children's self-expression.
Correlation of Arts with Other Areas of Curriculum	* Art is taught as separate area of curriculum. It is approached as an activity that warrants little attention or discussion	* The program utilizes concepts and skills taught in other curriculum areas. Art is taught as an integrated part of the curriculum.
Creating Art	* Children work in a tense and intimidating atmosphere. * Children are told to follow examples shown by the teacher and experimentation is discouraged	* Children work in a playful supportive setting. * Children are encouraged to create their own images and to use their own ideas
Display of Artwork	* Teachers display only the art work they like. * Work is displayed at adult eye level	* Teachers display the work of all children. * Work is displayed at children's eye level.
Responses to Work of Art	* Teachers discuss only the formal qualities or history of the art, lecturing children what they should and should not like.	* Children are given time to look closely at their own art and the work of others. They are encouraged to describe what they see and explain how they feel.

Note: Adapted from "Developmentally Appropriate Practices for the Visual Arts Education of Young Children" by C. Colbert and M. Taunton, 1992, Reston, VA: National Art Education Association. Copyright 1992 by the National Art Education Association. Additional copies of this paper may be ordered in packets of 50 from: NAEA Publication Sales, 1916 Association Drive, Reston VA 22091-1590.

1. sing tunefully.
2. respond rhythmically to music through creative movement and instrumental activities.
3. play simple classroom instruments that do not require fine muscular coordination.
4. develop attentive listening habits (Zimmerman, 1975, p. 75).

The early ability to recreate songs and engage in experimental creative music making is only the beginning of children's music potential. A variety of daily musical activities is essential to enhance the development of each child's musical artistry. Children's relationships with music include singing, dancing, creating, composing, and listening. It is not difficult to develop these relationships, because music is so readily available and easy to produce. Children's voices and bodies are natural musical instruments: Singing, chanting, humming, whistling, clapping hands, snapping fingers, and tapping feet are all ways in which children produce music with only their physical resources.

Music education has many developmental benefits. Rhythmic activities such as marching, clapping, or singing to a beat promote the development of concentration and gross and fine motor skills. Playing instruments also promotes the development of concentration and fine motor skills. Listening to music expands perceptive and attentive skills. Singing and creating songs enhance linguistic and emotional expression. Translating the symbolic language of music into sounds helps develop children's capacity to deal with abstract concepts. Successful creative experience with music builds children's self-confidence and self-esteem. Perhaps most important, music education fosters children's aesthetic growth, giving them the experiences and skills to appreciate and create the beauty of music throughout their lives.

Furthermore, music can be naturally incorporated into all curriculum areas. Music is science, made of sound waves, each with different frequencies, lengths, and intensities. Music is history, articulating the tenor, values, and events of every age. Music is social studies, expressing the nature and spirit of different peoples and cultures. Music is math, involving measure, counting, and dividing. Music is language, giving rich meaning and expression to words and ideas.

Young children bring to school an inherent love of music, natural musical abilities, and a wealth of musical experiences. Children are naturally receptive to music, and through music they develop, learn, and create. Music is an integral part of the creative learning environment, one that requires only the teacher's willingness to appreciate, support, and enjoy students' musical development.

The Music Program

All music is made up of certain elements or ingredients that may be mixed or scrambled to give it vitality and spice. Perception of these elements is essential to musical growth. As children become familiar with the components of music, they become more aware of how those components can be manipulated to

We are very serious when playing our musical instruments.

produce different sounds and effects. Knowledge of the whole is augmented by an understanding of the parts.

Katz and Chard (1989) suggest that four overlapping types of learning exist: knowledge, skills, dispositions and feelings. Musical knowledge refers to understanding of such concepts as rhythm, melody, harmony, form, timbre, dynamics, and style. Musical skills include easily observed behaviors: playing an instrument, singing in tune, and reading and writing music. Dispositions are nurtured rather than taught, representing "habits of mind" that children are apt to experience in a situation (Katz & Chard, 1989, p. 20). The disposition to sing, participate, be curious, experiment—all of these things are cultivated. A child may have the ability but not the disposition to sing. Feelings in musical situations are of two types: the emotional state resulting from interaction with others in a learning setting and the emotional response to music. Musical experiences are designed to take into consideration all of these forms of learning through singing, moving, playing instruments, creating, listening to music, and reading and writing music. Early childhood musical experiences generally are limited to the first five behaviors.

Objectives of the Music Program

The purpose of the music program is to provide children with opportunities to:

1. express themselves freely through music.
2. derive pleasure from musical experiences.

3. develop an understanding of the elements of music.
4. experiment with creating and performing music.
5. broaden their knowledge of music.
6. experience and respond to a wide variety of music.

The following activities are excellent avenues for achieving these objectives.

Singing

Children sing naturally and about anything at all: themselves, events, a variety of subjects that catch their fancy. For the young child, singing is a spontaneous musical activity tied closely to language development.

Exploration and imitation characterize the young child's earliest singing experiences. Up to age 3, children tend to imitate sounds and are capable of singing bits and chunks of songs. It is not until age 3 that they can begin to sing an entire song with reasonable accuracy (McDonald, 1979). Singing in tune with others is a skill learned and practiced over time, a skill that grows readily in an environment encouraging exploration, imitation, and the creation of vocal sounds and songs.

The skill of singing is tied closely to the disposition to sing. Nothing can cause longer lasting damage to this disposition than statements such as "His father can't sing either" or "Please just move your lips during the performance." Praise and encouragement are critical elements in the process of discovering a "singing voice." Although much of young children's singing does not appear to be very musical, this is deceptive! Their spontaneous song often is tuneful, based most often on the "teasing chant":

Jenny has a boyfriend!

Young children can joyfully imitate sounds from nature, sirens, and bells. Part of their spontaneous singing may be interspersed with speech as a way of telling a story, talking to or about a person or animal, or during play.

Research on song acquisition suggests that there is a sequence for learning songs: words–rhythms–phrases–melodic contour or shape (McDonald & Simons, 1989). As the child learns the song, the melodic accuracy improves as the words are retained. Simple songs such as question and answer songs or name games can help children make the transition from speaking to singing.

What's Your Name?

The children sit in a circle and the teacher, in center, rolls a ball to each child.

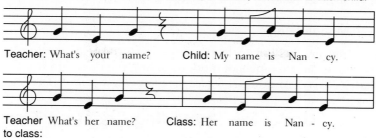

Teacher: What's your name?   Child: My name is Nan - cy.

Teacher   What's her name?   Class: Her name is Nan - cy.
to class:

Bye, Bye, Baby

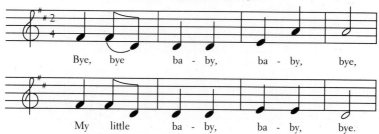

Bye,   bye   ba - by,   ba - by,   bye,

My   little   ba - by,   ba - by,   bye.

Variation: Bye, bye Angela, Dave, goodbye
My little Jimmy, Andrew, bye.

Treasure Song

Teacher has a small bag/box of items: paper clip, car, barrette, earring, button

1. Sing this song while passing out items to children, instructing them to close their hands after feeling an item between them.

Close   your   eyes,   open   your   hands

2. After all items are given out, sing

Close   your   eyes,   open   your   hands

3. Teacher sings the question and a child sings the appropriate answer.

Teacher: Who has   the   little   car? Child: I   have   the   little   car.
red   bar - ret?

You may want to change the items in the basket monthly, seasonally, or topically depending on classroom activities.

Suggested Activities

Motion Songs

Children are helped to learn songs by the use of motions or pictures. Two time-honored examples of motions aiding retention are *Itsy Bitsy Spider* and *I'm a Little Teapot.* Another is *Under the Spreading Chestnut Tree.*

Under the Spreading Chestnut Tree

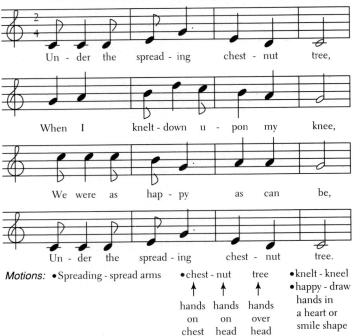

Motions: • Spreading - spread arms   • chest - nut   tree   • knelt - kneel
• happy - draw
hands   hands   hands   hands in
on   on   over   a heart or
chest   head   head   smile shape

Pictures can be used in two ways: to remind students of the text and to remind them of the contour or shape of the melody.

Snail

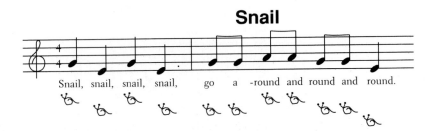

Bought Me a Cat

1. Bought me a cat, the cat pleased me,

Fed my cat under yon - der tree.

Refrain

The cat went fid - dle - i - fee

Use child-drawn animal pictures to facilitate recall

2. hen; chipsy-chops
3. duck; slishy-slosh
4. goose; qua-qua
5. dog; bow-wow
6. sheep; baa-baa
7. cow; moo-moo
8. horse; neigh-neigh

This is a cumulative song, so you sing one more each time

The range of popular recorded songs and the appropriate range for children are often different. The musically complicated songs heard on radio and television are integral parts of musical experience. However, teachers may find that children are more comfortable listening to these songs than singing along. The most appropriate range for the young child is from middle C to the A above.

Songs that contain relatively few leaps and make use of repetitive patterns of rhythm or melody are the easiest for children to retain and sing in tune. The ongoing development of singing skill is inseparable from the disposition to sing and from the joy of uniquely personal music making. Do not get discouraged; many children do not develop the ability to sing in tune until the upper elementary or middle grades. With continued practice and encouragement at home and in school, most children will learn to sing in tune by the end of sixth grade. Children are more likely to sing in tune with their peers than with an adult or a piano. The goal of singing activities is to have the child joyfully produce a sound that is light, flexible, and reasonably in tune within a limited melodic range.

Movement

As with singing, children gradually develop motor coordination as a result of maturation, practice, and encouragement. The expressive qualities of music are a natural enticement for young children. The body becomes an instrument to express feelings, stories, moods, images, objects and musical sounds. Several aspects of movement help to structure activities: exploration, imitation, use of space, variety of movements, and motions in time.

From birth, children use movement as a way of finding out about their world. Teachers can add to each child's repertoire of movements through exploratory and imitative activities. Begin with static shapes in space: statues, shapes, letters. Ask a partner to imitate, then to create a different shape. This exploratory/imitative pattern can be carried into motions in place and moving about the room "in your own space."

Another movement activity involves the imagination: "You are a piece of bacon in a frying pan. I am going to call out numbers 1 to 10, and I'd like you to show me what you'd look and sound like as the pan gets hotter." Another scenario might involve imitating animals, flowers growing, parts of a machine, or stirring water / pudding / peanut butter / cement in a big tub. Descriptive words will help children imagine the possibilities: "light as a feather," "tied to a string," "on a hot sidewalk," "walking up/down a big hill."

There are a number of singing games that lend themselves to creating motions.

Moving in time with music and when playing instruments presents a great challenge for many young children. They may have problems marching to music, particularly before the age of 6 (McDonald & Simons, 1989; Rainbow, 1981). A basic sequence of voice–small motor–large motor will help young children develop an inner sense of the beat. Begin with words: chants, nonsense rhymes, counting games, poems, songs. The next step is to ask the children to clap what they say, keeping a beat with their hands. The third step is to ask the children to "put the sound in their feet" as they say the words. This progression from inward to outward, always keeping the words or song as a reference point, will help children learn to walk in place or in space to music. One note: A young child's natural tempo tends to be much faster than that of an adult. So when a child uses the term *fast*, it has quite a different meaning than for an adult.

Getting creative input from individual children is important in making

Betty Martin

Hey,   Betty   Mar - tin,   tip   toe,   tip   toe

Hey,   Betty   Mar - tin,   tip   toe   fine

Hey,   Betty   Mar - tin,   tip   toe   tip   toe

Hey,   Betty   Mar - tin,   tip   toe   fine.

Substitute motions: running, hopping, dancing, etc.

Hop Old Squirrel

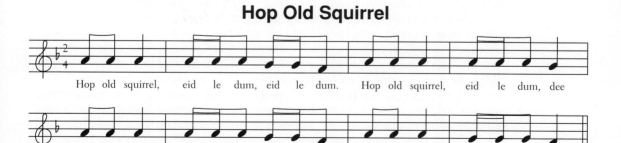

Hop old squirrel,   eid   le   dum, eid   le   dum.   Hop old squirrel,   eid   le   dum, dee

Hop old squirrel,   eid   le   dum, eid   le   dum.   Hop old squirrel,   eid   le   dum, dee

Improvise words and actions

fly old bird	wiggle old worm	gallop old horse
slither old snake	dig old mole	hop old toad
swim old fish	leap old frog	

Mary Wore a Red Dress

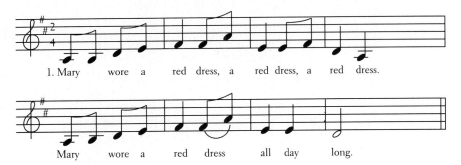

1. Mary wore a red dress, a red dress, a red dress.

Mary wore a red dress all day long.

2. Mary did a little dance
3. Let's all clap for Mary

Children sit in a circle, and move to center to dance if they fit the chosen characteristic.

Substitute:		
plaid on	glasses on	is in first grade
stripes on	has a sister, brother	wants to take a nap
brown hair	has a dog	wants to go to lunch
blue eyes	cat at home	wants to go outside
ten fingers	is five years old	
checks on	two?	
jewelry on	one?	
	zero?	

movement time fun for everyone. Encourage the children to give their own suggestions for changing the songs in some way, and respond positively to any ideas they might have. When they see that all answers are acceptable, many children will find the courage to share their ideas. As a facilitator, you can even help start their creative juices flowing by saying, "Okay, we've clapped and danced and jumped. Can you think of another thing we could do?" Accept any answer that is given, whether it has already been done or not. When a child answers "Jump!", for instance, ask, "Do you want to jump by yourself or with a friend?" and then, "How many friends?", "On both feet or just on one?", or "With your eyes open or closed?"

Rhythmic exercises with music, such as "aerobic mime," are fun learning experiences for children. Turn on some moderate-tempo instrumental music and narrate an interactive story, letting the children imitate your movements in pantomime. Such simple themes as "What You Do When You Get Up in the Morning" can make this repetitive action march fun and stimulating. Isolate one action for a certain number of beats, such as "pulling on your pants" and "opening up the refrigerator door," and then let the children take turns leading, coming up with their own daily rhythms. Children are encouraged to find and experience the rhythms present in everyday life.

The children perform a Chinese dragon dance for their parents at Seawell School's annual Folk Moot.

Instruments

Instruments allow children to reproduce and create music. They offer yet another outlet for expression. As children play, they also manipulate the elements of music and experience for themselves the effects of those elements.

Orff instruments are the ones most commonly used in early childhood education. The melodic instruments include glockenspiels, metallophones, and xylophones. Rhythm instruments include hand drums, tambourines, triangles, woodblocks, cymbals, rattles, and jingle bells. However, the lack of these instruments should not prevent the creative production of sounds. Many instruments are cheaply and easily made, and natural substitutes exist for others.

Any instrument serves as an extension of the body, a step beyond movement. So, it is natural to plan for exploration and imitation as the starting point for classroom activities. Explorative activities employ the young child's natural curiosity about instruments: What makes the sound? How long does it last? Can I change it? How many different ways can I make a sound from this instrument (some may be very unconventional!)?

Manufactured and homemade instruments are comparatively fragile in comparison to other objects in the early childhood environment. It is helpful for the teacher to introduce each instrument to the children, asking questions about the shape, size, sound, and means of sound production (Is it shaken? Bowed? Plucked? Hit? Rubbed? Scraped? Blown into?). The answers that the children give often lead to comparisons and alternative ways of viewing the same experience. For example, a 4-year-old girl in a local preschool was adamant that the college student was singing into the trumpet and trombone rather than buzzing his lips.

The exploration of instruments leads into the imitation of sounds to add to a poem, story, folk tale, or song. The nursery rhyme *Humpty Dumpty* lends itself naturally to the addition of sounds designed to illustrate it.

Humpty Dumpty sat on a wall	(sounds for Humpty climbing up to the top of the wall and plopping down)
Humpty Dumpty had a great fall	(sounds of a descent and crash)
All the king's horses and all the king's men	(sounds of horses' hooves)
Couldn't put Humpty together again	(sounds of small pieces breaking)

Hickory Dickory Dock is an example of an appropriate use of melodic instruments as the mouse moves upward and downward and the clock strikes. The counting rhyme

Engine, engine number nine
Going down Chicago line
If the train goes off the track
Do you want your money back?

is an example of sounds getting closer, the train crashing, and the sounds of coins being reproduced by instruments.

Wee Willie Winkie is a less familiar nursery rhyme that tells a story that could be musically illustrated and acted out.

Wee Willie Winkie runs through the town
Upstairs and downstairs in his nightgown.
Rapping at the windows, crying through the lock,
"Are the children in their beds? For it's eight o'clock."

Central to the popular Orff approach to music education is the idea of speech-to/movement-to instruments. The sequence of musical behaviors is easily adapted to classroom activities, and many books are available that use movement, speech, and instruments to illustrate songs and folk tales. (See the Suggested Readings at the end of the chapter.)

The Rhythm Band

Although the quality of manufactured instruments is superior to that of homemade instruments, the cost is sometimes prohibitive. The following activities allow children to create their own set of rhythm instruments and noisemakers.

Rhythm Sticks

1. Use 2 pencils or 2 ½-inch round dowels.
2. Play by striking the sticks together.

3. Describe the sound.
4. Experiment with creating sounds and producing beats.

Wood Blocks

1. Use a piece of wood that is easy to hold.
2. Sand the wood until it is smooth.
3. Play by hitting the block with a mallet.
4. Describe the sound.
5. Experiment with creating sound patterns.

Sandpaper Blocks

1. Nail or glue emery cloth or sandpaper to one side of a wooden block.
2. Prepare 2 wooden blocks.
3. Play by rubbing the sandpapered surfaces together.
4. Describe the sound.
5. Experiment with the blocks.

Clinkers

1. Use 2 coconut shells.
2. Play by hitting the shells together.

Gong

1. Use an old license plate (the older the better).
2. Strike it with a mallet to play it.
3. Describe the sound.

Shaker

1. Use 2 small paper plates.
2. Between them put a few beans or some rice.
3. Lace or staple the plates together.
4. Shake the plates to play them.
5. Describe the sound.
6. Experiment with sound patterns.

Chocallo (Latin American Shaker)

1. Use the cardboard tube from a roll of paper towels.
2. Put beans, rice, or popcorn into the tube.
3. Cover both ends and seal them.

4. Decorate the tube.
5. Play the tube by shaking it.
6. Describe the sound.
7. Experiment with the shaker.

Maracas

1. Use a frozen juice can that has a plastic lid.
2. Use a hammer and nail to make a hole through the center of the metal end.
3. Insert a dowel, pencil, or stick. Make it fit snugly.
4. Push the stick in until the top of it reaches the top of the can.
5. Put in beans or rice.
6. Cover it with the plastic top.
7. Nail the plastic to the stick.
8. Play the can by shaking it.
9. Experiment with playing the maracas.

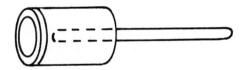

Tambourine

1. Use bottle caps and a Ping-Pong paddle.
2. Attach caps around the edge with cup hooks.
3. Screw each hook through the center of the cap.
4. Bend the hooks completely over.
5. Play the tambourine by shaking it.
6. Experiment with playing the tambourine.

Rattles

1. Use a plastic bottle, spice can, pill box, or similar container.
2. Put pebbles, beans, rice, or popcorn inside the container.
3. Decorate the container with paint.
4. Shake the container to play it.
5. Describe the sound.

Jingle Instrument

1. Use a set of metal measuring spoons.
2. Play them by slapping them into your hand.
3. Describe the sound.

Wrist or Ankle Bells

1. Lace a shoestring through 2 or 3 bells.
2. Tie it to your wrist or ankle.
3. Move to shake your bells.

Kazoo

1. Use the cardboard lining of a toilet paper roll.
2. Use a pencil to make a small hole about 1 inch from one end.
3. Cover that end with waxed paper.
4. Stretch the waxed paper tightly and secure it with a rubber band.
5. Hold the open end over your mouth.
6. Pucker your lips and blow.
7. Experiment.
8. Try to hum a melody.

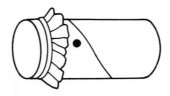

Shoebox Sound Production

1. Cut a circle or rectangle close to one end of a shoebox cover.
2. Put the cover back on the box.
3. Stretch different width rubber bands over the hole.

4. Pluck the strings.

5. Make as many different sounds as you can.

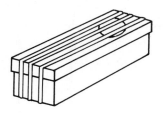

Garden Hose Sounds

1. Cut a garden hose into different lengths.

2. Blow through the end of a length.

3. Describe the sounds made by the different lengths of hose.

Folk Instruments for Children to Make

Bull-Roarer. This instrument is also known as the "thunder stick." The Native Americans used it to provide a roaring sound behind their drums. Take a soft, light piece of wood 2" wide and ½" thick. Shape it so that one end measures 1¼" across and the other end is rounded off. Sand off the edges and drill a hole into the untapered end of the wood. Run a piece of strong, lightweight string through the hole and knot it securely. Make a loop for your finger in the opposite end and whirl the roarer in a circle in front of your body. It can be decorated with painted Native American symbols.

Bottle Chimes. Construct a frame to hold a dowel rod from which bottles will be hung. Tie bottles with corks to the dowel rod after filling them with varying amounts of water. Tap them to produce different sounds.

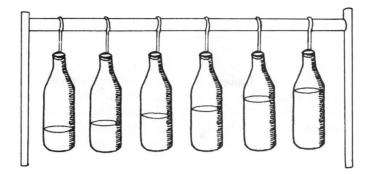

Double-Flowerpot Drum. This drum design is based on a Nigerian double drum. The lacings can be loosened or tightened to create different sounds. Glue or tape two plastic flowerpots together at the small end. Cut out inner tubing about 1" larger than the flowerpot openings. Puncture holes all around the edge of the tubing circle, 2" apart and ½" from the edge. Soak the inner tube and some heavy string or rawhide lacing in lukewarm water for 30 minutes before they are used. Thread the laces through the holes in the tubing evenly from the lower drumhead to the upper drumhead so that the heads are tight enough to elicit clear sounds. Dry it for 12 hours, and do not handle it until it is dry.

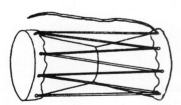

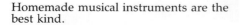
Homemade musical instruments are the best kind.

Creating

Creating is a musical behavior that can include one, some, or all of the others: singing, moving, playing, and listening. Learning about musical ideas or building skills is based upon the variations that the child can create, using the familiar as a reference point. When children are observed working with instruments, singing along, or moving, it is always with a progression from seemingly nonmusical to more musical sounds or movements. Many of the activities already suggested include elements of creation through exploration of sound; recombination of sounds; or the suggestions from children of ways to add sounds to a poem, song, or story. Teachers should create opportunities for creative endeavors, even at a very basic musical level.

For some reason, children are fascinated with feet and, most especially, with new shoes. What better way to incorporate their own interests and experiences than by creating "shoe music"? Shoe music is relatively easy to make, and different shoes make different kinds of sounds—high heels click, while heavy boots stomp and slippers patter. A variety of actions can also create new and unique sounds with shoes—tiptoeing, jumping, skipping, and dancing, for instance. Get the children to experiment with the sounds that they can make in their own shoes and have them share their discoveries with the rest of the class. A "shoe library" can be created as well, with children bringing in shoes from home to add to the classroom dress-up collection.

(while feeling their bare feet)
"They're soft, boney, bumpy, lumpy . . ."
"Big fat bumpy lumpy . . ."
"Yucky, stinky, feet!"
(for 4-year-old children)

We make beautiful music with our violins.

Poetry

Poetry is greatly encouraged in the musical curriculum of the British Infant Schools. One headmistress, Doris Nash of Sea Mills Infant School, has emphasized the importance of music in writing poetry, explaining that "most children take a natural delight in the joy of the words and music. Children need to extend their singing vocabulary in order to broaden their written vocabulary. Through music, children also achieve a sense of the rhythm and flow of words which they can then apply to their own creative writing" (Day, 1978, p. 230). Often, the children read their poetry aloud to the accompaniment of music by another child. Chants and their modern-day equivalent, rap, are also essential for children to discover the rhythm behind language.

Under imaginative teacher guidance, the interweaving arts of art exploration, music, and creative drama can extend basic vocabulary building into the art of creating with words. Children are encouraged to communicate in colorful language and poetic expression. Their standard and nonstandard words are sometimes startling in their beauty, especially when they arise from meaningful experiences.

> A lullaby is a quiet song your mother sings to you when you go to sleep—so you won't be afraid. (Four-year-old child)

> As quiet as a floor when no one is walking on it. (Five-year-old child)

> [Upon hearing Debussy] I feel like an angel was in my head. There was a dream in my eyes. (Five-year-old child)

For shy children, puppets are wonderful tools to help them come out of their shells. The children can sing *through* the puppets—their extended selves—until they feel confident enough to do it on their own.

Listening

Children are bombarded with music everywhere: on television, on radio, in stores, in medical offices, in the car. Teachers can help children learn to *listen* rather than merely *hear* by considering several types and uses for listening experiences.

Children need to listen to a variety of types of music ranging from adult voices to child voices, instrumental to choral, group to solo, classical to contemporary, and music from a variety of cultures. Music need not tell a story, but it may have a feature that the teacher feels will engage the children in some way, such as a fast tempo; graceful melody; or changes in texture, style, or tempo. It is important that children be engaged in attending and responding to the expressive qualities of the music rather than engaging in other activities such as drawing to music. If a musical selection contains singing, the teacher should listen to the vocal model presented: Is it pleasant to listen to (not raspy, grating, nasal)? Would I want the children to imitate that sound?

The choices the teacher makes have a significant impact upon children's musical preferences. If the teacher indicates a preference, the young child is likely to adopt that preference, particularly if a selection is repeated several times.

Active listening is preferable to passive listening. Young children will spontaneously want to dance, even to the music of television commercials. Children can play instruments, dance, or move in some creative way to what they perceive to be the beat of the selection. Many developmentally appropriate songs have instructions for movement as part of the text, as in the Hap Palmer and Ella Jenkins recordings. Listening experiences will help children integrate movement, singing, and playing into a response to the expressive qualities of music.

Elements of Music

Rhythm. According to Newman (1984), rhythm is the measured movement of music through time. Schafer (1976) says rhythm is direction, and he equates it to an arrow in a Klee painting. Definitions, however, are never adequate to describe rhythm. Rhythm is more easily felt than discussed.

Although rhythm is naturally employed and experienced by all children, they may not equate these common occurrences with the occurrence of rhythm in music. By helping them relate natural rhythm to musical rhythm, the teacher builds on familiar experiences to promote growth.

Many music teachers attempt to isolate the elements of music, hoping to enhance the probability that young children will learn them. Typically, rhythmic games are very popular as musical activities. Should the music specialist wish to use the Kodaly system, specific rhythmic syllables used are as follows:

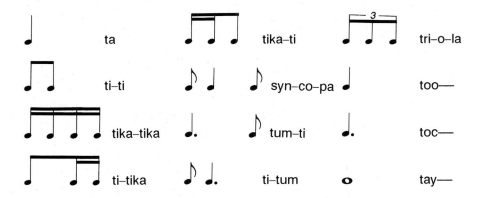

Tempo. Tempo is concerned with how quickly or slowly notes are produced. According to Newman (1984), tempo is the pace of music.

Dynamics. Dynamics is concerned with amplitude or how loud or soft the music is.

Timbre. Timbre or tone color is the element that gives an instrument a particular sound that distinguishes it from all other instruments.

Melody. The melody is often called the tune. It is the element that surfaces and is most easily remembered (White, 1968). Melody is composed of a line of single tones that has contour, that moves up, down, or repeats. Each tone has a definite *pitch* ranging from high to low.

Harmony. Harmony is created by playing two or more tones at the same time.

Form. The form of a piece of music is its construction plan. It is the design pattern by which the elements of harmony, melody, and rhythm are interrelated. Although form may be difficult to perceive in some music, it is quite easily detected in poetry and in the simple melodies of childhood. By dissecting a song into basic phrases, these patterns are made obvious. The ABA structure (verse, chorus, verse) is dominant in children's music, although other similar and equally simple arrangements exist.

(Body Movement)   **Simon Says for Everybody**

(Tune: If You're Happy And You Know It)   Words by Juanita Shippey

Simon says for everybody swing your arms Simon says for everybody, swing your

arms.   Simon says for everybody swing your arms, swing your arms. Simon

says for everybody   swing your arms.

2. When I'm happy, hear me play;
   When I'm happy, hear me play;
   I will play my Indian drum;
   Rum, tum, tum, tum, Rum, tum, tum, tum
3. Triangle; Ting, ting, ting, ting, Ting, ting, ting, ting,
4. Tambourine; Shake, shake, shake
5. Castanets; Clack, clack, clack
   Let the song continue with other instruments.

Being Me

(Self-concept)

Words and music by Dottie Rambo

1. If I were a bird I could fly High as the
2. If I were a bell I could chime, Ring ding-a-

stars in the sky. But a bird I'll never be so I'm-happy you
ling all the time. But a bell I'll never be so I'm-happy you

see just being me, being me. Being me, being
see just being me, being me. Being me, being

free, being all I can be. I can pass every test cause I'll
free, being all I can be. I can always be myself (better than

Say this part-
with feeling.

give it my best just being me, being me.
an-y-bod-y else) just being me, being me.

Sing.

This Is the Way the Worm Crawls

(Tune: Here We Go Round the Mulberry Bush)

Words by Juanita Shippey

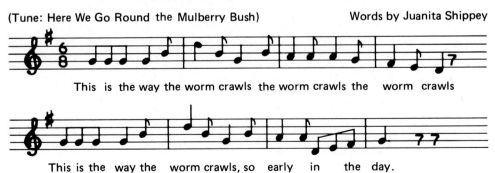

This is the way the worm crawls the worm crawls the worm crawls

This is the way the worm crawls, so early in the day.

2. the birdie flaps
3. the bunny hops
4. the frog jumps
5. the fishy swims
6. the elephant stomps
7. the lion roars

Johnny Works with One Hammer

(Tempo and Meter)

John-ny works with one hammer, one hammer, one hammer. John-ny works with

one hammer. Then he works with two.

Last verse Now he goes to sleep.

2. two hammers
3. three hammers
4. four hammers

Children begin hammering with one hand slowly to the beat. as the song progresses, it gets faster and children use both hands and feet as hammers.

Tunes Children Learn Easily
"If You're Happy and You Know It"
"Kumbayah"
"Here We Go Round the Mulberry Bush"
   ("The Wheels on the Bus)"
"Go Tell Aunt Rhodie"
"Are You Sleeping?" ("Frère Jacques"; "Where
   Is Thumbkin?")
"Old MacDonald's Farm"
"Goodnight Irene"
"B-I-N-G-O"
"Did You Ever See a Lassie?"
"Go Round and Round the Village"
"London Bridge"
"The Hokey Pokey"

"Here We Go Looby-Loo"
"The Muffin Man"
"Michael Row the Boat Ashore"
"Shoo, Fly, Don't Bother Me"
"Bear Went Over the Mountain"
"Da-ye-nu"
"Hey, Betty Martin"
"She'll Be Comin' Round the Mountain"
"Skip to My Lou"
"This Old Man"
"Zum-Gali-Gali"
"Hush Little Baby"
"We Wish You a Merry Christmas"
"The More We Get Together"

Classical Selections That Appeal to Children
"Peter and the Wolf" Prokofieff
"Sorcerer's Apprentice" Dukas
"Carnival of the Animals" Saint-Saens
"Danse Macabre" Saint-Saens

"The Sleeping Beauty" Tchaikovsky
"Til Eulenspiegel" Strauss
"The Firebird" Stravinsky

Suggested Readings

Art

Anderson, S. (1988). *Colors.* New York: Dutton.

Dodge, D. T., & Colker, L. J. (1992). *The creative curriculum for early childhood* (3rd ed.). Washington, DC: Teaching Strategies.

Hamilton, D. S., & Flemming, B. M. (1990). *Resources for creative teaching in early childhood education* (2nd ed.). Orlando, FL: Harcourt Brace Jovanovich.

Herr, J., & Libby, Y. (1990). *Designing creative materials for young children.* Orlando, FL: Harcourt Brace Jovanovich.

Kohl, M. F. (1985). *Scribble cookies and other independent creative art experiences for children.* Bellingham, WA: Bright Ring.

Mitchell, G. L., Bailey, N. C., & Dewsnap, L. F. (1992). *I am! I can! Keys to quality child care: A guide for directors.* Chelsea, MA: TelShare.

Shaw, C.G. (1988). *In looked like spilt milk.* New York: Harper & Row.

Testa, F. (1986). *If you take a paintbrush: A book of colors.* New York: Dial Books.

Wachowiak, F. (1985). *Emphasis art: A qualitative art program for elementary and middle schools* (4th ed.). New York: Harper & Row.

Wolf, A. D. (1984). *Mommy, it's a Renoir.* Altoona, PA: Parent Child Press.

Music

Songbooks

Beall, P., & Nip, S. (1985) *Wee sing* (series). (Cassettes available). Los Angeles: Price/Sloan/Stern.

Birkenshaw, L. (1977). *Music for fun: Music for learning.* Toronto: Holt, Rinehart and Winston of Canada.

Erion, C., & Monssen, L. (1982). *Tales to tell, Tales to play.* New York: Schott.

Feierabend, J. (1986). *Music for very little people, Music for little people* (with cassette). New York: Boosey & Hawkes.

Glazer, T. (1973). *Eye winker, Tom tinker, Chin chopper: Fifty musical fingerplays.* Garden City, NJ: Doubleday.

Glazer, T. (1980). *Do your ears hang low? Fifty more fingerplays.* Garden City, NJ: Doubleday.

Glazer, T. (1983). *Music for twos and ones: Songs and games for the very young child.* Garden City, NJ: Doubleday.

Kenney, M. (1974). *Circle round the zero: Play chants and singing games of city children.* St. Louis: Magna-Music Baton.

Kriske, J., & Delelles, R. (1987). *Making the most of the holidays: Songs, poems and dances for children.* Las Vegas: Kid Sounds.

Kriske, J., & Delelles, R. (1987). *Once long ago.* Las Vegas: Kid Sounds.

Kriske, J., & Delelles, R. (1988). *Tyme for a rhyme: Nursery rhymes with music for children.* Las Vegas: Kid Sounds.

Nash, G., & Rapley, J. (1988). *Holidays and special days: A sourcebook of songs, rhymes and movement for each month of the school year.* Los Angeles: Alfred.

Shotwell, R. (1984). *Rhythm and movement activities for early childhood.* Sherman Oaks, CA: Alfred.

Wirth, M., Stassevitch, V., Shotwell, R., & Stemmler, P. (1983). *Musical games, fingerplay and rhythmic activities for early childhood.* W. Nyack, NY: Parker.

Movement

Brehm, M. (1983). *Movement with a purpose: Perceptual motor-lesson plans for young children.* West Nyack, NY: Parker Publishing Co.

Curtis, S.R. (1982). *The joy of movement in early childhood.* New York: Teachers College Press.

Lynch-Fraser, D. (1991). *Playdancing: Discovering and developing creativity in young children.* Pennington, NJ: Princeton Book Co.

Mornighstar, M. (1986). *Growing with dance: Developing through creative dance from ages two to six.* Canada: Windborne Publications.

Pica, R. (1991). *Early elementary children moving and learning.* Champaign, IL: Human Kinetics Books.

Weikart, P.S., & Boardman, B. (1990). *Movement in steady beat: Activities for children, ages 3–7.* Ypsilanti, MI: High/Scope Press.

Recordings

The elephant tapes, by Sharon, Lois, and Bram. Ontario, Canada: Elephant Records.

The *Ella Jenkins* recordings. New York: Educational Activities and Folkways Records.

The *Hap Palmer* record series. Freeport, NY: Educational Activities.

Music for 1's and 2's by Tom Glazer. Mt. Vernon, NY: CMS Records.

Pica, R., & Gardzina, R. (1990). *More music for moving and learning* (2nd ed.). Champaign, IL: Human Kinetics Books.

Pica, R., & Gardzina, R. (1990). *Let's move and learn* (2nd ed.). Champaign, IL: Human Kinetics Books.

The small listener, The small singer, The small player. (Bowmar Records.) Distributed by Belwin-Mills Publishing Corp., Miami, FL.

Songs to grow on, by Woody Guthrie. New York: Folkways Records.

Sources

MMB Music, Inc. .P.O. Box 32410, 10370 Page Industrial Boulevard, St. Louis, MO 63132. 1-800-543-3771. Good source for music books, music, instruments.

Music for little people. Box 1460, Redway, CA. 95560. 1-800-346-4445. A comprehensive catalog of videos, books, and cassette tapes.

Chapter 6

Home Living and Creative Dramatics

The home living and creative dramatics center provides young children with a valuable opportunity to engage in stimulating, enjoyable play and learning experiences. Through dramatic play, children are able to investigate, learn about, and understand the world and their place in it. The developmental benefits of dramatic play are tremendous. Children grow intellectually, socially, emotionally, morally, and physically when they are allowed to engage in active, creative role playing (Van Hoorn Nourot, Scales, & Alward, 1993).

Teachers find this center especially useful for observing and learning more about the children in their care. Children naturally dramatize and imitate people, animals, objects, and experiences that are familiar to them. As children imitate what they have observed and experienced at home, teachers can learn about their home life. Teachers can learn about true feelings as their children speak through "pretend" characters. Fears or concerns that are otherwise hidden are easily articulated through puppets and other dramatized characters. When children reveal concerns related to school, such as fear of leaving the classroom or fear of the fire bell, teachers can actively and effectively address those concerns. Teachers may observe qualities such as leadership or organizational skill that the children can contribute to other areas of the classroom.

Teachers can also assess children's developmental levels and needs through observation of dramatic play (Eheart & Leavitt, 1985). This information can be used in planning an appropriate individualized program for each child (Hutt & Bhavnani, 1976). In order to do this, teachers should be familiar with how dramatic play generally evolves as children develop.

Mayesky, Neuman, and Wlodkowski (1985) have categorized play into the following four types:

1. *Solitary play.* The child plays alone. Young age - 1
2. *Parallel play.* Children play side by side with other children, but without direct involvement. 2 yrs ?

224

3. *Associative play*. The child is present in a group, for example, participating in finger play.

4. *Cooperative play*. Children are mutually involved in a play activity. *4-5yrs. example - McDonalds - window, cook, ordering, etc*

The initial stage of dramatic play can begin as early as 1 year of age. This stage of imitative role playing is characterized by the use of real objects as props (Dodge, 1988). Toddlers are beginning to engage in dramatic play when they hold the telephone and pretend to talk to someone. Teachers of toddlers can encourage dramatic play by planning for simple experiences and providing realistic objects. For example, 2-year-old children would enjoy feeding and petting a toy puppy after a real puppy had visited the classroom. Very young children may also need to imitate the teacher. Imitation is a stepping stone to original role playing and should not be discouraged.

Make-believe play is the second stage of dramatic play, beginning around age 3. Children begin to use their imaginations and no longer need to rely on realistic props. They can invent scenarios to act out that are not determined by real-life events (Dodge, 1988). A 3-year-old may still talk on the telephone, but now may use a banana or block for a receiver and may talk to someone in outer space rather than Mom or Dad. Pictures, stories, and field trips enhance dramatic play in 3 year olds. They may interact verbally, but their play will most often be parallel.

Around 3 or 4 years of age, children begin to engage in sociodramatic play. Elements of the earlier stages are included, but now children interact with one another in shared role playing (Dodge, 1988). The play becomes more complex as children negotiate and plan the roles they will act out. As children gain experience and knowledge about their world, a greater variety of roles is dramatized. Children spend more time engaged in this type of play because of its complexity than they did in the earlier stage of make-believe play. Teachers may be invited to join in the play, but their presence is not vital to sustaining the play. One of the best ways for teachers of older preschoolers to encourage dramatic play is to provide materials for the children to make props and to add props to complement the children's imaginations.

Each child develops at his or her own rate. The stages described here are only rough indicators of a child's level of development at a particular age. Other factors such as parental involvement and attitudes, real-life experiences, and media exposure also influence the stages of development (Dodge, 1988).

The dramatic play of most children centers around three themes. The first theme is domestic scenes. Children in the home living center who cook, clean, and care for the doll are exploring domestic situations. They are role playing from experience. The second theme is rescue. The "family" is busy in the home living center when suddenly the doll becomes sick or the daddy has a flat tire and cannot get to work. The children have to solve the problem. Often the most socially mature children will introduce the conflict and solve it as the rescue theme begins to emerge in role play. The third theme is sudden threat. Monsters come out from under beds as the mother is sweeping, or a mean animal chases the children as they play outside (Kostelnik, Whiren, & Stein, 1986).

Once children have played through these themes, they go back and forth through them to satisfy their play needs. One theme may interest them more, and they may spend a great amount of time engaging in that role-playing situation. Children's ages do not influence the themes they play out as much as do opportunities they have had to engage in any dramatic play.

The home living and creative dramatic center can provide endless opportunities for the teacher, as a facilitator of learning, to broaden a child's horizon. The center can be decorated and rearranged to represent an area that pertains to a specific unit of classroom study. Possibilities include creating a home, hospital, post office, grocery store, and more. The change of seasons, as well as certain holidays, can be easily incorporated in this center. For example, during fall, a child's rake, batons, sweaters, and pom poms might be included in the center. During the winter months, mufflers, mittens, a child's shovel, a holiday apron, candles, candlesticks, and bells may be additions to the center. For spring, the teacher may add baskets, plastic colored eggs, plastic or silk flowers, and a variety of bonnets and hats. The supplies in the home center should reflect the activities in the classroom and extend the skills being taught elsewhere in the classroom, as well as introduce new skills.

Cooking and puppetry are other components of home living and dramatic play. Activities involving food and cooking can be used to help children learn new information; gain new skills; develop positive attitudes about themselves and about learning; and promote good nutrition through nutritious recipes.

Puppets are invaluable in the classroom. The home living center should

Reading a book to the doll provides a quiet retreat and an opportunity to engage in oral reading.

have some ready-made puppets available, which can vary with the seasons, holidays, and units of study. In addition, the home living center should provide children the opportunity to make their own puppets.

In summary, the home living and creative dramatics center provides endless possibilities for learning activities that help all children in the classroom grow intellectually, socially, and physically. It also provides teachers, parents, and counselors with valuable opportunities to observe and plan for the enhancement of children's development.

Home Living

Many types of home living activities can be beneficial in preparing children for many areas of learning. Most children enjoy role playing a home life situation. The home center provides an outlet for children to act out feelings that often cannot be expressed directly. Generally speaking, people, including children, feel more comfortable sharing their feelings and ideas with others their own age (Jalongo, 1985).

Children can learn to deal with the anxieties as well as act out their fantasies through creative dramatic play. To pretend to do something, the child must have already experienced first hand (or on television or through stories and pictures) the concepts and roles used in dramatic play. A child's everyday life is the best source of such ideas (Mayesky et al., 1985). The home living center furnishes the appropriate background for this dramatic play. In the home living center dramatic play often begins with one child, and others later join in. The home living center presents a familiar and comfortable setting for learning, developing skills, and having fun.

Children will get the most benefit from the home living center if careful consideration is given to its location and organization. The center should be enclosed on three sides, if possible, to create a defined space. Dramatic play is enhanced when children have a cozy, secluded, home-like area in which to engage in role playing. It also makes it easier to keep the props and other materials in the center organized. The home living center should be located near other active, noisy centers. Children should be free to make noise as they act out their dramas without worrying about disturbing other children working in quieter centers (Dodge, 1988).

The center should reflect the various ethnic backgrounds of the children in the class. All children should feel comfortable and familiar with the setting so they will want to engage in dramatic play (Dodge, 1988).

Supplies

Child-sized furniture

Dress-up clothes, costumes, and accessories (jewelry, pocketbooks, dress shoes, slippers, scarves)

Blankets, pillows
Tablecloths, placemats
Flower vase with flowers
Tea sets, dishes, pots and pans, silverware, large spoons, aprons
Calendar
Clock
Telephone, a classroom telephone book, datebook
Books, magazines, newspapers
Mirrors
Cardboard chest, suitcase, or trunk
Baby equipment and accessories (dolls, bottles, cradles, blanket, toys, feeding
   dish, bibs, baby brush and comb, baby high chair, stroller, music box,
   rocker)

Objectives

1. To provide an environment for discovering the various ways in which
   one can set up a house and practice the manners used in living there.
2. To provide opportunities to role play people in familiar and community
   settings.
3. To develop and facilitate behavior modification within the child in a
   comfortable situation.
4. To provide an outlet for children to act out feelings that often cannot be
   expressed directly.

Suggested Activities

Role Playing Activity Objectives

1. The children will be given the opportunity to better understand their
   own feelings, and in some cases the feelings of others.
2. The children will become more aware of the duties of various family
   members.
3. The children will develop problem-solving skills when dealing with
   social situations.
4. The children will develop appropriate manners for the home.

Placemats Activity Objective

The children will be able to set the table correctly.

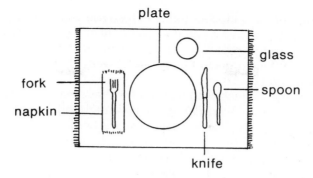

Flowermaking Activity Objectives

Simple flowers can be made from scraps of crepe paper, construction paper, and/or tissue paper. The children can draw and cut out basic flower shapes. Using a pencil or the edge of scissors, the children will curl the edges of the flower. For the stems and leaves, use straws, pipe cleaners, wire, or popsicle sticks covered with crepe paper. These may be put into an empty juice can that has been covered with yarn, wallpaper, fabric, or construction paper. This arrangement may be used as a centerpiece on the table.

1. The children will enjoy making an attractive addition to the center.
2. The children will become more aware of the basic parts of a flower (Cole, Haas, Heller, & Weinberger, 1976).

Cooking

Cooking in the classroom can provide children with many valuable learning experiences. Every area of the curriculum can be taught or reinforced through cooking activities. Mathematics concepts such as counting, measuring, and fractions can be taught. Language and reading skills are reinforced through following directions, learning new vocabulary, decoding symbols, following sequential order, and reading recipes. Children learn about health and safety when they wash before a cooking, activity and use equipment safely. Chemical changes occurring during cooking, and unlimited problem-solving opportunities provide a wealth of scientific experiences. Pouring, mixing, stirring, and measuring allow children to exercise and refine their fine motor skills. Social and emotional development occurs when children work together as a group, sharing, taking turns, cooperating, and gaining self-confidence and a feeling of success. Even social studies can be a part of the cooking experience. Children can learn about careers in the food industry and gain appreciation for the foods and customs of other cultures and countries (Feldman, 1991).

Cooking activities provide a natural vehicle for nutrition education. Nutrition education and health are key factors affecting learning and all areas of development. Nutritious cooking experiences can help lay the foundation for a lifetime of healthy eating habits. Good nutrition is essential to the well-being of young children. What they eat now affects their future health and physical growth and development. It also affects how they feel and act on a daily basis (Feldman, 1991).

Hungry and malnourished children have many problems relating to school, including problems concentrating, resisting fatigue, and staying alert. Malnutrition also increases susceptibility to infection and may cause children to have gaps in learning due to poor attendance (Oliver & Musgrave, 1984).

This center provides an excellent opportunity, through cooking activities, to alleviate hunger in the classroom, promote good nutrition, teach valuable cooking skills, and provide recipes that may be used at home. All of a child's senses are used in food or cooking experiences. Children see, smell, touch, and taste the food, as well as hear the food frying, boiling, and popping (Mayesky et al., 1985).

There are several important guidelines to follow when planning a cooking activity. Age-appropriate activities should be chosen. Younger children benefit more from recipes that allow them as much hands-on experience as possible. Recipes that require sharp utensils and heat may not always be the best choice. Safety is an important consideration.

In a group experience, there should be enough steps in the recipe so that every child is involved in some way. Pictorial recipe cards should be used so children can understand the entire process. Wholesome, nutritious foods should be the focus of recipe choices. Hygiene and cleanliness must not be ignored.

Breadmaking provides a natural vehicle for encouraging good nutrition.

Have adults and children wash up before participating and make sure utensils are clean. Give children their own spoons so that each may sample the food during the cooking process (Essa, 1992).

Supplies

Measuring spoons and cups	Muffin tin
Minute timer	Cookie sheets
Mixing bowls	Paper towels, plates, napkins
Hot plate	Recipe task cards or chart
Toaster oven	Spatula
Saucepans	Grater
Wooden spoons	Sifter
Eggbeater	Whisk
Paring knife	Blender
Cookie cutter	Aluminum foil
Potholder	Cutting board
Aprons and smocks	Electric fry pan
Dishpans	Colander
Rolling pin	Vegetable brush

Objectives

1. To provide opportunities to work together as a group to achieve a common goal.

This recipe calls for pouring, mixing, measuring, and following written and spoken directions.

2. To provide concrete experiences that promote understanding of concepts related to reading, science, mathematics, social studies, and health.

3. To provide practice in formal skills such as problem solving, following directions, predicting outcomes, and quantitative measurement.

4. To expose children to foods and customs of other cultures or times.

5. To provide practice in manipulative tasks, such as jar opening, pouring, sifting, and cutting, which help to develop fine motor skills.

6. To develop nutritious eating patterns.

7. To develop children's positive attitudes about themselves and learning.

Suggested Activities and Recipes

1. *Manipulation and exploration.* Use containers and cooking materials to encourage these activities.

2. *Language experience stories.* Use the cooking experience as a topic for a class or individual story.

3. *Tasting experiences.* Have the children identify familiar foods by tasting them (while unable to see them), compare and match foods with different textures, and taste foods that are opposites, such as sweet and sour.

4. *Smelling experiences.* Have the children identify familiar aromas (while unable to see the food) and match foods that have been placed in small containers by aroma only.

5. *Recipes.* Have the children actively participate in a variety of cooking experiences by pouring, mixing, grating, measuring, and following written and spoken instructions.

The first set of recipes is designed to be used with a small group of children and an adult helper. The second set is designed for individual use, perhaps located or set up in a learning center.

Recipes for Small Groups with Adult Helper

Energy Cookies

You will need:

oven	mixing spoon
large bowl	cookie sheets
eggbeater	

Ingredients:

4 C uncooked rolled oats	1 C brown sugar
3 C unbleached white flour	1½ C corn or peanut oil
2 C dates (pitted and chopped)	½ C maple syrup
6 T milk	

Directions:
1. In large bowl beat together sugar and oil.
2. Add oats, syrup, flour, and milk. Mix in dates.
3. Preheat oven to 350°. Oil cookie sheets, roll dough into small balls, and flatten them on cookie sheets.
4. Bake for 15 to 20 minutes. Let cool. (Makes 60 cookies.)

Gingerbread Man

You will need:

oven	mixing bowl
eggbeater	rolling pin
large spoon	cookie sheets

Ingredients:

½ C butter or margarine	1½ C flour
1 C sugar	1 tsp. baking powder
1 egg	1 tsp. ginger

Directions:
1. Cream butter and sugar together.
2. Add egg.
3. Mix in flour, baking powder, and ginger.
4. Roll out this dough.
5. Cut out shape of man.
6. Bake at 375° until brown.
   (Try making other shapes too.)

Apple Salad

You will need:

paring knife	measuring spoons
mixing bowl	wooden spoon
measuring cups	

Ingredients:

2 apples	½ C mayonnaise
3 celery sticks	½ C chopped nuts
½ tsp. lemon juice	

Directions:
1. Wash apples and cut into quarters.
2. Cut celery and apples into small pieces.
3. Put apples and celery into mixing bowl.
4. Sprinkle with lemon juice.
5. Add nuts and mayonnaise.
6. Mix.

Stuffed Potatoes

You will need:

oven	tablespoon
mixing bowl	mixing spoon
potato masher	cookie sheet

Ingredients:

baking potatoes	crumbled bacon
milk	(optional)
margarine	diced ham
cheese	choice of cooked vegetables

Directions:
1. Bake potatoes.
2. Cut them in half lengthwise.
3. Scoop the potato from the skin and put it in a mixing bowl.
4. Add milk and butter to creamy consistency.
5. Mash potatoes.
6. Add any optional ingredients.
7. Mix everything well.
8. Put back into potato skins.
9. Place on cookie sheets.
10. Reheat until warm.

Banana Wheels

You will need:
rolling pin
knife for cutting
knife for spreading

Ingredients:
banana
whole wheat bread
peanut butter

Directions:
1. Slice banana.
2. Spread peanut butter on one slice of bread.
3. Place banana slices on top of peanut butter.
4. Place another slice of bread on top and use rolling pin to roll sandwich flat.
5. Roll up flattened sandwich and slice into wheels.

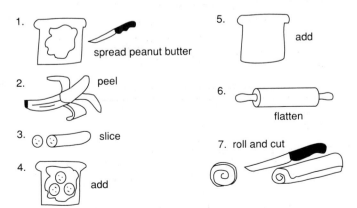

Mini Cherry Cheesecakes

You will need:

mixer   measuring cups and spoons
bowl and spoon   oven
small foil baking cups   cookie sheet

Ingredients:

2 8 oz. packages cream cheese   1 tsp. vanilla
2 eggs   1 can cherry pie filling
¾ C sugar   vanilla wafers
1 T lemon juice

Directions:

1. Soften cream cheese, add sugar, eggs, lemon juice, and vanilla. Blend with mixer for 5 minutes.
2. Set up foil baking cups on cookie sheet.
3. Put one vanilla wafer in each cup and spoon 2 T of cheese mixture on top.
4. Bake at 350° for 8–10 minutes.
5. Spoon 1 T of cherry pie filling on top when cooled.

Variety Muffins

You will need:

oven   muffin tins
sifter   paper liners
mixing bowl and spoon   cutting board
measuring cup   knife
measuring spoons   rubber spatula
blender

Ingredients:

1 C white flour   ½ C milk
1 T baking powder   1 banana, sliced
½ tsp. salt   fresh or canned fruit
¾ C whole-wheat flour   (optional)
1 egg   2 C bran flakes
½ C apple juice concentrate   chopped nuts
¼ C vegetable oil

Directions:

1. Sift the white flour, baking powder, and salt together.
2. Add the whole-wheat flour.
3. In a blender, blend egg, apple juice, vegetable oil, milk, banana.
4. Pour liquid ingredients into dry ingredients.
5. Stir.
6. Spoon into muffin tins.
7. Bake at 400°F for 20–25 min.

It is optional to add fresh or canned fruits and/or chopped nuts before filling muffin cups. For bran muffins add 2 C bran flakes in place of the whole-wheat flour.

Raisin and Nut Sandwich Spread

Ingredients:
1 lb. box raisins
2 C pecans
mayonnaise

Grind the raisins and nuts in a meat grinder. Add the mayonnaise until spreadable.

Pimento Cheese Sandwich Spread

Ingredients:

½ lb. grated sharp cheese	1 tsp. Worcestershire sauce
1 small can pimento	salt to taste
dash of Tabasco	mayonnaise or salad dressing

Mash pimento with fork and mix with grated cheese. Add Tabasco, Worcestershire, and enough mayonnaise to make spreadable. Add salt to taste.

Haystacks

You will need:

stove	teaspoon
large pot	wax paper
can opener	

Ingredients:
2 packages butterscotch bits
1 can chow mein noodles
1 can peanuts

Directions:
1. Melt butterscotch bits in a pot on the stove.
2. Stir in peanuts and chow mein noodles.
3. Drop a teaspoon at a time of the mixture on wax paper.
4. Cool.
5. Eat.

Remember: The careful cook leaves the center clean for the next cook.

Alphabet Pancakes

You will need:
measuring cups   frying pan or griddle
bowl and spoon   squeeze bottle (like those used for ketchup)
funnel

Ingredients:
Bisquick   water
oil   maple syrup

Directions:
1. Mix pancake mix according to Bisquick directions.
2. Use funnel to pour mix into squeeze bottle.
3. Heat oil in frying pan.
4. Squeeze pancake batter onto pan in the shape of letters.
5. Serve with warm maple syrup or eat plain like a cookie.

Edible Playdough

You will need:
wax paper
measuring cups
bowl and spoon

Ingredients:
1 C peanut butter
¼ C honey
1 C instant dry nonfat milk

Directions:
1. Mix peanut butter, dry milk, and honey together in bowl until smooth.
2. Knead in small pieces.
3. Roll and shape the dough on wax paper.
4. Eat your edible creations.

Peanut Butter Snowballs

You will need:
bowl and spoon
wax paper

Ingredients:
½ C honey   ½ C carob powder
½ C peanut butter   ½ C wheat germ
½ C sesame seeds   ½ C sunflower seeds
coconut

Directions:
1. Mix all ingredients together.
2. Roll mixture into balls on wax paper.
3. Fill small bowl with coconut and roll balls in it.

Honey Cocoa Pops

You will need:
5 oz. cups   measuring spoons and cups
Popsicle sticks   bowl and spoon

Ingredients:
2 T cocoa powder   1 C crunchy peanut butter
½ C honey   ⅓ C powdered milk
1 envelope unflavored gelatin   2 C boiling water

Directions:
1. Add boiling water to gelatin until dissolved.
2. Mix cocoa, honey, peanut butter, and powdered milk.
3. Add gelatin and water to mixture.
4. Pour into paper cups until half full.
5. Freeze partially, then insert Popsicle stick in center and freeze completely.
   Serves 10–12 children.

Spooky Biscuits

You will need:
oven   mixing bowl and spoon
rolling pin   measuring cups
cookie sheet cookie cutters in shape of ghost or pumpkin

Ingredients:
1 C canned pumpkin or fresh pumpkin puree (see below)
2½ C Bisquick baking mix

Directions:
1. Mix pumpkin puree and Bisquick together.
2. Knead and roll out.
3. Cut with cookie cutters and bake at 400° for 15 minutes.
4. Serve with honey and butter if desired.

Pumpkin Puree
1. Cut fresh pumpkin into pieces.
2. Wrap tightly in tinfoil and bake 1 hour at 350°.
3. Use food grinder or blender to puree pumpkin.

Cheese Wafers

You will need:

oven	mixing bowl
table knife	cookie sheet
cutting board	

Ingredients:

7 slices whole wheat bread	2 tsp. Worcestershire sauce
10 oz. cheddar cheese	shortening

Directions:
1. Tear bread into small pieces.
2. Cut cheese into chunks.
3. Mix in bowl with Worcestershire sauce.
4. Press crumbs together into small balls.
5. Place balls on lightly greased baking sheet.
6. Flatten slightly.
7. Bake at 350°F for 5 minutes.
8. Turn wafers and bake 5 minutes more, or until crispy.

Pumpkin Pudding

You will need:

oven	baking dish
blender	measuring cups
large bowl	measuring spoons

Ingredients:

4 pieces whole-wheat bread	1 ripe banana, sliced
½ C milk	¼ C apple juice concentrate
½ C orange juice	2 tsp. cinnamon
2 eggs	1 C canned pumpkin

Directions:
1. Break bread into small pieces and put into blender.
2. Blend well.
3. Place crumbs in a large bowl.
4. Add remaining ingredients to the blender.
5. Add mixture to bread crumbs. Stir together and pour into baking dish.
6. Bake for 50 minutes at 350°F.

Cracking an egg into the blender for this yogurt drink is no small task for a four-year-old. Under the watchful eye of the teacher, this one does it carefully.

Potato Latkes

You will need:

stove	chopping board
frying pan	sharp knife
grater	measuring spoons
large bowl and spoon	cooking oil

Ingredients:

6 large potatoes	½ onion
2 eggs	salt
1 tsp. minced parsley	pepper

Directions:
1. Wash potatoes and dry.
2. Grate potatoes into large bowl.
3. Add 2 beaten eggs.
4. Add 1 teaspoon minced parsley.
5. Add ½ chopped onion.

6. Add salt and pepper.
7. Mix well.
8. Flatten to form thin pancakes.
9. Fry until crispy brown.

Peanut Butter

You will need:
a blender

Ingredients:
1 lb. roasted peanuts
few drops of peanut oil
salt to taste

Directions:
1. Shell roasted peanuts.
2. Place peanuts in blender and grind.
3. Add a few drops of peanut oil.
4. Add salt to taste.
5. Refrigerate.

Applesauce

You will need:
plastic serrated knives
a pot
hot plate or stove

Ingredients:
6 apples
1½ C sugar
2 qts. water

Directions:
1. Peel and cut up the apples.
2. Put the apples in a pot of water. Cook until tender.
3. Mash.
4. Add sugar.
5. Cook for 10 more minutes.
6. Add cinnamon if desired.
7. Cool and serve.

Gazpacho

You will need:
sharp knife
bowl
refrigerator

Ingredients:

1 C chopped tomato	1 small clove garlic
½ C green pepper	½ T olive oil
½ C celery	1 tsp. salt
½ C cucumber	¼ tsp. black pepper
¼ C green onion	½ tsp. Worcestershire sauce
2 tsp. parsley	2 C tomato juice

Directions:
1. Chop all vegetables; crush garlic clove.
2. Combine all ingredients.
3. Chill overnight.
4. Enjoy.

(This is a good follow-up recipe after a trip to the market or a unit on foods.)

Cheddar Cheese Log

You will need:
refrigerator
mixing bowl and spoon
shallow dish
measuring spoons

Ingredients:

½ lb. Cheddar cheese	1 T Worcestershire sauce
3 oz. cream cheese	2 T chopped parsley
4 oz. cottage cheese	½ C chopped black walnuts
½ pack onion soup mix	variety of breads, bread sticks, crackers (optional)

Directions:
1. Have cheese at room temperature.
2. Place all ingredients except the walnuts in a mixing bowl and mix until well blended.
3. Refrigerate and shape into a log when the mix is cold.
4. Roll in the nuts and keep refrigerated until 2 hours before using.
5. Serve with a variety of crackers, breads, etc. (Selph & Street, 1975).

Fruity Cubes

You will need:
freezer
ice cube trays

Ingredients:
fruit juice
variety of colorful fruits (cherries, pineapple, strawberries, oranges)

Directions:
1. Cut fruit into small pieces.
2. Put several different pieces of fruit into the ice cube trays.
3. Pour fruit juice in trays and freeze.
4. Use fruit cubes in a glass of juice or wrap in napkin and eat.

Stone Soup

You will need:

large soup pot	cutting board
hot plate or stove	knife
mixing spoon	scrub brush

Ingredients:

1 stone	turnips
5 beef bouillon cubes	onions
1 qt water	tomatoes
1 can tomato or V-8 juice	celery
carrots	beans
potatoes	corn
cauliflower	peas
small bag of noodles	

Directions:
1. Scrub the stone well.
2. Dissolve 5 beef bouillon cubes in 1 qt water.
3. Add tomato or V-8 juice. Simmer.
4. Wash and chop all vegetables.
5. Add to soup pot all vegetables and cook for 30 minutes.
6. Add more water if necessary.
7. Add a small bag of noodles during last 10 minutes.

Tacos

You will need:
hot plate or stove
frying pan
taco shell rack

Ingredients:
2 lbs. ground beef
2 tomatoes
2 onions
½ lb. cheese
ketchup or salsa
medium can of prepared hot dog chili
taco shells

Directions:
1. Brown ground beef; add chili.
2. Shred and grate the vegetables and cheese.
3. Place all of these in the taco shell.
4. Top with ketchup or salsa.

(This activity is a little more advanced, but it is a very good one to follow a unit of study on Mexico.)

Personal Pizza

You will need:

baking sheet	frying pan
aluminum foil	cheese grater
knife	toaster oven
measuring spoons	hot plate or stove

Ingredients:

½ lb. ground beef	1 8-oz. jar spaghetti sauce
one can refrigerator biscuits	16 oz. package mozzarella cheese

Directions:
1. Brown ground beef.
2. Flatten biscuit with hand.
3. Spread 2 T beef on biscuit.
4. Pour 1 T sauce over beef.

5. Grate cheese and sprinkle 2 T over top.
6. Bake in oven at 400° for 10 minutes.
   Makes 10 servings.

Variations:
Use English muffins and cheddar cheese.
Add slice zucchini and mushrooms.

Vegetable Patties

You will need:

stove or hot plate	grater
oiled griddle	sharp knife
chopping board	measuring spoons
large bowl and spoon	

Ingredients:

2 T tofu	2 tsp. rolled oats
½ T beaten egg	½ T chopped onion
½ T grated carrot	1 tsp. chopped green pepper

Directions:
1. Mix all ingredients well in a large bowl.
2. Shape into one patty.
3. Cook 2 minutes on each side.

Fruit Tapioca

You will need:
hot plate or stove
saucepan
mixing spoon

Ingredients:

2 C fruit (apricots, cherries, raspberries, rhubarb)	4 T minute tapioca
2 C water	½ C sugar

Directions:
1. Place ingredients in a saucepan over low flame.
2. Boil until clear, stirring frequently.

Recipes for Individuals

Egg Salad

You will need:

small bowl	table knives
fork	tablespoon

Ingredients:

1 hardboiled egg	mayonnaise
salt	bread

Directions:
1. Peel and wash egg.
2. Mash egg in a small bowl.
3. Add 1 T mayonnaise and a pinch of salt.
4. Spread on bread.

Jack-O-Lantern Surprise

You will need:
table knife

Ingredients:
English muffins
spreadable orange cheese
olives, raisins, peanuts

Directions:
1. Spread cheese over muffins.
2. Use olives, raisins, peanuts to make surprise faces.

Banana-Ana Pudding

You will need:
measuring spoons
bowl and spoon

Ingredients:
½ small banana
3 T applesauce
1 tsp. plain yogurt

Directions:
1. Mash the banana in a small bowl.
2. Add the applesauce.
3. Stir in the yogurt.

Celery Racers

You will need:
sharp knife
spreading knife
toothpicks

Ingredients:

celery	peanut butter, cream cheese, or cheese spread
carrots	raisins

Directions:
1. Cut carrots into circles.
2. Cut celery into 4" lengths.
3. Use toothpicks to attach carrot circles to celery.
4. Spread your choice of filling in celery.
5. Put five raisins on top.

Honey Butter

Let's make honey butter Ingredients: Honey Whipping cream Salt	**1** Pour the whipping cream into the jar.	**2** Add one sprinkle of salt.
3 Put the lid on the jar and screw on tight. Take turns shaking the mixture until the cream separates.	**4** Pour the cream from the top into a bowl. Leave the butter in the jar.	**5** Pour the honey into the jar and stir the mixture.

6
Spread on a piece of bread with a knife.

Eat and enjoy your honey butter treat.

Proportions:
For group of 4 or 5, use 1C whipping cream
shake for 15-20 minutes
Add 2 + honey

Celery Boats

You will need:
toothpicks
table knife
sharp knife

Ingredients:

celery	apple
peanut butter or cream cheese	American cheese slices

Directions:
1. Cut celery into 4″ lengths.
2. Spread filling of choice in celery.
3. Slice apple into eighths.
4. Fold cheese diagonally to form a triangle.
5. Insert toothpick through cheese and into apple to form a sail.
6. Place apple with sail into center of celery.
7. Sail your boat right into your mouth!

Spanish Fruit Salad

2 T. pineapple chunks.
3 T. apple chunks.
2   banana slices.
8   orange slices.
1 t.   lemon juice.

In a cup, add
2 T. of pineapple
chunks.

Add 3 chunks
of apple.

Add 2 banana
slices.

Add 8 orange
slices.

Add 1 t. of lemon
juice.

Stir together.

Eat and Enjoy

Face Cakes

You will need:
plastic knives   small cups
small paper plates   serving tray with compartments

Ingredients:
rice cakes   sprouts
peanut butter   raisins
carrots   coconut
celery

Directions:
1. Put 2 T peanut butter in small cups.
2. Give each child a knife and peanut butter to spread on a rice cake.
3. Arrange vegetables, raisins, and coconut on tray and let children use them to create a face.

Variation: Use English muffins, cream cheese, or cheese spreads.

We are proud of the finished product, an edible face cake.

Skillet Bran Muffins

You will need:
Covered electric skillet
5 oz. paper cups
measuring spoons
large spoon

Ingredients:

1 T flour	⅛ tsp. baking powder
salt	1 T milk
2 T bran cereal	10 raisins
1½ tsp. molasses	

Directions:
1. Put flour in cup.
2. Add baking powder.
3. Put in a pinch of salt.
4. Add bran cereal and mix.
5. Stir in milk.
6. Add molasses.
7. Drop in raisins.
8. Place in skillet, cover, and bake 30–40 minutes at 375°.

(This recipe works well in a center where children can work independently. Adult should supervise use of skillet. This recipe can also be adapted for use with other recipes that require baking.)

Boy Salad

Face:
Canned pear half, using same material for features as girl

Hair:
Shredded carrots or grated cheese

Trousers:
Half a canned peach cut straight at the sides with a notch at the bottom in center

Legs and arms:
Pineapple wedges

Buttons and pocket trim:
Cut from marachino cherries

Girl Salad

Face:
Canned peach half, round side up

Eyes:
Raisins

Nose:
Clove

Mouth:
Cut from marachino cherry

Collar:
Stand half ring of pineapple on edge

Dress:
Hide a canned pear half under a lettuce leaf skirt and let pear show for petticoat

Slippers:
Tuck cherry halves under the petticoat

Walking Banana Salad

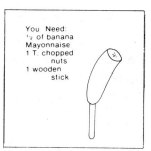

Variations:
Substitute honey mixed with granola to create another nutritious banana snack.

Flower Garden Treats

Ingredients:

whole-wheat bread   parsley
sliced carrots   sliced cherry tomatoes
sliced celery   cream cheese

Directions:
1. Spread softened cream cheese on slice of bread.
2. Arrange vegetables on bread to make flowers.
3. Use parsley for leaves.

Apple Smiles

You will need:
table knife
sharp knife

Ingredients:
red apple
peanut butter
jicama

Directions:
1. Slice apple into eighths.
2. Spread peanut butter on one slice.
3. Cut jicama into small cubes.
4. Place four pieces of jicama on top of peanut butter.
5. Put another slice of apple on top to form a smile.

Spooky Spiders

You will need:
table knife

Ingredients:
Round crackers   raisins
peanut butter or cheese spread   pretzel sticks

Directions:
1. Spread desired filling on one cracker.
2. Put eight pretzel sticks around sides of cracker for legs.
3. Place another cracker on top.
4. Use two raisins on top for eyes.

1. 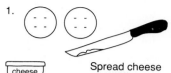 Spread cheese on crackers.

2. Put 8 pretzels around cracker.

3.  Stack like a sandwich. Make 2 ●● for eyes.

Ziploc® Salad

You will need:
sharp knife
Ziploc bags
measuring spoons

Ingredients:

lettuce	2 tsp. olive oil
carrots	1 tsp. apple cider vinegar
cucumbers	½ tsp. Italian seasoning
croutons	

Directions:
1. Tear lettuce into small pieces.
2. Slice cucumbers, carrots, and celery.
3. Place into Ziploc bag.
4. Add olive oil, vinegar, and Italian seasoning.
5. Shake bag to make a yummy tossed salad.

Cheese Constructions

You will need:
sharp knife

Ingredients:
variety of cheeses
pretzel sticks

Directions:
1. Cut cheese into 1″ cubes.
2. Push pretzel sticks into cheese cubes to form an edible construction.

Drinks

Peanut Butter Milkshake

You will need:
measuring cups and spoons
blender

Ingredients:
1 C milk
1 ripe banana
1 T creamy peanut butter

Directions:
1. Put all ingredients in blender.
2. Blend well.

Orange Cooler

You will need:
blender
measuring cups

Ingredients:
½ C orange juice concentrate
1 C plain yogurt
1 C milk

Directions:
1. Put all ingredients in blender.
2. Blend well.

Hot Spiced Cider

You will need:
sauce pan
hot plate

Ingredients:
apple juice
orange juice or cranberry juice
cinnamon stick

Directions:
1. Pour apple juice into sauce pan.
2. Add a small amount of orange juice or cranberry juice
3. Put cinnamon stick in pan.
4. Simmer for 5 minutes.

Strawberry-Orange Drink

You will need:
measuring cup
blender

Carefully pouring water is something we are learning to do with precision.

Ingredients:
1 C orange juice
2 crushed ice cubes
2 strawberries

Directions:
1. Wash and cap strawberries.
2. Put all ingredients in blender.
3. Blend well.

Cantaloupe Sip-Up

You will need:
blender
measuring cups

Ingredients:
2 C cantaloupe chunks
½ C apple juice concentrate
2 C milk

Directions:
1. Put ingredients in blender.
2. Blend well.

Hawaiian Drink

You will need:
blender
measuring cup

Ingredients:

2 C unsweetened pineapple juice	½ C nonfat dry milk
2 eggs	2 small bananas, sliced
2 tsp. vanilla	

YOGURT SHAKE

BLENDER

1 Cup Vanilla Yogurt

1 Banana

½ can frozen juice

Blend

Share with Friends!

possible additions: strawberries, wheat germ, pinch of nutmeg, cinnamon.

Use your imagination!

Directions:
1. Put all ingredients in blender.
2. Blend well.

Additional Information for Teachers

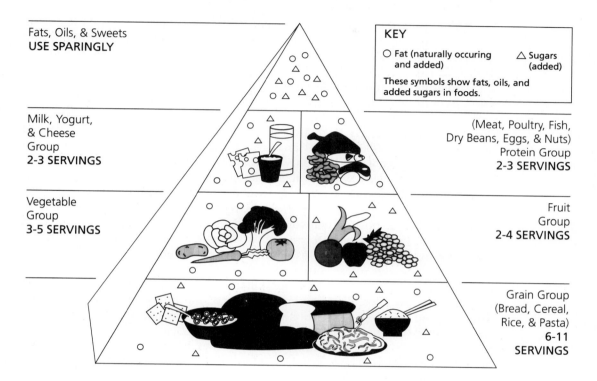

Fats, Oils, & Sweets
USE SPARINGLY

KEY

○ Fat (naturally occuring   △ Sugars
   and added)   (added)

These symbols show fats, oils, and
added sugars in foods.

Milk, Yogurt,
& Cheese
Group
2-3 SERVINGS

(Meat, Poultry, Fish,
Dry Beans, Eggs, & Nuts)
Protein Group
2-3 SERVINGS

Vegetable
Group
3-5 SERVINGS

Fruit
Group
2-4 SERVINGS

Grain Group
(Bread, Cereal,
Rice, & Pasta)
**6-11
SERVINGS**

What is the Food Guide Pyramid? The Pyramid is an outline of what to eat each day. It's not a rigid prescription, but a general guide that lets you choose a healthful diet that's right for you.

The Pyramid calls for eating a variety of foods to get the nutrients you need and at the same time the right amount of calories to maintain a healthy weight.

The Pyramid also focuses on fat because most American diets are too high in fat, especially saturated fat.

Dramatic Play

Children learn most effectively when they can learn actively. Dramatic play activities give children ample opportunities to engage in active, meaningful learning experiences. The dramatic play center provides unlimited learning opportunities in all areas of a child's development.

Through dramatic play, children gain competency in problem solving and divergent thinking, two skills that are necessary to be successful in our changing world. Other cognitive skills such as sequencing of events, classification, and number skills are also developed through dramatic play (Isenberg & Jalongo, 1993).

Role-playing activities allow children to experiment with a variety of societal roles. By putting themselves in another person's place, they begin to understand and empathize with other people's feelings. Social skills are learned when children work cooperatively to create a dramatic situation. Social rules are learned and moral growth is fostered (Hardacre, 1991). Children learn more about the world as they play with children with different backgrounds and experiences.

Dramatic play is a wonderful emotional release for children. It allows them to recreate frightening or stressful experiences and deal with them in a safe play situation (Pattillo & Vaughan, 1992). By being able to control their environment, children develop a positive self-concept and a sense of confidence and power in themselves. They also learn to trust themselves and each other (Taylor, 1985). Engaging in dramatic play helps children begin to define themselves and develop strong gender roles (Hardacre, 1991).

Children learn many self-help skills such as dressing themselves when they try on costumes. Their coordination and fine motor skills are enhanced through practice using tools, cooking utensils, and the many other props associated with dramatic play (Pattillo & Vaughan, 1992).

There are many opportunities for children to develop language skills in the dramatic play center. Through role playing, they practice communication skills, learn new vocabulary, and learn to listen to one another. Reading and prereading skills are enhanced with props such as store signs, price tags, and empty food packages (Pattilo & Vaughan, 1992).

The teacher has an important role to play in making the classroom a place for young children to experience the joy and benefits of dramatic play. By selecting materials and props and organizing and presenting themes or ideas, the teacher acts as a facilitator to encourage dramatic play. A teacher can intervene in children's play but must have good observation skills and know what kind of intervention would be most beneficial. Smilansky (cited in Saracho, 1991) has recommended two types of intervention. With the first one, the teacher gives suggestions or asks questions to promote play but does not become involved in the play. In the second type, the teacher assumes an active role to model behavior and encourage participation in the play.

Dramatic play is essential to the development of young children, and teachers have a responsibility to allow dramatic play to flourish in their classrooms. The following are suggestions for additional ways a teacher can help to encourage dramatic play in the classroom:

- Provide a variety of props and vary them according to classroom themes.
- Arrange for field trips and other new experiences that will stimulate role playing.
- Engage in fun activities for the children to role play later on their own.
- Take part in children's play activity when appropriate.
- At other times, let the children control the play.
- Guide children who seem to be having trouble by modeling.
- Allow the children to work out their conflicts as much as possible. Guide them, but do not solve all of their problems for them.
- Enjoy the children as they role play.

Supplies

Sufficient space to allow free movement

Child-sized furniture and appliances (table, chairs, sink, stove, bed, cabinet, ironing board and iron, baby carriage, baby high chair, etc.)

Clothes for dress up (including various occupational hats such as firefighter, police officer, hardhat, nurse, helmet, cap)

Props for cooking (pots, pans, tea set, dishes, pot holders, aprons, spoons)

Props for cleaning (broom, mop, dustpan, pail, sponge, empty spray can, rags, feather duster)

The dramatic play and home living area encourages children to use their imaginations. They become very grown-up in their costumes and props.

Full-length mirror
Added objects as needed for special emphasis

Objectives

1. To provide a setting for children to act out the world as they see it.

2. To provide an opportunity for children to act out feelings and emotions in a comfortable setting with an accepting adult.

3. To allow children to interact in a variety of roles.

4. To allow children to interact with other children and adults in a permissive and informal situation.

5. To help children develop oral language through creative expression.

6. To provide children an opportunity to imitate characters from stories and films.

7. To provide opportunities for children to create their own stories and actions for their stories.

8. To provide opportunities for children to practice standard American English through social amenities such as using the telephone.

9. To encourage creative expression through mask making and other activities.

In role-playing activities, children pretend to be ballet dancers and learn to understand the feelings of others.

10. To develop problem-solving techniques.
11. To enhance divergent thinking.
12. To encourage children to build social relationships with peers.
13. To enhance sensorimotor skills.
14. To help children develop a positive self-image.
15. To help children develop self-understanding.

Suggested Activities

Role Playing Goals

1. The children will be able to pretend to be very many different kinds of people and experience many social roles.
2. The children will be able to better understand the feelings of others and themselves.

Mask Making Activity Objectives

1. The children will make masks to represent themselves.
2. The children will make masks to describe their feelings about a certain subject.

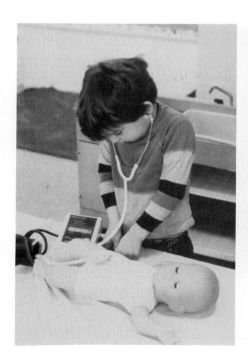

Children enjoy role-playing a variety of occupations. Here real "doctor clothes" and appropriate instruments help.

3. The children will make masks for use during a particular holiday or event.

4. The children will make masks for enjoyment and for the feeling of accomplishment.

Types of Masks

1. *Paper plate mask.* Use a round paper plate. Make two eyes in the paper circle. Decorate the mask with facial features using crayons or markers. Attach an elastic strip or rubber band to each side.

2. *Paper bag mask.* Draw a face on the flat side of a medium- or large-sized paper bag. Decorate facial features using paint, crayons, markers, or fabric scraps. Roll up a cuff at the bottom of the bag. Place the bag on the child's head and mark spaces for the eyes. Remove the bag and cut eye holes.

3. *Box mask.* Use a small box for a head mask and a large box for a body mask. Decorate the boxes using various materials to resemble such things as a robot, spaceman, or monster.

Hat Making

1. *Helmets.* Cut the bottom and a face-size section from a large plastic jug. The child will then decorate the helmet with stickers and bright paper to make a sports or astronaut's helmet.

2. *Paper hats.* Laminate a large sheet of red paper. Cut a semicircle, following the diagram. Staple the strip across the back to secure the hat. The child will paste a large number on the front to make a firefighter's hat.

Laminate a large sheet of white paper. Enlarge the following diagram onto it to make a nurse's hat.

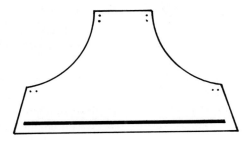

3. *Animal ears.* The child will make animal ears by cutting two ears from heavy paper and stapling them onto a band. Assist the child in measuring the band to fit his or her head. Provide pictures of the real animal whose ears the child is making.

Expand Play Center

Add materials to create a variety of situations in which the child will be able to role play numerous occupations.

1. *Post office.* A countertop or top of a bookcase or a window (or a puppet stage), stamps, play money, letters, old Christmas cards, telephone, postcards, mailbag or large shoulder bag, empty envelopes, stamp and ink pad, old magazines, advertisement flyers, badges, index cards, and file and postcards. Mailboxes, such as upside-down shoe boxes with the end cut out, can be placed in several other areas in the room for pick-up and delivery.

2. *Store.* A counter, cash register, play or real money, labeled boxes and cans, a price marker, newspaper ads, advertising bargains, a telephone for receiving orders, a calculator, and shopping carts.

3. *Beauty parlor and/or barbershop.* Full-length mirror (turned on its side) on a long table, combs, brushes, wigs, hair clasps, decorative combs, play razor, shaving cream, makeup, rollers, clips, pins, play shampoo, dryer, uniforms, capes, hair nets, and towels.

4. *Election booth.* Refrigerator box, paper ballots, pencils, names of candidates, curtain, official, clipboard with paper, voters.

5. *Public library.* Shelves, books, divider for quiet area, stamp and ink pad for dates, cards, record player, books with records, cassette player, books with cassettes, and posters about authors and/or books. This is a good place to share books the children have written and illustrated themselves.

6. *Playhouse.* A large refrigerator box with doors and windows cut out makes an exciting place to play. Let the children paint or decorate it as they wish. (This can make a good office, library, barbershop, doghouse, etc.)

7. *Laundry area.* A washtub and clothesline on an adjoining outside area add zest to this center. Allow the children to use the tub, with possibly a scrub board to wash the clothes they play with in the center.

8. *Grocery store.* Empty food containers, cash register, play money, plastic or papier-mâché fruits and vegetables, shopping carts, and paper bags.

9. *Hospital.* Stethoscope, masks, rubber hammer, tongue depressors, tissues, hospital gowns, doctor bag, scales, yardstick, measuring tape, clipboard with paper, cotton balls, adhesive bandages, empty pill bottles, play thermometer, hypodermic needle minus needle.

10. *Fishing pond.* An old wooden crate and a tackle box can turn any corner into a pond. Provide a fishing pole with a magnet in place of the hook, and fish with paper clip noses.

11. *Pet shop.* Stuffed animals, brush, towel, grooming supplies, cash register, cardboard boxes for cages, bowls.

12. *Camp site.* Backpack, sleeping bag, small tent, canteen, stones and sticks for fire, blankets.

13. *Airport/train station.* Telephone, tickets, travel brochures, suitcases, food trays, cardboard boxes, play money, chairs.

14. *Theater.* Tickets, puppets, cash register, empty food containers, puppet theater, costumes.

15. *Restaurant.* Notepads, pencils, apron, menus, play food, telephone, cash register, utensils, plates, cups, empty take-out containers.

Puppetry

Puppets can be used in the classroom to extend and enhance the dramatic play experience. They provide many of the same benefits as play acting as well as additional ones. When children make their own puppets, they are using fine motor skills and creativity. The use of puppets helps develop a positive self-

The use of puppets can help children improve their communication skills; it also provides an important outlet for expressing emotions.

image, stimulates and encourages communication and vocabulary, and improves social skills. It also provides a safe, acceptable outlet for expressing emotions. As they use puppets, children have the opportunity to experiment with different roles, gaining empathy and understanding for others. Children practice muscle control and eye-hand coordination while operating their puppets (Hunt & Renfro, 1982). The use of puppets also encourages abstract thinking and problem solving (Skelton & Hamilton, 1990).

Teachers can use puppets as valuable aids in their classrooms. They can learn more about how a child thinks and feels by observing the child's interaction with a puppet. They can also use the puppets themselves to lead singing, teach finger plays, act out nursery rhymes, help clarify abstract concepts, help demonstrate concrete concepts, and aid in reading (Mayesky et al., 1985).

Commercially made puppets have their place in the classroom, but the most beneficial puppets are simple ones children create themselves. Children get more satisfaction from designing simple puppets that are easy to manipulate. If a puppet is simple to operate, children can concentrate on role playing rather than the mechanics of puppet movement (Skelton & Hamilton, 1990). When working with puppets and young children, it is important to keep in mind that the child is a participant, not a performer, and that it is the creative process, not the product, that counts (Hunt & Renfro, 1982, p. 20).

Children can use puppets to create their own dramas or they can use them to reenact familiar stories and poems. Using puppets to recreate familiar stories improves reading comprehension and promotes speaking, listening, critical thinking, and reading skills (Isenberg & Jalongo, 1993).

When setting up the puppet area in your classroom, be sure to have puppets visible and easily accessible. Provide a mirror so children can experiment with movement, voice, and gestures. Allow children plenty of opportunities to practice with a variety of different kinds of puppets before they begin to create their own (Isenberg & Jalongo, 1993).

Supplies

Scissors, glue, pens, markers	Socks
Cloth scraps	Paper plates
Paper bags	Spools
Boxes	Cardboard rolls
Costumes	Pint-sized milk cartons
A stage	Clay or playdough
Materials to decorate puppets (yarn, buttons, trinkets)	Stapler
	Straws
Styrofoam balls	Gloves
Styrofoam cups	Mittens
Handkerchiefs	Pillowcases
Tongue depressors	Large cardboard boxes
String	Aluminum foil

Wooden spoons   Old pantyhose
Grocery bags   Wire hanger
Construction paper   Pompoms

Objectives

1. To provide a means of self-expression and role playing.
2. To promote verbal and dramatic expression in a variety of situations.
3. To promote an appreciation of various types of literature.
4. To help children learn how to become puppet makers.
5. To foster social skills through cooperation in making puppets and performing as a group.
6. To provide stimulation for creative writing and/or story telling.
7. To reveal the inner world of the child.

Suggested Activities

1. Performing with puppets.
2. Role playing with puppets.
3. Making puppets.
4. Teaching with puppets.
5. Using puppets in introductions.
6. Using puppets as icebreakers.

Finger Puppets

You will need:
an old glove   yarn
needle and thread   markers
fabric scraps

Directions:

Procedure 1:
1. Cut off the finger of a glove.
2. Sew facial features on the finger.

Procedure 2:
1. Draw a figure approximately 5" tall.
2. Cut it out.
3. Cut holes in the bottom for the child to stick his or her fingers through.
4. The child's fingers will be used for legs.

Peanut Pals

You will need:

glue   "google" eyes
peanuts   yarn, cotton balls
markers   acorn tops

Directions:

1. Cut the bottom off a peanut. (Teacher may need to do this.)
2. Draw faces with markers.
3. Glue on the google eyes.
4. Glue on yarn or cotton for hair.

Glove Puppet

You will need:

old glove   pompoms
scissors   felt scraps
yarn scraps

Directions:

1. Glue pompoms onto each finger of a glove.
2. Use yarn and felt scraps to make faces on pompoms or create different animals and characters.

This idea works very well for creating puppets for finger plays. For example, make five little monkeys, five little ducks, or five little Indians.

Sock Puppets

You will need:

an old sock	felt scraps
buttons	glue

Directions:
Sew facial features on socks and use for hand puppets.

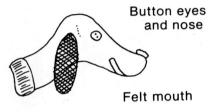

Button eyes and nose

Felt mouth

Felt ears

Wooden Spoon Puppets

You will need:

wooden spoon	material scraps
yarn	glue
string	construction paper

Directions:
1. Draw and cut out a character.
2. Glue it onto a spoon.
3. Glue on yarn, string for hair, and square or half-moon shaped cloth or paper for clothes.

Two-Faced Puppet

You will need:

two paper plates	markers
glue	stapler
sticks	scissors
yarn	

Directions:
1. Draw a face on the back of each plate.
2. Add features with varied types of materials
3. Insert a stick between the plates and glue it into place.
4. Staple the edges together.

Paper Plate Puppets

You will need:
two paper plates (one cut in half)
scissors
glue
yarn
construction paper scraps for features
paint

Directions:
1. Staple half a paper plate onto the back of a whole plate.
2. Cut out features from construction paper and glue them onto the front of the plate. The plate can also be painted if desired.
3. Slip your hand behind the half-plate to animate the puppet.

Variation: Follow the same directions but fold the puppet in half at the center. Cut out claws, legs, and eyes. Glue it on the plate to make a crab. (See illustration.)

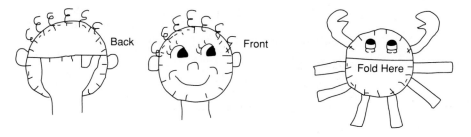

Recycled Rabbit Puppet

You will need:
recycled Styrofoam hamburger container
glue
construction paper
scissors
cotton balls

Directions:
1. Cut four slits in the top of the box for eyes and ears.
2. Cut out ears and eyes from the construction paper.
3. Slide them into the slits on top.
4. Glue a cotton ball onto the back for a tail.
5. To animate puppet, cut two holes in back, one above, and one below the hinge. Put your fingers in the holes to make the puppet's mouth move.

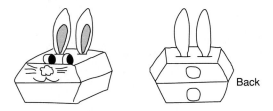

Milk Carton Puppets

You will need:

half-pint milk carton   glue
construction paper   scissors
yarn or string

Directions:
1. Cut through the center of a half-pint milk carton. Cut three sides only. Do not cut the fourth side.
2. Fold the carton in half (the uncut side becomes the hinge).
3. Cut facial features from colored paper and paste them to the carton.
4. Add string or yarn for special emphasis.

   To operate the puppet, place four fingers in the top section and the thumb in the lower section. Spreading and closing the hand makes the puppet's mouth open and shut (Platts, 1972).

Paper Bag Puppets

You will need:

brown lunch bag   markers
construction paper   glue
yarn or string   stick

Directions:

Procedure 1:
1. Stuff the lunch bag with newspaper.
2. Insert a stick.
3. Tie the bottom of the bag with the string.
4. Add facial features of yarn, construction paper, etc.

Procedure 2:
1. Using crayons or markers draw a character on the bag.
2. Add yarn for special emphasis.
3. The fold of the bottom of the bag makes a good mouth when hand is inserted (Collier, Forte, & MacKenzie, 1981).

Playdough Puppets

You will need:

playdough	toothpicks
raisins	fabric scraps
cereal	gravel

Directions:
1. Place a small amount of playdough onto your finger.
2. Mold the playdough into a face shape covering the finger.
3. Add raisins, cereal, gravel, toothpicks, etc. for facial features and add emphasis (Wolfgang, Mackender, & Wolfgang, 1981).

Styrofoam Ball Puppets

You will need:

Styrofoam ball	buttons
sticks	felt scraps
fabric scraps	

Directions:
1. Insert a stick into Styrofoam ball.
2. Cover the Styrofoam ball with fabric.
3. Tie the fabric around the stick.
4. Glue on buttons and felt scraps for facial features.

Finger-Face Puppets. Roll a rectangular scrap of paper into a tube and secure it with tape. Glue a face or sticker onto the tube. Wear the puppet on your finger.

Finger-Leg Puppets. Make a finger-leg puppet by cutting two small holes at the bottom of a posterboard character. Insert two fingers into the holes to make the puppet walk or dance.

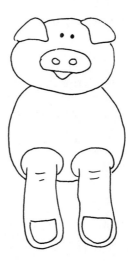

Stick Puppets. Either draw your own character on posterboard or cut large faces from a magazine and glue them onto posterboard. Attach this to a dowel stick with staples.

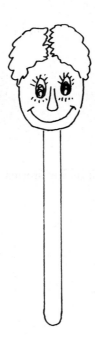

Large People Puppets. Draw a character on a piece of cardboard as tall as the height of a child. If need be, this can be easily done by using an opaque projector. Cut the figure out. Cut out a hole for the face as well as holes for the hands.

Body Puppets. Make large puppets by cutting people or story characters from posterboard. Make a small hole for the child's face and cut two small slits for the hands. These puppets are more durable if laminated. The child will wear the puppet in dramatic play. Animal puppets are especially appealing to very young children because they can make animal sounds as they wear the puppet.

Some suggestions for stories from which large character puppets can be made are:

The Three Little Pigs	The Elves and the Shoemaker
The Billy Goats Gruff	The Little Red Hen
Goldilocks and the Three Bears	The Brementown Musicians
The Wizard of Oz	Little Red Riding Hood
The Gingerbread Man	Henny Penny

Snowball Puppets

You will need:
Ivory Snow®	feathers, ribbons, shells, beans
Popsicle sticks	spoon and cup for mixing

Directions:
1. Mix 1 C of Ivory Snow and enough water to make a mixture the consistency of clay.
2. Model the mixture into snowballs.
3. Add feathers, beans, etc. to make faces.
4. Stick Popsicle stick into ball to make a handle.
5. Let it dry, then have a ball!

Clotheshanger Puppet

You will need:

clotheshanger	construction paper scraps
old pantyhose	scissors
yarn, fabric scraps	glue

Directions:
1. Bend the hanger into a diamond shape.
2. Stretch the pantyhose over the hanger and secure it at the top and bottom with yarn.
3. Glue on yarn and scraps to form hair and facial features.
4. The hanger provides a built-in handle to manipulate your puppet.

Puppet Storage Ideas

Children are more likely to use puppets if they are organized and displayed in an attractive manner. They must be accessible and easy to see. Following are some suggestions for keeping puppets organized:

1. Hang a clothesline along the wall and use clothespins to clip the puppets to the line.
2. Clip the puppets to a multiple-skirt hanger.
3. Store finger puppets in egg cartons.
4. Store puppets in tiered hanging baskets.

5. Use a shoe bag to organize puppets.
6. Place the puppets on an accordian clothes rack.
7. Set the puppets on a shoe rack. (Hunt & Renfro, 1982)

Simple Stages

You do not need a fancy stage to perform with your puppet creations. Here are a few simple ideas to make your own puppet stage:

1. Turn a table over on its side and get behind it.
2. Cut windows out of a large box. Hide inside the box and perform with your puppets peeking out of the openings.
3. Hide behind a chair and let your puppet peek over the top.
4. Hang a curtain on a rod or dowel and place it across the back of two chairs. (Hunt & Renfro, 1982)

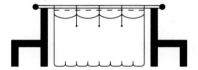

Suggested Readings

Additional Cooking and Nutrition Resources for Teachers

Children's Television Workshop Staff. (1989). *Parents' guide to feeding your kids right.* Englewood Cliffs, NJ: Prentice-Hall.

Walt Disney Staff. (1991). *Banana in a bandanna: A book about things to eat.* New York: Walt Disney.

Nonfiction Cooking and Nutrition Resources for Children

Berg, C. F. (1987). *What you've always wanted to know about nutrition.* New York: Vantage.

Bjork, C. (1991). *Elliot's extraordinary cookbook.* New York: Farrar, Straus & Giroux.

Brooks, F. (1989). *Food and eating.* Tulsa, OK: EDC.

Gross, R. B. (1990). *What's on my plate?* New York: Macmillan.

Kelley, T. (1989). *Let's eat.* New York: Dutton.

Llewellyn, C. (1991). *First look at growing food.* Milwaukee, WI: Gareth Stevens.

Children's Literature on Cooking and Nutrition

Barrett, J. (1978). *Cloudy with a chance of meatballs.* New York: Atheneum.

Brown, M. (1991). *Pickle things.* New York: Putnam.

Cushman, D. (1990). *Possum stew.* New York: Dutton.

Demarest, C. L. (1991). *No peas for Nellie.* New York: Macmillan.

Ehlert, L. (1989). *Eating the alphabet: Fruits and vegetables from A–Z.* New York: Harcourt Brace Jovanovich.

Harrison, J. D. (1989). *Saturn Storm's broccoli adventure.* Nashville, TN: Winston-Derek.

Mahy, M. (1986). *Jam: A true story.* New York: Little, Brown.

McLean, B. (1990). *The best peanut butter sandwich in the whole world.* Buffalo, NY: Firefly.

Modell, F. (1988). *Ice cream soup.* New York: Greenwillow.

Sharmat, M. (1984). *Gregory the terrible eater.* New York: Four Winds.

Stevenson, J. (1984). *Yuck.* New York: Greenwillow.

Thill, L. (1989). *The adventures of Alice in Nutritionland: A nutritional storybook for children.* North Highlands, CA: Impressive.

Chapter 7

Investigations in Science and Mathematics

Mathematics and science curricula are extremely important components in elementary education. Every child needs to learn the basic principles in these two subjects in order to excel in his or her overall education. However, the approaches for teaching these basic principles must be refined to a level that a young child can relate to, comprehend, and master. Once this is accomplished, children can use this strong base to build up their educational knowledge more effectively.

For almost 60 years, Jean Piaget examined and researched the development of children and how they acquire knowledge. According to Cliatt and Shaw (1992), Piaget's research described the following five factors involved in learning: social experience, physical experience, logical-mathematical experience, equilibration, and maturation. Social experiences derive from interactions with others. Physical experience is the process of working with and manipulating real materials. Through logical-mathematical experiences, children learn to classify objects based on their similarities. Equilibration involves taking in new information and organizing it into existing and changing mental schemes. Maturation is simply the passing of time. These factors indicate that children learn best through hands-on experiences and that these experiences can easily be incorporated into classrooms that are geared for this type of learning approach.

Jerome Bruner further complemented Piaget's research by stressing that children learn best through discovery (Cain & Evans, 1990). He went on to define three modes of presentation—action, imagery, and language—that can be used to provide more opportunities for children to discover knowledge, rather than being spoon-fed their ideas and thoughts.

The action mode presents a situation in which children manipulate real objects. This mode is appropriate for use not only with young children, but also when introducing a new concept into the elementary school classroom. Examples of this presentation include working with building blocks, sand and water activities, or live animals. The imagery mode uses representations of objects

Shannon and Susan manipulate real objects to discover number sequencing on the math board.

such as pictures or diagrams to teach various concepts. This mode is more effective with older primary grade children than with very young children. An example is adding sets of objects using pictures of various animals. Finally, the language mode relies on words and symbols to convey the meaning of concepts. This includes reading and verbal thinking. The action and imagery modes complement the language mode; and they should be experienced prior to introduction of the language mode.

Through these three modes of presentation—action, imagery, and language—children are able to become actively involved in learning by discovery, also termed *sciencing* (Coin & Evans, 1990). The sciencing approach requires a change in the traditional roles of both teacher and child. To be successful, the child must develop process-inquiry skills including observation, classification, measurement, computation, experimentation, and prediction (Cliatt & Shaw, 1992). These skills will provide a base for further science and mathematics learning.

Children, innately curious, are natural scientists. They eagerly discover as much as they can about the world around them. Children think, form concepts, and solve problems. They unconsciously use scientific methods as they observe, infer, classify, and reach conclusions. Encouraging the development of scientific and mathematical skills and methods of thinking requires an environment that is rich in interesting objects to explore and manipulate, one that fosters exploration of ideas. It is the teacher's responsibility to capitalize on children's natural curiosity as learning opportunities arise by helping them focus on relevant details; asking questions that require judgments and inferences; and providing opportunities to classify, experiment, and communicate their findings.

Establishing the Mathematics and Science Program _____

The experiences and activities in this chapter are designed to provide opportunities to develop basic process skills and an understanding of the patterns of science and mathematics through the use of hands-on materials. These activities are designed to help young children see relationships and interconnections between science and mathematics as they learn to deal flexibly with scientific and mathematical ideas and concepts. Children do best what they like to do. Although it may be hard work, the challenge of inquiry and discovery is stimulating and fun for children.

Objectives

1. To discover basic math and science concepts by exploration and experimentation (in incidental and contrived situations).
2. To enjoy science and math activities by engaging in various methods of discovery.
3. To use resource materials in problem solving.
4. To use a variety of materials for weighing and measuring.
5. To chart progress and results of experiences. *example- childs height, Bday*
6. To use the scientific method of problem solving—to observe, identify problem, predict, research, test prediction, and generalize.
7. To manipulate various objects to move from concrete experiences to the abstract.
8. To develop habits of thinking and investigation.
9. To share discovery with others.
10. To find success in these areas.

Environmental Resources

Rugs
Tables
Low shelving for puzzles, games, displays
Windows (preferably low enough for the children to see out)
Clear plastic containers with labels for "raw materials"
Plastic tubs for storing materials and supplies
A sink, preferably with hot and cold water

Science Supplies

Prisms, tuning forks, wood, wire, glass, soil, bottles, candles, batteries
Bolts, switches, pulleys, levers, screws, wheels and axles, planes, and pendulums

Pendulum frame, pendulum bobs, scales (balance, kitchen, spring), weights

Assorted materials for balancing, blocks of various weights, mirrors, lenses

Kaleidoscopes, electric bell, calendars, clocks, hourglass, egg timer, sundial

Bulbs, tape measures, yardstick, meter stick, rulers, dry and liquid measure containers

Rope, drinking straws, food coloring, stopwatch, stethoscope, sponges, keys

Kite, locks, iron filings, magnets, mechanical junk, slinky

An assortment of chemicals from home: vinegar, baking soda, table salt, baking powder, sugar, cream of tartar, rubbing alcohol, epsom salts, iodine, ammonia, hydrogen peroxide

Fibers: nylon, silk, rayon, linen

Magnifying glasses (hand and large on stand), compass, barometer, flashlight

Objects to smell, taste, touch; gears; strings; color paddles; telescope

Microscopes

Heat, water

Magazines (especially farm and science magazines)

Potting soil, variety of seeds

Hot plate

Thermometers (Celsius and Fahrenheit)

Aquarium and terrarium (empty)

Flowers and plants; animals (alive and preserved)

Rocks and shells

Cages and animal food

Paper and pen for labeling

Chart and graph paper

Resource material, pleasurable nature reading (e.g., *Ranger Rick*)

Watering can, trowel, seeds, flowerpots, incubators, bug house (to keep live insects)

Orientation

Children should have ample time and opportunity to explore materials on their own. No tasks should be introduced other than those the children devise for themselves. After a suitable time (days or weeks, depending on the age and developmental level of the children), simple tasks may be assigned.

Basic Earth Science

Water

Objectives

1. To learn the importance of water to living things.
2. To differentiate between the three forms of water.

Suggested Experiences

Free Inquiry. Provide an area (preferably outdoors), materials, and ample time for experimentation. Children will need containers of different sizes, sponges, funnels, strainers, etc. Discuss and record the children's observations.
Variation: Do this activity outside on a rainy day as well. Have the children observe and record their ideas about rain (e.g., through drawing or painting pictures with captions).

Sink/Float Experiment. Provide water and a variety of small items. Let the children discover which ones sink and which ones float. Ask them to record their results individually or as a group on a chart.

Water Use Experiment. Have the children think of all the ways water helps us. List these on a chart. Discuss the fact that water is essential to life. Plant some seeds. Water some but do not water others. Discuss the results.

Evaporation Experiment. This is a warm day activity. Provide paintbrushes. Allow children to "paint" on the outside of the building with water. When the children notice that the water dries, ask them to think about what happened to their pictures. Introduce the word *evaporate*.

Mixing Experiment. Have the children mix water in separate containers with various substances such as salt, oil, sugar, or food coloring. Ask them what they observed when the dry ingredients were combined with the water.

Ice Experiment. Ask the children to make ice in ice trays. Then let them observe the ice when it is put in hot and/or cold water, or as it melts to room temperature. Ask them why they think the ice melts or what causes it to melt slower or faster in different situations. Supply them with other materials such as scales, other liquids, salt, and a clock or timer.

Suggested Activities

Sink or Float? Make lamented cards of various household items such as corks, paper clips, erasers, and pennies. Provide the materials shown on each card as well. The child will choose a card and predict whether each object will float or sink. Then, have the child experiment with the objects to see whether or not his or her answers are correct.

Make a Boat (Woodworking). Provide scrap wood, glue, a hand drill, sandpaper, dowels, and construction paper. Following directions provided on task cards, the students sand the bottom of the boat until smooth. Have them drill a hole in the center to place a dowel. Students cut a mast from construction paper and glue it to the dowel. Students then glue the dowel into the hole.

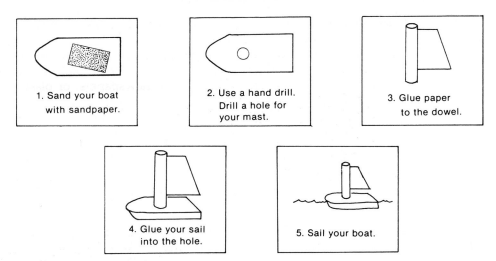

Water Volume. To develop the concept of volume, collect containers, two of equal size and one of a different size. Ask the children to first fill the two equal containers with the same amount of water. Have them observe and confirm that the two containers have the same amount and why. Then ask them to take one of the full containers and pour the water from it into the third container. Have them observe and comment on whether or not the two containers have the same amount of water.

Variation: A measuring cup can be added to further self-correct the children's theories.

Air

Objective
To learn about the properties and importance of air.

Suggested Experiences

Catch Some Air. Pull an opened plastic bag through the air. Twist the end of the bag so the air stays inside. Discuss with the children what is inside the bag. Tell the children to move their arms around rapidly. They will be able to feel their arms pushing air around. Give each child a plastic bag, and tell them all to catch some air. Collect the bags afterwards.

Variation: Have the children fill bags with other materials such as foam, water, or paper. Have them compare the characteristics of the bags filled with materials versus those filled with air (compare weights, shapes, etc.).

Moving Air. Take the children outside on a breezy day. Provide them with a streamer or pinwheel and ask them to find a way to make the wind move it.

Also, have them observe and/or record what else the wind can make move by drawing pictures or writing short stories.

Variation: Beforehand, have the children think of things that they can use to make streamers—what materials would work and what would not. Provide materials such as heavy and light fabrics, newspapers, or plastic and let them make their own streamer.

Air and Space Experiment. Demonstrate that air occupies space by pushing an upside-down glass (or clear plastic cup) down into a bowl of water vertically. This may be observed more readily if a cork is placed on the water first and is seen to float. If the glass or cup is pressed down over the cork it will sink, because the water is no longer there to lift it. Place this activity in a center for experimentation.

Balancing Balloons. Show that air has weight by carefully blowing up two similar balloons to the same size. Using thumbtacks or string, attach the balloons to opposite ends of a yardstick. Hang the yardstick with a piece of string at the center or balance point. Carefully burst one of the balloons with a sharp object. Notice that the end of the yardstick with the inflated balloon tends to be lower. Carefully break this balloon and notice that the yardstick tends to balance again.

Suggested Activities

Bubble Blower. Prepare a bubble solution as follows:

    2 C water
    1 to 2 T liquid soap
    ¼ C glycerine

Stir to mix well. Pour into two or three tubs or dishpans. Each child will need several straws and a paper or a Styrofoam cup. Make a hole in the side of the cup about 1 inch from the bottom for the straw to be inserted. Tell the children to place the open end of the cup in the bubble solution and then remove the cup. Call attention to the film that has formed across the opening of the cup. Tell the children to hold their cups upside down and blow slowly through the straws. Large bubbles will form as they blow. Make task cards asking such questions as the following: "What is inside your bubble? Can you think of a way to make your bubble smaller? Can you think of two ways to remove air from your bubble?"

Booklets. Make booklets with the title "Air Works for Us." Provide magazines for the children to find pictures of air at work. Sports magazines are good for pictures of sailboats, skydiving, parachutes, gliders, etc. The children can also find pictures of inflatables, auto and bicycle tires, kites, hairdryers, airplanes, windmills, etc. Have them cut and paste as many pictures as they can find.

Variation: Have the children separate the pictures into categories such as work and play activities. Also, have them write descriptive captions under the pictures, telling how the air is working.

Paper Airplanes. Provide materials for making paper airplanes. Demonstrate different methods of folding paper to produce the best glider. Provide a time outdoors for experimenting with these.

Parachutes. Supply materials for making parachutes using handkerchiefs, pieces of plastic, or paper tied to wooden spools or small balls. Experiment with different materials, making some with a hole in the parachute center. Observe which are more efficient in holding the parachute up the longest. Older children can record the results.

Weather and Seasons

Objectives

1. To become aware of changes in weather.
2. To observe different types of weather.

Suggested Experiences

A Walk in the Weather. Plan to take the children outside to observe the weather on several different days (e.g., warm and cold days, sunny and rainy days). Ask them what kind of day it is and what makes it that type of day. Point out the different clouds that form with each day. After experiencing several different days of weather, have the children imagine different kinds of weather and draw pictures about them.
Variation: If going outside is not feasible, have the children observe from the window. Ask them to describe or draw pictures of the different seasons of the year.

Temperature Experiment. Take the children outside. Have them stand in the sun and then in the shade. Let them tell about the difference in temperature. Fill two basins, each with 1 inch of water. Place one in the shade and one in the sun. Wait about an hour, then observe the temperature in both basins by feeling the water in each basin. Discuss the difference. Use a thermometer to see how many degrees difference there is in the two basins of water. Ask the children to think why it is warmer on a sunny day.
Variation: Fill two cups with cold water. Place one in a shady area of the classroom and the other in the window. Wait for a period of time and ask the children to compare the temperatures by feeling with their hands or measuring with a thermometer.

Suggested Activities

Weather Observation. On a large chart, keep a daily record of the weather. Make removable cards to hang on the calendar month with the date on one side and space to record the weather on the other side. Record the temperature and what type of weather is occurring (sunny, rainy, warm, cold, etc.).

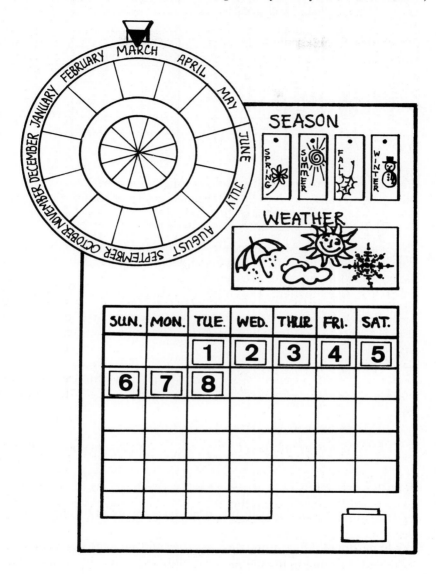

Charting Temperature. Chart the temperature on a graph. Some of the older children can do this as younger children observe. Place thermometers near the chart. The wind could be charted the same way using a weather vane.

The Date Game. Using tri-wall, cardboard, laminated tagboard, or material board, mount three pockets made with envelopes or library card holders. Label

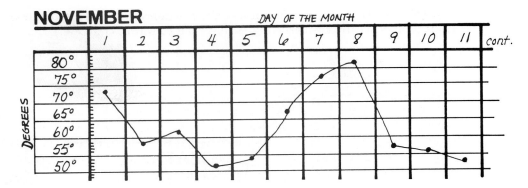

the four pockets *Day, Month, Holiday,* and *Season.* Make several picture cards and/or word cards; an individual or small group of children can sort them into the pockets accordingly. Label the back of the cards for self-correction.

The Seasons Game. Make a seasons matching game with tagboard and pictures from magazines of scenes showing different seasons. Select three pictures of each of the four seasons. Glue them on tagboard and cut them to fit a convenient card size. Laminate them. The children can match the picture cards to the poster, naming the seasons.

Space

Objectives

1. To become aware of the sky and the stars.
2. To discover and learn about the seven planets and the sun.

Suggested Experiences

Field Trip. Plan an outing to the local space museum or planetarium.

Sky Experiment. On a sunny day, ask the children to go outside and observe the sky. Ask them to do the same thing at night at home with a family member. The next day, discuss what they saw and what differences they found between the two observations.

Space Rockets. Provide materials for the class to make their own "spaceship." These materials can include toilet paper or paper towel cylinders, old juice cans, soup cans, construction paper, and glue. Have the children create a story—

either individually or in small groups—about where they would fly their space-ship.

Suggested Activities

Go to the Moon! Make a game board as shown in the diagram. Make or provide characters and dice. Players take turns rolling one die. If the person lands on a space with a star, he or she draws a card and answers the various questions such as Which planet is closest to the sun? Which planet has rings around it? When a player correctly answers the question he or she gets to move ahead one space. The winner is the first one to reach the moon.

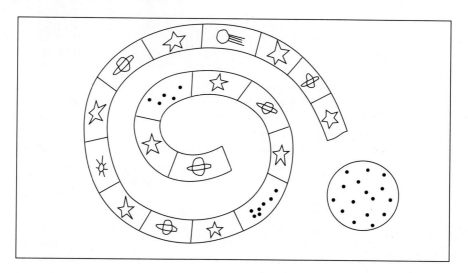

Health Science

The Human Body

Objective
To name, identify, and learn about the major parts of the body, including the head, neck, arms, elbows, hands, wrists, fingers, back, legs, knees, feet, and toes.

Suggested Experiences

Look in the Mirror. Provide a full-length mirror for children to observe themselves.

Identifying Body Parts. Play games such as Simon Says (Touch your neck, chin, earlobe, eyebrow, etc.).

Heather's mom comes to school to show us a skeleton and
talk about the parts of the human body.

Life-Size Portraits. Children trace each other on brown wrapping paper. (One child lies down on the paper while the other traces around his or her outline.) Each child paints or colors in his or her own facial features, hair, and clothing. The life-size portraits may be cut out and hung in the classroom.

Suggested Activities

Matching Body Parts. Draw the various body parts, unattached, on a single sheet of paper. Glue the paper to a piece of cardboard and cut out the various pieces. Have the children correctly piece together the puzzle. Have a copy of the puzzle available for self-correction.

Movement and Rhythm. While playing a tape of a simple song, have the children "be an instrument." They can clap their hands each time the drum is played, tap their feet when the trumpet sounds, or blink each time the cymbal is hit.
Variation: You can also use this activity while teaching music. Once you have taught the children a song that, for example, involves more than two voices, assign each child a part to "play their instrument" at the appropriate time.

The Five Senses

Objectives

1. To identify the five senses (sight, smell, taste, touch, and hearing).
2. To learn the basic functions of the body's senses.

3. To learn about the body parts associated with each of the senses.

4. To use the five senses to make observations.

Suggested Experiences

Sight

1. *Observing Pictures.* Show the children a bright, colorful picture and ask them to study it for a moment. Then, remove the picture and ask them to name some of the objects in the picture.

2. *Magnifying Objects.* Use a magnifying glass or a microscope to look at different objects or substances. Talk about how the magnifying glass helps us see things differently from the way we normally see them. Relate this to people who must wear glasses or to people who are blind.

Smell and Taste

1. *Identifying Smells.* Provide baby food jars, paper towels, spices, extracts of vanilla and lemon, and other food items such as fried bacon, onions, and so forth. Place a wadded-up paper towel in the bottom of each jar. Put a different object for smelling in each jar. Allow the children to smell and guess what the odors are with their eyes closed or blindfolded.

2. *Nature Walk.* Discover different smells by taking a nature walk and letting the children collect objects such as flowers, leaves, acorns, and pine cones. Bring them back to the classroom and have the children sort their findings into items with an odor and items without an odor.

3. *Sweet and Salty Experiment.* Provide salt and sugar in two cups. Discuss the difficulty in telling the difference between the two. Ask the children how they might tell the sugar from the salt. (By tasting them.)

4. *Sweet and Sour Experiment.* Provide lemon juice, vinegar, water, and sugar. Let the children taste each liquid. Discuss how each tastes. Add sugar and water to the lemon juice. Does the lemon juice still taste sour? Do sugar and water change the taste of the vinegar?

5. *Tasting Party.* Provide foods that are salty, sweet, sour, bitter, spicy, and bland. Include foods such as carrots, pickles, cheese, radishes, raisins, grapefruit juice, chocolate milk, and whole milk. Talk about the different tastes. Make a list of the foods in each category.

Touch

1. *Describing Attributes.* Provide a set of attribute blocks. Let the children handle the blocks and describe what they are holding. ("I have a large yellow circle"; "I have a small blue triangle.")

2. *Touch and Feel.* Provide a variety of materials for children to explore at a table. Materials can include cotton, pine cones, balls, metal, blocks, seashells, candles, Styrofoam, and a variety of fabrics.
Variation: Make it a game by providing a box or a bag to conceal the items. Ask the children to pull out a certain object or two things that feel similar.

Hearing

1. *Identifying Instruments.* Using a variety of musical instruments such as a drum, a song flute, a trumpet, bells, or a xylophone, have each child close his or her eyes while another child plays one of the instruments. Ask the first child to identify the sound.

2. *Listening to Your Environment.* Instruct the children to listen to their environment for about 30 seconds and make a list of the sounds they hear. Now ask them to arrange the sounds in order from softest to loudest.
Variation: Do this exercise outside and have the children list man-made versus natural noises (e.g., a car or a bird).

Suggested Activities

Poster of Senses. Make a poster with symbols for each of the five senses (an ear, an eye, a nose, a mouth, and a hand) and pictures of things to be identified. Match the pictures with the symbol that is most appropriate for identification.

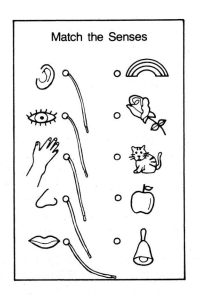

Identifying Noises. Make a tape of various sounds (e.g., weather such as thunder or rain; vehicles such as trains, car horns, or airplanes; or other sounds that go along with the current classroom theme). Play the tape and ask the children to identify the sounds.
Variation: To further practice grouping skills, instruct the children to categorize the sounds (e.g., loud vs. soft, man-made vs. natural sounds).

What Do I See/Hear? With a small group of children, choose an object or a sound you can hear in the classroom. Describe the object or sound by one attribute at a time until someone guesses the correct answer. Then have that child choose and describe an object or sound and repeat the game.

Life Science

Plants and Flowers

Objectives

1. To be able to distinguish living from nonliving things.
2. To become aware that seeds house dormant baby plants.
3. To understand that each plant has its own unique seed that can only grow into the kind of plant that produced it.
4. To understand that if seeds are planted in soil and are kept moist and receive sunlight, they have the potential to become mature plants.
5. To become aware that gravity, moisture, and sunlight affect plant growth.
6. To identify the parts of plants and flowers such as the root, stem, leaves.
7. To develop an awareness that the fruit of a plant is where the seeds for the plant are produced.
8. To become aware that dead flowers left on plants grow into fruits that will eventually contain seeds.

Suggested Experiences

Nature Walk. Go on a walk. Encourage the children to look closely at things outside. Encourage them to handle leaves, grass, soil, rocks, and flowers and to observe carefully. Return to the classroom and ask the children to name the things they saw that were living and those that were not. Make a chart in two columns listing the children's contributions.

Beans and Pebbles Experiment. Provide lima beans, small pebbles the size of lima beans, water, and two equal-size plastic containers. Show the children the

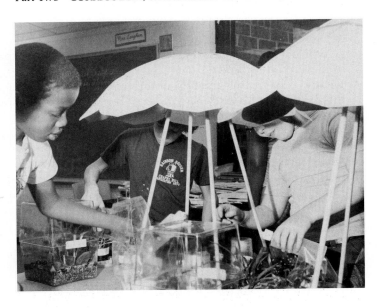

lima beans and the small pebbles. Ask them which of the two things is alive and which is not. Ask the children to sort out the lima beans from the pebbles. Ask them to count out equal numbers of lima beans and pebbles and place them in separate containers. Tell the children to fill the containers with water and leave them overnight. Ask them to predict what changes, if any, will occur in the beans and the pebbles overnight. The next day let the children observe the changes in the beans. Encourage them to describe what they observed.

Seeds Observation. Provide assorted fresh fruits and vegetables such as apples, oranges, cantaloupe, tomatoes, peas, and cucumbers; a knife; paper towels; and a magnifying glass. Ask the children where seeds come from. Allow each child to respond. Show the assorted fruits and vegetables and ask the children whether they know what is inside. Cut the fruits and vegetables and remove the seeds. Ask the children to place the seeds from each kind of fruit or vegetable on a separate paper towel. Allow the seeds to dry. Tell the children to examine the seeds with the magnifying glass. After the seeds have dried for a week, place them on a wet paper towel inside a jar or in a plastic bag to observe possible germination.

Seed Identification. The chart can be made by using tri-wall, cardboard, or tagboard. A sample of each kind of seed with the word under it may be put in the chart. Several additional seeds of the same varieties are placed in a box labeled seeds. Some children can find seeds that match and paste them on the chart. Others may want to do research on the various kinds of seeds.

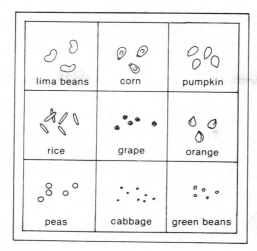

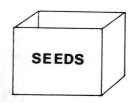

Collecting and Classifying Leaves. Ask the children to collect some leaves at home and bring them to class, or take the group on a nature hike to gather leaves. Beforehand, make a large poster with various leaves pasted on it, along with the name of each leaf. Hang this in the classroom. The children will then compare their leaves and label them by name as they match each one. Provide resource books in case they collect leaves that are not included in your collage.

Small Garden (for the Nature Center). This is a substitute activity to use when outdoor gardening is not feasible. Gardens aid children's understanding of the concept of change. (*Note:* With a little direction, the children can make such a garden for themselves.) Materials needed are:

A plastic or metal dishpan, although the ideal is a zinc-lined box with a hole for drainage.
A soil mixture (the children will help mix the soils and probably question why).

When the layout is ready, discuss it with interested children. They will offer suggestions. Research (and the teacher) will let them know what is possible in such small gardens. The children should decide on some workable plan, which should be accepted.

Plant Identical Seeds or Plants. Use different types of soil or different amounts of sunlight or water. Compare the groups.

Observation-Measurement Charting. Have the children observe the growth of seeds or plants in the room (height, new leaf, or bloom). Record their observations. Have them measure leaf spread and/or stem growth, and record it.

Animals

Objectives

1. To understand that the world is made up of living and nonliving things.
2. To become aware that most living things are either plants or animals.
3. To develop an awareness that animals live in many places.
4. To understand that all animals need food and water.
5. To understand that each animal needs its own kind of food.
6. To develop an awareness that animals are mobile and move in different ways.
7. To develop an awareness that most animals move, eat, and grow.
8. To develop an awareness that animals adapt to their environment in different ways to aid their survival.
9. To become aware that animals kept in captivity need to be cared for.
10. To begin to develop an appreciation and respect for life and living things.
11. To begin to develop an awareness of how to group animals with similar characteristics or attributes.

Suggested Experiences

Introduction to Animals. Provide a selection of assorted living and nonliving things such as various plants, goldfish, parakeets, hamsters, turtles, insects, snails, rocks, and seashells. Show the children the assortment. They should observe at least two or three live animals. Ask them to compare the animals to one another. Discuss how the animals are different, how they are alike, how animals are different from plants, what makes plants and animals alike, whether we are living things, whether we are plants or animals, and so on.

Ask the children to name the largest, then the smallest animal they can think of. Allow them to share their thoughts. Have the children find or make pictures of living and nonliving things. Tell them to sort the pictures into piles of living and nonliving things and then further sort the pictures of living things into plants and animals. The children can mount the pictures on appropriately labeled posters for display in the classroom.

Subdividing Mammals into Groups. Provide mammals to observe (e.g., children's or classroom pets, a trip to a pet store, or a trip to a farm or a zoo). Ask the children to observe the live mammals. Encourage the children to touch the mammals gently and to use their five senses to observe them. Ask questions that inspire the children's use of basic process skills. Include questions that require thinking: "What kind of animal is this? Can you feel its backbone? Does the

Touching an animal gently shows respect for life and living
things.

animal feel warm or cold when you hold it? How does your body feel when you
touch it (warm or cold)? What kind of covering does the animal have? Does it
have toenails? What body parts does the animal have that you have? How does
the animal move? Does the animal have teeth? Do the animal's teeth look like
your teeth?''

Suggested Activities

Pond or Stream Collections. When exploring these areas, children might use a plankton net to collect microscopic animals to observe with their field microscope or classroom microscope.

Animals and Appropriate Cages. Gerbils, mice, rabbits, chicken, and snakes are all appropriate for this activity. Learning to love and care for pets helps children develop a positive attitude toward living creatures.

Concentration Habitat Game. Have the children make 20 cards using tagboard and draw pictures of animals and their habitats. Play it like "Concentration." The person with the most matches wins.

Food Chain Train. Using posterboard, make a train. Find pictures of animals and plants in a food chain and paste them on cars. Color code different food chains. The dots make the activity self-correcting.

Variation: This game can also be used to show the water cycle; the sequence of seed to plant to flower to fruit; and the metamorphoses of various insects and frogs.

Match by Land, Water, and Air. Tape together three pieces of colored tagboard, with a picture on each one depicting land, water, or air. Mount several pictures of animals representative of each on cards. Have the children match each picture with the appropriate land, water, or air picture on the tagboard. Answers can be placed on the back of each card for self-correction.

Go Fishing. Prepare pictures of animals from both land and sea. Attach a paper clip to each animal. Have the child use a fishing rod with a magnet attached to the string to fish for the animals. As the children fish out the animals, they will sort them according to land and sea. Students can either list and label all the sea animals or draw, color, and label three sea animals, depending on their ability.

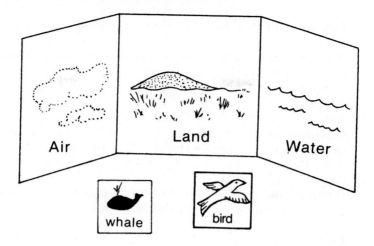

Physical Science

Objectives

1. To learn that matter has basic properties such as color, size, shape, and texture.
2. To state the properties of various common objects.
3. To distinguish between and classify objects according to a single property.
4. To describe the position of objects using words such as *up, over, under, beside, in front of, behind, left,* and *right.*
5. To describe comparative quantities of objects such as *more than, less than, the same as.*
6. To describe changes in the environment, such as seasonal changes, the differences in day and night, and how people change as they grow.

Suggested Experiences

Classification. Provide numerous opportunities for the children to classify objects (beads, attribute blocks, pattern blocks, pieces of cloth of different textures, pegs, Cuisenaire rods, etc.).

Location. Objects like those used for classification may be used to play position games in small groups. ("Place the blue bead under the chair, on the chair, behind you, on your right," etc.)

Nature Walk. Walks outside are valuable experiences as seasons change. Ask the children to observe changes.

Day and Night. Talk about appropriate activities for day and night. Let each child contribute to the discussion. The children will then make wall charts titled "Night" and "Day." Provide magazines for finding appropriate pictures to cut out and paste on the proper chart.

Suggested Activities

Classification Tasks. Task cards may be prepared for classifying activities and practice (e.g., "Place the red beads in the bowl"; or, for a greater degree of difficulty, "Place the round red beads in the bowl.")

Comparison Tasks. Make task cards for blocks and other manipulatives to reinforce the concepts of *more than, less than, the same as.*

Burning the Flame. Using a candle, children can learn about the properties of heat and fire. Light the candle, then have a child slowly place a glass jar over the candle. Ask the children why they think the flame went out. Experiment with many candles and different sizes of jars. Provide stopwatches, and the children can time and record how long it takes for the flame to go out using the different jars.

Mathematics

Mathematics Supplies

Dominos (large and/or small), flannel sets, and flannelboard
Magnetic letters and numbers, magnetic board, fractional parts, and fractional board
Playing cards, checkers and board, chess set and board
Rope (for encompassing areas), puzzles, logs, counting pegs and boards
Blocks of all shapes and sizes, number blocks, parquetry, attribute blocks
Sum stick, adding machine, play money, colored beads, math games, flashcards
Trundle wheel, compass, measuring rods and containers, Cuisenaire rods
Number line, abacus, collections of all types (buttons, coins, stones, sticks, stirrers, macaroni, beans, yarn, marbles, bottle caps)
Egg cartons for making sets
Books (interest and reference)
Catalogs, newspaper ads
Geometric wire forms and patterns
Metric step-on scale, metric platform scale, metric plastic measure set (spoons and cups, 1 ml to 250 ml), balance scale with metric weights 1 g to 50 g
Coin stamps
Calculator
Unfix cubes
Rice and sand (for measuring)

Measuring cups
Geoboards and rubber bands

Numbers

Objectives

1. To show skill in numeration by

    identifying numerals
    comparing sets
    rote counting
    using one-to-one correspondence
    using ordinal numbers
    classifying objects using specific attributes

2. To show knowledge of whole numbers by

    combining two sets of objects
    determining the larger of two sets of objects
    dividing a set into two equal sets
    determining the value of a set when objects are taken away

Number sequencing is fun when we help each other.

Suggested Experiences

Calendar Activities. Valuable learning occurs when children update the calendar on a daily basis. Children can learn recognition of numbers, ordinal numbers ("This is the second day of the month"), and before and after ("Today is Tuesday. What day comes after Tuesday?"), as well as the days of the week and the names of the months.

Using Ordinal Numbers. Teach ordinal numbers through such everyday experiences as lining up for lunch. ("John is the first in line today.")

The Grouping Game. Have the children line up in a row or a circle. Have them count off according to the number of groups to be formed (e.g., for five groups, go down the row, with each child counting off his or her number: 1, 2, 3, 4, 5, 1, 2, 3, and so on). Now ask the children to form groups with the other children who have the same number (all the "1s" in one group, the "2s" in another group, etc.). You expand this game further by asking the children to determine similar characteristics within their groups (e.g., all the girls, all the dark-haired).

Classifying Activities. Analytical thinking and clear expression of thoughts develop through classifying activities. Children learn to recognize particular properties of objects, focus on a certain attribute objects have in common, and label with words the property that certain groups have in common. The teacher shows several objects, such as pieces of plastic fruit, and one object that does not belong, such as a cap. The children are asked which object does not belong and why. This activity can be done with shapes, colors, sizes, and other attributes. It can also be done with people. The teacher selects four or five children, all but one of whom have a common attribute such as wearing tennis shoes or wearing jeans. Let the other children tell which one does not belong.

Suggested Activities

Sorting Task Cards. Make cards designating attributes of particular objects to be sorted, such as blue triangles and orange squares, white beans and brown ones.

Matching Game. Make cards for children to sort. Draw or cut out pieces of people in different professions (doctor, police officer, baseball player, grocery store cashier, etc.). Make other cards with pictures of single items used in each profession (bandage, medicine bottle, stethoscope, hospital bed, etc.). Laminate them. Have the children sort the cards according to the professional and the appropriate professional tool.

Booklets. Make booklets at science centers where children classify objects by attributes as they discover them, such as "Things That Float," "Things That Do Not Float," or "Things Magnets Will Pick Up."

Number Dog. Cut a dog and numbers from tagboard and laminate them. Have the children put the dog together in the correct number sequence. This activity is self-correcting by matching the dog's spots.

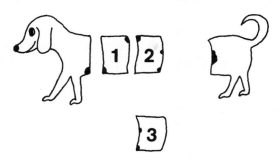

Counting Cards. Using a rectangular tagboard card, write the numeral. Make five small squares near the bottom of the card. Use clothespins to cover each of the little squares. On the back of the card, place the number word, five.

Number Concentration. Make 16 cards. On each pair of cards write a number and a set for that number. Use a piece of tagboard to make a game board for "Concentration." Place the cards face down on the game board. Play as you would "Concentration." The player with the most matches is the winner.

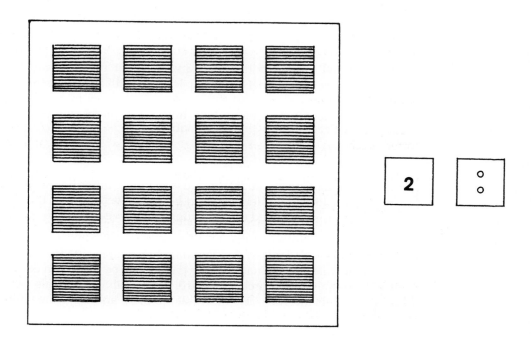

Addition and Subtraction Football. The game board or "football field" can be made with cardboard, laminated tagboard, or a window shade. Two or more children spin the spinner and advance that number of spaces. Yardage is gained if the problem is answered correctly. If not, the player must go back to the spot from which he or she advanced. The first person to get to the goal line wins.

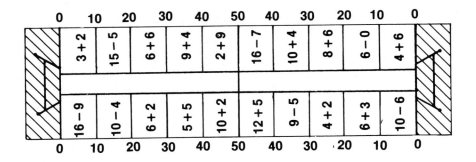

Fractions

Objectives

1. To identify objects that have been divided into two parts.
2. To identify objects that have been divided into halves.

Suggested Experiences

Using Fractions. Opportunities for learning about fractions can be found in classroom experiences almost daily. Experiences with food are often meaningful to children. ("I am going to cut this apple in half. How many pieces are there now? If you break your cookie in half, how many pieces will you have?")

Suggested Activities

Using Measuring Cups. Children can use water or other liquids to measure ½ cup and 1 cup. Provide other cups and bowls as well, so that the children can study and experiment to find out the difference between the two measurements.

Matching. Make task cards of various shapes or figures cut into two equal parts. (For younger children, the name of the picture can be placed on each part.) You can make two halves of a circle or square, or you can use animals such as a fish, a dog, or a cat. Hand the cards out disassembled, and have the children make the halves a whole.

Measurement

Objectives

1. To use direct comparison to classify and determine the size of objects.
2. To identify *before* and *after*.
3. To identify coins and use value.
4. To use hour and minute references in daily vocabulary.

Suggested Experiences

Using Coins. Names of coins can be learned through play in a school store using play money. Children can also learn the names of coins through the experience of buying their lunch at school. ("Lunch costs 75¢. How many quarters is that?" "You had a dollar today. What coin did you receive as change?")

Time Activities. Throughout the day, make the children aware of the time by showing them the clock as they begin a new part of the day. ("It is now 12:30 and it is time for lunch," or "We leave to go home at 2:30. It's time to go.") Not only will this teach the children how to tell time, but it will also help them get into a set routine that may contribute to their "time on task" behavior.

Suggested Activities

Number Relay. Make two sets of numerals 1 to 25 on different-colored pieces of tagboard and laminate them. Designate two teams. Place the numbers, scrambled up, on the floor in front of each team. Team members run to pick up the numbers to place them in sequential order. The first team to place the numbers in correct order wins.

Balance Scale. Use a balance scale to compare weights and sizes of various objects. Have the children record the results.
Variation: Select one object. Let the children sort the remaining objects according to which are heavier, lighter, or weigh the same.

Money Match. Make puzzles using coin ink stamps and an amount to match the coin. Use heads and tails of coins.
Variation: Make puzzles with different coin combinations.

Number Houses. Using colored tagboard, make several houses with windows, each window containing a number fact. The windows open to show the correct answers. Laminate the houses before cutting the windows. The children slip papers inside the house and the open windows to write their answers. Slide the papers out and check them. The answers are inside the windows.

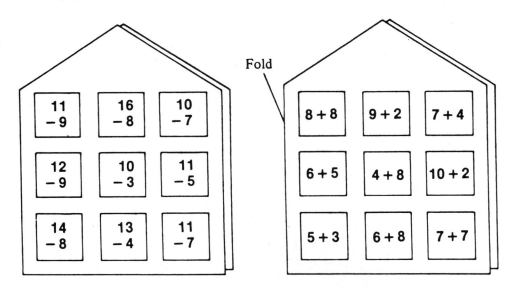

Geometry

Objectives

1. To recognize simple plane and solid figures.
2. To identify and repeat simple geometric patterns.
3. To classify objects by size, position, and shape.

Suggested Experiences

Imitating Patterns. Pattern is the underlying theme of mathematics. The skills involving recognizing and using patterns is a valuable problem-solving tool and can have a very real effect on the development of mathematical understanding.

Children can be introduced to this concept in activities such as reproducing clapping patterns. The teacher claps a pattern and the children join in. The teacher then claps a pattern, the children listen, and then they duplicate it. As the children become more familiar with this activity, individual children can initiate the clapping pattern as the teacher did and then the class repeats afterwards. This activity can be expanded to clap-and-snap patterns.

Making Patterns. Patterns can be made with children themselves. Seating can be arranged in a line of boy, girl or standing and sitting.

Identifying Patterns. Have the children identify patterns visible in the room or on their clothing.

Suggested Activities

Pattern Completion. Make task cards showing the beginning of a pattern for unifix cubes, pattern blocks, beads, or other objects. The children can duplicate these patterns and extend them as far as space or materials allow.

Pattern Creation. Cut shapes of different colors (yellow squares, red circles). Have the children paste the shapes on a large piece of paper in a pattern of their own design. As the children's skills increase, this activity can be expanded to several shapes and colors.

Same Shape and Different Shape. Use a manila file folder and paste pockets on the inside. One pocket is labeled "Same Shape" and the other pocket is labeled "Different Shape," with pictures illustrating same and different. Make 10 cards with 2 objects on each card: 5 the same and 5 different. The student is to sort the cards into the correct pockets. The answers are on the back of the folder to make the activity self-checking. For reinforcement, a ditto sheet can be made so that students can record their results.

Statistics

Objectives

1. To learn to read simple informational charts.
2. To learn to read simple horizontal and vertical bar graphs.

Suggested Experiences

Graphing. Simple graphs can be made with the children's help. Such things as the children's favorite ice creams can be charted on a simple graph. The children can readily see that more of them like chocolate, for example, if some visual evidence is placed before them. They could draw their favorite flavor, cut out the picture of the ice cream cone, and place their favorite in the appropriate column (all the vanillas together, the chocolates, etc.).

Class Graphing. Have the children think of ways in which they can divide themselves into groups (e.g., by the color of their hair or eyes, those wearing red and those who are not). Afterwards, talk about which group had more members and which had less.

Suggested Readings

Books for Children

Anderson, M. (1991). *Food chains: The unending cycle.* Hillside, NJ: Enslow.

Ardley, N. (1991). *The science book of magnets.* New York: Harcourt Brace Jovanovich.

Ardley, N. (1991). *The science book of things that grow.* San Diego, CA: Harcourt Brace Jovanovich.

Branley, F. (1985). *Flash, crash, rumble, and roll.* New York: Crowell.

Dewitt, L. (1991). *What will the weather be?* New York: HarperCollins.

Dineen J. (1989). *Let's look at rain.* New York: Bookwright.

Doubilet, A. (1991). *Under the sea from A to Z.* New York: Crown.

Gardner, R., & Webster, D. (1987). *Science in your backyard.* Englewood Cliffs, NJ: Messner.

Johnson, S. (1986). *How leaves change.* Minneapolis: Lerner.

Schneiper, C. (1989). *Amazing spiders.* Minneapolis: Carolrhoda.

Time-Life Books. (1988). *Things around us.* Alexandria, VA: Author.

Wyatt, V. (1990). *Weatherwatch.* Reading, MA: Addison-Wesley.

Reference Books for Teachers

Allen, D. (1988). *Science demonstrations for the elementary classroom.* Englewood Cliffs, NJ: Parker.

Atkinson, S. (1992). *Mathematics with reason.* Portsmouth, NH: Heinemann.

Cain, A. A., & Sund, R. B. (1989). *Teaching science through discovery.* Columbus, OH: Merrill.

Chaille, C., & Britain, L. (1991). *The young child as scientist.* New York: HarperCollins.

Clayton, L. R. (1991). *Explorations: Educational activities for young children.* Englewood, CO: Teacher Ideas Press.

Crosby, E. (1992). *Alligators to zebras! Whole language activities for the primary grades.* Englewood Cliffs, NJ: Center for Applied Research in Education.

Doris, E. (1991). *Doing what scientists do: Children learn to investigate their world.* Portsmouth, NH: Heinemann.

Harlan, J. D. (1992). *Science experiences for the early childhood years* (5th ed.). New York: Macmillan.

Harlen, W., & Jelly, S. (1990). *Developing science in the primary classroom.* Portsmouth, NH: Heinemann.

Hassard, J. (1990). *Science experiences: Cooperative learning and the teaching of science.* Wilbraham, MA: Wesley.

Hendrick, J. (1988). *The whole child.* Columbus, OH: Merrill.

Hohmann, C. (1991). *High/Scope K–3 curriculum series: Mathematics.* Ypsilanti, MI: High/Scope.

Jacobson, W., & Bergman, A. (1983). *Science activities for children.* Englewood Cliffs, NJ: Prentice-Hall.

Petrash, C. (1992). *Earthways: Simple environmen-*

tal activities for young children. Mount Rainier, MD: Gryphon House.

Poppe, C. A., & VanMatre, N. A. (1985). *Science learning centers for the primary grades.* Englewood Cliffs, NJ: Center for Applied Research in Education.

Reys, R. E., Suydam, M. N., & Lindquist, M. M. (1984). *Helping children learn mathematics.* Englewood Cliffs, NJ: Prentice-Hall.

Wasserman, S., & Ivany, J. W. (1988). *Teaching elementary science: Who's afraid of spiders?* New York: Harper & Row.

Chapter 8

The Social Studies: A Multicultural Emphasis

Social studies is the study of people and cultures. It provides the background for activities that increase students' awareness of their world, nation, state, and community. The social studies program in early childhood education helps children become discerning, capable, and caring citizens committed to a democratic way of life. Such a program prepares them to live in a constantly changing world and to be sensitive to social attitudes, values, and beliefs (Martorella, 1985). "Mastery of the social studies ensures that students will be informed and reflective when they begin to participate in both American culture and the global community" (Chapin & Messick, 1992, p. 4).

Social studies is the single curriculum area that deals entirely with human experiences. It prepares students to accept the rights and responsibilities of citizenship. The social studies program should provide skills, knowledge, attitudes, and values that enable students to become problem solvers and decision makers.

Reflective teachers in early childhood education plan appropriate social studies programs based on the cognitive, social, and physical growth of young children, as described by child development theorists Jean Piaget, Jerome Bruner, Lawrence Kohlberg, and Erik Erikson. The various theories of developmental stages provide meaningful observations on the learning capabilities and limitations of children 4 to 8 years old. Teachers who are familiar with these theories are aware of what to expect from young children and how to nurture their development. The theories imply that children learn through play, exploring, experimenting, and discovering (Martorella, 1985; Seefeldt, 1993).

According to Day (1983), a developmental approach in teaching works because it emphasizes the total child. A developmental program is organized around the needs, interests, and learning styles of children. An active program enables children to participate in experiencing and exploring their social and physical world through observing, predicting, and communicating.

To plan effectively, teachers must reflect on the social studies positions and guidelines published by national organizations such as the National Council of the Social Studies, as well as the goals and objectives of state and local educational agencies (Jarolimek, 1986).

Related Research

Competent teachers are interested in what research reveals about young children, data related to teaching, and how to apply them in the classroom. Current research studies on the human brain indicate that the hemispheres have different cognitive styles, identified as *systematic* and *intuitive*. Studies also suggest that individuals have a learning style preference and a hemispheric preference for perceiving and processing information used in problem solving. Some individuals may prefer the left side of the brain to process information systematically in a linear, sequential, logical way. Others may prefer the right side of the brain to process information intuitively in a holistic, abstract way. Still others prefer a left-right integrated way (Maxim, 1983).

There is an interrelationship between these separate and unique parts working jointly to process information in a complementary manner. "In all kinds of activities the brain uses both hemispheres, perhaps at times each carrying an equal share of a task" (Edwards, 1979). Traditional education programs and teaching strategies stress rational, logical, and analytical thinking, placing minimal value on innovative, experimental thinking. However, researchers and educators such as Roger Sperry, Robert Ornstein, Jerome Bruner, and Robert Samples advocate teaching strategies that exercise right-brain thinking. They also stress the use of techniques integrating both halves of the brain. "We must encourage in the social studies classroom not only systematic problem-solving experiences described in Dewey's description of the injury process, but also the inventive, intuitive thinking that is associated with *creative discovery*" (Maxim, 1983).

In reviewing early research in social studies education, Jantz and Klawitter

(1985) found support for the notion that in processing information children learn through a combination of the verbal, analytical left side of the brain and the nonverbal, synthetical right. Children in preschool and the primary grades are still in the formative stages of establishing their learning style and hemispheric preference and need instructional methods that use both hemispheres equally (Maxim, 1983). Teaching strategies incorporating both modes of thinking strengthen young children's awareness in learning that there is more than one way of solving problems. Thus, they assemble "a repertoire of problem-solving skills" (Wilkerson, 1986, p. 32).

The 4MAT is an instructional model designed by McCarthy (1980) in which teaching strategies speak to learning styles and hemispheric preference. Each of the four learning styles has concepts presented and taught through an eight-step cycle integrating the right-brain mode and left-brain mode of perceiving and processing information (Figure 8-1). Wilkerson (1986) applied the 4MAT system of instruction to evaluate its effects on academic achievement and retention of learning. The outcome of this study indicates that both academic achievement and long-term retention are facilitated significantly by the 4MAT system of instruction rather than by the textbook approach to instruction.

Importance of Social Studies

Students need assistance in understanding themselves and others. They come from many varied backgrounds, bringing with them many different views of life and their world. The way children view themselves and interact with others promotes a positive or negative self-image or awareness. For example,

John disrupts the class because he is impulsive. No one at home listens to him or pays attention to his needs.

Susan's parents spend a lot of time with her and she has traveled all over the world. She brings quite a different view of life to the classroom from John's.

Mark has a learning problem. He cannot read on his grade level. He is often ridiculed by his classmates.

Tonya has a constant fear of not being accepted because she is a minority and has had some unfortunate and unhappy experiences.

Rosa comes from another country and speaks very little English. Rosa and Tonya realize that being different causes them problems in relating to the other students.

Cole is a noisy, outspoken child whose family members have passed their prejudices on to him.

Thus, it cannot be assumed that all students will come to the classroom equipped with the knowledge and readiness required to study the structure of the social sciences.

Not only do children bring a wide range of experiences and interests to the classroom, but they also bring great differences in social, emotional, physical,

Left Hemisphere	Right Hemisphere
III. *Common Sense Learner:* Practice and Personalization	I. *Innovative Learner:* Integrating experience with "Self"
Step 5: Left mode, practicing defined concepts Instructional strategies: worksheets, workbooks, lab books, quizzes Step 6: Right mode, practicing and adding something of oneself Instructional strategies: set up experiments, design projects of own choice	Step 1: Right mode, creating a personal experience related to concept being taught Instructional strategies: guided imagery, simulations, brainstorming Step 2: Left mode, reflecting/analyzing experience and sharing results with others Instructional strategies: peer discussions, group discussions
IV. *Dynamic Learner:* Integrating Application and Experience	II. *Analytic Learner:* Concept Formulation
Step 7: Left mode, analyzing application for relevance, usefulness Instructional strategies: committee reports, murals, graphics, student demonstrations, debates, panel discussions, line graphs, drawings Step 8: Right mode, doing it and applying to new, more complex experience Instructional strategies: field trips, student presentations to the class	Step 3: Right mode, integrating reflective analysis into concepts Instructional strategies: informational films with holistic presentation of the concept, concept mapping, art projects Step 4: Left mode, developing concepts/skills Instructional strategies: lectures, reading assignments, reference reports

Adapted from McCarthy (1980) & Wilerson (1986).

Figure 8-1   Four Learning Styles

and intellectual abilities. These differences in abilities form the basis of other goals and objectives of the social studies for the groups and individual children. (Seefeldt, 1993, p. 24)

A social studies program and the teachers in early childhood education nurture a "sense of self-worth, dignity and a healthy self-concept in each child" (Seefeldt & Barbour, 1986, p. 394). Being valued and accepted in spite of limitations fosters the development of concerned citizens. Developing self-esteem, children learn they are unique individuals sharing similarities with others in their physical and emotional needs. "The more adequate children feel about themselves, the better able they are to reach out and relate to others, and to feel a sense of oneness with people and the things in their world" (Seefeldt & Barbour, p. 394). As young children develop a consciousness of who they are, they realize they have choices and decisions to make about themselves, their relationships with others, and their environment.

Research links the development of the young child's sense of self to school performance and social relationships. Self-concept is distinct from, but correlated with academic self-concept. There is evidence that final grades and certain higher-level thinking processes and self-concept are positively correlated (Stanley, 1985).

Banks and Clegg (1985) have suggested that people must clarify their feelings and values before they can make sound decisions. Children need to practice clarifying values as they solve problems and make decisions by recognizing possible alternatives and consequences, because values often determine what knowledge an individual will accept or reject. The age of the children and their level of moral and cognitive development dictate the appropriate materials and issues to be used in the social studies program on value clarification. Young children understand simple stories and dilemmas that involve values such as honesty, truth, and loyalty.

Young children have a personal form of knowledge (Jarolimek, 1986). Their personal knowledge is on a different level from an adult's, because they do not think logically or abstractly. Another way children develop their thinking capabilities is by depending on reliable and accepted sources such as parents, teachers, and books. However, the time comes when the authority sources are challenged (Jarolimek).

Appropriate Program Content and Methods

A questioning and curious attitude is a young child's natural way of learning. Piaget viewed children as being naturally curious about their surroundings and motivated toward exploration. Teachers must, therefore, capitalize on children's propensity to question and examine and provide them with activities designed to stimulate their curiosity about their environment. These activities should nurture a feeling of continuity with the past and develop a concept of time relating to the past and present (Hatcher, 1985). To reinforce this approach, wise teachers provide an environment in which meaningful learning takes place by presenting concepts within young children's frame of reference. Children are guided toward relating the known and familiar with new and unfamiliar information that broadens their knowledge and experience of the concepts (Jantz & Klawitter, 1985).

The content of such a complex subject is condensed into manageable proportions, which is essential for teachers in planning and teaching and for students in learning. How the concepts are taught is as important as the actual content being taught to young children (Day, 1983).

As part of the SPAN Project, the Research Triangle Institute conducted a survey interviewing social studies teachers in grades K through 12. The results of the survey showed that "commercially published textbooks were one of the central tools for teaching social studies" (Superka, Hawke, & Morressett, 1980, p. 79). In kindergarten through third grade, 65% of the classes were taught using textbooks. Lecture as an instructional strategy was used by 46% of the teachers "just about daily" and by 20% "at least once a week." Discussions were used by 60% of the teachers "just about daily" and by an additional 37% "at least once a week." Periodically teachers used other forms of instruction, such as student reports, library work, role playing, simulation, and "hands on" materials (Superka et al., 1980).

After interviewing 23 students in the 6th grade and 23 students in the 12th grade to find out "Why Kids Don't Like Social Studies," Schug, Todd, and Beery (1984) found that 48% of the students, of which 24% were elementary students, did not think social studies was important and relevant to them. The students found social studies to be boring and repetitious in content and lacking a variety of activities and teaching methods. These insights suggest improving social studies by giving students more opportunity to be actively involved in their learning, through group projects, field trips, discussions, and independent projects.

In the Wilkerson study (1986), both the 4MAT group and the textbook group experimented with concrete objects, drew pictures, saw a filmstrip, and completed worksheets. The teachers' appraisal of the textbook strategies and materials appears to confirm the students' reasons for not liking social studies as described by Schug and colleagues (1984). The textbook strategies were too hard, too rigid, and dull. However, "the 4MAT group was more interested in learning the material, had a more positive attitude toward the lessons, and demonstrated more on-task behavior" (Wilkerson, 1986, p. 92). The children's attitudes toward the two approaches were reflected in the number of activities they liked: The 4MAT group liked 100% of their activities, compared to the 48% of the textbook group.

Concepts, Skills, and Objectives

The study of *history* places human beings and their activities in a specific time frame, whereas the study of *geography* represents the stage for the unfolding of history, giving it a place. Developing the skills needed to make use of available resources so that a society can obtain what it needs and wants is accomplished through the study of *economics*. *Political science* provides an understanding of why and how governments exist, function, and relate to the world. Human behavior in group and individual activity is the emphasis in the study of *anthropology, psychology,* and *sociology*.

Traditionally history and geography have been the supportive pillars of the social studies program. Economics, political science, sociology, and anthropology have been blended into the curriculum through these two disciplines

(Jarolimek, 1986; Banks & Clegg, 1985). However, the program in the primary grades, kindergarten through fourth grade, has been predominantly focused on sociological studies. Units have been planned around narrow and limited topics of low-level concepts such as "Our Family" or "Our Town." But these topics can be extended and developed into interdisciplinary units of generalizations and concepts on the young child's cognitive level (Banks & Clegg). Jarolimek and Parker (1993) have suggested some appropriate terms for expressing concepts that make sense to children:

Concept	For Your Child This Means
Justice	Being or playing fair
Laws	Following rules
Equality of opportunity	Seeing that everyone gets a turn
Cooperation	Working with others
Responsibility	Doing your part or doing your duty

The concept of freedom is too abstract for young children to grasp. But through teaching strategies providing experiences, play, and discussion, they learn that rules and laws are necessary for orderly living. They also begin to understand their responsibility, as individuals in the group, to be considerate of others' rights.

There are three basic types of social studies skills: academic or intellectual skills, self-management skills, and social participation skills.

The *academic* or *scientific skills* relate to the ability to identify, define, and state problems; formulate hypotheses; test hypotheses; locate, organize, and interpret information; and draw conclusions (North Carolina Department of Public Instruction, 1985). Many references are available to help formulate behavioral objectives for the academic skills, such as Bloom's and Krathwohl's taxonomies of cognitive and affective objectives (Bloom, 1956; Krathwohl, Bloom, & Masia, 1964). The *cognitive* objectives include conceptual, skill, and process objectives. These are arranged by level of complexity. The first three categories are knowledge, comprehension, and application. They are prerequisites for the next three categories: analysis, synthesis, and evaluation. Students must have opportunities to move from knowledge and comprehension to higher levels of cognition. The *affective* objectives include values, interests, and attitudes. The awareness of values and attitudes, such as respect for the views of others, freedom of speech, fair play, and equal rights for all, must be developed through a variety of cross-cultural experiences. All of the categories of the affective domain—receiving, responding, valuing, organization, and characterization—will enable the student to experience a deeper dimension of meaning and feeling, in and out of school. The categories in the cognitive and affective domains are relevant to both social studies instruction and daily activities (Michaelis, 1976).

Instruction in *self-management skills* should include techniques to develop abilities that will enable students to deal with managing interpersonal and intergroup relations. They need to develop a sensitivity to others and deal with conflict, diversity, and the major societal changes that are currently taking place (North Carolina Department of Public Instruction, 1985). One of the major societal changes taking place is the widespread movement for freedom and equality of minority groups and women; a second is the increasing involvement in the decision-making and problem-solving processes of both groups and the individual.

Social participation skills deal with group discussion, planning, decision making, and accepting responsibility for such decisions. These decisions concern the problems and solutions of interpersonal and intergroup relations (North Carolina Department of Public Instruction, 1985). Social participation skills should be socially acceptable learned behaviors that enable students to listen and interact in ways that elicit positive responses and achieve the desired objectives set for interacting with other students.

In order to develop a basis for making decisions and become problem solvers, students need a historical perspective. Time is a concept that is slow to develop in a child's mind. It is not until about the age of 9 that a real understanding of time begins to develop (Schlereth, 1980). History begins in the here and now, but experiences of seeing and handling artifacts and visiting a museum, historical markers, or old houses can be a beginning in relating the past to young children. Recognizing holidays helps make children aware of the past and appreciate it (Jarolimek, 1986).

The study of geography provides young children many concrete-direct opportunities to observe, collect, and record data and to use simple charts. They become familiar with the various tools used to study the features of the earth. These tools are maps, globes, charts, graphs, tables, reference books, and photographs (Maxim, 1983).

Concepts related to anthropology are integrated into most of the other social studies disciplines. Yet children can begin to understand that people in all cultures share the need for love, protection, food, and recreation. Different cultures satisfy their needs in a variety of ways according to their customs and values (Banks & Clegg, 1985).

Transportation, communication equipment, and other forms of technology have made the world a smaller place in which to live. International problems and concerns face all who live on this planet. It is important to address global education in the social studies program. Opportunities and activities to enable children to recognize and appreciate the global society and its multicultural composition must be provided. Teachers and students must be broadened ethnocentrically. Judging another culture only from one's own point of view affects objectivity. Negative and biased feelings toward different groups must be discussed. Feelings need to be expressed and likes as well as dislikes acknowledged in order to help tomorrow's adults understand and feel the unity that underlies overt human differences (Martin, 1985). Young children learn about other countries through studying family structure. They learn about countries through music, art, literature, and resource people in the community (Jarolimek, 1986).

Modern technology is making it possible to solve some current problems more satisfactorily. However, along with these technological advances come more complex problems. The concern for quantity and quality of goods and services, energy and resource waste, the rising cost of satisfying basic needs, population growth in urban areas, pollution, and longer life expectancy, require concerted action using self-management skills and techniques (Michaelis, 1976).

Key sociological concepts integrated with economic concepts promote understanding of interdependence and self-worth in young children. Children learn about interdependence from the concepts *scarcity* and *plenty;* the meaning of *consumers* and *producers;* and the advantages of *division of labor* (Seefeldt & Barbour, 1986).

Social concerns and current affairs are important aspects of the social studies program. Learning about the unresolved problems of the present day helps children to become aware of being responsible and caring about people (Martorella, 1985). In the past, developing valuing skills and learning how to become an active participant in society have involved a collaboration among the family, church, and school. These basic social institutions are part of the major societal changes that are currently taking place. Schools must address an educational challenge of enormous magnitude as students enter school with a wide range of individual differences in values and ethics. Social expectations are also changing, posing still another challenge to the schools.

The media are powerful socializers. Television is the most influential medium. A 1981 Nielsen report found that the average viewing time for children between the ages of 6 and 7 was 26 hours a week and for 2- to 5-year-olds it was 29 hours a week. This is approximately 3½ hours a day. Schools have become less valued as television viewing has increased. Little influence is exerted by the schools in determining what children see and what television produces. Much of television's content conflicts with the schools' purposes and objectives. Emotion, instant gratification, and entertainment are the focus of television, while rational thinking and delayed satisfaction are among the objectives of the educational system (Cartledge & Milburn, 1986; Stephens, 1983).

Issues that voters must consider in this nuclear age are overwhelming to an intelligent, well-informed adult; yet an 18 year old encounters this responsibility also. Social concerns and issues to be addressed include global perspective education; energy and environmental education; career education; multiethnic, ethnic, and racial awareness; law-related education; and gender equity. Other issues include teaching about individuals with disabilities, the aging, and nuclear issues. Current affairs instruction is important for producing well-informed people. For young children, "making their own news may be the beginning of current events. The experience of contributing to the news story and of sharing news items and events helps children understand the concept of news" (Seefeldt, 1984, p. 111).

Social studies skills are taught within the content of the disciplines being studied. The teacher carefully plans the development of the skills in a systematic and sequential order. Ample practice is provided through the regular lessons and units. Social studies skills taught during the program are thinking skills, research skills, chronological and time skills, map and globe skills, writing skills, social skills, and new technological skills (Martorella, 1985).

Evaluation of achievement in a social studies program is intended to (a) assess the effectiveness of instruction; (b) determine whether or not instructional goals have been accomplished; and (c) provide feedback to students about their performance (Banks, 1985). Evaluation techniques are both informal and formal. Informal evaluation techniques include group discussions, observations, checklists, conferences, anecdotal records, work samples, portfolios, experience summaries, diaries, and logs. Formal evaluation techniques include teacher-made tests, criterion-referenced tests, and standardized tests.

The Social Studies Program

In this time of rapid change, increasingly finer judgments must be exercised to address more complex situations. Information alone seldom causes learning to take place and behavior to change. Motivation, incentives, and relevant activities that force choices and responses must be part of the social studies curriculum if the complex social changes are to be addressed.

It is hoped that the suggestions that follow will help teachers identify needs, state objectives, and implement activities that will help young children accept the rights and responsibilities of citizenship as they gain a better understanding of their world.

Objectives

1. To learn how to solve problems and make decisions at the appropriate level of development.
2. To accept and value the unique qualities of one's self and others.
3. To develop a positive self-concept.
4. To become more independent and responsible for one's own actions.
5. To recognize and accept one's own feelings and the feelings of others.
6. To express one's feelings in acceptable ways.
7. To develop social interaction skills.
8. To understand one's role within the family.
9. To understand the need for rules and laws.
10. To develop an awareness of one's own cultural traditions, as well as the traditions of other cultures.
11. To develop an appreciation of America's heritage.
12. To develop an awareness of varying life styles within one's own culture.

13. To develop a general awareness of community and the services communities provide.
14. To become aware of the need for civic responsibility and values.
15. To develop a beginning concept of the justice system.
16. To explore beginning concepts of politics and local government.
17. To study people and cultures around the world.
18. To learn about the community's relationship to the world at large.
19. To become aware of a need to change stereotyped attitudes about minority groups.
20. To learn about the environment and its relationship to human life and to investigate environmental problems and solutions.
21. To explore concepts of economics and use of economic resources.
22. To learn about economic processes, ideas, and problems and to be wise consumers.
23. To learn and practice skills in reading, following, and interpreting maps, globes, graphs, and charts.
24. To develop an understanding of time and chronology.
25. To develop an understanding of new technology.

Mrs. Drake introduces a new social studies unit on dinosaurs during total group time.

Environmental Resources

Table and four to six chairs
One or two individual desks
Bulletin board
Display areas on counters or bookshelves
Storage space for unit materials
Small display rack for books
Cubbie-style bookcases for games and activities
Carpeted floor space for children to play games, read, and do other activities

Materials

Globe and maps
Charts, posters, graphs, and cartoons
Study prints, photographs
Reference books
Biographies
Historical fiction books
Periodicals, magazines, and catalogs
Real objects (flags, coins, costumes)
World atlas
Cassette player with earphones
Flannelboard
Puzzle, games, models, and replicas
Filmstrip projector
Overhead projector and transparencies
Slide projector and color transparency slides
Television and VCR
Microcomputer and software
Works of art (paintings, drawings, sculptures, basketing, pottery)
Art materials (paints, easels, chalk, crayons, clay, paste)
Paper for writing, construction, art projects
Blocks and transportation toys
Cooking equipment and utensils
Clothing and props for dramatic role playing
Social studies textbooks

Self-Awareness and Interpersonal Relations

Suggested Activities

Life-Sized Body Outline. Have the children construct and stuff life-sized bodies. They have their bodies traced by the teacher or another student and then color or paint in their features and add fabrics, scraps, or other materials for detail. They cut out the traced body.

Variation. The children or the teacher staple the traced body to another large piece of paper. They cut out the second piece of paper to be the back of the body, then color the back to match the front of the body. They stuff the body with crushed newspaper and staple the edges.

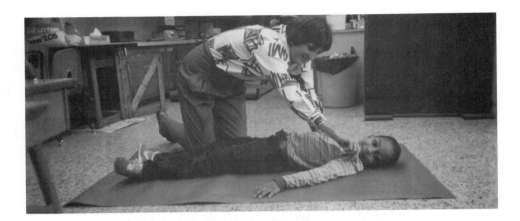

Autobiographies. Have the children write or dictate stories about themselves and their families.

"Me" Puppet. Ask the children to make a hand puppet to represent themselves. They can choose from a variety of materials such as paper plates, socks, paper bags, fabric pieces, buttons, yarn, shredded paper, crayons, paints, and colored markers to make the puppet.

Time Lines. The children first develop a time line showing important personal dates such as births of brothers and sisters, when they started school, and when they lost their first tooth. They then create a time line of the important dates and events of the community to help them develop a concept of time as well as identify historical events.

Feelings Chart. Have the children place a face on a chart that expresses how they feel during the school day.

Footprints and/or Hand Collages. Have the children paint or print their feet and hands on a large class mural to show individual differences.

Yum Yum! and Yuck! Books. Encourage the children to express their personal preferences by cutting out magazine pictures or drawing pictures to show things that they like or dislike.

Captions. Have the children write captions about feelings they see illustrated in pictures or drawings.

"Friendly Way to Talk" Game. Have the children enact appropriate ways to communicate with others.

People Collages. Ask the children to cut out magazine pictures representing a variety of cultural and ethnic groups and arrange these pictures on a large piece of construction paper or cardboard.

What Color Is Happy? Have the children write or dictate stories about the color(s) that make them happy. Ask them to illustrate the stories.

Feelings. Provide the children with a flannelboard to create faces that express different emotions. Cutouts of eyes and mouths are added to large flannel faces.

I Like. Have the children make a capital "I" out of paper and print the word LIKE at the top of the letter and their name at the bottom of the letter. They can draw or cut out pictures from magazines showing what foods, sports, subjects, games, places, and hobbies they like.
Variation: I Like, I Dislike. The children draw or cut out pictures showing their likes and dislikes to put on the poster.

Sociodrama. Provide the children with a variety of hypothetical problem situations and have them use role playing to act out appropriate responses.
Situation: Two children are in the math center creating patterns with parquetry blocks. A third child asks to join them.
Question: What would you say to the person? (A teacher or parent leads the discussions, asking further questions that will make the children think creatively about the situation.)

My Number Facts. Have the children make a chart writing the appropriate numbers for their birthdate, weight, height, address, telephone number, number of people in their family, and grade level.

My Number Facts

Birthday..........Feb. 10, 1988
Weight............................40 lbs.
Height............................45 ins.
Address.............1316 Elm St.
Phone number......368-0219
Family.......................................5
Grade.......................................2

Coat of Arms. Ask the children to assess their strengths and weaknesses by making their own coat of arms. A shield is drawn and divided into six equal sections. Each section is devoted to one of the following: (1) People in My Family; (2) Two Things I Enjoy Doing with My Family; (3) Two Things I Do Well; (4) Two Things I Would Like to Do Better; (5) One Thing I Do Most in My Spare Time; and (6) My Occupation When I Grow Up. Each section is illustrated.

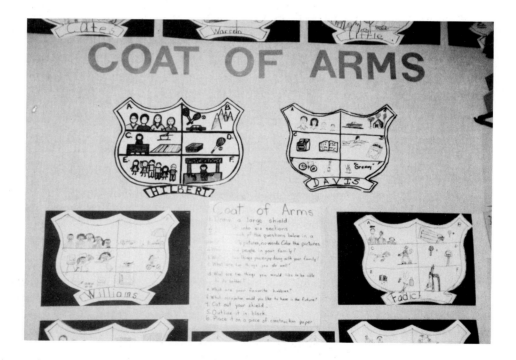

Big Cheese. Each week, select a child to be the Big Cheese. The child fills out a personal data sheet (Figure 8-2), draws a self-portrait, and furnishes a photograph. This will be displayed on the Big Cheese bulletin board. At the end of the week, each class member writes a paragraph telling specific reasons why this person is special. The Big Cheese takes these stories home in a special folder.

The Big Cheese

_____ is
the big cheese!
My address is _____

_____.
_____ is my phone
number. I was born in the town
of _____, in the
state of _____.
My eyes are _____ and the
color of my hair is _____.
I wear _____ sized shoes.
Some of my favorites:
Colors: _____
Food: _____
Song: _____
T V Program: _____
School Subject: _____
Friends: _____
The people who live at my house are _____

_____.
The things I like to do are _____

_____.

Figure 8-2.   Personal Data Sheet

Helpers Chart. Assign classroom responsibilities to the children using a helpers chart.

Assignment Sheet. Use assignment sheets to help the children become independent workers. A sample assignment sheet is shown in Figure 8-3.

Stereotyping

Intervention to reduce sex-role stereotyping and its effects on competencies, attitudes, and behaviors is needed in the early years. All children need to learn how to interact with people different from themselves, whether the difference is of race, sex, or learning style.

Suggested Activities

Mixed-Gender Small Groupings. Create interaction between the sexes by putting both boys and girls in all groupings.

Unisex Labels. Label all learning and play activities as appropriate for both boys and girls.

Leadership. Provide all pupils with equal roles of leadership in many different situations.

Feelings and Emotions. Have the children engage in role-playing situations that enable both boys and girls to express their feelings.

Daily Assignments			Name:		
Monday			**Thursday**		
Name and number of paper	Check when you finish	Teacher Check	Name and number of paper	Check when you finish	Teacher Check
Tuesday			**Friday**		
Name and number of paper	Check when you finish	Teacher Check	Name and number of paper	Check when you finish	Teacher Check
Wednesday			How many assignments did you complete this week?	what would you like to do better?	
Name and number of paper	Check when you finish	Teacher Check			

Figure 8-3.   Sample Assignment Sheet

Assertiveness Training. Provide puppets for the children to use to act out situations in which they need to speak up for themselves.

Communicating Positive Statements. Help the children improve their social and communication skills by having them complete sentences such as the following (Ellis, 1977):

I feel best when I _____.

I feel proud that I can _____.

I have learned that I can _____ as well as a member of the opposite sex.

I was surprised that I could _____.

Female Role Models. Present a unit of study on a selection of women to learn of their important contributions to society in the past and present. Some suggested role models are Abigail Adams (see box), Helen Keller, March Fong Eu, Sarah Winnemucca, and Carmen Delgado Cotaw. Have the children do research; read biographies; discuss the historical, social, economic, and political issues present; and study the family structures of each role model. They illustrate their findings by creating shadow boxes, dioramas, time lines, videos, movie-roll boxes, or murals (Women's Education Equity Act Program, 1985).

Abigail Adams
(Nov. 11, 1744–Oct. 28, 1818)

by Jean M. Molinari

When Abigail was growing up in the Massachusetts Bay Colony, she seemed to have three families. What do you think that would be like? Because of her health, Abigail was sometimes sent to live at her Grandmother Quincy's house. Other times she lived in the city with her Aunt Smith. Between her long visits to their houses she lived with her parents in the country eight miles away. How would you feel moving around this much? Abigail enjoyed it very much. She felt like a welcome guest in all three houses.

You may find this hard to believe, but girls couldn't go to school when Abigail was growing up. Luckily, her father had a large library of books. She was taught to read by her relatives. Her grandparents were very interested in politics and encouraged her to read, discuss and think about life in the colonies, freedom, people's rights and government. This was how she found out that women did not have any legal rights under British Colonial Laws. Abigail did not think this was fair, but what could she do about it?

When she was 19 years old, she married John Adams. He was a lawyer who wanted to change unjust British laws. It was because of these unjust laws that John became involved in starting a new government for the colonies. His work kept him away from the family home. This was difficult for Abigail. She was glad that John was working on the laws for their new country. She was eager to help him with her ideas about the new government.

Working on the new government in Philadelphia did not pay John any money. It was

(continued)

up to Abigail to take care of all their family business matters. Abigail ran their small farm in Braintree. She provided the food, clothes, and other supplies for the family.

In order to have a new government the Colonies had to become independent from the British. This is what led to the Revolutionary War. Sometimes the war was fought very close to the Adams farm. Abigail was afraid the children might get hurt. She thought that they might have to hide in the woods so the British army would not find them.

Abigail was a very brave woman. One time the British soldiers were very close to her house. Lots of her neighbors had left their farms because they were afraid that the British soldiers and the American soldiers would fight right on their land. People told Abigail to take her children and leave, too. She and the children stayed. When the American soldiers went by the farm, Abigail gave them food and water. She also gave the soldiers her dishes made of pewter metal. Even though she liked her dishes very much, she and the soldiers melted them and used the soft metal to make bullets. Instead of running away, she stayed to help, and she helped in many ways.

Abigail was responsible for her family's home and money for a long time. One way she earned money was by having John send her things from Europe when he was there working. Abigail made a list of things that were hard to buy in the Colonies, like straight pins. John would send these things to Abigail. She would sell them to her neighbors.

Under Abigail's care the farm grew bigger and bigger as she saved money and bought more land. She taught their five children to read, write, and do arithmetic. When they grew older the boys went to school, but there were still no schools for girls. Luckily, they could learn at home from their mother and the family books, just as Abigail had done.

The education of women was very important to Abigail. She wanted women to be equal with men. She wrote John many letters when he was working on the new government.

(continued)

She asked that the new laws take care of men and women equally. She wanted the new government to listen to what the women had to say.

Abigail taught her children that slavery was wrong. "No one should buy, sell or own another person," she said. When the laws of the new government were written, they allowed people to own slaves. Abigail knew that this was wrong.

To protest the new laws, she wrote many letters. She wrote to friends, family members, and statesmen. In fact, she wrote over 2,000 letters during her life!

Abigail Adams and her family were important people in the beginning years of the United States. Her husband, John, was the second President of the United States. Her son, John Quincy Adams, became the sixth President of the United States. Her husband and her son both learned from Abigail's leadership and often asked for her help.

Abigail did not give up! She was a leader. She was one of the first people in this country to talk and write about equality for women and freedom for slaves.

LISTENING QUESTIONS

1. How many families did Abigail have when she was growing up?
2. Why didn't Abigail go to school?
3. What did Abigail and the American soldiers do with her pewter dishes?
4. What did Abigail do when she thought something was not fair?

SUGGESTED ACTIVITIES

Discussion

Abigail Adams wanted women to have a voice in the new United States government after the Revolutionary War. She believed that women should have full rights to own property and to vote. Did women have these rights after the Revolutionary War? What are some of the rights women are working for today? Who are some of the leaders of today's women's movements?

Activities

1. Have the whole class imagine that they are growing up during the time of Abigail Adams. Remind them that books are scarce and that there are no public libraries. How will they learn to read and write? Have each student write and then give a short speech in class telling why they think there should be schools for both girls and boys. In their speeches, they should tell why being able to attend school is important to them.
2. To encourage your students to learn more about American government and how it works, discuss the school's system of authority. Have the class write and send a letter to the student council asking a representative to come to class and answer students' questions. What does the student council do? Who are the members? How does someone become a member? Have the class write a similar letter to the school's Board of Education. Discuss in advance what questions the visitor will be asked. Have each student write down three questions to ask. Have the students write down the answers when they learn them too.

(continued)

3. After reading the story of Abigail Adams have each student write a letter of advice to someone who decides on new laws: the city mayor, the state governor, or the president of the United States. The letter should offer advice about something the student feels is important.

4. Abigail Adams ran the farm business that supported her family. She conducted business in many different ways to raise money. What types of work do your students' mothers do outside and inside their homes to help support the family? Have each student write a short story about his or her mother and the various kinds of work she does.

Name _____

KEY WORDS

Fill in the blanks with the words that best complete the sentences. Choose from the following words:

business   rights   laws   colony   ideas

1. Abigail found out that women did not have any _____.
2. One _____ Abigail had was selling things to other people.
3. She told John her _____ about equality.
4. The United States was a _____ of the British.
5. Abigail Adams wanted the new _____ to include women's rights.

TRUE OR FALSE?

Write T if the statement is true. Write F if the statement is false.

_____1. Abigail sold her dishes to the soldiers so they could make bullets.
_____2. Abigail Adams was the wife of the second president of the United States.
_____3. She wrote over 2,000 important letters.
_____4. Abigail believed in freedom for all people.
_____5. She supported her farm and her family by her very hard work.

WRITE ON

On another sheet of paper, write a letter to Abigail Adams telling her what it is like to be a child living today. Think about what she would like to know.

Source: Women's Educational Equity Act Program (1985). *Women as Members of Communities: Third Grade Social Studies.*

Literacy Story Paper. Have the children write articles about the female role models for a literary story paper, recognizing and presenting these women as independent, worthwhile individuals with an intellectual, political, economic, and social life of their own (Chilcoat, 1985).

Famous African Americans. Have the children read available books, magazines, and newspaper articles to learn about and develop an appreciation of the contributions of some famous African Americans. They can also study entertainment programs and posters.

Community and Career Awareness

Suggested Activities

Careers or Places Riddles. Ask the children to write riddles about careers or places in the community. For example, "What would you be if you worked on a farm?"

Then and Now. The children can learn about their community and become historians by preparing a questionnaire about the types of schools, businesses, places of entertainment, shopping areas, and other aspects of the community. Using a tape or video recorder, they can administer the questionnaire to a grandparent or neighbor who has lived in the community for at least 50 years. Then they will compile the responses and make a comparison of the community *then* and *now* (Carroll, 1985).

Picture Album. Have the children bring pictures of old schools, the downtown, homes, fashions, and historical views of the community that their families allow them to borrow from the family album. They can make a display of the pictures.

Slide Show. The Chamber of Commerce may have a prepared slide show of important places in the community that it will share. Parents or other resource people may have slides available to help the children gain a better visual image of places in the community.

Community Helpers Task Cards. Have the children match pictures of helpers with the words that identify each picture. Colored shoestrings (or yarn) are used for matching, and the back of each card is color coded for self-correction.

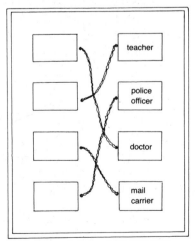

Other community helper charts can include garbage collector, electrician, plumber, firefighter, grocer, farmer, butcher, gardener, librarian, cashier, nurse

Mapping. After a walk around the neighborhood or community, ask the children to construct models or maps of streets and landmarks on a table or in the block area.

Build a Neighborhood. Have the children build a neighborhood or school community using cartons, boxes, or blocks.

Public Safety. Have the children draw roads and then discuss solutions to traffic problems that arise.

Puzzle: "People and Their Jobs." Have the children match pictures of workers with their job titles.

Places in the City Sorting Game. Provide the children with laminated cutouts of pictures associated with the zoo, library, park, supermarket, post office, department store, hardware store, school, dentist's office, doctor's office, bank, and restaurant. Ask them to sort and classify the pictures.

Working Moms and Dads. Have the children interview their parents about the kind of work they do. They can give oral or written reports about these occupations.

Career Awareness Centers and Materials. Set up a career awareness center including the following props:

A community within the classroom would be incomplete without a police station. This public safety officer is in the communication division.

Role-playing in a real bank is lots of fun. We learn all about banks
and the people who work there.

1. *Cosmetologist.* Wigs, rollers, clips and pins, comb, brush, mirror (turned
   horizontal) on table, hair dryer, apron, shampoo container.
2. *Barber.* Comb, scissors, shaving cream, apron, shampoo containers.
3. *Secretary.* Dictionary, telephone, typewriter, letters, paper, pen.
4. *Health worker.* First aid kit, thermometer, stethoscope.

This doctor is going through a practice session on
broken bones.

5. *Carpenter.* Tools, wood, yardstick, ruler, nails.
6. *Librarian.* Books, stamp, desk, computer.
7. *Construction worker.* Wooden trucks, hard hats.
8. *Truck driver.* Truck, traffic signs, cargo.
9. *Banker.* Puppet stage for window, checkbooks, play money, adding machine.
10. *Postal worker.* Window, stamps, letter scales, pencil, money, cash register.
11. *Baker.* Stove, cooking utensils, apron, hat.

Resource People. Invite people of different occupations to the classroom. Have the children interview them and draw pictures and write stories about these occupations.

Community Resources. Take the children on field trips to places in the community. Visit factories, plants, industrial bakeries, farms, radio and TV stations, stables, fish markets, pet shops, florists, grocery stores, lumber yards, zoos, museums, fire stations, and construction sites. Have them dictate or write stories and poems, draw or paint pictures, and cook or build something they saw on the trip.

Our class went on a field trip to the circus.

Community Worker Puppets. Have the children make puppets from lunch-sized bags to dramatize workers and their jobs.

Creative Writing. Have the children design a brochure telling why their community is a good place to live. They can include the places of interest, type of climate, location, natural and man-made resources, educational and health-care facilities, and recreation and entertainment opportunities. This could be a culminating activity to the study of the community.

Places

Suggested Activities

Imaginary Trips. Help the children plan a trip to the beach or mountains, a hike, a picnic in the park, or a trip to Washington, DC, or the capital city in their state.

Imaginary Place. Have the children make a map of a make-believe place and write a story. The map should include symbols and a key.

Tracing on Maps. Have the children trace routes from their city to other cities or places on maps.

My State. Have the children fill in pertinent information about their state on a map. They can draw in the state flower, bird, or tree.

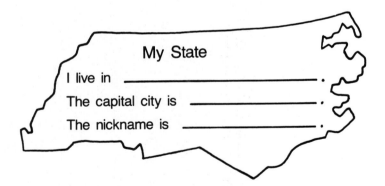

Where Do You Live? With the help of visuals, help the children learn where they live in relationship to the earth, continent, country, state, and city. Visuals can include a map of the community, pictures of the earth, continent, country, and state. Have the students locate their street on the map and with yarn connect a line from their street to their name card.
Variation: Have the children draw and color a picture of their home and label it with their address. They can use yarn to connect their picture with the community map.

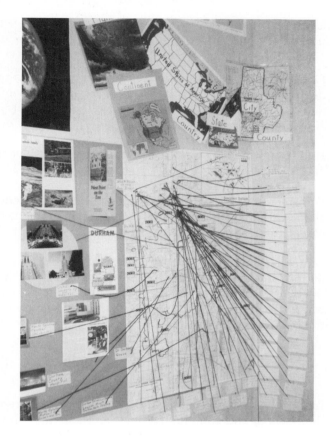

The Need for Rules and Laws

Suggested Activities

Classroom Rules. Help the children formulate a list of six or seven classroom rules.

Consequences of No Rules. Discuss with the children a hypothetical situation of a school that has no rules. Have them brainstorm both problems and solutions for this situation.

Conclude That Communities Everywhere Need Rules and Laws. Ask the children to research another culture and compare that culture's laws with the laws of the United States. This research can be done by interviewing people who have lived in other countries. A recording can be made of the interview and kept in a listening center.

Understanding the Justice System

Suggested Activities

Fair and Unfair Rules. Have the children engage in a problem-solving activity to determine whether the school rules most often broken are fair or unfair. If they determine that the rules are unfair, should the rules be changed or deleted? Have the children graph their data.

Understanding the Difficulty of Fair Judgment. Have the children read, discuss, and role play *The Little Red Hen* or similar stories.

Understanding Certain Aspects of the Justice System. Help the children learn about laws that protect and laws that constrain by having a lawyer and a police officer visit the class.

Understanding the Rights of Individuals. Have the children read and discuss the Bill of Rights. Cooperative learning groups can choose an amendment from the Bill of Rights and list examples of how it applies to daily activities. Groups can also categorize hypothetical activities as being protected or not protected by the Bill of Rights.

The Need for Civic Responsibility

Suggested Activities

Identifying Civic Responsibilities. Have the children participate in improving their school and community. Let them tour the school and list improvements that are needed. They can chart a course of action and set up committees to make the improvements. This idea can be extended into the community. Families, school administrators, and city or county officials can be called upon to help. An article can be written about the project for the school newspaper and local newspaper (McGowan, 1985).

Identifying Good Citizenship. Ask the children to list the rights and responsibilities of a good citizen at school. They can apply their knowledge within the classroom by using a "helpers chart" to share routine duties and by abiding by the classroom rules. Older students can extend their responsibility beyond the classroom by signing up to assist with duties in the library, computer and science labs, office, lunchroom, and playground.

Local Government

Suggested Activities

Elections. Have the children monitor local and national political campaigns by recording candidate's statements, collecting data about issues, and tabulating the number of broadcast appearances by each candidate.

Identifying Some Elected Officials. Ask the children to describe the position and duties of elected officials such as a judge, mayor, or commissioner. Invite local officials to visit the classroom and discuss their jobs.

Changing Stereotyped Attitudes About Officials and Leaders

Suggested Activities

Attitude Survey. Discuss with the children what makes a good leader. Have them fill out an attitude survey (see box) with the knowledge that it will not be graded (Women's Educational Equity Act Program, 1985).

Attitude Survey

Name_____

Write yes or no after each of the following statements.
1. Anyone can be a leader. _____
2. Different kinds of groups need different kinds of leaders. _____
3. Many women have worked to make laws fairer for everyone. _____
4. Leaders need help in making decisions. _____
5. Sometimes third graders are group leaders. _____
Finish this sentence with your own ideas.
I like leaders who are _____
_____

Name two things you think would happen if a woman were president of the United States.

1. _____
_____

2. _____
_____

Becoming Acquainted with a Leader. Students read about the life of Shirley Chisholm (see box). After they have read of her life and leadership, they take the attitude survey again to see whether they have changed their attitudes (Women's Educational Equity Act Program, 1985).

Shirley Chisholm
(November 30, 1924–)

By Dorothy L. Bristol

Have you ever been told to stop fighting? This is the story of a little girl who grew up to be a fighter. She didn't fight by hitting people. She fought by helping them. This little girl was poor. She was an African American and very small in size. She had trouble speaking.

(continued)

When this little girl grew up, she worked very hard to help people live better. For this reason, she is called a fighter.

The little girl's name is Shirley Chisholm. She was born in 1924 in Brooklyn, New York. Her parents were from Barbados, an island in the Caribbean Sea. Do you know where that is?

Shirley's mother did sewing for people and her father worked in a bakery. The family was very poor. Their apartment had no heat. Sometimes Shirley and her two sisters had to stay in bed just to keep warm in the winter. There was always a lot of love in Shirley's family. Their love for each other kept their hearts warm and feeling good.

Shirley's parents did not have enough money to take care of their children. One day Shirley's mother packed boxes with food and clothing. She took Shirley and her sisters to Barbados by boat. The boat trip took nine days. Shirley was just three years old.

Shirley, her sisters and her mother went to her grandmother's farm in Barbados. Shirley's mother stayed there with the children for six months. Then she went back to New York to work and save money. Shirley and her sisters did not get to see their mother and father again for seven long years.

Shirley loved the farm, and she loved her grandmother. The children had chores to do to help with the farm work. They carried water. They fed the ducks and chickens. They gathered eggs. They took care of the sheep, goats and cows.

Life on grandmother's farm was not all work. Sometimes the children went swimming in the blue Caribbean Sea. They played in the sand together and enjoyed each other's company. Shirley started school when she was four years old. By the time she was five years old she could read and write.

When Shirley was ten years old, she and her sisters returned to New York. The family was happy to be living together again. Shirley graduated from high school and went to college in New York. When she finished college she became the director of a nursery school. Later she was in charge of a child care center.

(continued)

Shirley Chisholm loved children. She also liked to work with adults. She felt many people weren't being treated fairly and she wanted to change this. She decided to try to get elected to the state government. In this way, she could help make laws that would protect people's rights in her state. Shirley told the voters what she wanted to do and they elected her! She served in the state government for four years. Next, she decided to run for a higher government office. Shirley Chisholm became the first African American woman in the entire country to be elected to the House of Representatives. Now she would be able to help decide on laws for the entire country.

While Shirley was working to make new laws, she called herself "fighting Shirley Chisholm." How Shirley did fight! She fought for health care, child care and good housing. She fought for laws to help make people's lives better. She fought for equal rights for women, for African Americans and for other groups of people who are not being treated fairly.

In 1972, Shirley Chisholm tried to be elected president of the United States. She did not win this, but she showed people something. She showed people that you can be a successful fighter even if you grew up as a poor, African American girl with a speech impairment.

Shirley Chisholm is now teaching, speaking, and writing. She especially likes to talk to students. She says that America's future depends on our girls and boys. She hopes that the new leaders will be women and men of every color. Shirley Chisholm hopes that these new leaders will be fighters for equal rights for all people, too.

LISTENING QUESTIONS

1. How does Shirley Chisholm "fight"?
2. What kind of work does Shirley do?
3. What does she fight for?

SUGGESTED ACTIVITIES

Discussion

1. After reading the Chisholm biography, have the students discuss leaders they know who are women. Who are they? What kinds of roles do they fill as leaders? What qualities do these women possess that make them leaders? Don't limit the discussion to elected leaders only. Consider the school principal, the president of the PTA, the head librarian, or school nurse, as well as other women in more political leadership roles.
2. Discuss an election. What does it mean to vote? Have the students hold an election with two candidates running for the same office (they can decide what the office will be). How are candidates chosen? Who gets to vote? Discuss the fact that men and women of all colors worked hard to get voting rights for African Americans and women. It was because of their work and the work of other women leaders that Shirley Chisholm was able to run for office. Help the class understand that Shirley Chisholm's candidacy for president was an important step toward the nomination of Geraldine Ferraro for vice president in 1984.

Activities

1. Help your class learn about their state representatives. Have the class write a letter to their representative. Have them write about issues that they think are important. Have them ask the representative about the issues on which she/he is working.

(continued)

2. Shirley Chisholm did not see her mother for seven years while she stayed at her grandmother's farm in Barbados. Ask your students if they have ever been apart from someone very special to them for such a long time. Ask them how they felt during that time. Have your students write a letter to someone very special in their lives whom they have not seen for a long time.

3. Have your students write a story about Shirley Chisholm. Ask them to write about ways they are like Shirley. Ask them to write about ways they are different from her.

Source: Women's Educational Equity Act Program (1985). *Women as Members of Communities: Third Grade Social Studies.*

Understanding Time and Chronology

Suggested Activities

Telling Time. Young children can grasp the concept of time by associating activities with the terms *today, yesterday,* and *tomorrow,* as well as *day* and *night.* Have them categorize pictures using these terms and sequence pictures of their daily schedule at school.

Calendar. The cyclical nature of days, weeks, and months can be represented by the use of a classroom calendar. The calendar can include birthdays, holidays, and special events. Have the children decorate each month's calendar with a seasonal theme.

History

Suggested Activities

Famous African Americans Crossword Puzzle. Have the children complete the crossword puzzle illustrated here, filling in the last name of the famous African American. The children will use pictures as clues, with or without name labels.

Across

1. A famous conductor of the underground railroad.
2. A famous professional male tennis player and civil rights activist.
3. A scientist and inventor who developed many uses for the peanut and over 500 new dye colors.
4. An important civil rights leader who was assassinated.

Down

1. A poet and short story writer.
2. A beloved jazz trumpeter.

Family Photos. Have the children bring two photos of their families to class, showing them in the past and present. They will compare and contrast the pictures by writing or dictating stories about the photos, giving informational data about their families.

Old Book Collection. Have the children bring old storybooks from home to compare with the present-day storybooks. Ask them to discuss what is alike and what is different.

Then and Now Museum. Have the children research how technology has changed life styles. They will look for kitchen utensils, clothes, toys, home appliances, communication and transportation products, and home and family care products that were used years ago and are no longer needed. They might find some of these items in attics, grandparents' homes, or other places, and they can bring appropriate ones to school to display (Hatcher, 1985).

New Treasures. Have the children determine whether the outmoded objects from the past still have value. They can make a chart, labeling the object, its original use, and suggestions for ways it can be used now (Hatcher, 1985).

Presidents. Have the children gather information about the current president and record their findings. They will record the president's full name, state of birth, occupation before becoming president, and three other interesting facts. *Variation:* Have them gather information on a previous president and record their findings. They will record the same information as above.

Treasure Hunt. Take the children on a field trip to fill out a treasure hunt list. They will observe different types of architectural structures to increase their sensitivity to the buildings in which people live today and have lived in the past (Hatcher, 1985).

Treasure Hunt List

1. Identify a structure that has been changed from its original use. For example, a home into a business, or a warehouse into a restaurant.

2. Identify a structure that has been modified from its original appearance. For example, a room has been added or remodeling has occurred.

3. Identify a structure that has been restored.

4. Identify a structure that is over 100 years old.

5. Identify a structure that is an example of a pure architectural style.

6. Identify a building or house of interest to you.

7. Identify a structure that has housed the same family for several generations.

Learning to Use Maps and Globes

Suggested Activities

Map Puzzles. Have the children put together wooden inlay puzzles of continents and oceans. They feel and see the shapes as well as develop spatial relationships by placing the continents and oceans in the appropriate place.

Map Construction. Help the children learn about space and dimension by providing them with blocks, milk cartons, Monopoly hotels, spools, and paper roll tubes to use as models for buildings and places in the community. A sand table, cabinet top, or block center can be used for the streets and roads (Van Cleaf, 1985).

Picture Maps. Have the children construct a picture map by cutting pictures of buildings and places out of magazines or old books. They place the pictures on a background of posterboard. They can see relationships among the locations of home, park, school, church, and shopping centers (Van Cleaf, 1985).

Matching Places with Directions. Give the children a matching activity to help them learn which direction a place of interest is in the community. Using a map of the community, number the locations of a few special places of interest. Number and label strips of paper or pictures of these places. The children match the numbers and determine in which direction these places are located (north, south, east, or west).

Draw Maps. Have the children select an area around the school ground or in the classroom to draw. This activity helps them develop an understanding of the relationship between objects in the environment and two-dimensional drawings (Van Cleaf, 1985).

East and West. Children can determine the directions east and west by observing the sunrise and sunset in relation to the direction their classroom is facing. Have them draw a picture of their school at sunrise and sunset and label its east and west sides.

Using the Globe. Have the children use a globe to develop the concept that north and south are at opposite ends of the earth, that the globe is a model of the earth, and that north, south, east, and west are cardinal directions.

Global Awareness. Have the children each construct a diagram with a small circle in the center with his or her name and address in it. Out from the center the child draws larger circles and writes the global dimensions in the circles (Peter, 1981).

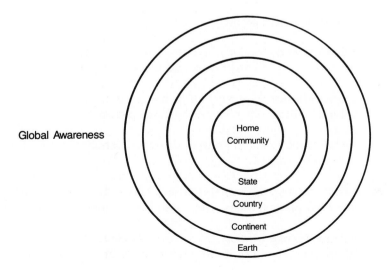

Environmental Problems

Suggested Activities

Litter Bags. Have the children make colorful trash bags from grocery bags to use at school or home.

Recycle, Reduce, Reuse. Have the children sort their classroom trash for recycling. Encourage the use of reusable canvas bags for lunch. Ask them to look for ways to have individual snacks that conserve packaging (Seefeldt, 1993).

Communication

Suggested Activities

Communication. Ask the children to list ways people communicate today and ways they communicated in the past. Have them suggest future methods of communication. The three lists are compared and contrasted.

Using the Telephone. Have the children practice correct telephone usage with model telephones.

Writing Letters. Have the children write to pen pals, friends, or relatives.

Keeping Journals. Have the children use a booklet to record their activities, thoughts, and special events.

Transportation

Suggested Activities

Box Cars and Trucks. Have the children make service and emergency vehicles from large cardboard boxes and draw or paint on details.

Transportation Mobiles. Have the children make transportation mobiles using colorful clotheshangers, string, and pictures of different modes of transportation.
Variation: Have them paint or draw with chalk a mural showing different modes of transportation.

 Land, Water, Air Transportation. Have the children sort laminated pictures of toy cars, planes, boats, trains, and other modes of transportation.

Future Transportation. Have the children design their own mode of future transportation, describing what it is and how it travels.

Transportation Safety Rules. In a group, ask the children to make a list of safety rules for riding the bus, going on a hike, riding in a car, or riding on a boat.

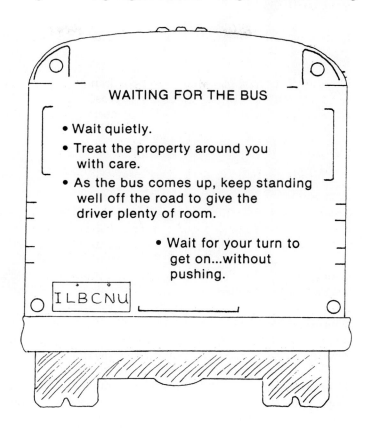

Life-Style Comparisons

Suggested Activities

Community Comparison. Ask the children to compare life in two different communities, such as city/farm, present year/1900, or city/small town.

Story Writing. Have the children research and write stories about what they think it would be like to live in different kinds of communities such as city, town, or farm. They can illustrate their stories with drawings or magazine pictures.

City Life and Farm Life. Ask the children to draw background scenes for city and farm life. They can then sort laminated figures associated with city and farm life.

Communities. Have the children build different communities such as farms, towns, or cities. They can build miniature communities or a community large enough to accommodate dramatic role playing.

Dioramas. Have the children make dioramas to depict farms, towns, or cities. They will construct their dioramas with shoe boxes, crayons, paints, and cardboard or construction paper cutouts.
Variation: The children construct dioramas representing farm, town, or city life from another culture.

Appreciating Our American Heritage

Suggested Activities

Pledge of Allegiance to the Flag. Reserve the pledge for special days: Earth Day; Lincoln's, Washington's, or Martin Luther King's birthday; Flag Day, or other holidays, so the children learn that the pledge has a special meaning and importance (Seefeldt, 1984, p. 290).

The National Anthem. Have the children become familiar with the national anthem by listening to a recording. Also expose them to other patriotic songs such as "This Land Is Your Land" that may be more meaningful to young children. Use the songs in context with holidays and historical events.

Native American Heritage. Native Americans wrote with pictographs. The children can use pictographs to construct their own stories.

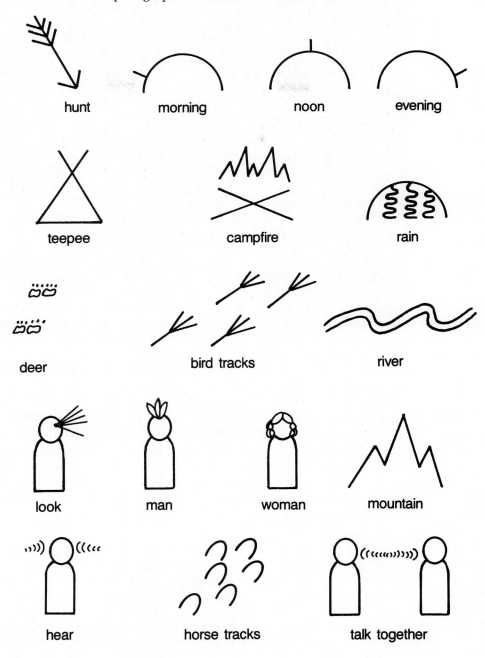

Variation: Have the children match word cards with symbols.

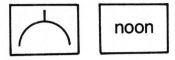

Special Holidays

Suggested Activities

Special Holidays. Use seasonal holidays to help the children compare and contrast the customs of people of different ethnic groups. Children can learn about the celebration of special holidays as they view videos, sing songs, read stories, and look up information appropriate for the special days.
Variation: Have the children make items used during a holiday, such as a piñata, kite, or Halloween costume.

Special Foods. Assist the children in preparing and cooking special foods eaten by different ethnic groups or in different countries during a holiday.

Halloween: Tasty Jack-O-Lanterns. The children can spread orange-colored cream cheese onto a rice cake or cracker. They can place raisins on top of the cheese spread to make facial features for a jack-o-lantern.

Thanksgiving. Guide the students to learn about the first Thanksgiving celebration through research and reading stories.

1. *Mural.* The students can illustrate the sequence of events of the first Thanksgiving by cooperatively drawing a mural.
2. *Turkey Bands.* The children trace their hands on fall-colored construction paper, cut them out, curl the fingers with a pencil, and glue the hands onto the back of a turkey body for its feathers. The body of the turkey is drawn on tagboard, cut out, and its physical features painted on.
3. *Thanksgiving Feast.* The children plan, cook, and serve a Thanksgiving feast at school.

Andrea helps Brian while on a field trip to the pumpkin farm. The children are getting pumpkins to make pumpkin pie for the Thanksgiving feast.

4. *Log Cabins.* The children construct log cabins from Lincoln logs, blocks, or boxes.

Exploration of Other Cultures

Suggested Activities

Resource People. Help the children learn about other cultures by inviting people who have lived or traveled in other countries to visit the classroom.

Letters. Have the children write to children in other countries.

Cook's Tour. Have the children prepare and share special dishes from different countries.

Art Forms. Have the children appreciate the art of other countries through the following activities:

1. *Japanese Paper Folding.* Show them how to make origami animals from 7-inch squares.

1. Fold in half

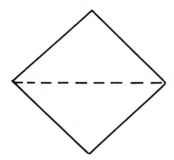

2. Fold over corners

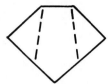

3. Draw face

b. *Origami Whale*

1. Fold in half and open again

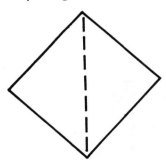

2. Fold top and bottom corners to center

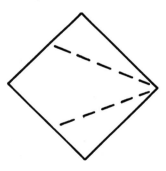

3. Fold left corner in

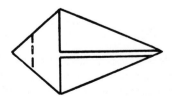

4. Fold bottom to the top

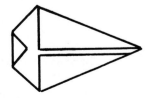

5. Fold right corner to the left and up

c. *Origami Bird*

*1. Fold in half and
   open again*

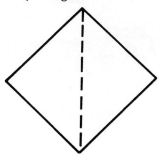

*2. Fold left and right
   corners to center*

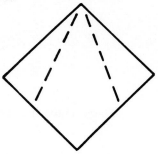

3. Fold top corner

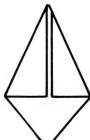

4. Fold left corner over

5. Pull out triangle from center

2. Have them listen to poetry from other lands such as haiku from Japan. They can then dictate or write their own poems.

Language. Help the children understand that people everywhere communicate. For example, the Japanese use a different form of writing. The children can write kanji characters, a Japanese writing form using Chinese characters. They will use black paint or ink and small brushes for this.

Paper People from Other Lands. Outline the children's bodies and then have them color in facial features and ethnic clothing with crayons, paints, or markers.

Flags. Have the children make flags of other countries.

Population Education

Suggested Activities

Language Arts

1. Read stories illustrating various roles of family members, community helpers, and careers to the children.
2. Have the children read about and discuss roles for adults such as two-parent families, one-parent families, and single adults.
3. Take the children on field trips to a large shopping center, airport, bus terminal, downtown district, or industrial complex to experience the effects of crowding; listen for noise pollution; and observe traffic, construction, and trash. The children can record their observations on a language experience chart or graph.
4. Have the children observe, list, and discuss the results of overcrowded conditions in the school, such as use of trailers and makeshift classrooms in the library, health room, and hallways.
5. Have the children research and write about population concepts such as advantages and disadvantages of small and large families and conservation.

Mathematics

1. Have the children chart or graph the number of people in their families. Discuss with them the average family size. Have them compare and contrast aspects of the largest family and the smallest family.
2. Give the children story problems to solve such as "If a family of two drinks 2 gallons of milk a week, how much would a family of four (six, eight) drink?"

Study this Chinese dictionary.

火 = fire	山 = mountain	天 = sky
口 = mouth	人 = person	木 = tree
大 = big	月 = moon	林 = forest (2 trees)

Write these Chinese characters in English.

口 _____   火 _____   大 _____

山 _____   木 _____   月 _____

Japanese Writing

The Japanese use three forms of writing. **Hiragana** is like our alphabet. It is made up of fifty-one letters. Each letter stands for a sound. **Katakana** is made up of the same sounds, but this writing is used only for foreign words and telegrams. **Kanji** is a set of Chinese characters. Some of these characters are "pictures" of what they stand for.

Use black paint or ink. Try writing some of these kanji!

① → ———	—— one	
① → — ② → —	二 two	
① → — ② → — ③ → —	三 three	
木	木 tree	
森	森 forest	

3. Have them solve money story problems comparing the basic needs of small families with the basic needs of large ones (lunch money, shoes, movies).
4. Have them take a census of their own neighborhood including people and pets.

Science

1. Have the children observe animals in the classroom and discuss reproduction.
2. Have the children grow and care for plants in the classroom. They can chart the growth of the plants and identify what plants need in order to thrive (sun, water, air).
3. Have the children make a bulletin board illustrating land, air, and water pollution. They can research and write about solutions.
4. Have the children observe the effects of land, water, and air pollution during nature walks.
5. Have the children make terrariums and aquariums to observe the balance of nature.
6. The children can collect newspapers, bottles, and aluminum cans to be recycled. They can practice conservation by using paper appropriately, turning off lights when they leave a room, and recycling paper or magazines.

Social Studies

1. Ask the children to explore the classroom for evidence of the social and economic interdependence of countries by looking at trademarks on items in the room. Graph the results.
2. Invite resource people who represent alternative roles for men and women (e.g., male nurses, female engineers) to speak to the class.

Understanding Economic Resources

Suggested Activities

Economic Exchange. To introduce money as an economic exchange, display examples of currency, checks, and credit cards. Use a flowchart showing the circular flow of money on a bulletin board. On another portion of the board, illustrate the concept of bartering.

Goods and Services. Help the children learn which jobs provide goods and which jobs provide services by having them brainstorm jobs. List them on a

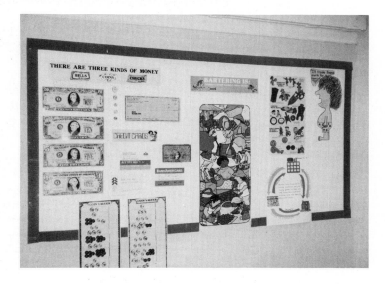

chart under the appropriate category: goods, services, or both goods and services.

Everyone Is a Consumer. To help the children understand how they are consumers, divide the class into groups. Each group should have access to Yellow Pages of old telephone books, newspaper ads, and magazine advertisements. They are to make a collage of all the goods that their families consume in a period of a week or a month (Atwood, 1985).

Pen Pals. Have the children compare their own economic way of life with that of a child in another community or country by having pen pals. Have them make a list of questions to ask in their correspondence in order to find out about economic resources as well as other aspects of life in their pen pals' communities and countries.

Cupcake Factory. Children can learn about margin of profit, division of labor, and productivity as they become "entrepreneurs," either simulating or actually carrying out an economic project. First have them do market research to find out whether the product they decide to produce will sell. They can sell shares of stock for investment purposes and in order to have capital to buy ingredients and materials needed to make the product. A banker could be invited to talk about loans and interest. Committees will be needed to finance the project, buy materials, make the product, advertise, sell the product, and handle profits (Yeargan & Hatcher, 1985).

Taxes. Ask the children to define the term *taxes* and make a list of the goods and services that are paid for by tax money. Have them engage in a critical thinking activity to determine the best use of tax money. For example, Why is it more efficient for tax money to buy fire trucks than for individuals to provide their own? Have the students try to determine another way to provide goods and services besides using tax money.

Decision Model. Have the children engage in a problem-solving activity that identifies an economic problem and uses a decision model to solve it. The children will learn that they can save or spend money and time, or save some and spend some, but not save and spend all at the same time (Speas, Martelli, Graham, & Cherryholmes, 1983).

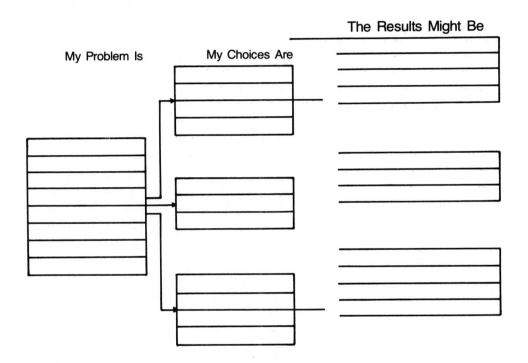

Computers in the Social Studies Curriculum

Suggested Activities

Graphics. Have the children use the computer to draw pictures and symbols and to design charts, tables, and graphs for reports.

Interactive Programming. Introduce the children to a simple interactive social studies program about historical events. They can then decide among possible choices concerning events and how history would be changed as a result of their choices.

General

Suggested Activities

Music. Provide the children with music activities incorporated into units of study in the social studies program. For example, during the study of transportation, teach them songs such as "The Glendy Burke" (steamboat), "Little Red Caboose" (train), and "Up, Up and Away" (balloon).

Museum, Hobby, or Special Exhibit Area. Set up areas in the classroom or hallways for the children to exhibit regalia from their various areas of study.

Classroom Newspaper. Have the children write and distribute a class newspaper. They can examine several newspapers to decide how to set up the editorial staff and what sections to include in the paper, such as classroom, school, community, current national events, comics, and sports. Let them decide how often to publish it and for how long.

Build Your Vocabulary. Have the children place a brick on a blank area of a large tagboard (or a house they have drawn themselves) when they can define or tell something about the vocabulary word written on the brick. They should use vocabulary words related to the unit of study.

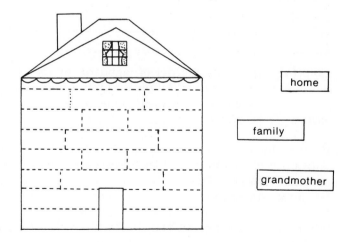

Game Board. Have the children play games on a versatile game board to reinforce information and skills learned in social studies. The players move one space on the board for each question answered correctly about a related theme at school, such as places and things in the community or famous people.

Understanding Life on the Farm

Suggested Activities

Alphabetical Fruits and Vegetables. Use a stand-up board with eight hooks positioned in it. (Drapery hooks work well on tagboard.) Provide a set of eight cards with a picture on each. The children put the cards in alphabetical order.

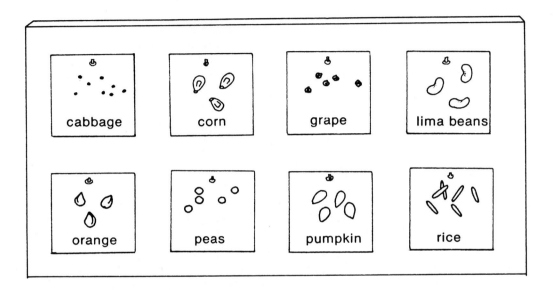

Colorful Pigs. Cut a pig out of tagboard for each basic color. Write the color word on the front half of the pig and put a color square on the back half of the pig. Cut the pig into two puzzle pieces. Be sure to vary the puzzle lines so that each pig is self-correcting.

Planting the Crops. Obtain a bottle crate to make the garden. Make a set of cards with a picture of a fruit or vegetable on each. Divide the cards evenly among two or three children. The children take turns looking at a card and giving the beginning sound of the item pictured on it. The correct answer is on the back of the card. If the correct answer is given, the child gets to "plant" his or her crop by placing it in the crate. The child with the most crops planted wins.

ABC Duck Puzzles. Cut a duck and an egg for each letter from yellow tagboard. Put a capital letter on the body of the duck and a lower case letter on the egg. Children match the eggs with the correct duck.

Animal Puzzles with Names of the Animals. Use a piece of tagboard for each animal puzzle. Draw one animal on each card (pig, cow, dog, and cat are good choices). Print the name of the animal across the top and cut the puzzle into three sections.

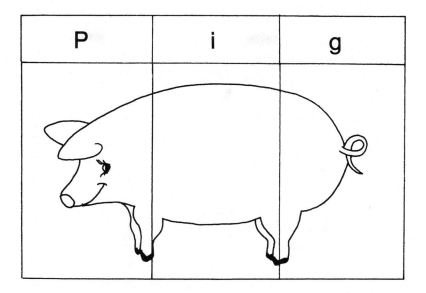

Word Search Fun Sheets. Use vocabulary words associated with the social studies theme being studied and hide them within a page of letters. The children circle each word as they find it (see art on page 360).

Vegetable and Fruit Match. Make a variety of cards. When the halves are fitted together, each card should represent a fruit or vegetable.

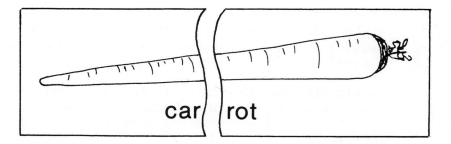

What's Your Name? Make one card for each animal. On the left side of the card, draw a picture of the animal. On the right side of the card, write the name of the animal. Cut the card into two puzzle pieces. Have the children match the animal to its name.

Barnyard Match Game. Draw a game board as shown on a piece of tagboard. Make available a set of cards with math problems and plastic animals to use as

```
i  c  e  c  r  e  a  m  l  v  x
c  x  o  v  t  o  l  t  s  v  d
h  a  y  b  a  u  k  d  i  z  a
e  v  w  l  z  d  r  p  l  l  i
e  n  m  r  d  d  x  o  o  u  r
s  t  i  t  l  e  h  h  d  l  y
e  s  l  w  h  r  n  t  c  s  o
l  r  k  t  y  o  s  b  a  r  n
v  x  z  c  o  w  s  y  l  k  p
f  a  r  m  e  r  x  p  f  r  q
h  o  m  o  g  e  n  i  z  e  x
```

Words to look for:

dairy	cheese	silo
farmer	milk	udder
calf	cows	hay
homogenize	ice cream	barn

markers. The first child picks up a card and answers the math problem. If the answer is correct, the child moves up one space. If it is incorrect, the child does not move. The children take turns, and the first player to reach the barn wins.

Animals Made from Shapes. Use attribute blocks for this activity. Form simple animal shapes from the attribute blocks. Trace the outer edges of these shapes onto tagboard. Label each picture with the name of the animal. The children use the attribute blocks to completely fill in the outline of the animal. On the back side of the card, the animal is drawn again with the outline of each block drawn in. This side can be used as a simple matching activity or to give the correct answer for the front of the card.

Egg Hatchery. Write numbers in the sections of an egg carton. Cut small eggs from tagboard. Write a math problem on each egg. The children solve the math problems on the eggs and place the eggs in their proper places in the egg carton. Answers to the problems can be written on the back of the eggs so that the children can check their own work.

Count Your Crops. Make a stand-up board with hooks. You can use tagboard with drapery hooks inserted. Make four sets of vegetable theme cards to count by 1s, 2s, 5s, and 10s. Each child takes a set of cards appropriate for his or her ability and hangs them in order on the board.

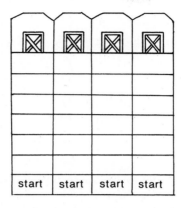

Going Fishing. An actual fishbowl can be used to hold fish cut from tagboard. Write a number on each fish and attach a paper clip to it. Make a fishing pole from a stick with a string and a magnet attached. A game board in the shape of a fishbowl is also made from tagboard. On it are pictures of fish that have number words on them. The children go fishing with the magnetic pole. When a child catches a fish, he or she looks at the number on the fish and then matches it to the fish on the game board with the appropriate number word.

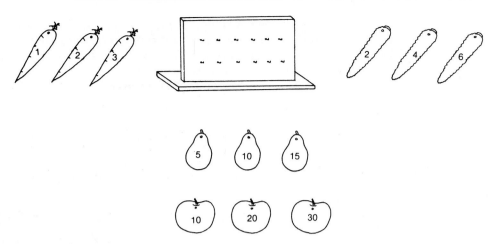

Farm Bingo. Five to six children play this game. Each child has a card with five vegetables across the top and five rows of numbers below these vegetables. Beans can be used to cover the numbers as they are called. Let one child be the "caller." Follow Bingo rules. Encourage the children to help each other.

🍅	🥕	🌽	◖◗	🥕
2	8	1	6	2
9	4	8	4	4
3	7	10	2	7
5	2	3	1	8
7	1	9	5	10

master card

🍅	🥕	🌽	◖◗	🥕
1				
2				
3				
4				
5				
6				
7				
8				
9				
10				

Barn Floor Game. Draw three barns on a large piece of vinyl as shown. Two children play, and each child gets a bean bag. The first child tosses a bean bag onto the vinyl. The child checks the number of the barn on which the bean bag landed and takes a card that has the same number on it. The child turns the card over and names the shape and color. The children check each other's answers. The game is over when each child has had five turns.

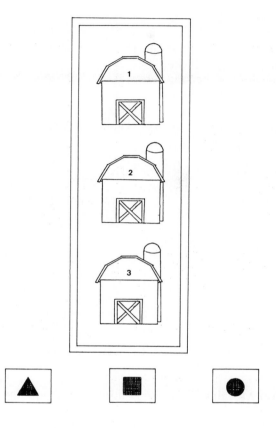

Mature Animal–Young Animal Puzzle. Using tagboard, draw or cut out pictures of a mature animal on half of the card and its young on the other half. Label each picture and cut it into two puzzle pieces.

Farm Animals and Their Products. Divide a piece of tagboard into six sections and paste on pictures of the following: a sheep, a turkey, a cow, a chicken, a pig, and a goose. Make small cards with pictures of the products we get from each of these animals. The children match each product to its appropriate animal source. Examples are as follows:

Sheep: sweater, scarf
Turkey: roast turkey
Cow: milk, butter, steak, cheese, shoes
Chicken: egg, chicken leg
Pig: sausage, bacon, ham
Goose: pillow feathers

Woodworking Activities. Make the task card as illustrated and have the children follow the directions.

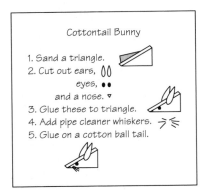

Farm Mosaics. Give the children small squares of construction paper and ask them to plan a farm scene on a background sheet of paper. Encourage the children to plan and "play" with their squares before they glue them down.

Playdough Farm Animals. Have each child shape the farm animal of his or her choice. These can be used to form a farm scene, grouping like animals together and placing them on appropriate areas of the farm.

Vegetable Printing. After they have examined and identified the vegetables, have the children dip them into paint and make prints on paper.

Block Center Task Cards. Draw a picture of a farm scene on each card. Ask the children to tell what they see in the picture. Let the children construct their own farm scenes similar to those on the cards. As a follow-up to this, the children may wish to dictate experience stories about their constructions.

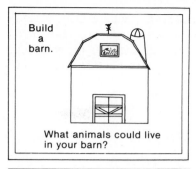

Build a barn.

What animals could live in your barn?

Build a henhouse.

How many blocks did you use?

Show it to a friend.

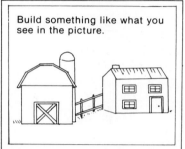

Build something like what you see in the picture.

Build a shed for the tractor.

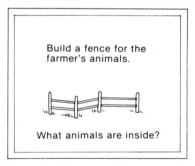

Build a fence for the farmer's animals.

What animals are inside?

Cooking Activities. The farm's emphasis on fruits, vegetables, and dairy products creates many opportunities for cooking activities. Two examples are illustrated on pages 366 and 367.

Making Butter. Pour small amounts of whipping cream into small jars (baby food jars are a comfortable size to handle). A bit of salt can be included for added taste. The children take turns shaking the cream until it becomes butter. Spread it on crackers and enjoy.

Checklist to Accompany a Field Trip to a Farm. A field trip to a farm takes the children beyond the ordinary realm of the classroom and helps to satisfy their natural curiosity. A checklist such as the one on page 368 is motivating and helps to define the goals of the field trip.

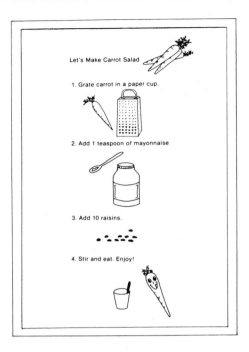

Farmer Brown's Apple Tree

Materials needed:
Lettuce (or Spinach)
Celery Stalks
Cherry tomatoes
Lemons

1.

Arrange 2 pieces of
lettuce to form
a tree top. Put it on a
paper plate.

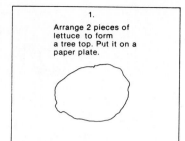

2.

Add 1 celery stalk
for the tree trunk.

3.

Place 4 cherry
tomatoes on
your tree for apples.

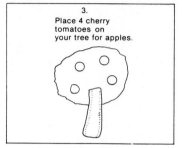

4.

Squeeze lemon juice
on your tree.

5.

Eat and enjoy!

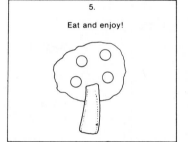

What did you see at the dairy?

☐ silo

☐ stall

☐ calf house

☐ udder

☐ calf

☐ cow

☐ milk truck

☐ hay

☐ dairy barn

☐ pasture

1. What was the best part of the field trip? _____

   _____

2. Name 3 things you did on the trip.

   _____

   _____

Learning Center Activity Planning Guide: An Example

Area: Social Studies

Unit Topic: Ecology

Concept: What is Ecology?

Days	Objective	Group Activity	Science/Social Studies Center Activity	Other Centers
1, 2, 3	Students will be able to define ecology as the relationship between living things and their environment and to demonstrate that the earth is shared by all living things.	-Introduce unit with globe. -Define ecology -Song "Big Beautiful Planet in the Sky" by Raffi	1) <u>Create a Bulletin Board</u> - Draw, color, and cut out yourself helping hold up the earth (Task Card #1). Add each child's self-portrait to the bulletin board. 2) <u>Earth Puzzle</u> (Task Card #2) - teacher made puzzle of animals and people sharing the world 3) Puzzle - Rauensburger: "Summer's Fun"	- <u>Writing</u> - Writing Card on "Seasons" - <u>Language</u> - game "seasons" by *Games for Growing*. - <u>Writing</u> - 6 Creative Writing Cards - <u>Research</u> - 6 Research Cards

Concept: Too Much Garbage!

Days	Objective	Group Activity	Science/Social Studies Center Activity	Other Centers
4, 5	Students will be able to demonstrate their awareness of the litter/garbage problem by pledging to help keep the earth clean.	Read: - Science Weekly Levels C & D <u>Tomorrow's World</u> - Mini Page on Earth Day, 4/16/90 - <u>How Come book</u>, pp.48-49 - <u>50 Simple Things You Can Do to Save the Earth</u>, p.14	1) Make <u>litter bags</u> (Task Card #3) 2) Make "I'm a litter picker upper" <u>badges</u> 3) <u>Litter Bug</u> board game	-Writing Card #1 continued - <u>Language</u>- game "Four Seasons" - Puzzles - "Playground Puzzle - Large Group Activity: Show <u>The Lorax</u> video by Dr. Seuss

369

Unit Topic: Ecology

Area: Science

Concept: Reusing/Recycling/Precycling

Days	Objective	Group Activity	Science/Social Studies Center Activity	Other Centers
6,7,8	Students will be able to state the differences between recycling, prescycling and reuisng.	- Show and discuss recycling posters - Read "What you should know about Recycling" pamphlet, pp. 16-17 for definitions of recycling precycling, and reusing. - Read: Chapters 5-8 of <u>Save It, Keep It & Use it Again</u>.	1) <u>Sorting Trash</u> - aluminum, paper, plastic into lableled containers. 2) 15 piece wooden "Earth" puzzle 3) Recipe for a Better World - children who read and write create their own recipe (Task Card #4). Younger children can write in amounts only on recipe.	- <u>Writing</u> - Writing Card #2 - <u>Research</u> - 6 Research Cards

Concept: Clean Air and Water

Days	Objective	Group Activity	Science/Social Studies Center Activity	Other Centers
9, 10, 11	Students will be able to classify the causes of clean and dirty air and water.	Read: -<u>The Magic Schoolbus at the Waterworks</u> - Science Weekly, "Acid Rain" (level C) -<u>50 Simple Things...</u>, p. 142 , colored water experiment - show and discuss "Ozone Poster Pack"	1) <u>Puzzle</u> - Ravensburger "Sunny Sunday" - shows activities good & bad for the environment. 2) <u>Duck Pond game</u> - Ravensburger (discuss why clean water is important to pond life) 3) <u>Sorting game</u> - causes of good & bad air - Task Card #5	<u>Puzzles</u> - move Ravensburger: "Summer's Fun" from ecology center to puzzle center

Area: Science

Unit Topic: Ecology

Concept: Water: Ocean Animals and Pollution

Days	Objective	Group Activity	Science/Social Studies Center Activity	Other Centers
12, 13	Students will be able to describe how polluted waters affect ocean animals.	Read: - Science Weekly - "Marine Science" (level E). Show balloons and discuss the consequences of releasing balloons. Demonstrate snipping 6 pack rings - The Brook Book - 50 Things... - p. 17	1) Sequence Puzzle - teacher made "Letting Balloons Go" (Task Card #6) 2) Living Things board game 3) Finger Painting Ocean (Task Card #7)	- Writing - add 6 creative Writing Card #3 on "weather" - Research - 6 Research Cards

Concept: Rainforest / Endangered Species

Days	Objective	Group Activity	Science/Social Studies Center Activity	Other Centers
14, 15, 16	Students will be able to explain how the rainforests affect the air we breathe and to state the difference between endangered, threatened & extinct species.	Read: Where the Forest Meets the Sea - Show illustrations of Wonders of the Rainforest. - Discuss the pander & elephant (Science Weekly, vol. 17, No. 3 & zoo books magazine). Read: Mini Page "There's No place Like Home" Read: - 50 Things... pp. 96-97.	1) Puzzle - "In the Jungle", Ravensburger 2) "Jungle Visions" paintings (Task Card #8)	-Art: "The Mixed Salad Tree" (vegetable printing) - (Task Card #11) - Large Group Activity: - Show You Can't Grow Home Again video from PBS

Area: Science

Unit Topic: Ecology

Concept: Endangered Species in North Carolina (substitute your own state)

Days	Objective	Group Activity (Home Base)	Science/Social Studies Center Activity	Other Centers
17, 18	Students will be able to identify endangered species in North Carolina.	Discuss: Endangered species in N.C. - Use "Wildlife" magazine, March, '91, pp. 16-17.	1) Make Bird feeders (Task Card #9) 2) Fisher Price Zoo 3) Skill sheets on endangered species: - Children who can read and write, categorize species as either endangered, threatened or extinct. - Younger children draw and color an extinct animal (a dinosaur) and an endangered animal (the manatee).	Writing Card #4, an "endangered species" - Task Card #12

Concept: What You Can Do To Help The Earth

Days	Objective	Group Activity	Science/Social Studies Center Activity	Other Centers
19, 20	Students will be able to explain how their small choices can help save the earth for future generations..	Read: Mini Page, 4/16/90 - "ABC's of What Kids Can Do..." - Your Choices Count, p. 3 - Mother Earth poem - 50 Things... p. 7 - It Zwibble and the Big Birthday Party!	- Each child adds their hand prints and thoughts to an "I will help save the earth" pledge - Task card #10. - Sequence puzzle about the earth's needs (pictures from the Environmental Protection Agency.)	Large group activity: Read book and show video of Johnny Appleseed - Also, video: It Zwibble: Earthday Birthday

Draw and color yourself helping save the earth.

I dream about the future. Will my world be different?

RECYCLE

TRASH

I can do things to change my world. It can be a better place.

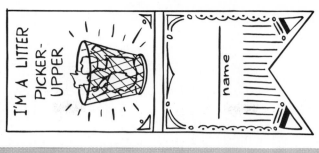

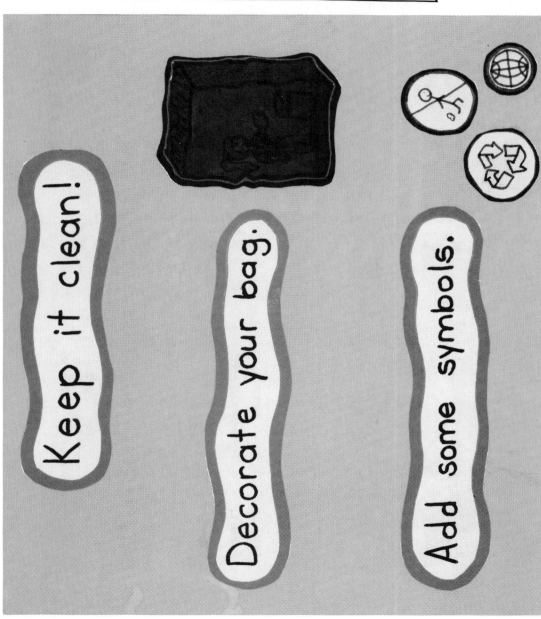

Note: A paper lunchbag is attached to the back of the chart.

Public transportation

A variety of pictures are laminated for children to sort.

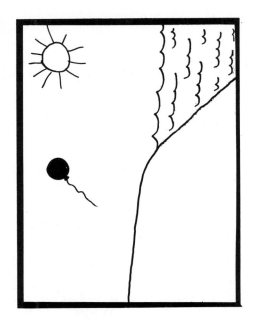

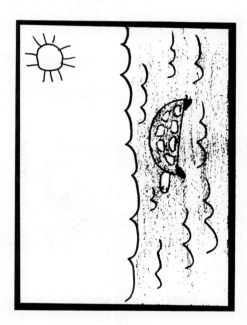

Create A Clean Ocean!

Finger paint an ocean!

Add some plants and fish.

Add some boats.

Jungle Visions

1. Paint your jungle animals.

2. Add your jungle.

3. Paint in your background.

Pledge To Help The Earth

Color your globe.

Cut and paste.

PASTE

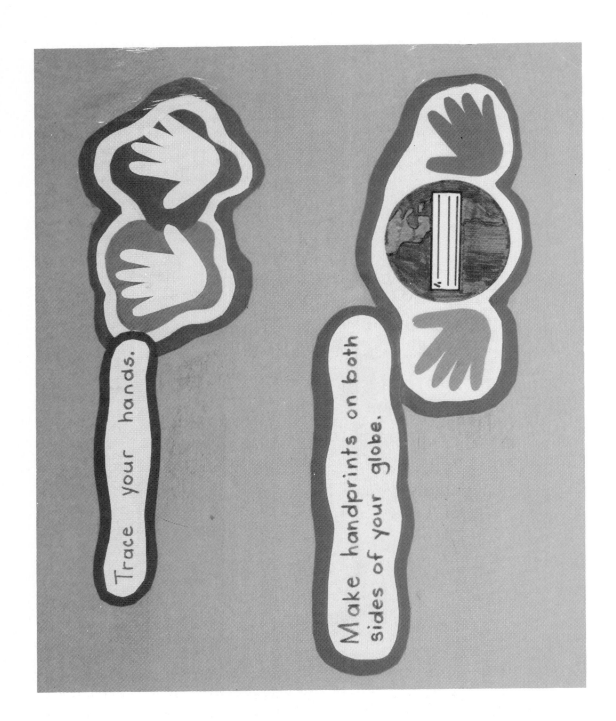

Trace your hands.

Make handprints on both sides of your globe.

Mixed Salad Tree

1. Take a piece of cabbage from the paint.

2. Press it in the outline of the tree.

Take a fruit, vegetable, or leaf from the paint.

Press it on a piece of white paper.

Cut it out.

Paste it on the tree. PASTE

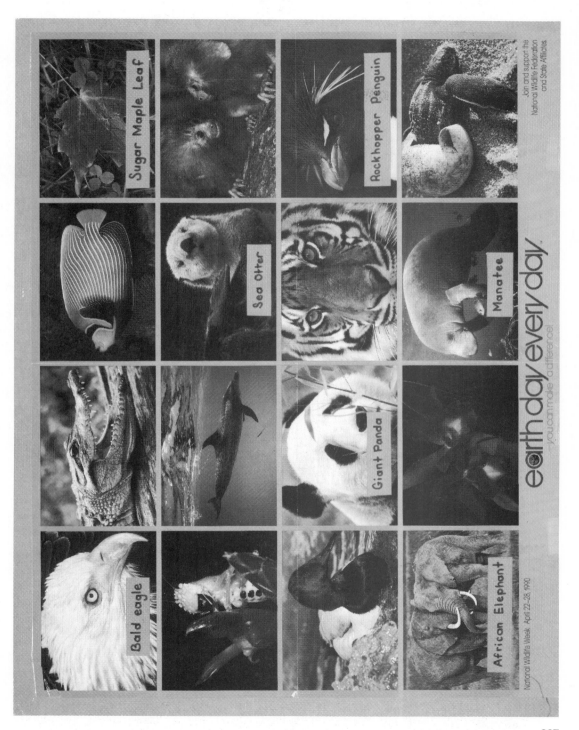

EXAMPLES OF RESEARCH CARDS FROM THE LEARNING CENTER ACTIVITY PLANNING GUIDE

I dream about the future. Will my world be different?

I can do things to change my world. It can be a better place.

Read about our world.

Look up world.

WEBSTER'S DICTIONARY

Look in the sky the next time it rains You just might see a rainbow. Do you know how a rainbow is made?

Rainbow

What season is it now? What is your favorite season? Why do you like that season best?

Look up rainbow.

p. 80

Do the activity.

Name _____

- A **threatened** species is one that loses too many members each year.

- An **endangered** species has so few members that it must be protected or it will become extinct.

- An **extinct** species is one that has no living members.

Fill in the blanks.

There are no more dinosaurs!
They are _____.

The Red Cockaded Woodpecker is disappearing quickly!
It is _____.

The manatee will soon be extinct if something isn't done!
It is _____.

Draw and color a safe habitat for an endangered species.

Name _____

Draw a Dinosaur

Draw a Manatee in Safe Waters

Dinosaurs are Extinct!

Lets Save the Manatee!

I, _____
pledge to help the earth by

Days 19–20

Parent Letter for Ecology Unit

Dear Parents,

In your child's classroom we are beginning a new unit on ecology. We will be learning about recycling, endangered species, the rainforest, pollution, littering, and how people affect the environment overall. We will be emphasizing what children can do to help save the earth.

One of our activities in the "All About" center will be sorting trash into three categories: paper, plastic, and aluminum. We are asking the students to help with our trash collection. If your child wishes to help, please make sure that the trash is thoroughly cleaned before sending it to school.

Thanks for your help!

Ms. Drake and Ms. Pringle

Chapter 9

Sand and Water Play

There is something natural and basic about playing in sand and water—having a tea party in the sun, watching a boat floating, or just engaging in pouring and sorting activities. The motivation and fun are built in. Younger children might simply enjoy the sensory experiences provided by sand and water, others may learn about letters by drawing in the sand, and still others can learn how cities are built by construction in the sand. As children work with sand and water, there are many possibilities for mathematics in measuring and filling, for language and communication in their play, and for science in experiments with the qualities of sand and water.

Lay-Dopyera and Dopyera (1990a) state that materials such as sand and water offer rich learning possibilities for children. These materials take on whatever form and meaning a child imposes upon them and replicate something specific in the real world. Activity becomes increasingly detailed and elaborate as the child matures and becomes more experienced with the possibilities inherent in the material. When children construct a highway with a sand tunnel or create a rainstorm at the water table, they symbolize these objects and events in their thinking. Their activity may lead them to new discoveries. "For example, as the sand caves in on cars in the highway tunnel, they may begin to wonder what keeps the ground from falling on cars in real tunnels" (Lay-Dopyera & Dopyera, 1990a, p. 274). Lay-Dopyera and Dopyera stress that as the incompleteness of children's knowledge becomes apparent, their curiosity will lead them into more precise observations and further experimentation.

Stages of Development in Sand and Water Play

Dodge (1991) says that children's methods for approaching sand and water play are not always the same. One child may be more experienced with sand than the next child, and that child may be more experienced with water than the first. This inequality in abilities is due to previous exposure to sand and water. Since the developmental progress of each child in sand and water is not always at the same stage, Dodge believes that teachers should encourage children to explore both.

Dodge (1991) believes that children work through similar stages in both sand and water play, even though they are not always at the same stages of development simultaneously. The first of three stages of development is sensory-motor exploration, when children become acquainted with the properties of sand and water. At this stage children discover the sound of rain on a roof and the splish, splash of stomping in a puddle. They also experience the sensation of sand or water as it runs through their fingers or even the sight of water as it is absorbed by soil or sponges.

According to Dodge, in the second stage of development children use what they have learned and apply it to a purpose. In this stage, play is more of an activity, and children involve themselves in planning events and experimenting with sand and water. In the third stage of development, children perfect the gains of the previous stage. In this stage, children's experiences are exhibited in their intricately planned activities (Dodge, 1991).

Benefits of Sand and Water Play

Lay-Dopyera and Dopyera (1990a) also note that large muscle activities are predominant in outdoor sand play. Children develop strength, balance, and endurance by constantly transporting sand. They gradually increase their ability to perform these actions with ease and agility. Children also engage in activities that foster small muscle development during sand and water play. Moreover, they are able to reduce tension as they become involved in various sand and water activities.

Children can become engrossed as they play with sand (Lindberg & Swedlow, 1980). They can hold sand in their hands and feel the mass of it get smaller and smaller as it sifts between their fingers. In damp sand, they can leave footprints, handprints, or the print of their whole body. They can transfer sand from containers of many shapes and sizes by pouring, spooning, dumping, or sifting.

Lindberg and Swedlow (1980) stress that children learn many concepts because of the versatility of sand. They learn mathematical concepts as they compare shapes they make with wet sand, discover that wet sand is heavier than dry sand, and use measuring cups to measure amounts of sand. They engage in scientific processes as they find ways of controlling sand in order to build tunnels, bridges, or roads. In addition, they gain experience in communication as they talk with other children about what they are doing.

Children can also become engrossed in water play (Lindberg & Swedlow, 1980), either alone or in groups. There is no feeling of failure during water play because water can be used over and over again. If children enjoy what they are doing, they can repeat their actions. If not, they can stop and do something else with the same water.

Children can make many scientific discoveries during water play. For example, some things float on water, while other things sink. When pushed, water generates force. Water takes the shape of its container. It can change from liquid to vapor and become ice or snow. When things are mixed with water, their properties may change. For example, salt forms a solution and dirt forms a mixture.

Playing with water in its various forms commands children's attention. The discovery that some objects float is remarkable to them. At first children test one object after another, yet eventually they observe that some objects always fall to the bottom, whereas others always remain on top. When detergent is added to water, a child can fill the air with bubbles by blowing through a straw. Ice and snow are particularly exciting to children. Children can catch snowflakes on their tongues, and if there is enough snow, they can build snow figures.

Sand and water play presents various learning possibilities. Through this play, children can gain scientific and mathematical knowledge, as well as develop language and communication skills. No matter what the activity, sand and water play results in fun and exciting experiences for children as they learn, develop, and mature.

The Sand and Water Program

For a sand and water play area in the classroom to be successful, it must be in an area of the room that is away from the class traffic flow. This will lessen the chance that someone will slip and fall on a wet floor and decrease the number of distractions for the children exploring in the sand and water centers. The following are lists of items that should be obtained for the classroom sand and water play environment and materials—both permanent and expendable—that will enhance these centers. These are followed by program objectives and suggested activities.

Environmental Resources

Sand and water table and/or a large galvanized (or plastic) tub
Sheets of plastic, an old shower curtain, or an absorbent rug to place under the tub
Scales (balance)
Plastic aprons for the children
A hose and/or pitchers to fill the tub (the teacher can mark the water line with a colored marker so the children can fill the tub to the best level)
Sponges and a pail, a mop for cleanup
Storage space for materials

Materials

Permanent

Plastic containers and lids (all sizes and shapes)
Plastic dishes (cups, bowls, mugs, and beakers)
Measuring spoons, cups, and containers
Weights (ounces, grams)
Eggbeaters, whisks, and spoons
Bubble pipes
Meat basters

Corks, sponges
Plastic eyedroppers
Funnels (all shapes and sizes)
Sieves (all shapes and sizes)
Seasoning bottles with sprinkler tops
Paintbrushes of several sizes
Clear, flexible plastic tubing (several lengths and diameters)
Scoops (ice cream, sugar, and flour types)
Rolling pin
Trowels
Sand combs
Dump trucks, small cars
Shovels
Ladles
Buckets
Seashells or pebbles
Colander
Muffin tins
Cookie cutters
Squeeze bottles
Boats
Siphons
Water wheels
Molds
Pots and pans

Expendable

Straws
Cakes of soap, soap flakes, liquid soap
Food coloring
Tempera paint
Small sponges
Pieces of wood
Styrofoam, cork
Chart paper, markers
Box of objects for sinking and floating (sponge, nail, rubber eraser, pencil, leaf,
    nickel, paper clip, rock, cork, crayon, twig, acorn, peanut, rubber band,
    wooden bead, lengths of sticks, spools, odd pieces of wood, scissors)
Substitutes for sand that add variety (beans, rice, bird seed, popcorn, sawdust,
    macaroni, paper confetti, nonmenthol shaving cream)

Teacher-Made Materials

1. Tin cans with varying numbers of holes punched into the middle of the
   closed ends with a large nail. A variation might be cans with holes
   punched into the sides. These can be used for both sand and water play.

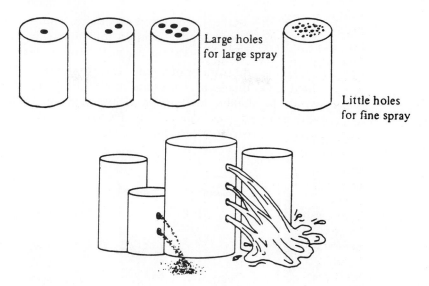

Large holes
for large spray

Little holes
for fine spray

2. Pie tins with holes punched into the bottom. These can be used for both sand and water play.

3. Larged-sized plastic detergent bottles that are cut across the middle. These can be used as funnels in sand and water play.

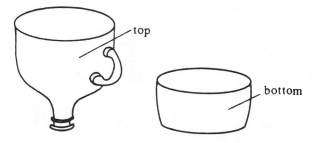

top

bottom

4. A balance for weighing sand and water. The bottoms of the large-sized plastic detergent bottles and some cording can be used to make the buckets for the balance.

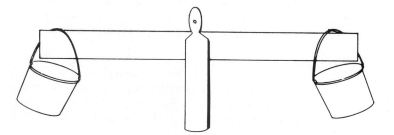

5. A cloth doll that gives children experience pouring. The doll is made of strong cloth, and sand is poured into her with a large tablespoon or wooden spoon. Drawstrings are at the top of her head for closing.

6. Shakers made from orange juice cans that have rubber tops. These are filled to various levels with sand (both fine sand and gravel). A variation would be shakers made from plastic medicine bottles filled with sand with a round stick nailed to the lid for a handle. These can be used as a rhythm instrument for music.

7. Large containers for water and sand play.

Indoor play

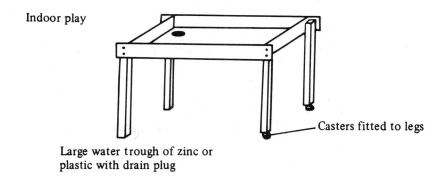

Casters fitted to legs

Large water trough of zinc or plastic with drain plug

Wood sand tray made of a 6″ × 1″ softwood frame and hardboard base strengthened with battens. Stood on chairs for play. Sand may be stored in tin cracker box.

Dishpan and towel on low table or box

Another crude type of sand-box might be cinder blocks just put together to keep sand in an area. Children could sit on the blocks.

Wood-frame sandpit with metal strips across corners. Allow 6" space for foot room from top to level of sand.

Tub of water on two crates

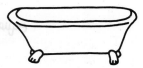

An old bathtub would be ideal for water play.

8. Sand combs made from rectangular shapes of plywood to make patterns in sand. Cutting different shapes into the edge of the rectangular pieces varies the look of the patterns.

Objectives

1. To play creatively in the sand or water alone or with others.
2. To use the sand, water, and available materials to seek answers to open-ended questions.

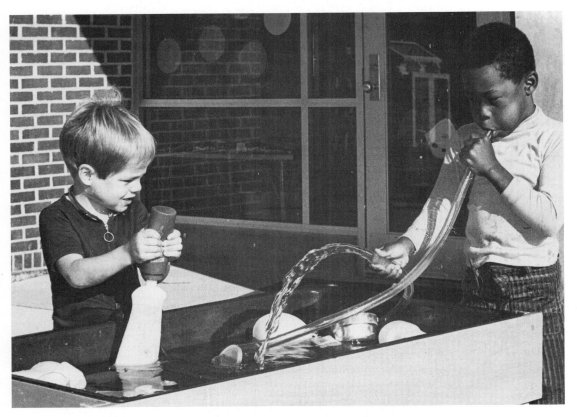

Observing the rate of water flow through tubes and tunnels is a good outside water table activity.

3. To discover equivalences ~~equal~~ through the use of water and other materials.

4. To use large muscles while digging, hauling, and building with sand.

5. To classify materials that will and will not float; that are absorbent and nonabsorbent. *Cotton, cork (could graph)*

6. To develop writing skills by labeling bottles filled with sand or water and calling them cola, milk, juice, etc., or by writing a story about an experience with water that made the children feel happy, sad, or scared.

7. To explore roles and relationships through use of dramatic play; for example, playing fire chief with hose lengths, yellow coats, and firehats.

8. To develop sensory awareness skills; for example, seeing the difference between water when it is frozen and water when it is heated and feeling the differences between ice and steam through touch.

Measuring the amount of water various containers hold is a challenging task.

We built a community in our classroom and now we are building it in the sand.

Suggested Activities

Experiment with Food Color and Water. Mix colors with water to discover how all colors are made from the primary colors (red, yellow, and blue).

Task Card

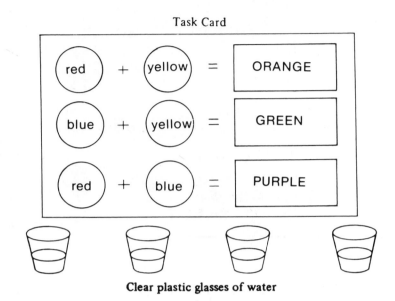

Clear plastic glasses of water

Boat Races. Divide a pan into racing lanes. The children blow boats with straws. Number the boats for a math experience; make a chart to record wins and losses.

Creative Water Painting. Use brushes, sponges, or other materials to make wet imprints on the chalkboard.

Water Play Related to Other Centers. Other activities that involve water play are cleaning, washing dishes and/or clothes, and imaginary cooking.

Therapy. Use sand or water play as a therapeutic technique (playing for the sake of play and for relaxation and release of tensions).

Task Cards. Use teacher-made work cards or directions to suggest methods to help the children discover the effects of weight on flotation.

Can floating in water

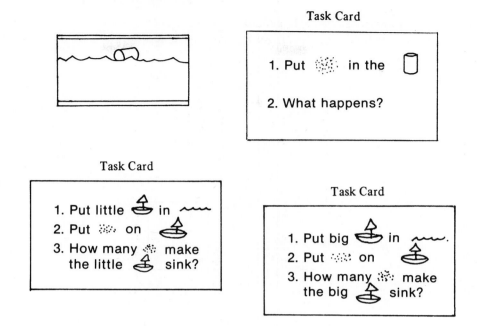

Task Card

1. Put ⬚ in the ⬚

2. What happens?

Task Card

1. Put little ⛵ in 〜〜
2. Put ⬚ on ⛵
3. How many ⬚ make the little ⛵ sink?

Task Card

1. Put big ⛵ in 〜〜
2. Put ⬚ on ⛵
3. How many ⬚ make the big ⛵ sink?

Floating and Sinking Experiment. Have a collection of objects that sink and float. Provide two shoe boxes labeled "Things That Sink" and "Things That Float." See the activities presented in Table 9-1. To extend these activities, add

TABLE 9-1 Sinking and Floating Activity Guide

Day	Objective	Group Time	Water Center	Other Centers	Research	Language
1, 2	To observe objects that sink and float.	Discuss the meaning of *sink* and *float* as related to water. Talk about things that sink and float. Introduce activities in centers. Discuss gravity.	Have a tub of clear water in center. Place various objects in the center to experiment with sinking and floating; then classify. Containers for classifying are coded by color and symbol. Plastic trash bags are in the center for use as smocks to cover clothing. Background of the center (or bulletin board) demonstrates, pictorially, the concepts of sinking and floating.	Art—Draw an object floating or sinking and label it. Sink and Float float sink	Look up *sink* and *float* in reference to water. Read books about things that float and discuss with the class.	Dictate a language experience story to go with art center picture, or a story about a mysterious object that sank or floated.

408

| 3, 4 | To guess which objects sink and float, test guesses, and record results. | Discuss what was learned about sinking and floating and the idea of guessing and testing.

Introduce the chart to be filled in on individual and small-group basis. (The chart could be written on the contract as part of an individual assignment.) Be sure the children understand the assignment. | Same setup as before, including the tub of water, but only objects to be tested are placed in the center. A wipe-off chart is hanging nearby. Individual containers for water could be included in lieu of the tub. Chart is as follows:

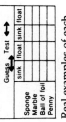

Real examples of each object are glued to the chart to aid in matching. | Math—Discuss weight and how it may affect the ability to sink or float. Social Studies—Look at a life preserver and talk about how it works. Guest speaker: A lifeguard or a scuba diver discusses sinking and floating under water. | Look up and write about what you learn about why some objects float and others sink.

Tell or write a story about a sunken boat or sunken treasure. |

5, 6	To test the concepts of *wet* and *dry*. To observe how equilibrium is achieved when a wet object is placed in water. To observe effects of wetness and dryness on flotation. To reinforce previously learned concepts about sinking and floating.	Discuss how wetness and dryness might affect ability to float. Reiterate previously learned information in relation to sink/float. Discuss outcomes of previous testing. Discuss new activities and how to use the chart.	Individual tubs of water and specific objects (both wet and dry examples of each object) are in the center. A wipe-off chart is hanging nearby. Children test objects in wet and dry states and check off the chart. Additional activities could involve wetting objects with a substance other than water and testing whether or not that made a difference.	Art—Paint the sidewalk with water. Block—Try floating various sizes of blocks. Sand—Feel wet and dry sand.	Find out about substances, such as oil, that float on water, as well as those that sink. Look up *gravity*; find out how it affects sinking and floating.	Tell a story about floating on a raft down the river. Write about floating in outer space and what it might feel like.

Investigate

	DRY		WET	
	Sink	Float	Sink	Float
Sponge				
Paper towel				
Stick of Wood				
Piece of towel				
Cotton ball				
Kleenex				

7, 8	To observe how salt and sugar change the properties of water in respect to taste and flotation.	Discuss salt and its effect on water. Discuss what happens to salt and sugar when they are placed in water.	Make a clay-salt water animal. Music—Listen to recordings of ocean waves, whale sounds, etc. Movement—Pretend to be swimming in the ocean.	Find out about plants and animals that live in salt water. Look up the *Dead Sea* and find out how salt affects life under water. Find out where salt and sugar come from.	Make up a story about how the sea became salty. Make a list of what salt does. Tell or write about the difference in the taste of sugar and salt.
9	To reinforce learning with reading, music, and movement activities.	Introduce activities.	Small containers, paper cups, and a large pan of water are provided along with salt and sugar. Children can add salt, in various amounts, to a container of water. Objects can be placed in the water to see whether salt changes their ability to sink or float. Children may do the same for sugar. Children may taste-test samples of salt water and sugar water.	Books—Read about ocean life. Water play—Watch colors mix under water through clear container.	Find out about, and make a list of, things that taste sugary and salty.

| 9, 10 | To build a boat that floats, using materials in the center. | Discuss materials that sink and float. Discuss boats and their uses and special designs. Introduce activities. | A large container of water is provided, along with plenty of aluminum foil, clay, or Styrofoam for constructing boats. Children may test materials and determine how to form their boat. After making and testing the boat, the children may put it on display in the center. | Art—Paint a picture of a boat on water. Dress-up—Act out a play about a boating adventure. Books—Read a story about a boat. Math—Measure and record the length, width, and weight of your boat. Social studies—Look at maps and find out where boats go. | Find out about boat construction and design. Look up different types of boats and write about your favorite. Draw a picture of that boat (sailboat, houseboat, tugboat, steamboat, motorboat, aircraft carrier, submarine, canoe, etc.). |

salt to the water and have the children observe whether there is a difference between the items that sink and those that float. Another extension would be to have the children hold a floating object and let it go. Have them observe what happens when the object is released.

Vocabulary and Concept Development. Encourage the children to describe what they are doing and to answer questions about how and why they are doing it.

Water Experiments. Undertake experiments dealing with the following:

1. How water affects different materials (textures of sugar, cotton, cork, and material, etc.) and how and why different materials absorb water.
2. The rate of water flow through various tubes and funnels.
3. The ability of water to take the shape of its container by freezing water in paper cups, balloons, or milk cartons and peeling the container away to show the shape. This demonstrates water's ability to change forms, liquid to solid.
4. Measurements: Have the children pour water from large to small and fat to skinny containers.
5. Evaporation: Have them fill two clear containers with identical amounts of water, mark them on the outside, and observe the differences daily.
6. Mixing: Have the children add oil to water and observe what happens. Have them feel the oil in the water.

"Watch this! I can make the water wheel spin."

Digging Activities. Use the sand table or outdoor digging area with spoons, cups, trowels, sticks, and shovels to dig for enjoyment, to experiment with floating and damming, to build canals, and so on.

Map Study. Use sand (in a sand table) for simple map study. Streets, houses, and stores can be constructed and placed on the sand or can be drawn with fingers.

"Cooking." Use sand and water for an imaginary "cooking" experience. A recipe and directions might be placed over the tub to suggest this. This activity is a good follow-up to role playing in the home-living center.

Letters in the Sand. Use a tactile approach to learning letters, numbers, and shapes by having the children write in the sand or mix sand and water to form letters and numbers.

Exploring Scientific Properties. Have the children explore the various textures of dirt, the temperature of water, and the science of waves.

Health. In conjunction with home living, let the children give the dolls a bath or wash their clothes. This is a good way to teach them about health practices.

Outdoor Digging. Have an unconstructed digging pile as a part of the outdoor play area.

Comparing Weight. The children can use a balance scale to discover differences in the weight of wet and dry sand.

Comparing Quantity and Capacity. Discuss how liquids and solids (drinks, medicine, flour, sugar) are measured in everyday situations to introduce measuring experiments. Use transparent measuring containers so the children can easily see differences in quantity and capacity.

1. *Comparing Quantity.* Use two different size containers (e.g., pint and quart) for discovering relative differences in units of measure. The children can chart how many spoonfuls or cups of water or sand each container holds in order to determine which holds more or less.
2. *Comparing Capacity.* Provide containers that are different shapes but hold the same amount to compare capacity.

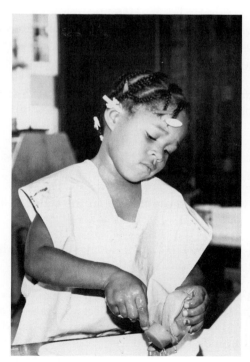

Washing the measuring cup before using it to measure the water for Jello is important.

Measuring Water for Eating or Drinking. The children can measure water to make gelatin, lemonade, popsicles, and ice cubes.

Dictating or Writing Stories. Have the children write or dictate stories about experiences playing in the sand (e.g., "How I Made Muffins," "The Sand Village," "If I Were a Sand Castle I Would . . .").

Aquarium. Make an aquarium with sand on the bottom. Have the children plant water plants in the sand.

Planting and Watering Activities. Develop planting and watering task cards and have the children perform the tasks over a period of a few days.

1. Put soil in a cup. Plant a seed in the soil. Put water on the seed. Look at the cup every day. Make pictures of what you see.
2. Plant two seeds in two paper cups. Put water in one cup. Do not put water in the other cup. Which seeds grow?
3. Water one plant. Do not water another plant. What happened? Then water both plants. What happens?
4. Instead of growing something in soil, cover a damp sponge with grass seed. Compare the amount of time it takes grass to grow in soil to time it takes to grow on a sponge.
5. Make soil instead of purchasing it. Hammer rocks such as slate and sandstone to the consistency of sand and have the children mix it with crushed decayed leaves and water.
6. Start a compost pile as a class project.

Observation of Water Conduction. Color a glass of water. Place a stalk of celery in it. Have the children observe how the colored water rises up through the celery.

Plastic Toys. The children can play with plastic ducks, dolphins, and fish in the water.

Listening Experience. Boil water in a teakettle and let the children listen to the boiling water and the whistle.

Ripples. Throw stones and rocks in water at a local lake to see the ripple effect. Perhaps some children can make a stone skim the water.

Weather Activities. Experiments with rain, snow, and ice can be part of a unit on weather. On two rainy days, the children can collect rainwater in a pan, pour it in clear measuring cups, and compare how much rain fell each day. After a winter storm, the children can melt snow and ice.

Explore Occupations and Services Related to Water. Discuss what a plumber does. Visit the basement of the school to see the water pipes. Take a field trip to the city water works facility to see how water is processed and how it gets to homes and buildings.

Water Glass Chimes. Fill glasses of the same size with different amounts of water. Strike the rims of the glasses lightly with various instruments.

Sand and Water Play—Art-Related Activities. Make boats for water play.

1. Spool boats

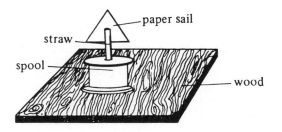

2. Scrap lumber boats
3. Newspaper boats
4. Leaf boats
5. Jar lid boats

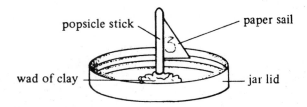

6. Cork boats

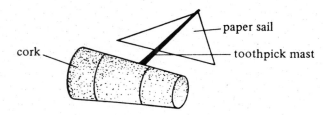

7. Walnut boats

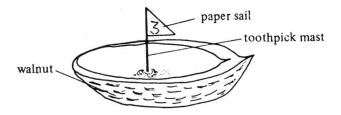

Geography. In the sand area, have the children make landscapes like mountains and volcanoes.

Graphing. To aid in math, map locating, geography, create an archeological dig. This activity requires a sandbox that is plotted out. Bury rocks, figures, and other items of interest in the sandbox. Have the children dig up three items and identify them by naming them and the locations where they were found. Instead of letters and numbers, label the buried objects by colors and shapes. This activity may help younger children learn colors and shapes.

Telling Time. Sand can be used to tell time, and this is handy if all of the children want to be in one center that is a favorite. Punch a hole in a can and hang it. Let the children fill it with sand; time, for example, 5 minutes while the sand is seeping through the hole. When the 5 minutes are up, empty the remaining sand. The amount of sand that seeped out will be used for the timing. This is time-telling that young children can do on their own.

Sandpaper Projects. Make sandpaper numbers and number charts, letters, and pictures.

Painting with Water Colors. The children learn that depending on how much water they use, their color will get darker or lighter.

Sand Candles. Make a roundish indentation in the sand. Fill it with melted (colored) wax and put in a wick. Let it dry, then remove it from the sand and brush it off.

Cutouts. Cut out pictures of water in its various forms from magazines.

Sand Painting. Add 1 part paint powder to 4 parts sand and combine them in large shakers. The children shake them on paper they have covered with paste.

Elmer's Glue Sand Painting. Design a picture on a colored piece of construction paper with Elmer's Glue. Scatter sand on top, then brush it off. Sand remains where the glue was.

The sand table is designed so that children with special needs (i.e., wheelchairs, walkers) can fit directly under the edge of the table.

Chapter 10

Blocks

"All human beings are active seekers of knowledge; play is an integral facet of this ongoing quest" (Bergen, 1988, p. 12). Children like to examine the world around them by exploring their environment. Blocks give children the opportunity to create their own images of the adult world around them through play.

Blocks are dynamic tools for the early childhood classroom. Children who have the opportunity to use blocks develop creativity; their ingenious creations may range from simple square dwellings to large megastructures. Children can

Blocks promote sharing and cooperation.

build and rebuild things based on their own perceptions. Block building enables children to gain self-satisfaction, which helps to promote good self-esteem at an early age.

Moreover, blocks aid young children on an emotional level as they experiment with role playing. For example, if a child's parent is an important business entrepreneur, the child might build a new building of blocks and supporting material. By doing this, the child can play out the role of what it is like to own a business and realize that at times it is scary and stressful.

Blocks also promote sharing and cooperation. A group of children may decide to organize and plan the creation of a circus or an amusement park, for example. They must work and plan together to make their structure a success.

My teacher, Mrs. Turchi, can tell me many things about the airport. She goes there often.

This experience teaches responsibility and the ability to follow instructions given by others.

Through blocks a child can gain the necessary skills for future academic success. Math and science concepts learned through blocks include counting, area, fractions, size relationships, classification, shapes, gravity, and stability. Reading and language skills are put to use in the block center as well. Children must understand printed letters and words that are symbols for objects and actions. Children use language to discuss their buildings as they engage in dramatic play. In addition, building stores, houses, airports, schools, post offices, government buildings, and streets helps children understand mapping skills.

"It is the supreme art of the teacher to awaken joy in creative expression and knowledge" (Albert Einstein). A teacher must challenge children to want to create in the block center by providing enough materials that are interesting to them. The instructional presentation should be clearly stated with relevant examples such as the following:

"You used a lot of blocks." "He has only a few blocks." "He needs five more blocks." (number concepts, language development, comparison of quantity)

"Can you find another block just like this one?" (matching, classifying according to size and shape)

"How can you make this road as long as that one?" "How can you make this side as high as that one?" (language development, measurement, defining spatial relationships, problem solving)

"I wonder what would happen if we put this block here?" (experimentation, testing)

"How can we connect these two blocks?" (problem solving, language development)

"Look, two square blocks are as long as, or equal to, one rectangle." "This rectangle is half as long as this rectangle." (fractions, measurement, spatial relationships, language development, labeling)

"Can you make the same pattern with your blocks that I have made with my blocks?" (comparison, patterns)

"Try to make the other side the same as this side." (symmetry)

"Can you think of a sentence/story to tell about your block creation?" (written language)

These comments enable children to understand their constructive work. Subsequently, the teacher must provide an atmosphere conducive to block building. This includes large space to construct block structures, a storage area, and the blocks.

Stages of Block Building

Just as children undergo stages of development, they also progress with their building techniques. The stages of block building as described by Harriet Johnson (1982) are as follows:

Stage 1:   (under the age of 2) Blocks are not used for building. The child carries one or two blocks around, making vast discoveries about the blocks themselves, turning them over and over, throwing them, pushing them, standing them on end. The child at this stage learns all facets of one block before moving to two, three, or more blocks.

Stage 2: (age 2 or 3) Actual building begins. Rows become the fascination, either horizontally or vertically; repeated patterns are typical to this stage—one block is often pushed along to become a car or a train.

Stage 3: (age 3) Bridging begins to occur. Two blocks with a space between them are spanned by a third one; there is still some horizontal or vertical building at this stage, and bridging illustrates a problem-solving technique discovered by the child builder.

Stage 4: (ages 2, 3, or 4) Four blocks are placed so they form an enclosed space. Children learn about the insideness and outsideness of space; combined with bridging, sophisticated building occurs.

Stage 5: (age 4) Patterns begin to appear. Symmetry can be seen at this level of ability in building; buildings do not have names but become more elaborate.

Stage 6: (ages 4 to 6) Prior to this stage, a structure was named as an exercise in itself; now the child begins dramatic play and the name of the building is related directly to the function of the building.

Stage 7: (ages 5 and up) Block play begins to reproduce or symbolize true-to-life structures. Building becomes an integral element of dramatic play ideas.

The Block Center Environment

The block area should be separate from the rest of the classroom. Figure 10-1 shows a possible classroom set-up.

The floor of the block center is important. It must be even so that the children's structures will stand alone. Carpeting is helpful because it breaks the sound of falls and reduces the occurrence of accidents. Pile carpeting is usually best.

Blocks require a large amount of space. They should be stored either on shelves or in freestanding cabinets accessible to a child's reach. They should be arranged on the shelves in an orderly fashion but should not be so neat that they say "Don't touch me!" Children should not build structures close to the storage areas, because incomplete structures stand in danger of being destroyed accidentally. Refer to Figure 10-2.

All areas of the classroom have rules, and the block center is no exception. The rules should be simple and stated clearly:

use positives!

- Blocks are for building. Please do not throw them!
- Please do not knock someone's building down. Show your consideration for fellow classmates!

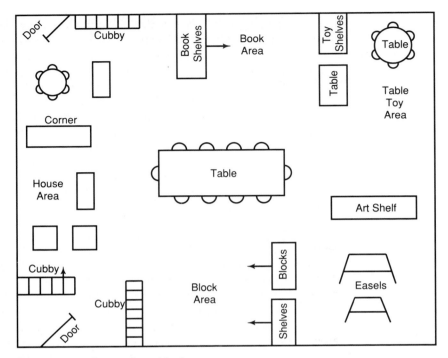

Figure 10-1   Set-up for a block center

- Please build buildings only as tall as you can reach without help from another person or a chair!
- Remember, only a few people can play in the block center at one time!
- Please do not build close to anyone else's construction!

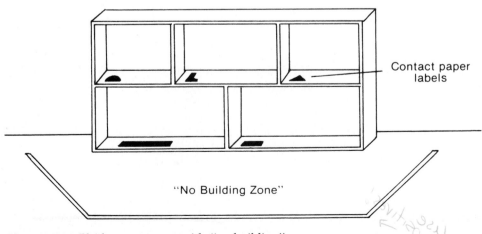

Figure 10-2   Block storage area with "no building" zone

If possible photograph some of the children's buildings so that they may reflect upon them at a later time, especially when it is impossible to allow buildings to remain for longer than a short period of time.

Supervising clean-up time in the block center is like having multiple personalities for some teachers: how it proceeds depends on the approach taken. Children need time signals to alert them that clean-up time is coming. A certain song or a flash of the lights could signal when it is 10 minutes to clean-up. Suggestions to help make clean-up a pleasant experience include the following:

- Clean-up should be a purposeful, satisfying activity in its own right, with enough time allowed for it to prevent rushing.

- Children need a future orientation; that is, they need to know what activity follows clean-up.

- Confusion and destruction should be kept to a minimum. Knowing where the blocks go provides a feeling of security. Having a teacher hand down the blocks from the upper story of a high building, thus avoiding a collapse, prevents destructiveness. There should be a quick response should a building topple.

- Waiting or inactivity makes anxiety rise. No child should be kept waiting at any time during transition periods, even if this means that some have snacks or go outdoors before everyone has completed clean-up. Children should know where to go once they are finished.

- A clear expectation of purposeful activity and a follow through by actively participating teachers eliminates the feeling of helplessness.

- Teacher presence and help also make the task seem more manageable and more worthwhile. (Hirsch, 1984)

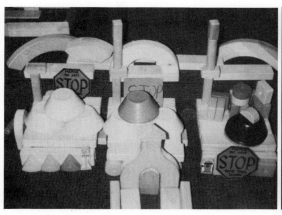

The Block-Building Program _____

The materials, objectives, and activities described in the following sections can help facilitate creative learning in the block center.

Materials

Caroline Pratt's unit blocks are the main source of block construction. A unit block is 5½″ × 3¾″ × 1⅜″ (13.47 cm × 9.53 cm × 2.21 cm). These solid wooden blocks consist of half units, double units, and quadruples as well as curves, ramps, triangles, arches, pillars, switches, and cylinders. It is important that children have access to enough blocks to keep their activities interesting. The names and shapes of unit blocks are shown in Figure 10-3.

Depending on the child's age, the number of unit blocks needed for the block center varies. Suggested numbers are given in Table 10-1.

Accessories are a must in the block center. Children have access to many different resources, which provide opportunities for wonderful creativity. Marbles, magazines, and alphabet blocks are just a few accessories to enhance play in the block center. Here is a list of many more.

Small plastic or wooden people figures (often available in family or community
    worker sets)
Tiles, carpet squares, wallpaper (can be used as floors)
Large- and small-wheel toys such as trucks, trains, tractors, and airplanes
Miniature traffic signs

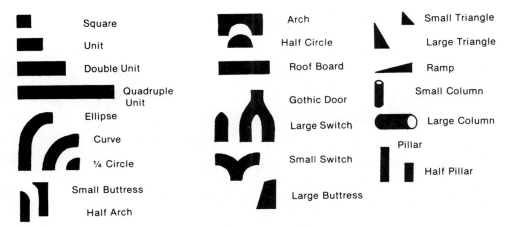

Figure 10-3   Unit block shapes
Note. Reprinted by permission of Monroe D. Cohen and the Association for Childhood Education International, 3615 Wisconsin Avenue, N.W., Washington, D.C. Copyright © 1976 by the Association.

TABLE 10-1 **Number of Unit Blocks Needed According to Student Age and Block Shape**

Block Shape	At 3 Years	At 4 Years	At 5 Years
Half units	48	48	60
Units	108	192	220
Double units	96	140	190
Quadruple units	48	48	72
Pillars	24	48	72
Small cylinders	20	32	40
Large cylinders	20	24	32
Circular curves	12	16	20
Elliptical curves	8	16	20
Pairs of triangles—small	8	16	18
Pairs of triangles—large	4	8	12
Floor boards—11"	12	30	60
Roof boards—22"	0	12	20
Ramps	12	32	40
Half pillars	0	12	16
Y switches	2	2	4
Right angle switches and/or switches	0	4	8

Note. Jessie Stanton, Alma Weisberg, and the faculty of the Bank Street School for Children, *Play Equipment for the Nursery School* (New York: Bank Street College of Education, 1967). Reprinted by permission.

Small wooden or rubber animals (containers labeled "Zoo" and "Farm" provide
    a good sorting activity at clean-up time)
Miniature furniture
Colored markers, pencils, small cards, sentence strips (for labeling; store in
    small boxes or cans covered with contact paper)
Puppets
Tool kits (for dramatic play)
Thin pieces of rubber tubing (for gasoline pumps)
Pulleys
Dry cell batteries with lights (to illuminate building interiors)
Planks
Packing crates, boxes, ropes
Old steering wheel
Books related to building and construction
Objects used to "decorate" buildings:
    Dominoes
    Shells (scallop, clam)
    Variety of small plastic containers, lids
    Popsicle sticks
    Large dried beans
    Small colored cubes (1" or 2 cm)

    Spools (thread and textile mill)
    Parquetry blocks
    Assorted colored wooden table blocks
    Lumber scraps (sanded)
    Pebbles, stones
Other building materials:
    Interlocking blocks (large and small)
    Tinker toys
    Lincoln logs
    Large hollow blocks (plastic or wooden)
Easter grass (excellent for animal food)
Scraps of fabric
Styrofoam pebbles
Small flags
Art box (paper, crayons, string, clay, scissors, cellophane tape, masking tape)
Block cart (use a wooden crate and add wheels and a handle; this will make an excellent cart for the children to move the blocks outside)
Milk carton blocks (cut off the pouring end of two milk cartons; put one inside of the other; these will make good hollow blocks; use half-pint, pint, quart, and half-gallon cartons)
Blocks from wood scraps (sand and varnish or paint scrap 2" × 4" (5.08 cm × 10.16 cm) bits of wood from a construction site)

Objectives

1. To enjoy the block area by working with the blocks for fun.
2. To orient the builder to his or her body in space.
3. To improve small- and large-muscle coordination by working with and building with blocks.
4. To role play with the animals, people, and/or puppets.
5. To learn to share ideas and work together in a group while taking turns with the blocks.
6. To develop genuine respect for others' work.
7. To develop concepts of big, little, more than, less than, equal to, shapes, and sizes.
8. To make the inquiry approach to learning valuable and real to the child.
9. To develop a sense of pattern and symmetry.
10. To use materials to create the child's world as he or she sees it.
11. To learn to express oneself nonverbally and to release emotions in an acceptable form.
12. To explore the dynamics of balance through construction.

Suggested Activities

Math and Science:

Counting. Ask a small group of children to count out several blocks—perhaps 15 or 20—and build a building. Make sure they agree on the correct number of blocks.

Adding. Put several sets of blocks together that are about the same size, and ask each child to pick a friend who has one more block than he or she. A small worksheet may be used (see illustrations).

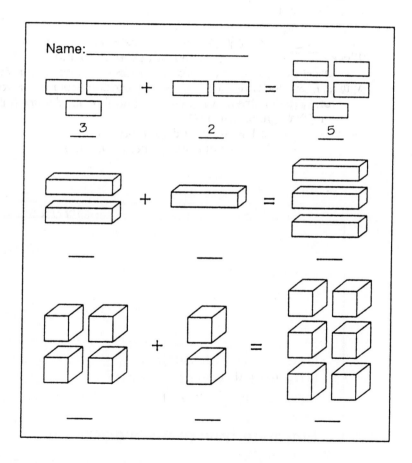

Marble Rally. This teaches children about gravity. A series of blocks is used to build a pathway for the marble to travel from a high point to a low point, as illustrated.

Write the number blocks of each kind
that were used inside the block shape.

I built

_____

....

_____

Name_____Date_____

Write 2 sentences about your
building.

_____

_____

Use ☐ to measure:
How tall is your building? _____
How long?_____
How wide? _____
Estimate how many blocks you
      used. _____

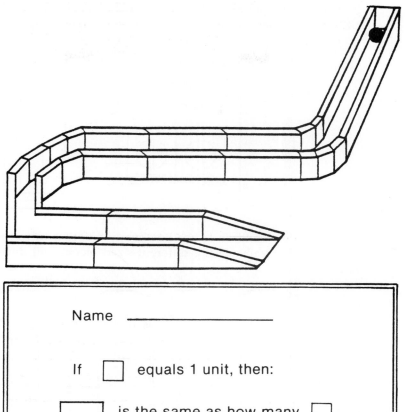

Name _____

If ☐ equals 1 unit, then:

▭ is the same as how many ☐

◰ is the same as how many ☐

▭ is equal to how many ☐

BONUS*BONUS*BONUS*BONUS*BONUS*BONUS

◺ is the same as how many ☐

◺ ◺ is the same as how many ☐

Fractions. Use blocks that represent halves, quarters, and wholes. Show the children the relationship among parts of a whole.

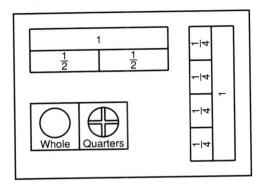

Ratio. Ask the children to see how many different ways they can reproduce a structure identically. Using different-sized blocks will develop the concept of *ratio*.

Trace and Match. Trace around the shapes of several blocks and have the child match the shapes to the blocks. This activity is good to use with young children learning shape recognition.

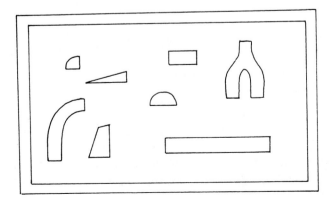

Sequencing. Sequencing activities can also be structured with prepared mats of traced shapes. Provide a limited number of blocks to be used. Move the other blocks out of the center.

○ □ ○ □ ○ □ ? ?

△ □ △ □ △ □ ? ?

⬡ ⬡ ○ ⬡ ⬡ ○ ? ?

□ □ △ □ □ △ □

⬡ ⬡ ○ ○ ⬡ ⬡ ○

Make a pattern and
try it with a friend.

Blueprints. Full-sized sheets of posterboard can be prepared as "blueprints" by tracing block shapes in various designs or sequences. When these are taped vertically to the side of a storage cabinet or "cubbie," the children can match and reproduce the designs exactly—a fine exercise in visual discrimination and sequencing.

Horizontal Blueprints. Posterboard sheets can also be placed directly on the floor for the children to build on top of; these "horizontal blueprints" prove to be valuable exercises in open-ended problem solving.

Language Arts

Alphabet Blocks. Ask the children to get alphabet blocks that match the words spelled either on the board or on flashcards. This helps children learn how to spell as well as to recognize letters.

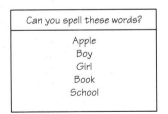

Can you spell these words?

Apple
Boy
Girl
Book
School

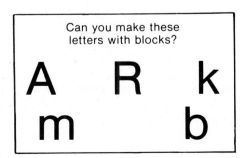

Can you make these
letters with blocks?

A   R   k

m   b

Story Creation. Ask children to write stories about their creations using different types of blocks. For example: "If you build a building such as this one, what would you name it?"

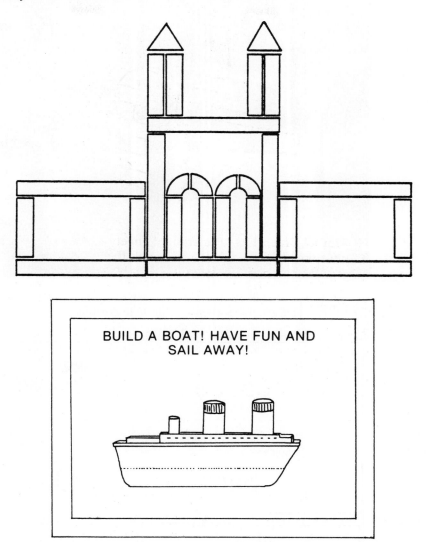

BUILD A BOAT! HAVE FUN AND
SAIL AWAY!

Sentence Strips. In addition to allowing children to make their own labels, the teacher can prepare a set of labels on sentence strips in advance. Once laminated, these strips may be stored in a small can near the center; the children come and select the label they need. A small picture or illustration added next to the word may help prereaders.

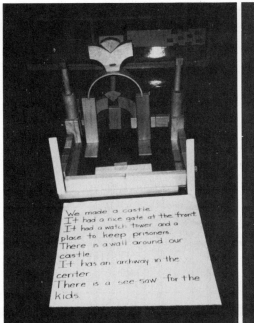

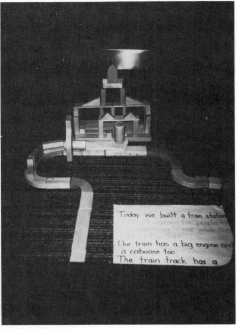

Writing stories or making charts about block structures teaches sequencing and descriptive writing, and generates a sense of pride in creating.

 castle

 windmill

 barn

 bank

 garden

 school

Role Play. The children can gather clothing from the housekeeping area to pretend to be another person and use the blocks to demonstrate what that particular person does (e.g., a train conductor, public safety officer, clown, zookeeper.

Emotions. The children can build happy and sad faces with the blocks and then write stories about how they feel at different times.

I am happy when_____.
I am sad when_____.

Creative Construction. Children's books may instigate creative construction, particularly if one is occasionally placed in the center as a visual reminder. For instance, Virginia Lee Burton's *Little House* may result in a large replica of the city, with the "little house" right in the middle. Likewise, David Macaulay's *Cathedral* (Houghton Mifflin, 1973) can produce miniature Notre Dames, complete with flying buttresses.

Weekly Theme. Use the block center to reinforce the weekly theme in the classroom. For example, for winter/snow, the children can build a snow fort, make a snowmobile, and "drive away" in it.

Small-Scale Constructions. Lincoln logs, Tinker toys, and other toy sets can be used to do small-scale construction on a table or a designated floor area. (These can be easily stored.)

Partnership Activity. Assign partners and have them work together. This is effective when children have had vast experience with blocks and it encourages new friendships.

Outside Block Party. Move the blocks outside. Some of the large pieces from the center might remain out at all times. Outdoor space is more conducive to building of larger objects (forts, submarine, etc.).

We paint pictures of Doge's Palace and we build Doge's Palace in the block center.

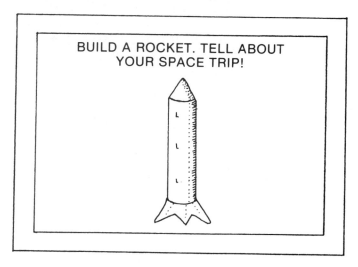

BUILD A ROCKET. TELL ABOUT YOUR SPACE TRIP!

Mapping

Children could go on a tour of the neighborhood surrounding the school or to a nearby community. They are to construct what they saw along the way on their trip.

Defining Special Areas. Colored (or plain) masking tape can be used to define special areas such as coastlines, rivers, and streams (blue) and roads, highways, streets, and airport runways (gray or red). A whole community might be planned this way that could later be "mapped out" with crayons and paper, allowing the children to make a two-dimensional representation of their three-dimensional model.

Signs. Have children bring in shopping bags displaying store logos or labels. These designs and words can be cut out, pasted on small pieces of posterboard, and laminated, resulting in miniature "signs" that children can use to label their buildings. Best of all, even very young children and other "nonreaders" can usually read and recognize familiar signs.

Computers

The children can explore graphics, typing, and learning games with blocks. A game like *Tetris*, which is a block game in which you try to make all the blocks fit, is a good option.

Chapter 11

Woodworking

The woodworking center has been accepted for the most part in good schools for young children (Rudolph & Cohen, 1984). The National Association for the Education of Young Children adopted 22 goals for children's learning as guidelines for woodworking in early childhood programs (Skeen, Garner, & Cartwright, 1984). Decker and Decker (1992) have stated that woodworking centers are popular with children. Rudolph and Cohen, in monitoring children's reaction to the center, found much interest and lasting satisfaction from the time spent there. Most children have watched a grownup use tools at some time or other and long for a chance to use them too (Adams, 1967).

In addition to children's enthusiasm for woodworking activities, child development theory and research support the developmental appropriateness and value of woodworking. Piaget (1966) emphasized that young children learn and develop by interacting with their environment. They touch, pour, taste, or in woodworking activities, hammer, saw, and drill objects in order to learn about them. They obtain important information on the basis of interaction with tangible materials (Leeper, Witherspoon, & Day, 1984).

Motivational theory points to children's need to interact with their environment to cause change, not to maintain the status quo, and "a variety of stimuli presented across varying sensory modalities will have the effect of maintaining optimal arousal" (Evans, 1975, p. 282). According to Rudolph and Cohen (1984), children "derive sensory pleasure from handling wood and learning the mechanics of fitting, fastening, connecting, and cutting"(p. 161). They enjoy hands-on experience with the physical attributes of the materials employed (roughness, softness, sharpness). As Leeper and colleagues (1984) have emphasized, in order to ensure children's development, the teacher and the school need to offer many avenues of manipulation that children might not otherwise experience. Woodworking is one such avenue.

Woodworking and carpentry activities incorporate skills from traditional school subjects such as language arts, math, and science, and provide children with opportunities for cognitive, psychomotor, and affective development. As children compare sizes and shapes, note different textures, and decide which materials and tools to use, they are learning to experiment and solve problems.

Measuring, counting, and sorting lead to practical understanding of mathematics. Children learn new vocabulary as they name each tool and woodworking action (Davis, 1980). They develop expressive skills and vocabulary as they describe what they see, hear, do, and feel in woodworking. Manipulating tools promotes the development of large and small muscles. Hammering and sawing provide emotional release. In addition, woodworking fosters creative expression, respect for property, and appreciation for the child's efforts and those of others.

Piaget stated that children may gain as much from their errors as from completed tasks (Evans, 1975). "As children grow they acquire more complex and sophisticated means of interacting with their environment" (Honman, Banet, & Weikart, 1979, p. 97). "There is a progression from simple one-step activities to more complex ones" (Pitcher, Feinburgh, & Alexander, 1984, p. 198). Adams (1982) has differentiated children's stages of development according to how they grow in woodworking proficiency. "Therefore, by making available activities designed to meet the developmental characteristics found in the specific stages, the needs and interests of each child can be more appropriately met and challenged" (Adams, 1982, p. 220).

Croft also agreed that children go through developmental stages in woodworking. Croft identifies these stages as exploring, combining, and representing. The first is essential to development but is dependent upon the child's experience with woodworking. In this stage, the child will explore the center and spend time familiarizing himself or herself with the tools and materials. In the combining stage, the child experiments with putting two or three pieces together. The third stage is when the child plans the outcome ahead of time. Children are more concerned and get more joy from the process of woodworking than from the product (Croft, 1990).

In spite of the many developmental benefits from woodworking activities, they are often excluded from the curriculum, or if they are included, they are underutilized by teachers. Woodworking is often one of the first activities eliminated from kindergarten programs (Davis, 1980). Adams (1982) cites many instances of carpentry materials put aside or left in a corner.

Why does this part of the curriculum tend to be ignored? Anderson and Hoot (1986) suggest that the noise is objectionable, the dust and shavings create a mess, and there are unnecessary safety dangers. This may be one reason woodworking centers are excluded. Another factor may be the cost and availability of woodworking materials, tools, and equipment.

Teachers can overcome obstacles to implementing woodworking centers in many ways. To build confidence, they might invite a carpenter or carpentry instructor to visit the classroom and teach them and the children basic woodworking operations and safety techniques. To obtain resources for a woodworking center, teachers can solicit donations of scraps, tools, and equipment from parents and local businesses. To ensure safety, teachers can carefully supervise and establish clear rules and procedures for woodworking activities.

An important consideration for teachers operating woodworking centers is avoiding sex-role stereotypes and biases (Anderson & Hoot, 1986). Sometimes females play in home living centers while males are encouraged to engage in woodworking activities. Teachers should encourage both to participate in woodworking activities, and should provide the support and assistance needed to make woodworking a successful experience for both sexes.

Day and Drake (1983) urge teachers to set clear expectations in early childhood classrooms. The establishment of specific rules sets the appropriate atmosphere for learning. Adams (1982) has established the following four rules for the carpentry center:

- All equipment and tools have a home. When something is taken out of its home, it needs to be returned to its home.
- Each tool has a particular use and is limited to that use only.
- No one should hold equipment or a tool for anyone else. Use a tool instead of a person.
- If a tool doesn't work or if you need help, ask the teacher or another adult for assistance.

Another set of rules by Adams (1967), in *Creative Woodworking in the Kindergarten*, also establishes guidelines for using woodworking tools:

- Keep hands off cutting edges.
- Keep both hands on the saw handle.
- Always have the piece of wood to be cut held firmly against the table with a vise or a clamp, or even two.
- The teacher or other resource person should check the tightness of vises or clamps.

Allen and Hart (1984) emphasize that woodworking is a teacher-structured activity that must be supervised at all times. Good monitoring involves listening to and observing children while they are building, in order to gain insights into their behavior and growth (Leeper et al., 1984). With appropriate structure, direction, and monitoring, children can learn basic woodworking skills that will be useful throughout their lives.

The Woodworking Program

Environmental Resources

Essential

Center area, free from distractions, away from flow of traffic, in a side room, yet not isolated from supervision, and access to other areas for dramatic play (Skeen et al., 1984)

Storage for tools on a wall rack or pegboard

A workbench or table set out from the wall so that children will not have to reach over the work table to get tools

Color coding on the floor or carpet to indicate the proper places for equipment and supplies within the woodworking area

Color coding on the tool rack and/or pegboard to indicate which tools go where. Outlines of tools and clean-up equipment can also be color coded (Day & Drake, 1983, Skeen et al., 1984)

A sturdy workbench or table with

Height proportionate to size of child (approximately waist high)

Top that allows for carrying out basic operations without fear of damage

Space sufficient to allow movement

Storage space (a tool cabinet with pegs, shelves, drawers, and containers for other materials)

Important

Sawing bench (may be placed in an outdoor woodworking area)

Nailing block: (30″ × 10″ × 6″; 76.3 cm × 25.4 cm × 15.2 cm) with carpet squares underneath to cut down on noise. This can be moved outdoors (Skeen et al., 1984).

Recommended

Rollers on workbench or table to allow for movement inside and outside

Rollers with locks on them so table/bench stays still

Shop vacuum for quick pick-ups

First aid kit for splinters and cuts

Sink, wash-up area

Equipment

Essential

Hammer: 7- to 10-oz. claw with wooden handle

Screwdrivers: assorted sizes of both slot (standard) and Phillips

"C" clamps: 4″–6″ (10.2–15.2 cm) in length

Nails: variety of penny and heads

Screws: assorted sizes and types

Ruler, measuring tape, and yardstick (that includes metric measurements) (Rudolph & Cohen, 1984)

Keyhole or compass saw that is light and easy for young children to handle (Skeen et al., 1984)

Rasp: a good, safe tool for children to handle (Rudolph & Cohen, 1984)

Hand saws: crosscut and coping

File: cabinet, half-round 8″ (20.3 cm)

Brace and bit

Hand drill and bits or push drill and points

Important

Vise for workbench
Pliers: combination, 6″ (15.2 cm)
Sawhorse
Sure forms: are handled like rasps and files, but cut smoothly and easily (Skeen
    et al., 1984)

File card for cleaning file
Monkey wrench
Wire cutter
T-square
Awl

Recommended

Planes: block and smoothing
File
Miter box
Paint scraper

Materials

Large-wood supply—many varied shapes and sizes
    Soft pine or spruce
    White pine rather than yellow pine, grown in United States (eastern, western, and sugar white pine)
    Spruce (white, black, red, Sitka, and Engelman, grown in United States) (Skeen et al., 1984)
    Some finished and unfinished wood
    Molding and doweling
    Plywood
Small-wood supply
    Toothpicks
    Popsicle sticks
    Tongue depressors
    Paint stirrers
    Small branches and sticks
    End grain scraps
    Box of assorted scrap wood
Cardboard
    Tri-wall
    Large posterboard boxes

Wood Supply Sources

Local lumber companies
Local hardware stores
Local paint stores
Local cabinet shops
Construction sites
High school industrial arts classes
Parents of students and friends

Supplies

Pencils, scissors, string, wallpaper scraps, tacks, tapes, leather, wire, chicken wire, paper clips, glue
Small wheels, Styrofoam, bottle caps, pop-tops from cans

Formica, tile, linoleum
Sandpaper, paint, shellac, brushes
Hinges, knobs, nuts, bolts, hooks
Pulleys, rope
Broom, dustpan, rags
Safety glasses
Work gloves
Magnet
Paint shirts
Bandages
Mild bath soap
Babyfood jar lids (for wheels)
Spools
Rubber bands

Yarn
Cardboard tubes

Objectives

1. To use wood as a medium of expression.
2. To discover relationships of equality, inequality, and proportionate comparisons while building and constructing with wood and other materials.
3. To communicate, plan, and work cooperatively with others to solve common problems.
4. To use woodworking as an emotional release and/or as a means of nonverbal expression.
5. To develop fine muscles by working with hammer and nails, and large muscles by working with saw, lifting.
6. To improve eye-hand coordination by manipulating tools.
7. To experience a legitimate way of making noise.
8. To refine sensory awareness.

Seven Basic Woodworking Operations

1. *Sanding.* The sanding operation underlies almost all woodworking activities. Its purpose is to smooth and shape wood. Mounting sandpaper on wood blocks makes this operation much easier for children to master and reduces waste of sandpaper supplies.

Steps to Follow

a. Fold a section of sandpaper to accommodate the approximate area of the wood block.
b. Bend the sandpaper along the fold several times.
c. Tear the sandpaper along the straight edge of a table or workbench.
d. Use a staple gun or glue to secure the sandpaper. Do not allow children to manipulate a staple gun. It is a tool that requires strength and precision to use properly. Its potential danger is great.

Sanding is accomplished with long, even strokes away from the body. Sand with the grain of the wood. If the piece of wood to be sanded is small, the students may wish to hold the wood in one hand while using the sanding block with the other. For larger pieces of wood, securing the wood with a "C" clamp or vise will make the sanding operation easier. Allow the children to discover the difference varying grades of sandpaper make in the smoothness obtained.

2. *Gluing.* The second woodworking operation is generally not difficult for children to master since they have had previous experience with glue. However, make sure that the glue used with wood is suited to that purpose. Popsicle sticks are handy for spreading glue evenly on the two or more areas of wood to be glued together. Putting small amounts of glue in recycled plastic food containers cuts down on waste.

Steps to Follow

a. Spread the glue on the surfaces.
b. Wait for the glue to get tacky. Provide a related activity for the children during the waiting time.
c. Apply a very thin second coat of glue.
d. Hold or clamp the wood together until the product can be put aside to set.

3. *Hammering or nailing.* This basic woodworking operation is for fastening material together.

Steps to Follow

a. Use an awl or a nail with a large head to make a pilot hole. The pilot hole anchors the nail and makes it easier for the child to hammer the nail in straight.
b. Insert the nail in the pilot hole.
c. Hold the hammer near the end of the handle. While holding the nail with the thumb and forefinger of the other hand, tap the nail lightly with the hammer until it stands by itself.
d. Remove the fingers from the nail and hit harder until the nail is in place.

    If the wood splits during the operation, the reason(s) may be that the nail is too near the edge of the wood, the nail shaft is too thick, or there are too many holes in the same grain of wood. The nail is likely to bend if it is too long and thin. Having the work too high may cause the child to hit the nail on an angle. This, in turn, may also cause the nail to bend. A safety precaution for this operation and others is wearing safety glasses. Protective lenses help to prevent getting wood or metal particles into the eyes, and most children find them fun to wear.

4. *Holding.* Vises and "C" clamps hold the wood securely to the work surface during sanding, sawing, drilling, and some fastening operations. For most efficient use of a vise, have it permanently attached to the workbench or table. Placing a piece of heavy cardboard or thin wood between the holding device and the finished product will prevent marring.

5. *Drilling.* The drilling operation has two distinct purposes. The first is to drill holes through wood, and the second is to make pilot holes in which to insert screws. There are many types of drills and bit sizes. One used frequently with children is a hand drill with a ¼" (.64 cm) chuck that works like an eggbeater. Bits ranging in size from ⅛" to ¼" (.32 to 64 cm) are available to use in this type of drill. The push drill is easy for young children to use for making holes ¼" (.64 cm) and smaller. The bits for this type of drill are commonly called "points." A brace and bit is used for holes larger than ¼" (.64 cm). For young children, the appropriate drill point or bit could be chosen and secured by an adult.

Steps to Follow

a. Secure the wood to the work surface.

b. Make an initial pilot hole for the drill with the awl.

c. Use the appropriate drill and bit for the intended purpose.

6. *Fastening with screws.* The initial step in this operation is choosing the appropriate type of screwdriver—slot or Phillips. The size of the screwdriver should be equal to the size of the screwhead. Select the necessary bit or point for the predrilling according to the screw's shank size.

Steps to Follow

a. Select a screwdriver and bit.

b. Insert the bit into the drill. Test to make sure it is secure.

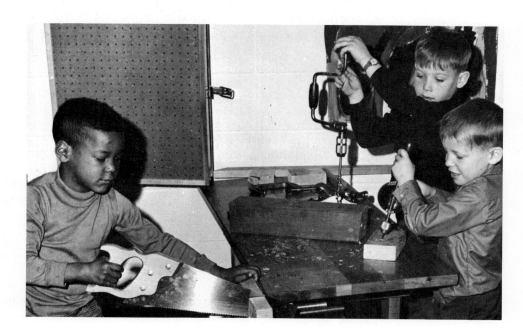

    c. Punch an initial pilot hole with an awl.

    d. Predrill a hole for the screw.

    e. Insert the screw and turn it with the selected screwdriver (clockwise to insert, counterclockwise to remove).

    f. Screwdrivers are dangerous. They should be used only by children who have shown advanced coordination and only under strict supervision (Skeen et al., 1984).

7. *Sawing.* This operation is the most difficult woodworking operation for the majority of children to master. The basic carpenter's saw, a crosscut, 12"–16" (30.5 cm–40.6 cm) long is used for this operation. A good one will have 11 to 16 points per inch (2.54 cm). Look for the number of points per inch on the heel of the saw. Before buying a saw, in addition to looking for the appropriate size and number of points per inch (2.54 cm), bend the blade over to test the metal. If the blade does not spring back straight, do not buy it. A coping saw is used to cut gradual curves and interior shapes. Buy extra blades, because they tend to break frequently.

Steps to Follow

    a. Mark a saw line with a pencil.

    b. Secure the wood with a vise or clamp to saw on the waste-wood side of the line. Use a wood file to make a groove for the saw blade.

    c. With the saw resting in the groove, begin slow, rhythmic back-and-forth motions. Hold the wood with your free hand.

    d. Increase the speed of the motions as the groove deepens.

    e. Slow your motions near completion to help prevent breaking or splintering the wood.

        A work glove on the holding hand protects the child from abrasions if the saw happens to slip out of its groove. Lubricate the saw blade with mild bath soap to keep it working smoothly. Also, be sure to have the blade sharpened occasionally.

        In addition to the seven basic woodworking operations, children enjoy painting what they construct. Brannen (1978) suggests using a mixture of easel paint and white glue, which covers the wood well and does not rub off easily. Brannen also suggests having a rule that some construction must occur before painting; otherwise some children will only paint.

Introduction to Woodworking

1. *Tools and wood.* Touching the tools and wood helps young children feel secure. By holding and feeling all the materials, children acquire infor-

mation about weight, balance, strength, and texture. The children will move the wood from one place to another, shake the work table, and take out and replace the tools. When they have learned the motions and behaviors appropriate for the center, they will move to the next level (Davis, 1980).

2. *Demonstration.* Always demonstrate the proper use of tools to the children. Go through the actual steps they will be using to duplicate a specific woodworking activity. If sequence is important to the process, help the children understand the rationale for the progression.

3. *Simple activity attempts.* The children will begin to enlarge upon their awareness of carpentry by experimenting with some of its uses and the processes involved. Hammering, sanding, gluing, sawing, and placing pieces of wood securely into the vise and removing them are among the basic skills explored (Davis, 1980).

4. *Experimentation.* After the children have had an opportunity to produce a directed product in woodworking, allow them to experiment with

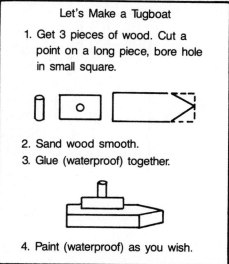

Let's Make a Napkin Holder

1. Get 3 pieces of wood

2. Sand wood smooth

3. Glue sides to bottom

4. Paint, if you wish.

Let's Make An Airplane

1. Get 3 pieces of wood like these:

2. Sand wood smooth.

3. Glue front wing on.

4. Glue back wing on.

5. Paint.

Let's Make a Serving Tray

1. Get 3 pieces of wood.

2. Sand wood smooth.

3. Nail together.

4. Paint as you wish.

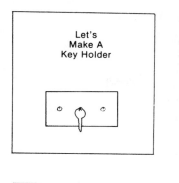

Let's
Make A
Key Holder

1. Punch wood at
the 3 dots on
the front.

2. Punch wood at
dot on back.

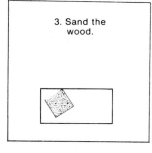

3. Sand the
wood.

4. Paint wood
with varnish.

5. Let dry
overnight.

6. Drill the 3
punched holes
on the front.

7. Nail hanger
at back
punched hole.

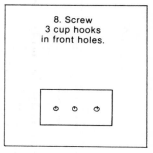

8. Screw
3 cup hooks
in front holes.

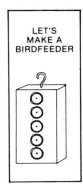

LET'S MAKE A BIRDFEEDER

1. Sand a piece of wood like this:

2. Nail 5 bottle caps into each large side of wood.

3. Punch and drill a hole at dot on top of wood.

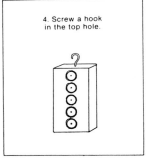

4. Screw a hook in the top hole.

5. Full bottle caps with peanut butter.

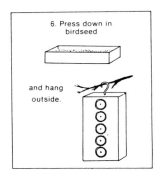

6. Press down in birdseed

and hang outside.

Let's Make a Stoplight.

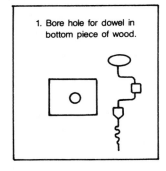

1. Bore hole for dowel in bottom piece of wood.

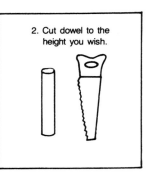

2. Cut dowel to the height you wish.

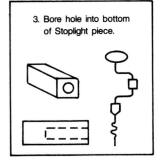

3. Bore hole into bottom of Stoplight piece.

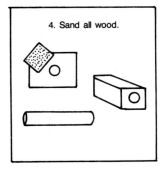

4. Sand all wood.

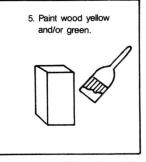

5. Paint wood yellow and/or green.

(Continued)

6. Let dry overnight.

7. Tack bottle caps to Stoplight block.

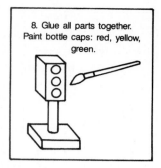

8. Glue all parts together. Paint bottle caps: red, yellow, green.

another, similar project. The product may be identical to the one produced earlier, or it may vary in every way from the original. The product is not the goal. What is important here is giving the children an opportunity for expression.

5. *Recipes.* Chart paper or posterboard may be used to make woodworking recipes. Directions for specific woodworking activities are numbered sequentially and written in concise sentences. Illustrations and varying colors for each step in the sequence help the children follow written directions. See the accompanying "recipes."

6. *Task cards.* Use posterboard cards with illustrations and written directions for specific woodworking activities. If a precise sequence is necessary, number each card. Otherwise, leave the cards unnumbered and use them to evaluate the children's understanding of the activity. To preserve task cards, laminate or cover them with transparent adhesive. Sample task cards follow.

Suggested Activities

Resource Person. Invite a local carpenter (preferably a parent or relative of one of your students) to demonstrate proper usage of major tools, the importance of measuring for proper proportions, how to smooth wood with sandpaper, and so on.

Field Trips. Plan field trips to a construction site, a cabinet shop, and/or a lumber yard.

Large Tree Stump. Add a large tree stump (inside or outside) to this center to use for hammering.

Musical Instruments. Have the children cut two squares of wood to make sand blocks. Using the squares, have them trace the shape onto the sandpaper, cut the sandpaper shape out, and glue it onto the square (rough side out). On the smooth side, have the children glue a dowel length or spool on for a handle.

These can be painted and used as musical instruments when dry (Croft, 1990).

Ideas for Using Cardboard. Cardboard can be purchased or obtained as industrial scrap.

1. *Stool.* Make the base from a large tube and the top from thin plywood or triwall. Fasten with tape or glue. Small telephone wire spools can also be used to make stools.
2. *Table.* Same as above using several tubes for the base.
3. *Storage containers.* Fasten several tubes together.

Ideas for Using Wood. Simple objects such as animals and boats can be made by the children. They can build their own creative structures; older children may use simple pictorial directions. The finished product may be painted.

1. *Trucks and cars.* Use assorted sizes of wood blocks for the body of the vehicle. Thumb tacks with red and silver heads serve as lights. Faucet washers, jar lids, or dowels may be used as wheels. All basic woodworking operations are incorporated into this activity.
2. *Trains.* This is similar to the preceding activity with the addition of hooks and catches for connecting train cars.
3. *Marvelous monsters.* Make these with one or a combination of fastening operations and lots of imagination.

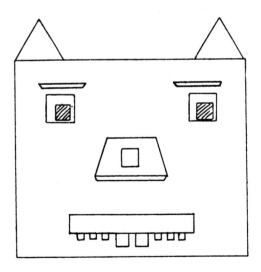

4. *People.* Use one or more fastening operations combined with various sizes and shapes of wood. Have newspaper or material scraps available for clothes and other special features.

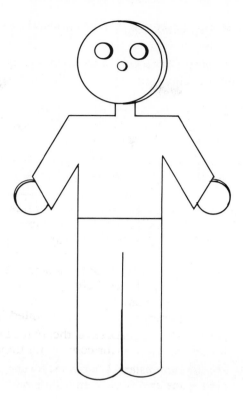

5. *Animals*. Imagination makes this an especially creative activity using different sizes and shapes of wood and a combination of fastening operations.

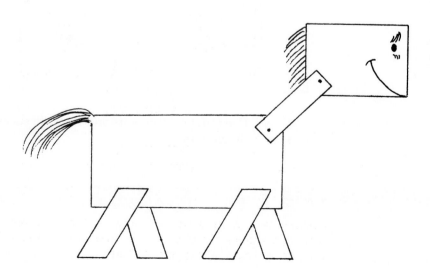

6. *Animal wrap boards.* Use yarn or wire to trace outlines of animals on nails.

7. *Buildings.* With small modifications, the initial structure may be a house, barn, school, or church. Entire mini-cities may be built.

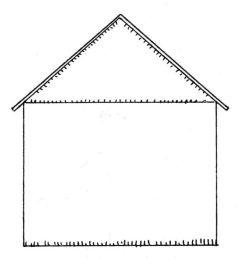

8. *Fences.* Wood blocks serve as corner posts and supports, with tongue depressors or Popsicle sticks for rails.

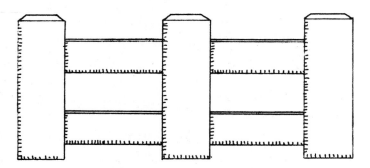

9. *Animal cages.* Use tongue depressors and Popsicle sticks. Glue on paper wheels for a circus train effect.

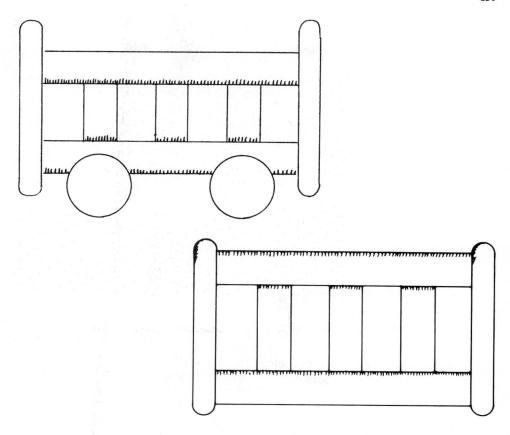

10. *Recipe holders.* This may be an all-gluing activity or a combination of any of the fastening operations (gluing, nailing, and/or fastening with screws).

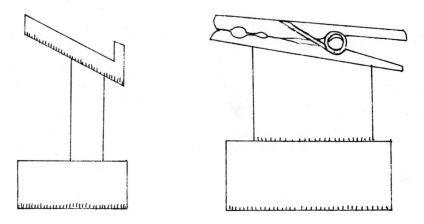

11. *Tomahawks.* This is a simple nailing activity.

12. *Puzzles.* Use simple shapes with straight edges and/or slight curves.

13. *Rubber band letter boards.* Use printed numbers and arrows on boards to help ensure accurate letter formation.

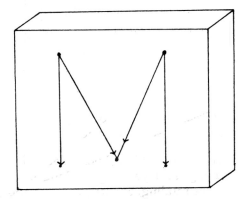

14. *Geoboards.* This is a good activity for even very young children who have some hammering experience.

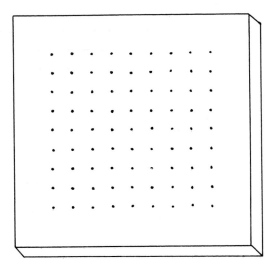

15. *Signs.* Let children make traffic signs for use later in the block center, sand area, or outside.

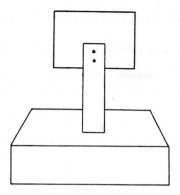

16. *Birdhouse*. This may be a gluing and/or nailing activity. Make sure that the glue is waterproof for use outside.

17. *Bookholders*. Making bookholders with fixed ends uses skills in sanding, nailing, and painting. Making bookholders with adjustable ends requires sanding, sawing, drilling, and painting skills.

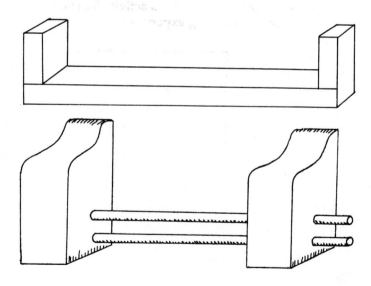

Combined Use of Wood and Cardboard. Make a mobile with several scraps of decorated wood and cardboard.

Interrelated Center Activities

Language Arts

1. Show pictures of construction sites, tool catalogs, tool boxes, and so on to the children. The children are to find and discuss specific woodworking tools in the pictures.
2. The child draws an object made of wood on a Language Master card. They tape-record information about the object drawn and listen to their own recordings and those of other students.
3. The children match picture cards of tools with word cards of tool names, rhyming words, and scrambled letter cards.
4. The students look up information about trees, leaves, paper, and so on.
5. The students write about what they would like to be made into if they were a tree or what they would build from wood if they had their choice of anything in the world.
6. The children make journals of activities completed. Ask them to share the journals in circle time (Koppelman, 1976).

Games

1. Have the children classify pictures and/or objects into correct categories such as tools, toys, clothes, and books.
2. The children cut and paste classification cards of tools, wood products, and people who work with wood, from magazines and catalogs.
3. Make Lotto games with pictures or word cards for the children to match.
4. Design and develop open-ended game boards and information cards in the shape of tools.
5. Have the children play sorting games for different sizes and/or types of nails or screws.

Blocks. Have the children build various structures such as houses, schools, trains, and space stations.

Science and Math

1. Have the children count the annual rings of a tree trunk to determine its approximate age.
2. Have the children measure and mark several pieces of wood both in inches and centimeters.
3. Have the children add and subtract various marked wood lengths.
4. Have the children use scales to weigh different kinds of wood of like size. They chart and compare the different weights.

5. Ask the children to identify 10 objects made of wood.

6. Have the children make an insect jar by pounding holes in jar lid with hammer and nail (Oklahoma State Department of Education, 1983).

7. Have the children experiment with nailing different materials (e.g., different types of wood—hard and soft, cardboard, and Styrofoam. Have them label these *hard* and *soft* and discuss texture, size, and shape of the items (Croft, 1990).

8. Have the children sand varying grains of wood (rough and semirough) and use different grades of sandpaper. Have them compare what the different grades of sandpaper do to the varying grains of wood by touching and feeling. Discuss why this difference happens (Croft, 1990).

Art

1. Make a tree collage. Cut brown and green paper and paste it onto a baking sheet.

2. Paint woodworking projects.

3. Make seasonal trees. Draw four trees; paint and/or color according to each season.

4. Make block pictures. Use pictures cut from magazines and decoupage onto wood.

5. Make leaf prints. Cover leaves with thin paper and color over them with the flat side of a crayon.

6. Draw and color carpenters' tools.

7. Make tool boxes with shoe boxes and string handles. Add paper tool cut-outs.

8. Crush old crayon pieces in a paper or cloth bag using hammers. Spread crushed crayon on construction or waxed paper. Fold and melt with a warm iron.

9. Make a design with glue on paper. Sprinkle sawdust on wet glue. Shake the excess into a wastebasket.

10. Paint on different textures of wood products such as paper, cardboard, paneling, and wood blocks.

Drama

1. Have the children pantomime tools being used.

2. Provide props for role playing people who work with wood-forest rangers, lumberjacks, carpenters, and so on.

3. Stimulate creative dramatics with songs such as "London Bridge" and "If I Had a Hammer."

Social Studies

1. Have the children discuss future use for woodworking in their homes.

2. Ask the children to draw the tools they think a carpenter or an architect uses (Koppelman, 1976).

3. Have the children research other jobs that use woodworking and/or carpentry.

Computer-Enhanced Learning

Using Technology to Aid Instruction _____

> Technology should be integrated into curriculum areas in experiences that enhance the educational process for students. Technology should facilitate instructional management for more individualized instruction and assessment. Technology should support administration for greater efficiency and focus on learning. (*Orange County Schools Technology for Learning*, 1991)

Benefits of Computer-Enhanced Instruction

Research on the effectiveness of technology used with instruction indicates that educators should emphasize *technology that supports learning*, rather than focusing on technology itself.

Computers lend themselves especially well to the self-discovery style of young children for the following reasons (Beaty, 1992b, p. 70):

1. "The computer's style of interaction favors young children."
2. "The computer's combination of visual and verbal learning is especially helpful to young children." According to Beaty, children are especially responsive to visual stimuli before they can read and write. Seeing words on the screen, combined with visual images and even words they hear, helps them make the "transition to verbal thinking."
3. "The computer makes it easier to individualize learning." Beaty finds that educational software provides students a bounded range of choices and monitors their progress to help them adjust their choices appropriately.
4. "The computer serves as an equalizer for children from different backgrounds." According to Beaty, all children should have equal access to classroom computers, children with disabilities can use technology to level the learning field, and disadvantaged children are less intimidated by hints and corrections from a computer than those from a teacher.

5. "The computer is an effective promoter of young children's positive self-image." Students can proceed at their own speed and experience success.

Beaty and Tucker (1987) emphasize that if visually oriented computer software is used to support learning early and continues into the elementary and secondary school years, the visual element can help preserve and develop the creativity that often diminishes as children develop verbal skills in school. Having a computer for every student in early school years is unnecessary, because having students share a computer as part of an activity enhances social skills, cooperative learning, language skills, and creativity.

Constructivist Theory

It has been observed that children go through three developmental levels in computer use. At the manipulation level, they press different keys and watch for effects of their actions on the screen until they figure out how a program works. At the mastery level, they have learned how the program works and use this knowledge to create the effects they want. At the meaning level, they invent new uses for favorite effects (Beaty, 1992b).

Beaty's descriptions of children's uses of computers are examples of a constructivist theory of learning, which holds that children combine new sensory input with their prior learning to construct and retain their own meanings. Thus, according to this theory, "learning is a reconstruction rather than a transmission of knowledge" (Molinhar, 1990).

Wirth (1993) advocates a constructivist approach to learning to ready students for the work patterns of the future, quoting from Piaget: "To understand is to discover, or reconstruct by rediscovery, and such conditions must be complied with if in the future individuals are to be formed who are capable of production and creativity not simply repetition" (p. 361). Wirth describes the essential conditions of a learning environment as "freedom to play with ideas, to experiment, and to enter into dialog" (p. 362). He states that "an inquiring collaborative style of learning can be combined with the power of computer technology to produce an education appropriate for our time" (Wirth, p. 364).

Integrated Learning

The interdisciplinary character of much educational software makes it useful in supporting integrated learning—integrating content areas such as math, science, and communication skills and utilizing thinking skills, real-world applications, cooperative learning, and technology. Jacobs (1989) emphasizes that learning within individual disciplines should not be eliminated; rather, it should be complemented by interdisciplinary learning to give separate disciplines more impact, because students then see them as relevant to each other and important for their own lives.

Students may also develop better thinking skills, such as being flexible, valuing multiple points of view, and making analogies, so that the whole of the integrated learning may be greater than the sum of its parts. Interdisciplinary education is "the pinnacle of curriculum development" (Ackerman, 1989).

The Computer-Enhanced Learning Program

The following are examples of the kinds of early childhood learning objectives that computer use can support (Dodge & Colker, 1992).

Objectives for Socio-Emotional Development

- Work cooperatively with others (working in pairs at the computer).
- Take responsibility for one's own work (directing the flow of a program).
- Develop perseverance (seeing a program or task through to completion).

Objectives for Cognitive Development

- Identify and sort objects by attributes such as color, shape, and size (using programs that develop classification skills).
- Learn sequencing and order (using programs that focus on size and patterning).
- Develop early reading skills (relating word labels to graphics).
- Understand cause and effect (seeing what happens when keys are pressed and feedback is given during a program).
- Extend creativity (using programs that encourage free explorations or simple graphics-creation programs).

Objectives for Physical Development

- Develop small muscle skills (putting a disk in the disk drive, clicking a computer mouse, using the keyboard).
- Refine eye and hand coordination (moving the cursor to a desired place on the screen).
- Improve visual skills (tracking movement on the screen).

Teachers' Experiences

At the Triangle J New Hope Model Elementary School in Orange County Schools, Hillsborough, North Carolina, technology supports learning as one of six components of an effective school: site-based management, parent partici-

TABLE 12-1   K-3 Objectives for Technology Use from the Computer Skills Curriculum Adopted in July 1992 by the North Carolina Department of Public Instruction*

 **School Level Strands Guide**

Elementary Grades K

	Societal Uses	Ethics	Terms & Operation	Curriculum Software Use	Keyboarding	Word Processing
	1.1.....Identify the computer as a machine that helps people work and play.		2.1.....Identify the physical components of a computer system (e.g., monitor, keyboard, disk drive, printer). 2.3.....Demonstrate correct use of a computer.		2.2.....On a keyboard, identify letters, numbers, and other commonly-used keys (e.g., RETURN/ENTER, space bar).	
	1.1.....Identify uses of technology at home and at school.	1.2.....Demonstrate respect for the computer work of others.	2.1.....Identify the physical components of a computer system (e.g., monitor, keyboard, disk drive, printer). 2.2.....Identify fundamental computer terms (e.g., disk, software, hardware, booting/starting, cursor). 2.4.....Demonstrate correct use of hardware and software.		2.3.....On a keyboard, demonstrate the use of letter keys, number keys and special keys (e.g., shift key, delete/back-space, space bar, arrow keys).	
	1.1.....Identify uses of technology in the community.	1.2.....Describe the right of an individual to owner-ship of his/her created computer work.	2.1.....Identify the function of physical components of a computer system (e.g., monitor, keyboard, CPU, disk drive, printer). 2.6.....Demonstrate correct use of hardware and software.		2.2.....Locate and use symbol keys and special function keys (e.g., period, question mark, Caps Lock, arrow keys, shift, ESC). 2.3.....Demonstrate correct keyboarding pos-ture and finger placement for the home row keys.	2.4.....Identify word processing terms (e.g., word processing, cursor, load, save, print). 2.5.....Demonstrate begin-ning word processing techniques of entering selected home row words, saving, printing, and retrieving text.
	1.1.....Identify the ways technology has changed the lives of people in com-munities.	1.2.....Explain that the copyright law protects what a person or a com-pany has created and placed on a diskette.	2.1.....Identify the physical components of a computer system as either input, output, or processing devices. 2.5.....Demonstrate correct use of hardware and software.	2.4.....Use commercial software in content areas.	2.2.....Demonstrate proper keyboarding tech-niques for keying all letters.	2.3.....Use a word pro-cessing program to load, enter, save, and print text.

pation, staff development, developmentally appropriate instruction, technology, and program evaluation.

Gilbert (1989) describes first grade teachers at Running Creek Elementary School in Colorado, who started with one 2-week interdisciplinary unit. After 5 years, they were doing 80% of their teaching with interdisciplinary units and this approach had spread to the rest of the school. Gilbert found that interdisciplinary work at Running Creek resulted in "better student self-discipline, improved attendance, fewer visits to the school nurse, increased homework completion, and better attitudes" (p. 47).

Teacher Chris Held (Instructional Materials Services, 1989) finds that technology support has helped him move to a more effective role in relation to students. He observes that "the reality has been [that] it was the teacher, me, up in front of the class, kind of the sage on the stage. The good news is that today we can really take advantage of technology. . . . I've left that sage on the stage, for much of the day, and become the guide on the side, who's working individually with children or working with small groups of children."

Gillings and Griffiths (1989) describe primary students using *Logo*-like commands to program a real toy robot to perform tasks. They point out that this work "involves the children in planning, predicting, and testing. It also involves measurement and the use of numbers" (p. 132).

Myers (1991) helps her students integrate communication skills and social studies using telecommunications: "Students from across the country and around the world answered four basic questions: Who am I? What do I want to do when I grow up? How do I want the world to be better when I grow up? What can I do now to make this happen?" (p. 34). Myers finds that sharing their answers with students around the world through telecommunications results in a dramatic increase in her students' interest in school. "With the help of technology—and an encouraging push from a fellow teacher—[she found that her] students were able to reach out and touch the world" (p. 35).

Learning Goals

Learning should be strengthened by technology use to make learning *relevant, appealing, developmentally appropriate,* and *successful* for students.

Making learning *relevant* means relating it to the world in which students live now and will live in the future. This includes relating concepts to real applications, being able to think and solve problems, and working and communicating effectively with others in the same class and farther away, as in other schools and other parts of the world.

Making learning *appealing* means arranging for learning experiences in which students get involved, that seem relevant to them, that are fun, and that help students want to be lifelong learners.

Making learning *developmentally appropriate* means providing for each student's developmental stage and learning style with concept development moving from concrete, hands-on experiences to abstract concepts.

Making learning *successful* means making sure that each student experiences success and makes significant progress in learning.

Suggested Activities

Develop the attitude that the teacher should not always be the "sage on the stage" (Instructional Materials Services, 1989); rather, the teacher should be the "guide on the side" (Instructional Materials Services, 1989), modeling lifelong learning alongside children while continuing to help them make those critical connections between the software they are using and the concepts they are learning.

Word Processing and Publishing
Help the students use word processing and publishing software to facilitate, illustrate, and publish their writing. "A word processor is a critical tool for the writing process because it makes editing so simple and fun that students are willing to do it" (*Orange County Schools Model School Technology Committee Educational Recommendations,* 1990). Have the students use the spelling checker included with the word processor to identify their misspellings. They can correct these using the word processor dictionary or a paper dictionary. Let the students compete with the spelling checker to see whether they can "catch" it not identifying a misspelled word. Then they can add the word to the software dictionary.

Students love to publish their work for their class and wider audiences. Desktop publishing software makes their work look attractive and enhances their pride in publishing and desire to write more.

Electronic Mail
Help the students compose messages to communicate through electronic mail with students in other classes, giving them another real reason to write well. Let them exchange their story files with other classes.

Examples of Communications Technology in the Classroom. Following are illustrations of students and staff using technology to support the development of communication skills in New Hope Elementary School, Orange County Schools, Hillsborough, North Carolina.

Logo
Help the students integrate math, thinking skills, the writing process, art, and music through *Logo* software. *Logo* was developed to teach students geometry as they give keyboard commands to a turtle to move through distances and angles to draw shapes. Help the students use *Logo* to make the concept of angle intuitive. Encourage them to analyze and communicate about what they are doing as they solve problems in getting the turtle to draw the shapes they want and illustrate stories they write with turtle drawings and sounds and

A grade 2–3 student is working on her story about dinosaur bones. Using a primary publishing program, she is able to publish the story she wrote in her journal yesterday.

This K-1 student has just finished keying in his story, "About Baseball." He composed his story at the computer, which is in the Story Writing Center. This student's story, as well as others written by K–1 students, are also illustrated.

music. Help them make connections between what they do and concepts such as shapes.

Microcomputer-Based Science Laboratories
Help the students use simple sensors attached to a computer and motorized simple machine-building kits and robots to enhance measurement and science exploration. For example, a temperature sensor measures temperature in air and

About Baseball

I hive a baseball game on monday. I hive baseball pids on satday. I pay sote stop. We tow to bases. And i pay sekt base. I like baseball. Baseball is fon. I like to hit the mods. I like to rone to. We hive som gud payrs. Er kohe is nise. I kowte 16 fiy bose.
    By cole woodside.

SCIENCE

a exspereens is fun, but dajeris! so if you'er a frend of a mad Sientest be shor to sta bac. do you know a mad sientest? no! is ther a mad sientes ineway? yes! i know ther is! haw created a sientst is! i like sientests. thoms up for Sientest! do you know wot a sientest dos? yes he wrks and wrkr!

March 31, 1992

All About Spring

I liic Spring. Spring is hot. Spring is god. In spring tam i liic to sweym. In spring tam I liic to play weth my Sestre. Today is Sixte togres. In Spring tam I liic to plae. Spring das god theing. Spring dos wadrfl theing. Spring is pretey. Spring is vare halfol.

March 25, 1992

My Famaly

I like my Famly. I like to play weth my Sester. Wen my Dad wrxe I like to help. Wen my Mom fexis brafest I help. My Dad pecx me up. Sum times my Sesetr gets me wen my Dad is wating. My Mom pcxe me up. Som times I am not at home. Som times my Sester is not at home. Som times my Dad gos to taks off the trash. Seom tiems my Mom gos to wrke. Seom times my Sesetr gos to school. Bus 4 taekx me to school. My Famley is spashol.

Puppys

Puppies are freandly and nice. Puppies can be all dafret colors. You neda to fede your baby puppy four time each day. I love puppies very, very, very mouch becos thy love you. Do you like puppies? Yes!

The five Senses

The senses are seeing, smlling, hearing, touching and tasteing. You see with your eyes. You smll with your nose. You hear with your ears. You taste with your mouth. You touch with your hands. If you can not see you are blied and you neda a gade dog to halp you go plases so you will not get rade over by a car. If you can not hear you neda to yous sine lagweg so ether pepla can ader stand you. If you can't see ferry will you neda gllasiy. You have taste buds on your toug to halp you taste. You can fael with your hole body even your feet. You have all of your senses on your body. You tipe with your hands on the computer key brod. I do not know ene pepla who are blied.

Today is Friday, April 10, 1992

A Spring Day
 Spring is fon bech fliirs blom. Rosis blom and a ranbow choms out. Spring is vare, vare, vare spshl bech it's butofol. I Love Toolips bech thay are butofol. I Love Spring bech it's prete. The sun helps the flaowrs.

MY CAT

Mi ct liks to et. mi ct liks to gt n the trsh kn. hr liks to gt ondr the bd. mi ct liks to gt on the coch.

June 1,1992

FISHES

FISHEIS liv in a gas bol. or in the sae. and i like fisheis. my sistr's gold fisheis dide.and win the gold fisheis dide she pot it in a big box . and we wer oseoop . me and my sistr corid. we we wer coiing bcos my sistr's fisheis dide. thet wes the liat tim we seol my sistr's ogin. vrie list tim we evr sel gldlks. i hadid thet we wed navr see her aing. the resn i sid thet i nive sel her aing is thet she wes dide. and thet is wie i said thet. and it wes not fonney. becos wet if you dide wet wed you do. i weid yal dade mama. so dot do thet rembr thet ok ok so dot. ok ok so you shd not do thet ok ok. it wes a sad day. itwes a vare sad day. win the day wes over we cried and cried. wen mama sel use she said wei are you crieing and we said arer gold fesh dide. it wel be ol rit we wer going to getb a new one see now you are oe'l rit see becos you lisnd to me. and my sistr said i am going to get oen for my brthday she wes going to get me a new fish and then i said me and you can shr

it. i promes i wed shr it so laura cod play weth it to beces if i did not lat her play she wed cal me. then i wed not be alve reley. som fish are gold fish. and som fish are not gold fish. som of the theaing in the sae are crabs. and som of the other theaings.and I well till som more theaings obat the sae. ther are oil kins of fish and crabs. ther are weas in the sae.and ther are shrks in the sae to. ther are all kies of theaings in the oshin. ther are a lit of theaings in ther are olit lit lit .becos tha are itspntiv. las not tokobat it ok.las tlk obt estr. sins it is april. sins april the 19 well be son.   and my brthday is april the 29. and I git to be a carridr. it well be a god day for me and my clss to have a prte at school.wet it be fun I thek so mab il have theing to give you insd of reeseeving prass.   now li s go bak to tiking obotd anmls. rabbits run fast.kittens are nis.fish live in the sae.dogs are at my house.cat.horuses are in a fins.now lis tlk obot alt sid ther are hills olt sid.ther are houses olt sid.

liquid and software instantly converts this information to other measures and graphs the results, so students can focus on what is happening rather than becoming bogged down in successive measurements and recordkeeping (*Orange County Schools Model School Technology Committee Educational Recommendations,*

This K–1 student looks in his folder for his contract to read his teacher's feedback and see which center he will visit next.

1990). The machine-building kits and robots create excitement about studying simple machine concepts and help students integrate science and math.

Help the students use simulation software to perform and repeat science experiments that are impractical to do in class. As they repeat the experiments, help them try different variables and help them link variables and results. Help them make the concepts of *hypothesis* and *variable* commonplace.

Telecommunications

> There is nothing like a personal relationship with someone in a distant place to nurture a desire to cooperate and know more about that place. This is the essence of globalization, which many see as essential to future economic and political cooperation worldwide.
>
> [Telecommunications] links students with others in the world outside the school faster and in a more exciting way than the postal service. It creates a need to learn communication skills and social studies.
>
> Through [telecommunications] students can also participate in a project to collect data in scattered locations and share results. (*Orange County Schools Model School Technology Committee Educational Recommendations*, 1990, p. 9)

Help the students dial up an electronic bulletin board to select and participate in telecommunications projects with students in other geographic locations.

Video/Audio Production

> Children are great imitators. For example, they see television programs and want to produce their own. With video camera(s), monitor/receiver, video cassette recorder, and access to an in-house television network, they can share with audiences elsewhere in the school and outside the school. In the process they are integrating subject matter; preparing presentations from that subject matter for real audiences makes learning motivating and increases retention. (*Orange County Schools Technology for Learning Plan*, 1991, p. 10)

Hypermedia

Help the students use hypermedia-controlling software; the varied media of videodiscs and CD-ROM discs; and related hardware such as videodisc players, CD-ROM players, digitizing cameras, scanners, microphones, and speakers to make content come alive. Ultimately, help them create their own hypermedia presentations to show on television screens to culminate their work on cooperatively learned units.

> Hypermedia are built on associative thinking. Associative thinking is a cradle of creativity because it leads to synthesis of things/ideas sometimes in new ways. The student chooses a starting concept and then explores successive menus in the controlling software to pull in and interact with related images, video, graphics, music, databases, and text. Thus the exploration is multisensory, which appeals to a variety of learning styles. It is interdisciplinary,

which makes subject matter more meaningful. It harnesses television, which students like, without the passivity television engenders, because it's interactive. (*Orange County Schools Model School Technology Committee Educational Recommendations*, 1990, p. 12)

Database Access

Help the students use databases. "The ability to search a database for information related to specific criteria becomes ever more critical as the amount of information explodes. Databases are especially useful in social studies and science" (*Orange County Schools Model School Technology Committee Recommendations*, 1990, p. 12). An increasingly familiar form of database is the multimedia encyclopedia. The popularity of this kind of encyclopedia with children can help lead them to developing facility with paper encyclopedias as well.

Media Center Automation

Another example of a database is the media center catalog. Students find an on-line catalog fun and easy, motivating them to explore more sources for their research. Help them integrate this activity into cooperative learning units. A computer network can make a media center catalog available to the classroom, thereby making the media center more efficient to use and the research more immediate.

Electronic Support Systems for Students with Disabilities

Identify and incorporate electronic support systems appropriate for students in your classroom who have disabilities. For example,

Beginning his work with computers as an early childhood student, this student, now in grade 4–5, is using a multimedia encyclopedia to complement his other ways of learning science concepts.

augmentative communication systems . . . eliminate one of the most frustrating barriers that a nonverbal person encounters—the inability to communicate his/her needs and wants. Electronic environmental control systems provide access to computers, telephones, TV, and other electronic and mechanical equipment which allows even the most severely physical handicapped person to have some control of his/her life. (*Orange County Schools Model School Technology Committee Educational Recommendations*, 1990, p. 14)

These support systems help level the learning field for students with disabilities.

Computer-Managed Instruction
Help the students use software that incorporates concept reinforcement, monitoring of progress, recordkeeping, and reporting. Use these capabilities to individualize practice, reinforcement, and monitoring. Make sure the students' use of this software is connected to concepts they are learning in their other activities.

Suggestions for Teacher Use of Technology

Student Information Management
Use software to make information management more efficient. Use it to record and calculate attendance; maintain a student database; create reports on student progress; create and update inventories of resources; and create lesson plans, presentations, handouts, and evaluation instruments.

Voice Mail
Use voice mail to facilitate and increase contacts with parents. For example, record a daily greeting and homework message. Parents who are reluctant to speak directly with a teacher may try initial contact through listening to a home-

Ms. Jones helps children ages 7 and 8 use the main menu to access programs linked to concepts they are learning.

K–1 teachers Ms. Eubanks and Ms. Holman use word processing/database software to create templates and narratives to report student progress to parents, students, and the school. In this school, teachers use narrative reports in place of grades. Portfolios contain samples of students' work and are shared with parents in parent/teacher conferences.

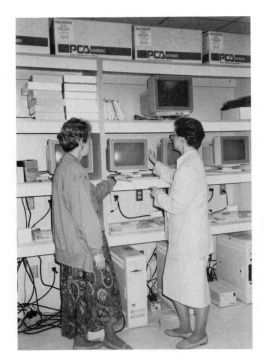

Media specialist Ms. Solomon and lead technology expert Ms. Efland confer on backing up the instructional file servers.

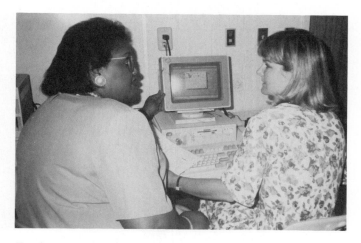

Teachers on the same multi-age team work on writing and developing the narratives for the portfolio.

work message. Other parents may call and leave messages, to which the teacher can respond when convenient.

Resources

Software Selection Criteria for Age 4 to Grade 3

1. The software has been reviewed and recommended in a reliable source, such as the *Advisory List of Computer Courseware* provided to school

Ms. Holman is printing a narrative report on the laser printer.

Ms. Holman calls on Ms. Efland to help send printing from the teacher's computer in the classroom through the computer network to the laser printer in the teacher workroom.

media coordinators by the Media Evaluation Services Section of the North Carolina Department of Public Instruction, or in software periodicals such as *Incider*.

2. Technical support is readily available.

Ms. Eubanks contacts a parent to set up a conference to review a student's portfolio. Each classroom has a telephone and voice mail to facilitate parent contacts.

3. Thorough documentation is included.

4. The producer is reputable.

5. The software is noted for being "user friendly."

6. The software is appropriate for student developmental level(s).

7. If appropriate, the software provides recordkeeping capabilities.

8. The software provides options for the teacher to tailor the software to class or individual needs.

9. The software provides for selection of a variety of activities with a progression of skills developed through the program.

10. Individuals within the school or district who may have access to or knowledge of review sources or programs have been consulted.

11. The software has been previewed if reliable review is unavailable.

12. The cost is proportionate to need and use.

13. The software contributes a balanced collection including simulations, utilities, and management, as well as tutorials.

Integrated Learning System Selection Criteria

1. The system enables the user to access other software that is not directly included in the system.

2. The system is highly correlated to the curriculum the school is using.

3. The system develops higher-order thinking skills, in addition to lower-order thinking skills.

4. The system promotes integrated learning through a variety of subjects and applications.

5. The system provides initially for at least K–5 math and communications skills concepts.

6. The system is designed to complement noncomputer instruction.

7. When the system is used to complement noncomputer instruction, the result is short- and long-range improvement in appropriate test scores and/or other assessments.

8. The format appeals to students and promotes continued use by means of:

   a. Providing graphics, sound, and animation appeal, but not to the extent that they detract student attention from concepts.

   b. Giving hints that promote understanding following incorrect answers.

   c. Returning the student periodically to missed items.

   d. Making explanations/illustration available.

e. Requiring the student to go through just the lesson(s) needed, rather than every lesson in a sequence.

9. Teacher options and control are easy and extensive.

10. Reports are available for teacher diagnostic use and for parents.

11. Overall costs are affordable:

   a. The start-up cost is the highest of the costs.

   b. Annual follow-up costs are low.

   c. Service support is available at minimal cost.

   d. A full-time manager just for the Instructional Materials Services/Integrated Learning System (IMS/ILS) is not required; a network manager can also manage the IMS/ILS.

Software

Abacus Instructional Management System (Abacus Educational Systems, Inc.)
Animal Homes and Stories (Troll Associates)
Bouncy Bee Learns Letters (IBM)
Bouncy Bee Learns Words (IBM)
Children's Writing and Publishing Center (The Learning Company)
Circulation Plus/Catalog Plus (Follett Software Company)
Cleanwater Detectives (Minnesota Educational Computing Consortium)
Compton's Multimedia Encyclopedia (Encyclopaedia Britannica)
Conquering Whole Numbers (Minnesota Educational Computing Consortium)
Estimation Strategies (Minnesota Educational Computing Consortium)
Exploring Math with Manipulatives (IBM)
Exploring Measurement, Time, and Money (IBM)
Geometry Workshop (Scott, Foresman and Company)
Gertrude's Secrets (The Learning Company)
Graphing and Probability Workshop (Scott, Foresman and Company)
Grolier's Multimedia Encyclopedia (Grolier Electronic Publishing, Inc.)
IBM Classroom LAN Administration System (*ICLAS*) (IBM)
IBM Math Concepts Series (IBM)
IBM Math Practice Series (IBM)
Josten's Learning Systems (Josten's Learning Corporation)
Just Grandma and Me (Broderbund)
Kinder Critters (Microgram Publishing)
Linkway Live (IBM)
LogoWriter (Logo Computer Systems Inc.)
Mammals: Multimedia Encyclopedia on CD-ROM (National Geographic)
Measure Works (Minnesota Educational Computing Consortium)
Microsoft Works (Microsoft Corporation)
Milliken Math Sequences (Milliken Publishing Company)
Moptown Hotel (The Learning Company)

Moptown Parade (The Learning Company)
Muppet Math (Sunburst Communications)
Mystery Objects (Minnesota Educational Computing Consortium)
Paper Plane Pilot (Minnesota Educational Computing Consortium)
Patterns (Minnesota Educational Computing Consortium)
Picture a Story (Minnesota Educational Computing Consortium)
Primary Geometry (Scott, Foresman and Company)
Primary Graphing and Probability Workshop (Scott, Foresman and Company)
Problem Solving with Nim (Minnesota Educational Computing Consortium)
Procom Plus (Datastorm Technologies Inc.)
PSL Personal Science Lab (IBM)
Puppetmaker (Sunburst Communications)
Reader Rabbit (The Learning Company)
SpeechViewer II (IBM)
Stories and More (IBM)
Storybook Weaver (Minnesota Educational Computing Consortium)
Take a Chance (Minnesota Educational Computing Consortium)
The Tale of Peter Rabbit (Discis Knowledge Research, Inc.)
Teaching and Learning with Computers (IBM)
Touch Typing for Beginners (IBM)
Windy City (Minnesota Educational Computing Consortium)
Woolly Bounce (Minnesota Educational Computing Consortium)
Woolly's Garden (Minnesota Educational Computing Consortium)
The Writing Center (The Learning Company)
Writing to Read (IBM)
Writing to Write (IBM)

Work Stations

IBM Model 25 or higher with at least a 386 processor, if possible, at least 2 megabytes of RAM (preferably 4–6 Mb), at least 40 megabytes of fixed disk drive space, a 3.5-inch high-density floppy drive, at least 16 megahertz speed (preferably higher), a sound device such as *Digispeech* or an audio capture/playback adapter card, a mouse, a VGA or higher color monitor, and a self-booting appropriate network adapter card if a local area network exists or is being planned.

Macintosh LC II or higher with at least 2 megabytes of RAM, preferably 4–6 Mb, at least 40 megabytes of fixed disk drive space, a 3.5-inch high-density floppy drive, at least 16 megahertz speed, a mouse, a color monitor, and an appropriate network adapter card if a local area network exists or is being planned.

Printer and cable, such as IBM Personal Printer Series II or Apple Imagewriter II.

Complementary Hardware

CD-ROM drive
Laserdisc player

Motion video adapter card
Still-video digital camera
Video capture/playback adapter card
Scanner
Speakers
Microphone
Headphones
True-color overhead projector palette
Overhead projector
Screen
Cart(s)
Telephone set
Modem
Camcorder
Tripod
Monitor/receiver
Videocassette recorder
Surge protectors

Network(s)

Design
Installation labor
Cable and connectors
Cable support system
Conduit
Concentrators/hubs
Network adapter cards
Network adapter cables
File servers with back-up tape drives
Communications server, network modem(s)
Network operating system software
Network menuing software
Electronic mail software
Asynchronous communications software
Uninterruptible power supplies
School-wide telephone system with voice mail
School-wide video/audio communications system with at least three in-house
    channels, preferably two-way between classrooms and headend

Supplies

Blank floppy disks
Printer paper
Videotapes
File server tape drive back-up tapes

Using Technology for Implementation of Effective Student Assessment ___

The North Carolina end-of-year testing program is moving from nationally standardized multiple-choice tests to a multifaceted assessment program. The program combines open-ended as well as multiple-choice items, items in which process is evaluated and that involve the writing process, tool selection and use (such as calculators and computers), and student hands-on demonstration items. This shift in assessment is helping teachers move with students toward greater focus on problem solving, reasoning, communicating, using tools, and applications.

In an effort to move toward authentic/alternative assessment techniques, teachers are using student portfolios, narrative reports, and parent conferencing as primary assessment vehicles. They revise their narrative report format in response to parent concerns as needed.

Software can be added to aid student assessment, as well as lesson planning, in the form of a software shell to which goals, objectives, corresponding resource titles, assessment items, and student results can be added. This software shell can be a vehicle to align curriculum components with each other and align what the various teams of teachers are doing with students. Teachers may refer to goals, objectives, and resource titles as they plan each lesson and thematic unit. They may use corresponding assessment items to assess student progress.

Portfolios are used as vehicles for assessment. Illustrated writing samples are included in the portfolios. Journal *writing samples* are collected throughout the year. Each child has a journal and writes in it daily.

Ms. Eubanks, a K–1 teacher, is looking at a *self-portrait* of a student aged 5 years, 2 months and another self-portrait when the student is aged 5 years, 9 months, in May. These portraits are included in the child's portfolio along with other items such as narratives printed on the laser printer.

Software can include some formative evaluation items, with feedback to students and recordkeeping and reports for teachers and parents. Integrated learning system software may include varying degrees of evaluation, diagnosis, prescription, recordkeeping, and individual and group reporting.

Databases of all media center resources, other school resources, and who has what resources checked out should be available. Teachers and students should be able to use the computer network to access this information from their classrooms.

In order to use the technology effectively to enhance and support learning in an early childhood program, a technology committee may be helpful in the following ways:

1. Planning innovative uses for technology, such as the narrative reports and addition of the assessment shell.
2. Applying for grants.
3. Helping with troubleshooting.
4. Helping lead and organize staff development.
5. Coordinating with site-based management and curriculum committees.

Acknowledgments

This chapter is based on valuable input from the following people: Carlynn Ashley, Nancy Cheek, Carolyn Cook, Knox J. Efland, Cindy Eubanks, Sue Florence, Cindy Hackler, Trinia Holman, Jo Hunt, Barbara Jones, Pam Lamason, Stephen Kegg, Ruth Murphy, Jennie Parrish, Lynn Poythress, John Schaenman, Deb Sievert, Lexie Simpson, Gerry Solomon, Diane Starrett, Lorraine Tuck, Bob Warren.

Chapter 13

Movement

The need to move and the need to express feelings are present in all human beings at birth. Both needs can be satisfied through a movement education program for young children. Movement education provides opportunities to use movements for creative expression and to develop confidence in the ability to move. An educational movement program can encourage the child to apply problem-solving techniques to explore fantasies and relationships with others. With movement exploration activities children can develop motor skills and knowledge of the operation of their own bodies. In addition, a child's self-concept can grow through the teacher's use of nonjudgmental techniques to show respect for each child's ability (Sullivan, 1982).

Most young children are comfortable with movement. It is through movement, through acting upon objects and people, that they begin to learn about their world. Children solve problems and respond to questions with their bodies long before they can express themselves verbally. When a question calls for movement, rather than for a verbal response, children are not limited by their verbal activities (Dodge & Colker, 1992).

Children's skill levels vary according to their experience and development. The amount of encouragement, freedom, and space available will determine the child's overall competence in movement. An atmosphere that contains these essentials must be provided for all children to develop their potential.

Elements of Movement Education

For many years, movement has been a part of the curriculum for young children, often disguised by terms such as *rhythm*. It continues to be an integral part of the total curriculum, reinforcing and extending the concepts of mathematics, language arts, science, social studies, and other basic areas. Movement can serve as a unifying factor and can enhance the interrelated nature of the curriculum. The elements of a standard movement and dance approach have been defined by Rudolf Laban. These elements are described by Sullivan (1982) as follows:

Body Awareness. The shape of the body in space, where the different body parts are, how the body moves and rests, the body's behavior when combined with other bodies, how the voice is a part of the body.

Force and Time. Being limp, being energetic, being light, being fluid, being staccato, being slow, being quick.

Space. Where the body is in a room: the level (high—erect posture or in the air, crawling or stooped; low—on the floor), direction (forward, backward, sideways), size (bigness, smallness), path through space, and extensions of the body parts into space.

Locomotion. Movement through space at various levels (lowest—wriggling, rolling, scooting; middle—crawling, crouching, using four limbs (ape walk); highest—walking, running, skipping, galloping, sliding, leaping, hopping, jumping).

Weight. Relationship of body to ground, ways to manage body weight in motion and in relation to others, understanding momentum.

Working with Others. Combining with others to solve problems, to develop trust, to explore strength and sensitivity, to feel a sense of union with others.

Isolations. How various individual body parts (head, shoulders, arms, hands, elbows, wrists, neck, back, upper torso, ribs, hips, legs, knees, ankles, feet) can move (swinging, jerking, twisting, shaking, lifting, tensing, relaxing, becoming fluid, pressing, gliding, floating, flickering, slashing, punching, dabbing).

Repetitions. Getting to know a movement and how it feels when repeated often; being able to repeat a shape or action. (p. 3)

Activities for development of each of these elements are available in the Suggested Activities section.

Two main types of movement are personal movement and functional activity. Personal movement shows the mood or inner state of an individual, whereas functional activity serves a practical purpose (Lynch-Fraser, 1982). It is appropriate to focus on personal expressive movement with developing young children.

Teacher's Role

The teacher's role in movement is to provide a series of problems that challenges the child and leads to the development of greater skill and expression. Activities must be presented in a developmental sequence, teaching easier movements before more difficult movements. The order of presentation is determined by the needs of the children. For example, preschoolers are not mentally or physically ready for sports. These children need freedom to express themselves in a different way through movement and dance (Coleman & Skeen, 1984–1985). Their large muscles have not been fully strengthened. Teachers should provide creative activities to develop large muscles.

The teacher begins with a simple problem involving one element of movement and progresses to other elements and combinations according to the ma-

turity and skill demonstrated by the children. Each problem is structured carefully and has specific objectives to be accomplished. The teacher must anticipate possible responses to the problem and plan additional questions and activities that will help the children to refine their solutions.

When a problem is presented, the children explore it in various ways. There is no one correct response, and all individual efforts must be encouraged. Imitation of other children is to be expected and, for some children, it provides needed security. Most children progress quickly to more original solutions. The teacher does not demonstrate in most instances. Imitation of adult movement is difficult and frustrating for most children and can hinder the development of self-confidence. In movement, the learning process is as important as the product.

During the period of exploration, the teacher circulates, noting problems and progress, asking questions, and occasionally suggesting ideas. Some children may be asked to share their solutions with the group. In general, demonstrations for anyone other than classmates should be avoided. The success of the movement program depends largely upon the attitude and skill of the teacher. If the teacher is enthusiastic, observant, and skillful in phrasing questions, the program will be rewarding for all. The children are naturally motivated, and they learn quickly and easily when they are actively involved and are experiencing success.

Having a permanent movement area in a regular classroom may not be feasible, but movement activities can be done outdoors, in a gymnasium, on a stage, or even on a field trip. A teacher may, however, want to set up a special place for movement occasionally in the classroom. This may require moving furniture to provide a large open area, as well as providing musical instruments;

a tape recorder; and a variety of props such as scarves and streamers, hoops, and capes that swirl. Children enjoy seeing themselves in motion. This is accomplished by providing a full-length mirror or by arranging a strong light in a dimly lit room so the children can see their shadows (Dodge & Colker, 1992).

The Movement Program

The activities that follow begin with general exploration of the individual's body movements and progress to combined movements. Teachers are encouraged to start their movement program with activity 1 and continue in sequence. Skills that are too difficult for particular children or age groups should be omitted.

Notes to the Teacher

1. Discuss with the children and agree on a signal to be used when it is time to stop and listen.
2. State the problem or challenge briefly, in direct terms.
3. When a piece of equipment is involved, indicate what the children are

to do as soon as they get their equipment. Immediate involvement is preferable to waiting until each child has his or her rope, ball, or bean bag before beginning the activity.

4. Remind the children to avoid collisions with one another when they are working in the general or shared space. This requires constant attention and good body control. It is, therefore, a better learning condition than having the children always move in the same direction.

5. Encourage the children to wear comfortable clothing that does not bind or impede free movement of any body part. Barefoot participation is highly recommended if the floor surface is splinter-free. The muscles of the feet work more efficiently and tactile sensation is enhanced when walking barefoot.

6. Avoid demonstrating the movement to prevent preconceived notions about the solutions. Once the children are involved, they themselves will provide good examples of the solution to the problem. You can point out these solutions to the class with the suggestion that others might want to try that particular solution. Make it clear that such examples represent *another* way of responding, not the *right* way to respond.

7. Allow time for practice and creativity. Free choice of any activity for a given time will allow you to observe and suggest individual problems to be solved. Encourage the children to make up games to be played with the equipment or apparatus. That way, they become responsible for stating the problem or challenge.

8. Assign and/or allow the children to choose a partner they will work with throughout the movement activities. Change partners often (each week) so that the children learn to work with different people.

9. Praise and reinforce the children's efforts to explore the limits of their motor ability. Challenge them to create new ways to solve the problems you give.

10. End each movement activity with a closing statement based on the children's experience.

Environmental Resources

Large open area
Audio equipment (record player and record, cassette player and tapes)
Tambourine or drum (for signaling)
Partners

Suggested Activities

Where the Body Moves

Objective

To understand and explore personal and shared space; also to learn movements of direction, level, and pathways.

Materials

Large room
Tambourine or drum for signaling
Partners

Directions

1. Discuss with the class the definition of *personal space* and *shared space*. Personal space is space occupied by the individual that does not infringe on the space of another. Shared space or general space is the space the group as a whole uses.
2. Direct the students to the signaling device, explaining that they are to stop moving at the signal of the tambourine or drum.
3. Encourage the students to explore their own space.

   a. How tall is your space? How wide is it?
   b. If you keep one foot still and move the other, can you make your space wider?
   c. Touch as much of your space as you can at one time. Can you do this standing up? How about sitting down?
   d. See how little of your space you can fill at one time.
   e. In your personal space be a telephone pole—standing tall and straight.
   f. Now be a jelly fish—you can't stand at all.

4. Encourage the students to explore their shared space.

   a. Can you travel about the room, moving quickly, without touching anyone? Try it again and change directions each time you hear the signal. (Use the drum or tambourine every 2–5 seconds.)
   b. How would you move if all our space were filled with cotton balls? Show me how you would move the cotton balls with different parts of your body.
   c. Can you travel about the room staying very close to one another without ever touching? How would this look in slow motion? How would you move if you were late to school?
   d. Pretend you are a cloud. How would you move on a very windy day? Now move on a very calm day.

5. Encourage the students to work on directions (forward, backward, sideways, diagonally, up, down) in their personal space.

   a. Can you move your arms in different directions? in front of you? sideways? behind you? How about your feet, can they be moved in different directions? in front of you? sideways? behind you?

   b. Who can stretch one arm in one direction and the opposite leg in another direction? (This assumes that the concept of *opposite* has been learned).

   c. Lie on your back and lift your legs. Can you lift one at a time? Can you lift an arm and a leg at the same time?

6. Work on directions in the shared space.

   a. Can you change directions each time you hear the signal?

   b. Who can hop in more than one direction?

   c. Can you walk, change directions, and still face the same direction? Can you walk backward without touching anyone?

   d. In shared space be a glider plane with your arms spread making straight wings. Change directions each time you hear the signal.

   e. Stand in one place and pretend you are a teapot. Pour out some tea. Be careful not to lose your balance.

   f. With your partner, see if you can both move in the same direction when the tambourine rattles and in different directions on the tap of the tambourine. (Indicate the different sounds from the tambourine so that the class recognizes the two signals; establish a firm, rhythmic beat.) Try this with music and small groups of three or four. Allow a brief time for practice and then share each group's "directional pattern" with the class.

7. Work on some different levels (high, middle, low) in students' personal space.

   a. Put yourself at the lowest level possible in your space. Can you move your whole body at this level?

   b. Is it possible to have your head lower than your feet? Is there another way?

   c. Show me how you can keep two different body parts low and one body part high. Can you do it another way?

8. In the shared space, work on different levels.

   a. Begin your run at one level and end your run at a different level. Can you think of another way to do this?

   b. What level is best for stopping at the end of a run? What level is best for a quick change of direction? (Encourage experimentation with the idea of lowering the body level with a wide stance to stop or turn.)

   c. Can you travel, changing your level and direction on the signal?

9. Explore pathways as another way to move around (straight, curved, twisted, zigzag).

   a. Can you move forward with a pathway that is not straight? Can you show us a different way?
   b. Who can move like a corkscrew? Can you do it the opposite way?
   c. How would you move if you were an arrow shot from a bow?
   d. Can you make a zigzag pathway? Can you make the same zigzag pathway when you are hopping?
   e. Can you move in one pathway? At the beat of the tambourine, move in a different pathway. Repeat.

Note. Below is a list of movements that can be used by the teacher to extend any of the given activities. Each of the levels (low, middle, and high) has activities arranged according to difficulty.

Low Level

long body roll
belly crawl
moving forward; sitting
moving backward; sitting
back on ground; scooting
hip walking

seal walk (using arms, legs dragging)
sitting up roll (palms; hips; and legs on the floor)
curled-up roll

Middle Level

crawling
knee walk
squatting walk
frog jumps
four-legged walk—belly down

walk on knees and elbows
walk holding onto ankles
semicartwheels
four-legged walk—belly up

High Level

walk
run
pogo jumps
run through held-up large scarf
run and hit drum or tambourine with two hands
march/high-knee walk
stomp
straight-leg walk

walk on heels
shuffle (without lifting feet from ground)
slide walk (without lifting feet from ground)
kicking walk
crossed-over steps—one swings out and around in front of other
tip-toe walk

giant steps	run and leap
hop	run and freeze in a shape
gallop	run and fall down and roll
turn	swinging arm broad jump
punch air with fists as you walk	skip
run and jump to hit drum	run and slide
lunge	
run and jump	(Sullivan, 1982, p. 62)

The activities should be spread over a number of days. *Repetition* of these activities will help the children understand each concept.

How the Body Moves

Objective

To understand and explore time, force, flow, tensed-relaxed, and relationships associated with different movements.

Materials

Large open space
Musical equipment
Tambourine or drum for signaling
Bean bags (one per child)
Partners

Directions

1. When moving your body in both personal and shared space you can use different time (fast, medium, sudden, sustained).

   a. Can you be a machine that begins very slowly and then moves faster and faster? Repeat with a change of levels. (Remind the students of low, middle, high levels.)

   b. When you are ready, travel very quickly until you hear the signal, then stop. Repeat, but on the signal stop and slowly change your level on four drum beats (or tambourine taps). Can you show me a different level this time?

   c. Move like a train that is having trouble starting. Now move like a race car or a racing horse just out of the gate.

2. Your body can also move using forces (strong, light).

   a. How would you travel if you were pushing a heavy box? pulling a loaded wagon?

   b. Can you walk like a giant? run like a deer?

    c. While the music plays, change from heavy, strong movements to light ones each time you hear the signal.

    d. Again, listen to the music and try to change your movements by force each time the music changes.

3. In the next activities, see if you can show tensed-relaxed movements.

    a. Can you show us what happens to a popsicle in the sunshine? Move as if you are a cup of water that changes to an ice cube.

    b. Can you slowly tighten all your muscles as the tambourine beats four counts? Now relax them with the next four counts. This time show us a change of body shape (curled, twisted, stretched) as you tighten. Are you able to change your level as you relax?

    c. Can you tighten all at once on one tambourine beat and relax on three counts? Can you slowly tense on three beats and relax completely on one tambourine beat?

    d. Move like an iron man and then like a rag doll when you hear the signal. (Try this to music, letting the children alternate their movements at will. Praise any sense of rhythmic pattern exhibited.)

4. Relationships (near-far, alongside, in front-behind, over-under, leading-following, unison-contract) can also be expressed in movements. For this activity, pass out bean bags to each child.

    a. Can you place yourself over the bean bag? alongside it? under it? behind it?

    b. On the signal, can you move as far as possible from your spot and then return to your spot on the second signal? Change the level or the force of your movement this time.

    c. Be very still and listen to the music. Then let some part of your body move to the music; let the movement grow bigger until it takes you all over the room. Repeat with a different body part leading.

    d. Mirror your partner's movements when the tambourine rattles and try to contrast your movements with his or hers on taps of the tambourine. (Precede this challenge with a discussion of what it means to mirror and contrast movements. Examples of contrast: fast-slow, up-down, strong-weak, and so on. This may be done to music.)

Note. These activities should be conducted over a number of days. Provide much repetition in order to promote thorough understanding.

What the Body Does

Objective

To explore and understand changes in body shape, positions, locomotion movements, nonlocomotion movements.

Materials

Large open space
Tambourine or drum for signaling
Musical equipment (record player, cassette player with a variety of fast/slow music)
Floor mats (one for every two children)
Partners

Directions

1. One way we can see how the body moves and changes is by shape (stretched, curled, twisted, wide, narrow, tall, short).

   a. Try to make your body as small as possible, now as large as possible.
   b. Show us a tall, twisted shape; a curled shape at a low level; a wide, stretched shape.
   c. Is it possible to curl one body part and stretch another?
   d. First stretch, then twist, then curl your body. Show us a different way as you change your level. Can you make three different body shapes as you travel about the room?
   e. When you hear 4 beats of the tambourine, change your body shape.
   f. With your partner, combine body movements to make a statue.

2. Now let's move our body parts in different positions (leading, supporting, transferring, receiving, initiating).

   a. Show us how many ways you can move your head, your arms, your feet and legs, your trunk. (This can be done to music as the children combine different body parts in movement in personal space or as they travel the shared space.)
   b. Find a way to make a bridge, supporting your weight on three body parts. Who can show us another way?
   c. Can you support your weight on one body part and shift your support to two body parts with a smooth movement? Now move from standing on two body parts to three body parts smoothly.
   d. What is a good way to land after you jump or leap? Why? (Stress the best way to absorb force: by giving with the force [i.e., bending in the hips, knees, and ankle joints when landing].) What is a good way to catch a ball that is moving very fast? Why? ("Give," as if pulling the ball into your midsection.)
   e. Pretend like you are catching a ball that is moving very fast. Then catch a ball that is moving slowly.
   f. How would you toss a ball, catch it, and go into a roll on the floor? Can you think of another way to do this? Try another.

3. Locomotor movements include movements of running, walking, crawling, rolling, hopping, skipping, jumping, leaping, climbing, sliding, galloping, pushing, and pulling. Try some of these locomotor movements.

   a. When you are ready, move about the room as quickly and quietly as possible, changing directions on the signal. Remember not to touch anyone.

   b. Can you jump from one foot and land on two? Can you jump backward?

   c. Who can skip at a high level? Can you skip backward? (Progression for nonskippers: hop two times on the right foot, lifting the left knee high; hop two times on the left foot, lifting the right knee high. As children become proficient, alternate one hop right, one hop left, emphasizing lifting opposite knee high each time. This is the basis for skipping.)

    d. Let us see you travel about the room at a low level, changing your way of moving on the signal (crawling to rolling, to running, to giant steps, and so on).

    e. Begin doing one of the locomotor movements. At the signal, change to another. Repeat.

    f. Find a partner. How many ways can you and your partner pull, push, roll each other? (Point out examples of good body mechanics [i.e., getting down low and close to one's partner in order to apply force for pushing or rolling; lining up one's body in the direction of applied force in pulling].)

    g. Do three movements in a row. See if your partner can follow your sequence. Switch roles with your partners.

4. Nonlocomotor movements include swinging, swaying, twisting, turning, curling, and stretching. The activities we are going to do now will work on these nonlocomotor movements. In addition, we will combine some of the other movements we have previously learned.

    a. Can you swing one body part and then another? Can you swing your whole body? Can you swing with a partner? (Try this with music and/or rhythmic accompaniment.)

    b. With a partner, can you make a twisted shape? a combined high and low, stretched shape?

    c. As you sway back and forth or from side to side, can you show us different body shapes (curled, stretched, twisted, and so on)? Do this to music.

    d. Can you combine two of these movements? Try to do it another way.

Using Movements of Manipulation

Objective

To explore and use manipulatives effectively; also to understand how the body is able to manipulate these materials.

Materials

Bean bags
Balls
Hoops
Wands
Balance board
Partners
If possible, all children should have their own pieces of equipment

Directions

1. Using balls, let's explore some movements.

   a. How many ways can you move your ball?
   b. Can you move your ball at a different level?
   c. Can you travel and move your ball at the same time (walk, toss, and catch; run, tap ball with your feet, and so on)?

    d. Each time you hear the signal, change the way you move the ball or your body. Remember you don't always have to be bouncing the ball. (Repeat a few times in order to allow the children to experiment with different movements.)

    e. Can you and a partner move the ball from one to the other with good control? What helps you to control the movement of the ball?

    f. Bounce or pass the ball to any person who does not have a ball; keep balls moving all over the room. (Use as many balls as the group can control.)

 2. Bean bags can be used to explore movements.

    a. What body part can you use to move your bean bag? Is there another part? yet another?

    b. Toss and then catch your bean bag with a different body part—other than your hands.

    c. Can you toss your bean bag so it lands in front, behind, beside you?

    d. Can you toss your bean bag and clap once (twice, three times) before you catch it?

    e. Balance your bean bag on a part of your body. Can you move (walk, skip, hop, sway, etc.) while you balance the bean bag?

    f. Can you balance it at a different level? Now try to move at this level.

3. Let's see if we can use ropes in movement.

    a. How many ways can you move over your rope? What ways can you travel from one end of your rope to the other? Can you move backward along your rope?

    b. Can you jump over your rope while turning it? Can you jump while turning your rope backward?

    c. Can you travel about the room while you turn and jump your rope?

    d. Use your rope at a different level. Can you think of something else to do with your rope at this level?

    e. Can you combine a body movement and a movement with your rope? Is there another way?

4. Another tool we can use in movement is a hoop. Let's manipulate the hoop while moving.

    a. Lay the hoop on the floor, show us different ways to move around the outside of your hoop. Around the inside of the hoop.

    b. Now pick up your hoop and show us ways to move inside and outside of your hoop.

    c. Can you stretch as you move into your hoop and curl and roll as you move out of your hoop?

    d. Show us a way to stretch as you move into your hoop at a different level.

    e. Who can twirl the hoop around some body part? Show us a different way. Is there another way?

    f. Can you balance the hoop on a body part? Show us a different place to balance the hoop.

    g. How many ways can you move through the hoop as your partner holds it? Can you move through a rolling hoop?

    h. Hold the hoop at a different level. Now see how many ways your partner can go through it.

5. Wands can help us explore movements, too.

    a. Move around the room slowly using your wand. Can you do it at another level?

    b. Can you stand in your personal space and balance your wand? Is there another way? Now can you move forward or backward balancing the wand?

    c. Now balance the wand on a body part. Then stand up or sit down. Is there another way you can move while balancing the wand?

    d. As you hold the wand with both hands, can you step forward and then backward over the wand?

e. Can you stand the wand in front of you, turn quickly, and catch the wand before it hits the floor?

f. Can you and a partner have a tug-of-war holding the wand? Can you do it at a different level?

g. Can you draw a pathway with your wand, then hop along it?

h. Show us another way to use the wand that we have not done.

6. Balance boards are another piece of equipment that we can use to expand our movements.

a. Show us how you can move from one end of the board to the other with good balance.

b. Can you walk and dip a foot at the same time?

c. Try to walk to the middle of the balance board, then extend one leg forward—now backward. Can you do it with the other leg?

d. Can you walk halfway across, then balance, leaning forward with arms held out to the side and the other foot held high in back? *Hint:* Look straight ahead, not down.

e. Who can walk halfway across, stop, and then change direction to finish?

f. As you move across the board, show us two balanced positions before you finish. (Balance is aided by a wide base of support and/or a position that is lower to the floor.)

g. Can you get into a kneeling position without falling off the board? How about a sitting/squatting position?

h. Sit on the balance beam and make your body into a V position (legs and arms extended).

i. As you move across the board, toss and catch a bean bag.

j. Who can jump off the end of the balance beam, land softly, curl, and roll? (Mats are needed.) *Hint:* Roll on the rounded parts of your body.

Rhythmic Activities

Objectives

To encourage exploration of large and small motor movements with music; in addition, to use combinations of all previously learned movements.

Materials

Large space
Partners
Music (It is helpful to prepare a cassette with a variety of music pieces so that you will not have to stop the lesson to change the music.)

Directions

1. We will begin our rhythmic activities working individually.

   a. Sit comfortably on the floor, close your eyes, and listen to the music.
   Can you move just your head in time to the music? Now move your
   head in one direction, pause, and then in another direction, pause,
   and so on. (Stress the "pause" as being a positive element rather
   than merely an absence of movement. Such rhythmic pauses are
   either the logical ending for a movement or the preparation for a new
   movement. The concept of pause and stillness as a positive element
   is basic to confident rhythmic responses; it indicates purpose and
   control.)

b. Move a joint in you body. Can you move two joints at a time?

c. Show us how you would use your muscles. Is there another way to move your muscles?

d. There are some muscles we often forget about—facial muscles. Make your face sad, happy, scared, excited, frustrated.

e. Show us how many ways your hands and arms can move in response to the music. Now your feet. Can your movements lead you as you dance around the room? How about your feet?

f. Stand like a floppy rag doll and listen to the drum. Can you start a movement in your trunk that takes you all about the room? (Vary the rhythm of the drum beat, and stress pauses that end a movement or begin a new one.)

g. Pretend you are an instrument. Can you make your instrument play to the rhythm of the music you hear? Change the way you move when the rhythm of the music changes.

h. As you move, can you make different body shapes each time you hear a different sound? (Shapes—curled, stretched, twisted, tall, short, narrow, wide. Varied sounds—drum, bell maracas, tambourine, vocal sounds.)

i. Listen carefully to the music. Make up a dance that follows the music. (Use a variety of music types in order to encourage changes in movement.)

j. (Ask the children to suggest various words that describe or depict movement—*creeping, dashing, springing, balancing, rising, sinking, growing, flowing,* and so on. Make a list of these words and ask each child to choose one or two of them as a theme for a dance. Rhythm instruments or body percussion can provide accompaniment. If the children feel secure, have them share their dances and let the class guess which works served as the themes for each dance. This can also be done as a group effort when working with partners and groups.)

2. Creative movements with music can also be done with a partner. With your partner, we can do the following activities.

a. Face your partner and do a "mirror dance" with your hands and arms. Can you do a mirror dance with your feet and legs? How about with different facial expressions?

b. Hold hands with your partner and skip (slide, leap, gallop) until you hear the signal; then find a new partner and continue to move to the music.

c. Move the same way your partner moves until you hear the tambourine; then move in a different way. (Encourage contrasting movements as well as strong unison movements. This challenge can be either locomotor or nonlocomotor.)

d. What interesting body shapes can you and your partner make? Can the two of you create an interesting design in the space you share? Practice until you two can make three different designs with various body shapes and levels; then let's do these designs to music. (The concept of purposeful pause is basic in this problem; the children finish one design and prepare for the next, holding the final design longer to give a strong ending to their dance.)

3. The final way we will explore movement with music is in a group.

   a. Can you move toward the center of the room on the signal and away from the center when you hear the signal again? *Hint:* Remember not to bump anyone. (Recorded music may be used for this. Allow time for controlled movement in the center, occasionally, before sounding the signal to move away from the center.)

   b. (With all the children seated in a circle on the floor, have them take turns leading a rhythmic pattern with body percussion.) Can you work out a rhythmic pattern to your name and share it with the group?

   c. (Assign each small group of three or four children a movement theme and let them make up a short dance. Suggested themes: "Grow and stretch as flowers do, opening their petals"; "Move as if you were leprechauns creeping out for a frolic in the moonlight"; "Move as if you were calm ocean waves that become rough and tossed by a storm." The theme from a favorite story or poem may be chosen. Remind the children of elements that make movements interesting—change and contrast in direction, level, strength, tempo, pathways, body shapes, and relationships in movements.)

Movement to Music

"Music and movement are like happily married partners, each able to function alone but with added joy when they are together" (Mitchell, Bailey, & Dewsnap, 1992, p. 165). Although music enters spontaneously into many non-teacher-directed activities in which children make up their own songs or chants to accompany their actions, it is also a "natural" in teacher-directed movement activities. Some children may initially have difficulty moving to the beat of the music, particularly a slow tempo, but they will soon master the skill and move on to adjusting their movements to accompany contrasts in the music, such as fast and slow or light and heavy (Dodge & Colker, 1992).

Musical instruments are also natural accompaniments to movement activities. Children can move in response to how a certain instrument makes them feel. Children also enjoy playing rhythm instruments while moving, matching the tempo of another instrument or a recording (Dodge & Colker, 1992).

Movement and music can be used to expand children's vocabularies. Children may use such words as *smooth, jerky, gliding,* or *bouncy* to describe the music they hear and the way they move in response to it. Movement may also allow children to demonstrate their understanding of musical terms, such as *high* and *low,* better than words can (Dodge & Colker, 1992).

Movement Throughout the Curriculum

Movement cannot help but be integrated throughout the curriculum. It can be used easily to follow up, expand, and reinforce concepts taught in all subject areas (Mitchell, Bailey, & Dewsnap, 1992). A sampling of movement activities used throughout the curriculum follows.

Language Arts

1. Choose a letter and think about how you can express that letter with your body. Can you make it with your fingers? With your whole body? Using different body parts? With a partner?
2. Think of some action words that begin with your letter and demonstrate them.
3. Use the pattern of your letter to make a dance.
4. Use large sheets of paper and paint your letter as you listen to the music.
5. Choose a favorite book character and describe him or her through movement.

Note: Activities 1, 3, and 4 would also work with numbers.

Science

1. Play animal charades. The children choose different animals and demonstrate as many characteristic actions as they can. For example, a cat may arch its back when frightened, wrap its tail around itself or carry it high in the air, rub against a person's leg, sharpen its claws, move in quick leaps, stretch out very long, and so forth.
2. After a study of the solar system, have the children pretend that they are on the moon, where their bodies are much lighter than on earth. Then select a familiar game such as softball, tag, or dodge ball and have the children play it, without balls or bats, as if they were on the moon.
3. Demonstrate the movement of the moon around the earth, how we get night and day, and the movement of the planets around the sun.
4. Play chasing games and demonstrate predator and prey. As a variation, have a child hold the hand or waist of one or two other children while pretending to be the predator or prey.
5. Have relay races with the children moving like different animals. For example:

   Bunny: Hop, squatting and folding arms around knees.
   Elephant: Bend body forward and swing arms like a trunk.
   Caterpillar. Inch along like a caterpillar.
   Crab: Walk on heels and palms with back parallel to the floor.

As a variation, have the children move like different farm animals or jungle animals.

6. Be a flower. Pop up through the dirt, stretch tall, open your buds toward the sun, blow in the breeze, and so on.

Social Studies

1. Show through movement the kind of things people do in various occupations. Vary the movements. Do them fast and slow, large and small, high and low, in different directions. Add sound effects.
2. Select a holiday and discuss objects, actions, and feelings related to it. Then demonstrate these through movement.
3. Demonstrate various modes of transportation through movement.

Art

1. Play music in the art area and see how this affects the way children paint or draw. Their movements may become larger, smaller, faster, slower, more fluid, jerky, and so on.
2. Focus a child's attention on how his or her hand moved when making certain lines in fingerpainting. Have the child repeat the movement with another color or make a pattern by doing it larger or smaller.

Warm-Up and Relaxation

Warm-up activities are important before starting movement activities with children. The warm-up will not only prepare them physically for the upcoming activities, but also give them a chance to regroup and slowly work their way up to larger, more active movements.

Relaxation activities are important after a session of physical activity. Relaxing will help the children calm down and get settled before they move on to another phase of the day. Relaxation at the end of an active period helps children release tension and become more fluid (Zion & Raker, 1986).

Warm-Up Activities

1. Tell the children to stand up and stretch as high as they can. Have them sit on the floor with their legs out in front of them and try to touch their toes. Also have them stand up with their feet together and bend down to touch their toes.
2. Have the children perform the following movements:

   a. Jumping jacks
   b. Running in place
   c. Rocking horse (lie on stomach, grasp feet with hands and rock)

     d. Upper body twists

     e. Alternate touching right toe with left hand, left toe with right hand

Relaxation Activities

Tell the children to lie down on the floor with their hands out to their sides. Have them "feel" their bodies against the floor. Ask them to imagine they are floating and all the muscles in their body are very relaxed. Show them how to breathe deeply and slowly.

Suggested Readings

Brehm, M. (1983). *Movement with a purpose: Perceptual motor-lesson plans for young children.* West Nyack, NY: Parker Publishing Co.

Curtis, S.R. (1982). *The joy of movement in early childhood.* New York: Teachers College Press.

Engstrom, G. (Ed.). (1971). *The significance of the young child's motor development.* Washington, DC: National Association for the Education of Young Children.

Joyce, M. (1973). *First steps in teaching creative dance: A handbook for teachers of children, kindergarten through sixth grade.* Palo Alto, CA: Mayfield.

Kamii, C., & DeVries, R. (1980). *Group games in early education: Implications of Piaget's theory.* Washington, DC: National Association for the Education of Young Children.

Kogan, S. (1982). *Step by step: A complete movement education curriculum from preschool to 6th grade.* Bryron, CA: Front Row Experience.

Lynch-Fraser, D. (1991). *Playdancing: Discovering and developing creativity in young children.* Pennington, NJ: Princeton Book Co.

Mornighstar, M. (1986). *Growing with dance: Developing through creative dance from ages two to six* Canada: Windborne Publications.

Pica, R. (1991). *Early elementary children moving and learning.* Champaign, IL: Human Kinetics Books.

Stecher, M. B., McElheny, H., & Greenwood, M. (1972). *Joy and learning through music and movement improvisations.* New York: Macmillan.

Warren, J. (1984). *Movement time: Early learning activities for parents and teachers of young children.* Palo Alto, CA: Monday Morning Books.

Weikart, P.S. & Boardman, B. (1990). *Movement in steady beat: Activities for children, ages 3–7.* Ypsilanti, MI: High/Scope Press.

_____ Chapter 14 _____

Outdoor Play

Young children learn and grow from play. According to Frost and Klein, play is universal and essential to humanity. "Since the dawn of civilization, people have left artifacts and records depicting the importance of play to physical, intellectual, emotional, social, and spiritual well-being of the individual" (Frost & Klein, 1983, p. 1). Play is the child's means of communication, discovery, and expression (*Criteria for Selecting Play Equipment*, 1981). Loving guidance and adequate equipment can open a world where children can unfold and learn to understand themselves and those with whom they live. Therefore, educators of young children must acquaint themselves with the crucial role of play in child development.

Why Children Play _____

Children have always played. There is not, however, general agreement regarding why children play. Early play theorists believed that play was merely the expenditure of surplus energy. A shortcoming of this theory is that children often play even when they are near exhaustion (Frost, 1992). Another early play theory, the recapitulation theory formalized by G. Stanley Hall in 1906, originated in Darwin's view that humans evolved from lower species. This theory holds that play mirrors the behavioral evolution of mankind and rehearses the activities of the race in ages past. According to Frost, the recapitulation theory, like the surplus energy theory, breaks down under scrutiny. While water play may be linked to origins in the sea and tree-climbing may be related to ape-like ancestors, piloting space ships and firing laser guns can hardly be considered rehearsals of the past.

In actuality, play has many functions, all of which are important to the child. Van Hoorn, Nourot, Scales, and Alward (1993) emphasize play as the center of a developmentally appropriate early childhood program. In a play-centered curriculum, children grow in long-term, broad, inclusive competencies such as self-direction and industry, competencies much needed and valued for adults in our society. In the short-term, a play-centered environment is one with

Outdoor playtime puts children in a world where they can unfold and learn to understand themselves and others.

an atmosphere of cooperation, initiative, and intellectual challenge (Van Hoorn et al.).

The different forms of play represent mastery of various skills, capabilities, or experiences determined by the child's current developmental status and personal life experiences. According to Rogers (1985), the primary function of play is active mastery. Play is psychically active if and when children are free to enjoy it and to impose something on the environment. Play involving motor skills such as climbing and jumping demonstrates the child's exercise and mastery of developing motor skills. Play involving creative and constructive activities such as making paintings or working with clay or blocks demonstrates the joy of self-expression. Play centered on acting out unhappy incidents from the past demonstrates the child's active attempts to master traumatic experiences. Play contributes to mental health by helping the child to regain or maintain emotional equilibrium. Social play involving role taking with peers demonstrates the child's attempts to understand and master complex social life roles and situations. Play helps the child develop positive personality traits or attitudinal styles involving perseverance, self-confidence, and social competence.

In addition to the functions just mentioned, Frost and Klein (1983) reiterate the significance of the Roberts and Sutton-Smith study—which hypothesized that children compensate for stress by playing games to relieve it—and point out that playing games aids in the enculturation of the child. Frost and Klein also present the instinct-practice theory of Karl Gross, in which play is viewed as a vehicle for perfecting instincts and skills needed in later life. For example children around the world rehearse for adult roles by playing house.

Safe Play

For play, children need an environment free from physical or emotional fear or stress. Jerome Bruner, an American cognitive theorist, maintains that play minimizes the consequences of actions and maximizes learning because in play one can test limits without risk. Play provides opportunities to try combinations of behavior that would never be tried under pressure. Frost (1986) developed a Playground Maintenance Checklist to keep outdoor play areas safe (Figure 14-1).

In providing a pressure-free, safe environment for children to play, the selection of appropriate playthings is important. It helps to recognize that a playground is not just a place for children to let off steam; it is an outdoor classroom (Mitchell, Bailey, & Dewsnap, 1992). *Criteria for Selecting Play Equipment for Early Childhood Education: A Reference Book* (1981) states that good play equipment should have the following characteristics:

- Be as free of detail as possible.
- Be versatile in use.
- Be easily comprehended.

Instructions: Check the entire playground at least once each month. Train all personnel to be alert to playground hazards, and report them promptly. Avoid the use of hazardous equipment until repaired.	Date Checked	Repair Needed	Date Repaired
1. Is there an 8- to 10-inch-deep (20.32–25.4 cm) resilient ground cover (sand, pea gravel, shredded wood) under all swings, merry-go-rounds, slides, and climbing equipment? Is the resilient surface compacted or out of place? If concrete or asphalt is under equipment, is the manufactured impact attenuation product in place?			
2. Are there foreign objects or obstructions in the fall zones under and around fixed equipment?			
3. Are there obstructions to interfere with normal play activity?			
4. Are there climbing areas that would allow children to fall more than their reaching height when standing erect?			
5. Are concrete supports sticking above the ground? Are they secure?			
6. Are there sharp edges, broken parts, pinching actions, or loose bolts?			
7. Are there openings that could trap a child's head?			
8. Are there frayed cables, worn ropes, open hooks, or chains that could pinch?			
9. Are timbers rotting, splitting, termite infested, or excessively worn?			
10. Are portable toys such as tricycles and wagons in good repair?			
11. Are there protrusions that can catch clothing?			
12. Are there crush points or shearing actions such as hinges of seesaws and undercarriages of revolving equipment?			
13. Are swing seats excessively heavy? Do they have protruding parts such as animal noses or legs?			
14. Is the fence at least 4 feet (12.19 cm) high and in good repair? Can gates be secured?			

Figure 14-1   Playground Maintenance Checklist

Instructions: Check the entire playground at least once each month. Train all personnel to be alert to playground hazards, and report them promptly. Avoid the use of hazardous equipment until repaired.	Date Checked	Repair Needed	Date Repaired
15. Are there electrical hazards on the playground such as accessible air conditioners, switch boxes, or power lines?			
16. Are there collections of contaminated water on the playground?			
17. Are there toxic materials on the playground?			
18. Do the grass, trees, and shrubs need care?			
19. Do children wear inappropriate clothing such as capes on climbing and moving equipment?			
20. Does the adult-to-child supervison ratio equal ratios required for indoor activity?			

Source: Frost, J. L. (1986). *Playground Maintenance Checklist.* Austin, TX: Texas Department of Human Services. Reprinted with permission.

Figure 14-1   *(Continued)*

- Have large, easily manipulated parts.
- Involve the child in play, including large muscles.
- Encourage cooperative play.
- Have material that is warm and pleasant to touch.
- Be durable.
- Work as intended.
- Be safe.
- Be generous in proportions and quantity.
- Have a price based on durability and design.

A good plaything should involve the whole child—body, mind, and spirit—because such a toy will stimulate children to do things for themselves. Frost and Klein (1983) suggest that the novelty of a toy is a primary reason for children to explore it. The introduction of a novel object stimulates the child to explore its properties.

Types of Playgrounds

Playgrounds are divided into various categories: traditional, contemporary, adventurous, creative, and commercial (Frost & Klein, 1983). Traditional playgrounds are usually part of schools, housing projects, or neighborhood parks

Playing games outside promotes physical development and friendship.

and typically contain swings, slides, seesaws, and climbing bars. Contemporary playgrounds are frequently designed by architects and emphasize textures, novel designs, and different heights in aesthetically pleasing arrangements. Most often these playgrounds are somewhat sculptured, frequently based on sand or concrete. Adventure playgrounds provide children raw building materials and tools with which they can build their own play structures. Creative playgrounds include an inexpensive mix of handmade equipment and loose parts. Commercial playgrounds may consist of a massive unit structure containing interior and exterior space for climbing and dramatic play, horizontal tire swings, slides, and a firefighter's pole and ladder. Some commercial playgrounds comprise an array of specially treated wood structures, including balance beams, chinning bars, obstacle climbers, suspension bridges, and the like.

In each of these types of playgrounds mentioned, Frost and Klein (1983) report that certain activities are prevalent. They also present general conclusions from the Frost and Strickland study of creative and commercial playgrounds. The most widely used piece of equipment on traditional playgrounds tends to be the swing, whereas on contemporary playgrounds the sand areas are the most widely used. At adventure playgrounds, the clubhouse is used most.

Slides are common items on many playgrounds. Mitchell, Bailey, and Dewsnap (1992) maintain that a stand-alone slide is expensive in relation to its value for physical satisfaction, social growth, emotional release, and intellectual stimulation. A slide incorporated into a total climbing configuration is much more valuable. A child might climb a ladder or ropes to reach the top, walk a plank, and then choose between going down steps, sliding down the slide, or even going down a firefighter's pole. With this in mind, it is not surprising that slides on traditional playgrounds are rarely used, while they are heavily used on contemporary playgrounds due to the variety of ways of climbing to the top. Of traditional, contemporary, and adventure playgrounds, children stay the shortest lengths of time at the traditional playground and the longest at the adventure playground.

General conclusions from the Frost and Strickland study on creative and commercial playgrounds are as follows:

1. Action-oriented equipment is preferred by children.
2. Equipment designed primarily for exercise play is not sufficient to provide for the wide range of children's developmental play needs.
3. Children prefer equipment that can be adapted to their play schemes.
4. Among equipment tested, only loose parts have equal appeal to children across all grade and age levels.
5. Inexpensive play environments can be superior to expensive ones.

Mitchell, Bailey, and Dewsnap (1992) believe that a sandbox should receive top priority when designing a playground, even if it occupies a fairly large proportion of limited space. To be effective, sand must be combined with water, enough to make it adhere, so children are not left to just sift and pour.

Playgrounds should be developmentally relevant to the play needs of children. Frost and Klein (1983) state that the complexity and variety of playground equipment influences play types, equipment choices, social behavior, and verbal interaction. High complexity in the play environment sustains greater interaction with play objects and less interaction with peers. As the amount of equipment increases, the amount of play increases, and the amount of undesirable behavior and social behavior decreases. On traditional playgrounds children engage in exercise play over 77% of the time and in dramatic play less than 3% of the time. On creative playgrounds, children engage in dramatic play 40% and in exercise play 43% of the time. In addition, on traditional playgrounds over 35% of the time is spent in solitary and parallel activity, but on creative playgrounds this activity occupies less than 25% of the time.

The Outdoor Classroom

In the child's world of outdoor play, life is an adventure of sunshine, imagination, and freedom. The outdoors is a natural learning environment for children, and its endless possibilities should be explored at every opportunity. It can be a place for noisy, active pursuits such as kickball or carpentry, or a place for quiet reflection while studying a flower or reading under a shady tree. The outdoor world is limited only by the imagination.

The advantages of using the outdoor classroom are many, and the limitations are few. The health benefits of fresh air, sunshine, and exercise for children

Inexpensive play environments can be superior to expensive ones.

are obvious. Rarely is the weather too cold or damp for children to go outside. The teacher should be appropriately attired for daily outdoor activity as well. Some teachers will scold a child for not wearing a coat on a chilly day and yet they will not be wearing one of their own (Mitchell et al., 1992). The addition of a roofed patio area greatly expands the possibilities for using the outdoor classroom during inclement weather. Children have a real need for freedom—free-

There are many activities to choose from in the outdoor learning center.

The Popular Waterway.

The Seasaws.

The Sand Table.

Bubbles.

dom to move, make noise, and sometimes make a mess. The outdoors gives them this freedom far beyond the possibilities of the indoor learning environment.

Opportunities for learning in the basic curriculum areas are present both indoors and out. The outdoor environment simply adds another dimension to the learning process. In mathematics, the skills of counting, sorting, classifying, and measuring can be practiced using natural outdoor objects. Creative materials for language arts abounds in the outdoor classroom. There is much to see, hear, talk about, write about, and read about. Science concepts are learned more easily through hands-on experience with actual objects. The plants, animals, rocks, and sky in the outdoor environment provide this opportunity.

Certain activities such as art, water play, sand play, or carpentry may be offered intermittently in the outdoor classroom because of a lack of space or housekeeping restrictions indoors. The freedom of the outdoors allows these activities to continue on a daily basis with plenty of space and no clean-up difficulties. In fact, virtually all classroom activities may be conducted outside, allowing greater flexibility in scheduling, using equipment, and balancing quiet and active tasks. Thus the indoor and the outdoor environments become one world—a world in which children can explore, create, learn, and grow.

Play and Children with Special Needs

Considerations regarding play must also be made for children with special needs. The principles that underlie Public Law 94-142, the Education for All Handicapped Children Act (renamed the Individuals with Disabilities Education Act by P. L. 101–476 in 1990) should apply to children's play and play environments as well as to formal classrooms and educational settings. Play is a situation in which the child is free of pressure to achieve a specific goal. Because of this, it provides a teacher with a good opportunity to see the child as he or she really is and to identify areas of strength that may not emerge under stress (*Criteria for Play Equipment,* 1990).

In addition to physical disability children may experience difficulty in skills such as extent of exploration; response and approach to others; initiation of activities; respect for others; understanding of limits; attention span; and self-esteem (Frost, 1992). Equipment designed to foster both positioning and improvement is important for progress in children with physical disabilities. Equipment that allows a child to sit or stand or self-propel can make a difference that is nearly miraculous. Durability of the equipment is of particular importance because it must hold up to the hard treatment of poorly controlled muscles. Equipment for children with special needs may stretch an already thin budget. Hard choices must be made, but it is worth it (*Criteria for Play Equipment,* 1990).

Frost (1992) believes that adults who work with children with special needs must understand their individual differences. They must approach these children with expectations for growth. Children with disabilities can learn and they want to learn. They have normal human needs, but because of their disabilities it is more difficult for them to meet their needs.

Frost (1992) points out two prominent but inaccurate beliefs about children with disabilities and play: (1) Children with disabilities do not play, and (2) Play is merely a good way for children with disabilities to pass the time. Frost believes that these children fail to play because their environment is not stimulating and does not take their disabilities into account, or because they are not given the opportunity for play. Children with disabilities do learn through play when given support and appropriate materials, equipment, and opportunity.

The Outdoor Play Program

Environmental Area

150 square feet (13.935456 m^2) of play area per child
Variety of topographical features: mounds, flat, sod and turf, pine needles, and sand
Balance of space in the sun and shade
Hard-surfaced area for wheel toys and bouncing balls
Grassy plot for running and romping
Spot for pets, garden, and digging
Sandpit with cover (with brick or concrete surroundings for a place to sit)
Space for water play
Storage space for equipment
Safety precautions
Natural areas with a variety of plant life: trees, shrubs, grass, weeds, flowers
Outdoor weatherproof electrical outlets
Paved walkways (so entire playground is accessible by wheelchair)

Equipment and Materials

Stationary Equipment

Interesting structures or sculptures for climbing
Swings (tire or leather seats)
Platforms for climbing and/or swinging
Large sewer pipes set in concrete
Equipment for crawling and tunneling
Tree trunks
Low horizontal ladders
Low climbing ropes
Wading pool
Raised area for woodworking, play with vehicles, etc. (accessible to children in wheelchairs)
Raised area for sand and water play (accessible to children in wheelchairs)

Portable Equipment

Walking boards of various lengths
Sawhorses of various heights
Wooden steps, wooden ladder

A place for quiet reflection is an important part of a playground.

Heavy wooden benches
Low balance beams
Bales of straw
Tires (tractor, automobile, bicycle)
Balls
Bean bags
Jump ropes: long and individual
Transportation equipment: wagons, tricycles, wheelbarrow, go-carts, broomstick with sock head
Sand toys
Tools for gardening: shovels, rakes, hoes
Building blocks
Tools for woodwork
Scrap lumber for large construction
Wooden boxes, packing crates, rope handles, cardboard cartons
Planks
Steering wheel and column attached to a heavy box

Loose parts have equal appeal to children across all grade levels.

Children prefer equipment that can be adapted to their play schemes.

Parent-Made Equipment and Materials

1. Storage unit to build

2. Wooden climbing structure

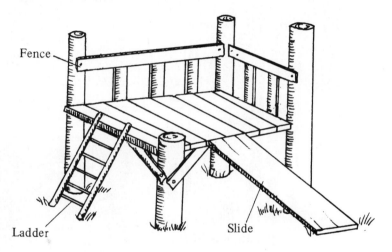

3. Telephone spools

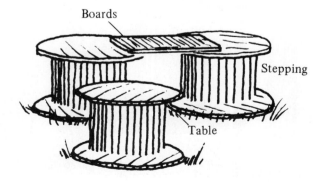

4. Wooden bridges and structures

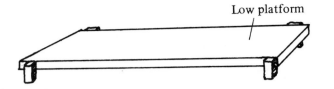
Low platform

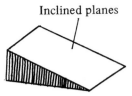
Inclined planes

5. Cans and barrels

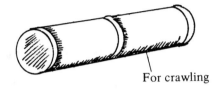
For crawling

6. Tires

Swing (punch holes in bottom
to let out water)

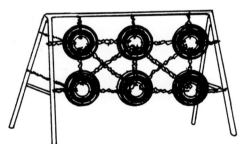

Old swing-set frame held together with rope

Tire bed swing-bolt tires together

7. Rolling slide

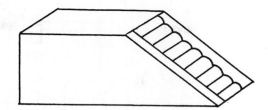

Walk up area (slide is made of
pipes app. 20 inches long)

8. Trees encircled with brick (may be used as a quiet area for small-group
teaching, storytelling, or dramatic play)

9. Nets for climbing

Rope should be knotted
at intersections

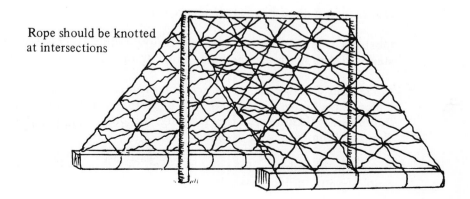

Climbing nets is challenging and fun.

Suggested Activities

Spontaneous and Directed Play. Structure the outdoor environment so that the children will have many opportunities for spontaneous, creative play as well as directed play. Children should be free to engage in either or both.

Hopscotch. Paint a hopscotch square on an asphalt area.

Obstacle Course. Plan an obstacle course requiring crawling through pipes, stepping through tires, climbing, crawling under bars, and similar activities.

Movement Courses. Instigate active movement courses such as "Station one, gallop like a horse; station two, leap like a frog; station three, bend like a tree in the breeze." Include walking, running, jumping, hopping, galloping, leaping, skipping, climbing, and dodging.

Extension of Indoors. Take out as many indoor activities as possible—for example, painting, blocks, dolls.

Task Cards. Make task cards of games that the children might enjoy. Remember to make the wordings as simple as possible.

Change Equipment. Create interesting situations for climbing, crawling, and so on by changing the equipment frequently.

Jump Rope. Use the jump rope on the ground to create geometric designs and shapes; have the children "walk" the shape.

Large Bags of Rags. For emotional release, hang a large bag of rags from a tree and have the children use it as a punching bag.

Tussles. When tussles occur on the playground, allow the children to fight it out—in slow motion.

Rope Net. Hang a rope net between two trees (good for swinging or climbing).

Exercising. When they are exercising, ask the children to suggest an exercise and let them lead it.

Playhouse Change. From time to time, place an interesting playhouse on the playground, such as a camping tent or teepee.

Nature Trail. Create a nature trail for the children to walk through, explore, and enjoy (creek, trees, animals, plants, natural habitats of animals).

Carpentry. Keep tools, wood scraps, nails, and paint in an outdoor storage area for the children to build and paint small, temporary objects and structures. Adult assistance is advised here.

Animal Cages. Keep animals and cages near both indoor and outdoor play environments for the children to observe and enjoy throughout the day.

Collage. Have the children collect objects found outdoors and create a collage.

Sand Castles. Encourage the children to build large sand castles.

Habitat Play. Ask the children to use sand and water or other outdoor objects to build a habitat for creatures the class is studying.

Natural Happenings. Have the children study the effects natural events have on the play area. For example, they can explore differences after rain, make cakes in the sand, or observe the snails in the sandbox.

Splatter Paint. Encourage the children to create interesting designs by dipping a brush into paint and splattering it onto paper in different ways.

Magic Corner. Attach a shelf to a fence or use a table to display items for children to explore that are related to a topic currently being studied by the class.

Math Games. Have the children use outdoor objects to sort, estimate, quantify, build symmetrical designs, and so on.

Language Activities. Have the children write or tell about their activities. Focus on sequencing or comparing. The children might also enjoy writing stories or plays inspired by outdoor activities such as a nature hike or a sandbox creation.

Playground Suggestions

1. Give support and encouragement to timid and unsure children.
2. Plan activities for uncoordinated children so that they may succeed.
3. Be patient with all types of children in their endeavors.
4. Make the playground an interesting learning situation by adding art, music, reading, sciences, and other activities.
5. Make sure slides have top platforms. Slides built into hills and mounds are safest.
6. Situate swings away from heavy traffic areas.
7. Place sawdust or sand under all climbing apparatus.
8. Place trash cans on the playground.

Additional Playground Equipment

1. Wading pool

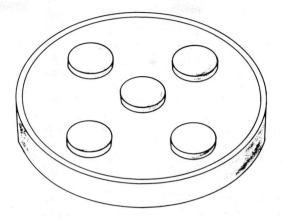

2. Sand trough

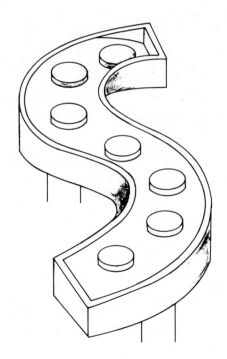

3. Play sculpture

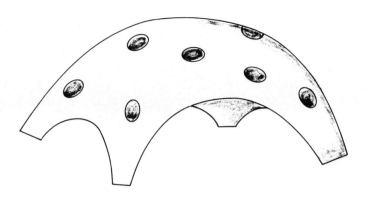

4. Outdoor room

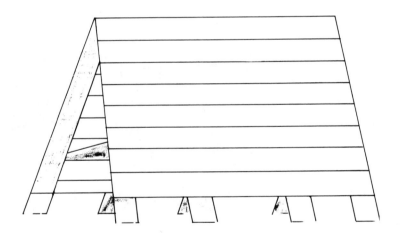

5. Blocks

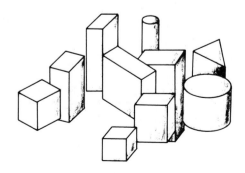

6. Tire walk

7. Slides and tunnel

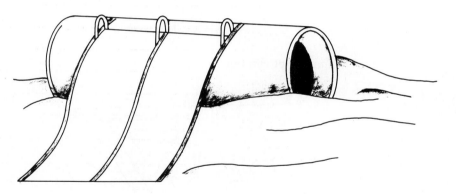

8. Mound

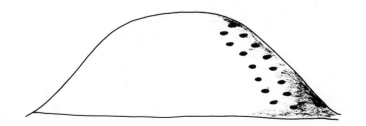

9. Free play area
10. Trees for climbing

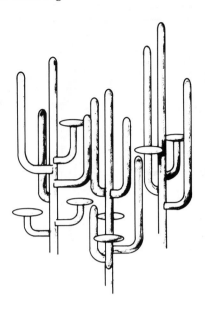

11. Cargo net climber

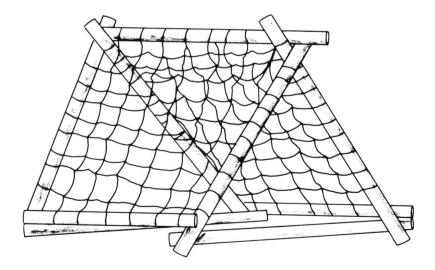

12. Swings

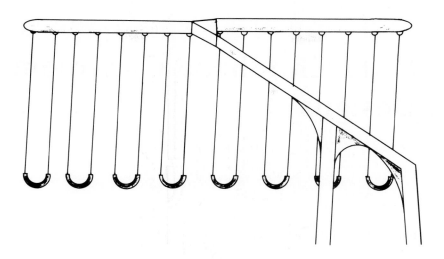

Chapter 15

Early Childhood Classroom Designs

Early childhood classrooms encourage the flow of movement from center to center and provide for social interaction. Clearly defined, well-equipped interest areas promote independence, foster decision making, and encourage involvement (Dodge & Colker, 1992). There is flexibility in the use of space, and the space is designed to be shared rather than compartmentalized into individual territories. This extension of space expands children's interaction with peers and materials. Communication flows between students and teachers as well as among the students.

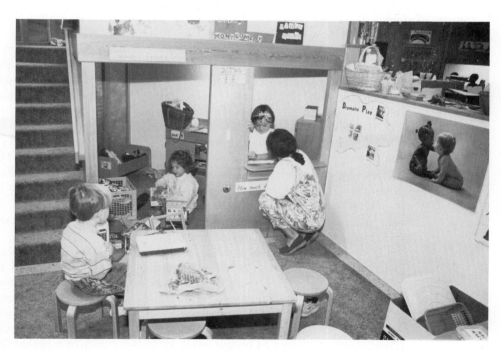

Children have created a grocery store in their multi-level learning space.

When assessing the effectiveness of interest areas, it is important to consider several questions. First, consider how children select interest areas and materials (Dodge & Colker, 1992). Which are used most often and which are rarely used? Do the children select a variety of areas and materials from day to day? Are they able to access the materials independently? Are the traffic patterns safe?

Second, consider the way children use the materials (Dodge & Colker, 1992). Are they able to use the materials successfully, appropriately, and creatively? How do different children use the same materials? Which materials hold the children's interest longest? Do the children care for the materials appropriately?

Third, consider how the materials affect children's interactions with peers and adults (Dodge & Colker, 1992). Do the children join in naturally, or do they wait to be invited? Do the same children usually play together? How do the children ask for help from peers and adults? Which materials lend themselves to cooperative play and which to solitary play?

An effective early childhood classroom should provide areas suitable for large-group, small-group, and individual activities. A loft is a good way to provide space for many types of activities.

A good classroom is a place where children feel safe and comfortable. Physical limitations must be clear. Materials should be arranged so that the children know which materials they may use and which are for the teacher only. It is also important for the classroom to have "safe" spaces where children who are not yet ready to join into an activity with other students can watch from a comfortable distance. Finally, although much of the space in the classroom is shared, each child should have a place such as a cubby or a basket that is his or her own.

The following layouts are meant to be used as guides for opening spaces in the classroom. Many require no specific architectural features but can be created within any four walls. Learning occurs in good self-contained classrooms just as it does in good open-space environments.

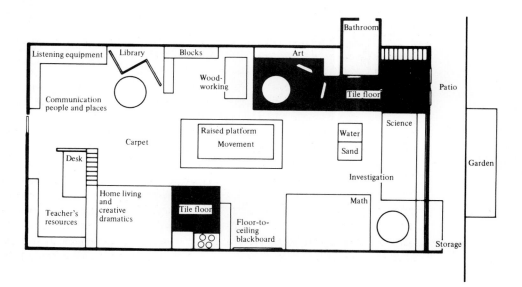

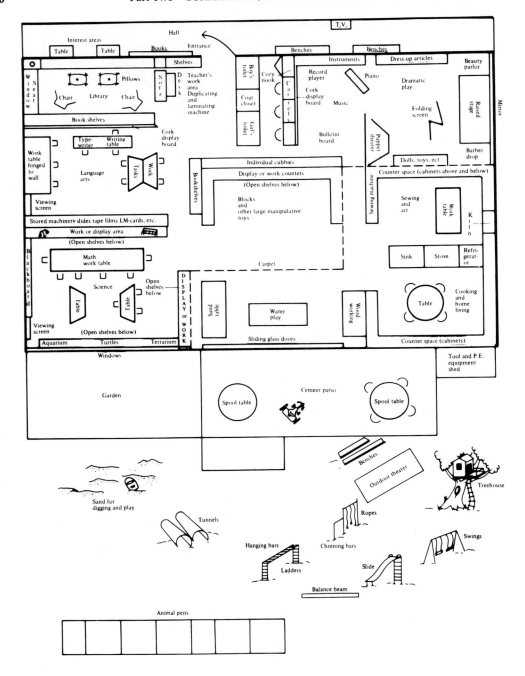

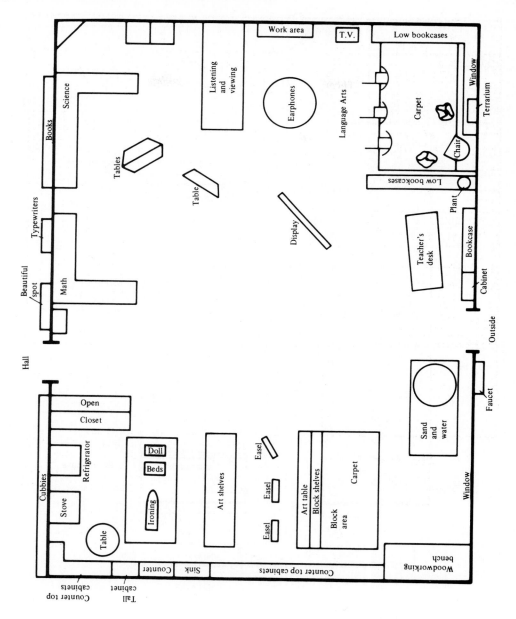

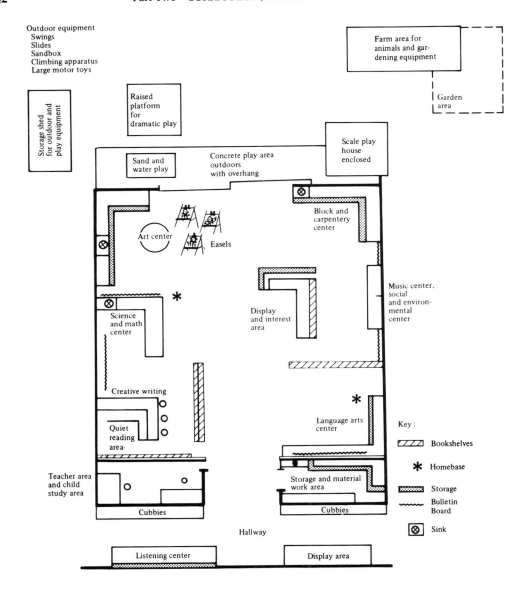

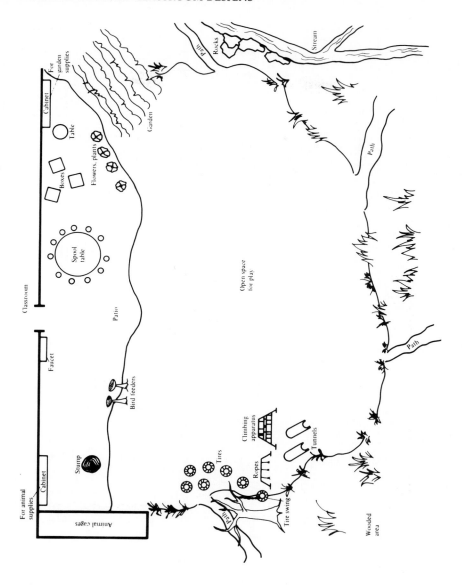

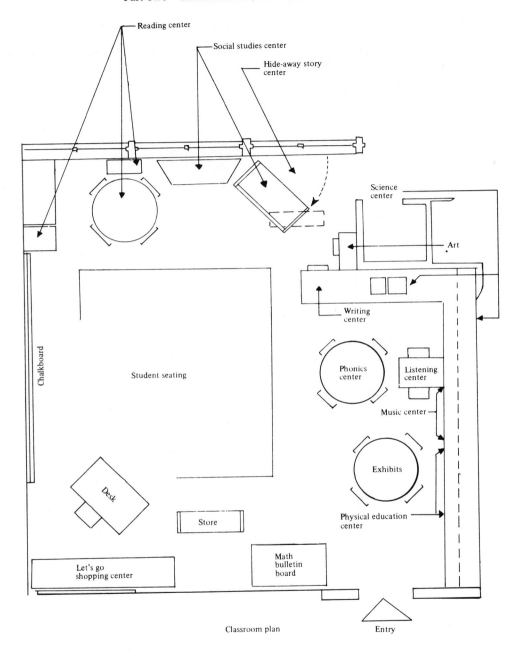

Reading center

Social studies center

Hide-away story center

Science center

Art

Writing center

Phonics center

Listening center

Music center

Exhibits

Physical education center

Chalkboard

Student seating

Desk

Store

Let's go shopping center

Math bulletin board

Classroom plan

Entry

Suggested Readings

Greenman, J. (1988). *Caring spaces, learning places: Children's environments that work.* Redmond, WA: Exchange Press.

Wolfgang, C. H., & Wolfgang, M. E. (1992). *School for young children: Developmentally appropriate practices.* Boston: Allyn and Bacon.

Appendix A

Resource Materials

RESOURCE BOOKS FOR TEACHERS

The Alphabet Activity Book, by Betsy Verne Franco. Oak Lawn, IL: Creative Publications, 1993.

Balancing the Basics: A Handbook for Teachers of Reading (K-8) (2nd ed.), by Trevor Cairney. Portsmouth, NH: Heinemann Boynton/Cook, 1990.

Child, Family, Community (3rd ed.), by Roberta M. Berns. Fort Worth, TX: Harcourt Brace College Publishers, 1993.

Children and Computers Together in the Early Childhood Classroom, by Jane I. Davidson. Albany, NY: Delmar Publishers, 1989.

A Child's World (6th ed.), by Diane E. Papalia and Sally Wendkos Olds. New York: McGraw-Hill, 1993.

Classroom Teaching Skills (2nd ed.), by Kenneth D. Moore. New York: McGraw-Hill, 1992.

Creating Reading Instruction for All Children, by Thomas G. Gunning. Needham Heights, MA: Allyn & Bacon, 1993.

Creative Activities for Young Children (4th ed.), by Mary E. Mayesky. Albany, NY: Delmar Publishers, 1990.

Creative Expression and Play in the Early Childhood Curriculum, by Joan P. Isenberg and Mary Renck Jalongo. New York: Macmillan, 1993.

Critical Issues in Education (2nd ed.), by Jack Nelson, Kenneth Carlson, and Stuart Palonsky. New York: McGraw-Hill, 1993.

Developmental Continuity Across Preschool and Primary Grades: Implications for Teachers, by Nita Barbour and Carol Seefeldt. Wheaton, MD: Association for Childhood Education International, 1991.

Developmentally Appropriate Practice in Early Childhood Programs Serving Children from Birth Through Age 8, S. Bredekemp (Ed.). Washington, DC: The National Association for the Education of Young Children, 1987.

A Different Kind of Classroom: Teaching with Dimensions of Learning, by Robert Marzano. Alexandria, VA: The Association for Supervision and Curriculum Development, 1992.

Discipline with Dignity, by Richard Curwin and Allen Mendler. Alexandria, VA: The Association for Supervision and Curriculum Development, 1988.

Effective Teaching in Elementary Social Studies (2nd ed.), by Tom V. Savage and David G. Armstrong. New York: Macmillan, 1992.

Elementary Classroom Management: Lessons from Research and Practice, by Carol Weinstein and Andrew Mignano Jr. New York: McGraw-Hill, 1993.

Elementary School Science for the '90s, by Susan Loucks-Horsley, Roxanne Kapitan, Maura Carlson, Paul Keurbis, Richard Clark, G. Marge Melle, Thomas Sachse, and Emma Walton. Alexandria, VA: The Association for Supervision and Curriculum Development, 1990.

Elementary and Secondary Science Projects in Renewable Energy and Energy Efficiency. Boulder, CO: The American Solar Energy Society, 1992.

Expanding Student Assessment, Vito Perrone (Ed.). Alexandria, VA: The Association for Supervision and Curriculum Development, 1991.

Experiences in Math for Young Children (2nd ed.), by Rosalind Charlesworth and Deanna J. Radeloff. Albany, NY: Delmar Publishers, 1991.

Explorations with Young Children: A Curriculum Guide from the Bank Street College of Education, Anne Mitchell and Judy David (Eds.). Mt. Rainier, MD: Gryphon House, 1993.

Getting Along with Others: Teaching Social Effectiveness to Children, by Nancy F. Jackson, Donald A. Jackson, and Cathy Monroe. Champaign, IL: Research Press, 1992.

Globalchild: Multicultural Resources for Young Children, by Maureen Ceck. Denver: The University of Denver, CTIR Publications, 1991.

The Great Big Multicultural Pattern Book. Carthage, IL: Good Apple, 1993.

Growing Teachers: Partnerships in Staff Development, E. Jones (Ed.). Washington, DC: The National Association for the Education of Young Children, 1992.

Guided Discovery Activities for Elementary School Science, by Arthur A. Carin. New York: Macmillan, 1993.

Health, Safety, and Nutrition for the Young Child (3rd ed.), by Lynn R. Marotz, Marie Z. Cross, and Jeanettia M. Rush. Albany, NY: Delmar Publishers, 1993.

Healthy Young Children: A Manual for Programs. A. S. Kendrick, R. Kaufmann, and K. P. Messenger (Eds.). Washington, DC: The National Association for the Education of Young Children, 1992.

Helping Children Explore Science: A Sourcebook for Teachers of Young Children, by Mary Jo Puckett Cliatt and Jean M. Shaw. New York: Macmillan, 1992.

Helping Kids Learn Multi-Cultural Concepts: A Handbook of Strategies, by Michael G. Pasternak. Champaign, IL: Research Press, 1992.

Home, School, and Community Relations: A Guide to Working with Parents (2nd ed.), by Carol Gestwicki. Albany, NY: Delmar Publishers, 1992.

How to Help Beginning Teachers Succeed, by Stephen Gordon. Alexandria, VA: The Association for Supervision and Curriculum Development, 1991.

Human Diversity in Education: An Integrated Approach, by Kenneth Cushner, Averil E. McClelland, and Philip L. Safford. New York: McGraw-Hill, 1992.

Improving Classroom Reading Instruction (3rd ed.), by George G. Duffy and Laura R. Roehler. New York: McGraw-Hill, 1993.

Integrated Language Arts for Emerging Literacy, by Walter E. Sawyer and Jean C. Sawyer. Albany, NY: Delmar Publishers, 1993.

Integrated Learning Activities for Young Children, by Susan L. Trostle and Thomas D. Yawkey. Needham Heights, MA: Allyn and Bacon, 1990.

Joinfostering: Adapting Teaching Strategies for the Multilingual Classroom, by Christian J. Faltis. New York: Macmillan, 1993.

Language Arts Activities for the Classroom (2nd ed.), by Sidney W. Tiedt and Iris M. Tiedt. Needham Heights, MA: Allyn and Bacon, 1987.

Leading Young Children to Music: A Resource Book for Teachers (4th ed.), by Joan E. Haines and Linda L. Gerber. New York: Macmillan, 1992.

Literature for Young Children (3rd ed.), by Joan I. Glazer. New York: Macmillan, 1991.

Literature-Based Reading Activities, by Ruth Helen Yopp and Hallie Kay Yopp. Needham Heights, MA: Allyn and Bacon, 1993.

Making a World of Difference: Creative Activities for Global Learning, by the Office on Global Education, National Council of Churches. Denver: The University of Denver, CTIR Publications, 1989.

Math Excursions 2: Project-Based Mathematics for Second Graders, by Donna Burk, Allyn Snider, and Paula Symonds. Portsmouth, NH: Heinemann Boynton/Cook, 1991.

Math and Literature (Grades K–3), by Marilyn Burns, White Plains, NY: Cuisenaire Company of America, Inc., 1993.

Math and Science for Young Children, by Rosalind Charlesworth and Karen K. Lind. Albany, NY: Delmar Publishers, 1990.

Mathematics Assessment, The National Council of Teachers of Mathematics. White Plains, NY:

Cuisenaire Company of America, Inc., (1993).

Mathematics Their Way, by Mary Baratta-Lorton. Oak Lawn, IL: Creative Publications, 1993.

Multicultural Education: A Teacher's Guide to Content and Process, by Hilda Hernandez. New York: Macmillan, 1989.

Music: A Way of Life for the Young Child, by Kathleen M. Bayless and Marjorie E. Ramsey. New York: Macmillan, 1991.

Organizing and Managing the Classroom Learning Community, by Joyce G. Putnam and J. Bruce Burke. New York: McGraw-Hill, 1992.

Recycling Activities for the Primary Grades, by Jean Stangl. Carthage, IL: Good Apple, 1993.

Renewable Energy: Activities (Grades 6–9). Albany: New York Science, Technology and Society Education Project, New York State Education Department, 1991.

Renewing the Social Studies Curriculum, by Walter C. Parker. Alexandria, VA: The Association for Supervision and Curriculum Development, 1991.

Science Experiences for the Early Childhood Years (5th ed.), by Jean D. Harlan. New York: Macmillan, 1992.

Serious Players in the Primary Classroom: Empowering the Young Child Through Active Learning Experiences, by Selma Wassermann. New York: Teachers College Press, 1990.

Skillstreaming the Elementary School Child: Teaching Prosocial Skills to the Preschool and Kindergarten Child, by Ellen McGinnis and Arnold P. Goldstein. Champaign, IL: Research Press, 1992.

Social Studies in Elementary Education (9th ed.), by John Jarolimek and Walter C. Parker. New York: Macmillan, 1993.

The Sourcebook: Activities for Infants and Young Children (2nd ed.), by George W. Maxim. New York: Macmillan, 1990.

Stories in the Classroom, by Bob Barton and David Booth. Portsmouth, NH: Heinemann Boynton/Cook, 1990.

Story Problems with Teddy Bears and Dinosaurs, by Shirley Hoogeboom, Judy Goodnow, and Ann Roper. Oak Lawn, IL: Creative Publications, 1993.

Storytime Around the Curriculum: A Comprehensive Early Childhood Curriculum Presented Through Literature, by Linda W. O'Berry, Robin G. Little, and Ann W. Fields. Mt. Rainier, MD: Partner Press/Gryphon House, 1993.

Teaching About Cultural Awareness, by Gary Smith and George Otero. Denver: The University of Denver, CTIR Publications, 1989.

Teaching Science to Children (2nd ed.), by Alfred E. Friedl. New York: McGraw-Hill, 1991.

Tools for Learning: A Guide to Teaching Study Skills, by M. D. Gall, Joyce Gall, Dennis Jacobsen, and Terry Bullock. Alexandria, VA: The Association for Supervision and Curriculum Development, 1992.

Who Am I in the Lives of Children? An Introduction to Teaching Young Children (4th ed.), by Stephanie Feeney, Doris Christensen, and Eva Moravcik. New York: Macmillan, 1991.

Worldways: Bringing the World into the Classroom, by Pamela Elder and Mary Ann Carr. Denver: The University of Denver, CTIR Publications, 1987.

VIDEO PROGRAMS FOR TEACHERS

Appropriate Curriculum for Young Children: The Role of the Teacher. Washington, DC: The National Association for the Education of Young Children, 1992.

Building Quality Child Care: An Overview: Washington, DC: The National Association for the Education of Young Children, 1989.

A Century of Childhood Education, 1892–1992, by S. Wortham and M. Wortham. Wheaton, MD: ACEI Publications, 1992.

Discipline: Appropriate Guidance of Young Children. Washington, DC: The National Association for the Education of Young Children, 1992.

Early Childhood Education: Classroom Management and Curriculum Organization, by Barbara Day, Kay Drake, and Markie Pringle. Alexandria, VA: The Association for Supervision and Curriculum Development. (Winner of the CINE Golden Eagle Award.) 1991.

Experiential Learning in Early Schooling. New York: Insight Media, 1992.

Good Talking with You: Language Acquisition Through Conversation. Portland, OR: Educational Productions, 1991.

Hand-in-Hand: Supporting Children with Play Problems. Portland, OR: Educational Productions, 1993.

Math on the Street. New York: Insight Media, 1991.

Multicultural Education: Valuing Diversity. New York: Insight Media, 1991.

The Nongraded School, by Robert H. Anderson and Barbara Nelson Pavan. Bloomington, IN: Agency for Instructional Technology, 1992.

Play and Imagination. New York: Insight Media, 1992.

Play Power: Skill Building for Young Children. Portland, OR: Educational Productions, 1992.

Quality Schools, by William Glasser. Bloomington, IN: Agency for Instructional Technology, 1992.

Teaching People with Developmental Disabilities, by the Oregon Research Institute, Kate Marquez, Producer. Champaign, IL: Research Press, 1992.

BOOKS FOR CHILDREN

ABC: Museum of Fine Arts, by Florence C. Mayers. New York: Abrams, 1986.

Adam Mouse's Book of Poems, by Lilian Moore. New York: Atheneum, 1992.

The Animals of Buttercup Farm, by Judy Dunn. New York: Random House, 1981.

Any Room for Me? by Leok Koopmans. Mt. Rainier, MD: Floris/Gryphon House, 1993.

Aster Aardvark's Alphabet Adventures, by Steven Kellogg. New York: Morrow, 1987.

Back Home, by Gloria Jean Pinkney. New York: Dial Books, 1993.

Beautiful Junk II, by Karen Brackett and Rosie Manley. Carthage, IL: Good Apple, 1993.

The Best Town in the World, by Byrd Baylor. New York: Macmillan, 1983.

Big Book for Peace, by Ann Durell and Marilyn Sachs. New York: Dutton, 1990.

Black and White, by David Macaulay. Boston: Houghton Mifflin, 1988.

Blue Sea, by Robert Kalan. New York: Greenwillow, 1979.

Bugs! by Patricia McKissack and Fredrick McKissack. Chicago: Children's Press, 1988.

Building a House, by Byron Barton. New York: Greenwillow, 1981.

Chin Chiang and the Dragon's Dance, by Ian Wallace. New York: Macmillan, 1984.

The Cloud Book, by Tomie dePaola. New York: Holiday House, 1975.

Counting, by Diane Wilmer. New York: Macmillan, 1988.

Desert December, by Dorian Haarhoof. Boston: Clarion Books, 1992.

An Early American Christmas, by Tomie dePaola. New York: Holiday House, 1987.

The Easter Craft Book, by Thomas Berger and Petra Berger. Mt. Rainier, MD: Gryphon House, 1993.

A Farmer's Alphabet, by Mary Azarian. Boston: Godine, 1981.

A Farmer's Dozen, by Sandra Joanne Russell. New York: Harper & Row, 1982.

Festivals, Family, and Food, by Diana Carey and Judy Large. Mt. Rainier, MD: Hawthorne/Gryphon House, 1993.

Fireman Jim, by Roger Bester. New York: Crown, 1981.

Forest, Village, Town, City, by Bernice Loewenstein. New York: Harper & Row, 1982.

Handful of Stars, by Rafik Schami. New York: Dutton, 1990.

Hands Around the World, by Susan Milord. Mt. Rainier, MD: Gryphon House, 1993.

Hiawatha: Messenger of Peace, by Dennis Brindell Fradin. New York: McElderry Books, 1992.

Holes, by Joan Elma Rahn. Boston: Houghton Mifflin, 1984.

Icebergs and Glaciers, by Seymour Simon. New York: Morrow, 1987.

Just Enough Is Plenty: A Hanukkah Tale. New York: Viking, 1986.

Katie's Trunk, by Ann Turner. New York: Macmillan, 1992.

The Magnificent Nose and Other Marvels, by Betsy Duffey. Boston: Joy Street Books, 1992.

Monkey-Monkey's Trick: Based on an African Folk Tale, by Paul Meisel. New York: Random House, 1988.

Nice or Nasty: A Book of Opposites, by Nick Butterworth and Mick Inkpen. Boston: Little, Brown, 1987.

A Northern Alphabet: A Is for Arctic, by Ted Harrison. Estes Park, CO: Tundra, 1987.

Old, Older, Oldest, by Leonore Klein. New York: Hastings House, 1983.

Oliver and Amanda's Halloween, by Jean Van Leeuwen. New York: Dial Books, 1992.

One, Two, Three, and Four—No More?, by Catherine Gray. Boston: Houghton Mifflin, 1988.

One Duck, Another Duck, by Charlotte Pomerantz. New York: Greenwillow, 1984.

Puppets, Poems, and Songs, by Julie Catherine Shelton. Carthage, IL: Good Apple, 1993.

The Raggedy Red Squirrel, by Hope Ryden. New York: Lodestar, 1992.

Rain Forest, by Helen Coucher. New York: Farrar, Straus & Giroux, 1988.

A Rainbow Balloon: A Book of Concepts, by Ann Lenssen. Colchester, VT: Cobble Hill, 1992.

Richard Scarry's Best Counting Book Ever, by Richard Scarry. New York: Random House, 1975.

The Samurai's Daughter: A Japanese Legend, by Robert San Soucci. New York: Dial Books, 1992.

Scott Gustafson's Animal Orchestra: A Counting Book, by Scott Gustafson. New York: Harper & Row, 1984.

Seeing Earth from Space, by Patricia Lauber. New York: Orchard Books, 1990.

Seven Little Monsters, by Maurice Sendak. New York: Harper & Row, 1977.

Soccer Sam, by Jean Marzollo. New York: Random House, 1987.

Spiderwebs to Skyscrapers: The Science of Structures, by Dr. David Darling. Minneapolis: Dillon Press, 1991.

Sundianta: Lion King of Mali, by David Wisniewski. Boston: Clarion Books, 1993.

This Farm Is a Mess, by Leslie McGuire. Bowling Green, KY: Parents Press, 1981.

This Same Sky: A Collection of Poems from Around the World, by Naomi Shihab Nye. New York: Four Winds, 1993.

Three Up a Tree, by James Marshall. New York: Dial, 1988.

Toby in the Country, Toby in the City, by Maxine Zohn Bozzo. New York: Greenwillow, 1982.

Train Ride, by John Steptoe. New York: Harper & Row, 1971.

Visiting the Art Museum, by Laurene Krasny Brown and Marc Brown. New York: Dutton, 1986.

We Learn All About Protecting Our Environment. Carthage, IL: Good Apple, 1993.

A Weekend with Rembrandt, by Pascal Bonafoux. New York: Rizzoli, 1993.

What Is Beyond the Hill? by Ernst A. Ekker. New York: Harper & Row, 1986.

When Summer Ends, by Susi Gregg Fowler. New York: Greenwillow, 1988.

Why the Sky Is Far Away: A Nigerian Folktale, by Mary-Joan Gerson. Boston: Joy Street Books, 1992.

The Wing on a Flea: A Book About Shapes. Boston: Little, Brown, 1988.

Wish Again, Big Bear, by Richard J. Margolis. New York: Macmillan, 1974.

FOR MORE INFORMATION ON THESE AND OTHER BOOKS FOR CHILDREN, THE FOLLOWING SOURCES ARE AVAILABLE

Adventuring with Books, A Booklist for Pre-K Thru Grade 6 (9th ed.), M. J. Simpson (Ed.). Urbana, IL: The National Council of Teachers of English, 1989.

Best Books for Children, Preschool Thru Grade 6 (4th ed.), J. Gillespie and C. J. Naden (Eds.). New Providence, NJ: R.R. Bowker, 1990.

The Best in Children's Books: The University of Chicago's Guide to Children's Literature, by Z. Sutherland, B. Hearne, and R. Sutton. Chicago: University of Chicago Press, 1991.

Beyond Picture Books, A Guide to First Readers, by B. Barstow and J. Riggle. New Providence, NJ: R.R. Bowker, 1989.

Books Kids Will Sit Still For (2nd ed.), by J. Freeman. New Providence, NJ: R.R. Bowker, 1990.

Children's Book Review Index (Vol. 17), N. E. Walker and B. Baer (Eds.). Detroit: Gale Research Inc., 1992.

Children's Catalog (16th ed.), J. Yaakov (Ed.). New York: The H. W. Wilson Company, 1991.

FILM / VIDEO PROGRAMS FOR CHILDREN

101 Things for Kids to Do. New York: Random House, 1987.

The Animal Alphabet. Irvine, CA: Karl-Lorimar Home Video, 1985.

Big Bird in China. New York: Random House, 1987.

Dinosaur! Stamford, CT: Children's Video Library, 1985.

Don't Eat the Pictures: Sesame Street at the Metropolitan Museum of Art. New York: Random House Home Video, 1987.

Get Ready, Get Set, Grow! New York: Brooklyn Botanical Gardens, 1986.

Here We Go (Vol. 1) and *Here We Go Again* (Vol. 2). Woodland Hills, CA: Celebrity Home Entertainment, 1986.

Kids in Motion. New York: Playhouse Video, 1987.

Learning About Numbers. New York: Random House, 1986.

The Macmillan Video Almanac for Kids. New York: Macmillan, 1985.

The Magic World of Art. Cincinnati, OH: Congress Video Group, 1987.

Mr. Wizard's Word: Air & Water Wizardry. New York: Playhouse Video, 1983.

National Geographic Series: Among the Wild Chimpanzees. Stamford, CT: Vestron, 1984.

Raffi in Concert with the Rise and Shine Band. Hollywood, CA: A & M Video, 1988.

Strong Kids, Safe Kids. Los Angeles, CA: Paramount, 1984.

Too Smart for Strangers, with Winnie the Pooh. Los Angeles, CA: Disney, 1985.

The Wonder of It All. Culver City, CA: Media Home Entertainment, 1987.

FOR MORE INFORMATION ON THESE AND OTHER CHILDREN'S FILMS AND VIDEOS, THE FOLLOWING SOURCE BOOKS ARE AVAILABLE

Best Videos for Children and Young Adults, by J. J. Gallant. Santa Barbara, CA: ABC-CLIO, 1990.

Media Review Digest (Vol. 22). Ann Arbor, MI: The Pierian Press, 1992.

Notable Children's Films and Videos, Filmstrips, and Recordings, 1973–1986. Chicago: The American Library Association, 1987.

Parent's Choice Guide to Videocassettes for Children, D. H. Green (Ed.). New York: Consumer Reports Books, 1989.

MEDIA PROGRAMS FOCUSING ON DEVELOPMENTALLY APPROPRIATE TEACHING AND LEARNING

Filmstrips/Cassette Tapes

Early Childhood Education: Curriculum Organization and Classroom Management (1983).

This program applies the current research on how children learn the process of creating an appropriate early childhood learning environment. Emphasis is on managing and organizing the classroom in a way that provides for active participation, observation, exploration, and verbalization on the part of the child. The program seeks to meet the needs of the total child—cognitive, affective, and psychomotor—and to match the curriculum to the developmental needs, interests, and learning styles of each child.

The kit includes four sound filmstrips accompanied by materials that allow early childhood practitioners to assess their own philosophies of teaching; plan a learning environment that meets children's developmental needs; design their own contracts; organize plans and develop materials for teaching through learning centers; implement small-group instruction in mathematics and reading; and apply management techniques such as color coding, contracts, and internal and external discipline to their own classrooms. The program is intended for use by early childhood teachers, administrators, curriculum specialists, and university educators and can be used as the basis for staff development workshops or teacher education classes or as self-instruction by individuals.

For information regarding this program, contact Dr. Barbara Day, the School of Education, CB #3500, Peabody Hall, the University of North Carolina at Chapel Hill, Chapel Hill, NC 27599-3500.

Video Program

Early Childhood Education: Classroom Management—Curriculum Organization. (1991). Program consultant: Barbara Day, the University of North Carolina at Chapel Hill; featured teachers: Kay Drake and Markie Pringle.

This 40-minute video program presents a state-of-the-art, K–1, multiage early childhood classroom and shows how an interactive learning environment can be designed to meet the social, emotional, cognitive, and psychomotor needs of each child. Kay Drake and Markie Pringle, two experienced early childhood teachers, offer many suggestions for organizing an early childhood curriculum and managing the classroom. A 200-page *Facilitator's Manual* provides learning and discussion activities to help organize a workshop to accompany the video presentation.

Part One of the program introduces a curriculum that integrates developmental approaches through learning centers, units of study, and small groups. Viewers tour a classroom featuring 14 learning centers including language, research, listening, reading, art, dramatic play, mathematics, creative writing, outdoor activities, and more. Units of study are examined as to how they integrate children's experiential learning with broader academic concepts. Skill groups are discussed as a way of incorporating into the curriculum specific concepts and skills in reading, language, and mathematics. Part Two presents a typical day in Kay Drake's and Markie Pringle's K–1 classroom, where the developmental needs of children are met in a creative learning environment.

For more information on this program write to the Association for Supervision and Curriculum Development, 1250 N. Pitt Street, Alexandria, VA 22314-1403 or call (703) 549-9110.

Materials for Learning Centers

LANGUAGE ARTS CENTER

1. Bingo ABC game
2. Book jackets
3. Booklets, blank
4. Books, wide variety, of interest to children
5. Cans labeled with a letter each: small cans with small letters, large cans with capital letters in another color
6. Cards for children to write their own words on
7. Cards, groups with ryhyming words (self-correcting)
8. Cards with rhyming pictures (self-correcting)
9. Chalkboards
10. Dictionaries
11. Dramatic play equipment (dress-up clothes, props, furniture)
12. Feel box
13. Filmstrips, tapes, records, and videos related to reading
14. Flannelboards and cutouts
15. Large alphabet blocks
16. Magazines and catalogs
17. Magic slates
18. Magnetic board
19. Manipulative devices for visual discrimination and motor coordination
20. Manipulative letters: wood, sandpaper, pipe cleaners, plastic, cardboard
21. Mirror (full child body length)
22. Paints and brushes
23. Paper: lined and unlined, white and colored

24. Pencils, colored marking pens, crayons
25. Pictures, groups with one different for visual discrimination
26. Pictures and objects for classifying
27. Pictures, series (for putting in correct sequence)
28. Pictures: wild and farm animals, vegetables, fruits, birds, flowers, various other pictures of different groups of things and places
29. Poems and story starters
30. Puzzles
31. Reading games, commercial and teacher-made
32. Reading skills kits
33. Scrap materials that can be used for book covers
34. Sentence strips
35. Sequence cards
36. Tape recorder, earphones
37. Telephones, play and real
38. Tiles with letters on each
39. Typewriter
40. Word boxes
41. Word cards
42. Writing paper of different sizes and shapes

READING CENTER

1. Books, assortment (library books, basal readers, classroom-made)
2. Books, child-made
3. Book rack and open storage for records and tapes
4. Calendars, schedules, lunch menu
5. Carrels for individual use
6. Charts: color, number, and alphabet
7. Crossword puzzles
8. Easy chairs and couch
9. Encyclopedias
10. Filmstrips of stories
11. Flannelboard, story characters, and objects
12. Lists: words, songs, books
13. Magazines and catalogs
14. Magnetic board and letters

15. Matching picture and letter games
16. Newspapers: class, local, and city (current)
17. Pillows or floor cushions
18. Puppets
19. Puzzles (variety of types and number of pieces)
20. Records and tapes with corresponding books
21. Rocking chairs
22. Rug or carpet for large area
23. Shelves (low)
24. Spelling and reading games
25. Stories: child-written and commercial
    a. Stories of the country, seasons, and nature
    b. Stories of other countries and cultures
    c. Folk and fairy tales, nursery ryhmes, poetry
26. Tables, 1 to 2, with 2 to 4 chairs each
27. Table, small, with typewriter
28. Talk-starter picture cards
29. Tape recorder, for children to tape themselves reading
30. View masters and slides of stories

BLOCK CENTER

1. Art box (paper, crayons, string, clay, scissors, transparent tape, masking tape, etc.)
2. Batteries, dry cell with lights (to illuminate building interiors)
3. Block bin
4. Block cart
5. Blocks, set of hollow-ply (varying in size)
6. Blocks, set of solid wooden unit blocks, double unit blocks, quadruple unit blocks, ramps, curves, (elliptical and circular), Y shapes, triangles, cylinders
7. Books related to building and construction
8. Building materials: interlocking blocks (large and small), Tinker Toys, Lincoln Logs, large hollow blocks (plastic or wooden)
9. Easter grass (excellent for animal life)
10. Fabric scraps
11. Flags, small
12. Furniture, miniature
13. Markers, colored pencils, small cards, sentence strips (for labeling; store in small boxes or cans covered with contact paper)

14. Objects used to "decorate" buildings: dominoes, shells (scallop, clam), variety of small plastic containers and lids, popsicle sticks, large dried beans, small colored cubes (1" or 2 cm), spools (thread and textile mill), parquetry blocks, assorted colored wooden table blocks, lumber scraps (sanded), pebbles, stones
15. Packing crates, boxes, ropes
16. People, rubber (farmer, police officer, firefighter)
17. Planks
18. Pulleys
19. Puppets
20. Styrofoam pebbles
21. Thin pieces of rubber tubing (for gasoline pumps)
22. Tiles, carpet squares, wallpaper (can be used as floors)
23. Tool kits (for dramatic play)
24. Toys, riding wheel (tractor and trailer, derrick truck, open van truck)
25. Traffic signs
26. Vehicles, small (airplane, helicopter, dump truck, steamroller, train, fire truck)
27. Zoo, rubber (and farm animals)

MATH CENTER

1. Abacus
2. Balances
3. Bead or counting frame
4. Blocks of all shapes and sizes, number blocks, parquetry, attribute blocks
5. Books (interest and reference)
6. Cards, problem or activity
7. Catalogs, newspaper ads
8. Clocks
9. Coin stamps
10. Collections of all types (buttons, coins, stones, sticks, stirrers, macaroni, beans, yarn, marbles, bottle caps)
11. Counters (blocks, beads, sticks, straws, buttons, clothespins, bottle caps)
12. Cuisenaire rods
13. Dominoes
14. Egg cartons for making sets

15. Flannelboard and cutouts
16. Flash cards
17. Fractional parts and fractional board
18. Games, commercial and teacher-made (see directions for making)
19. Geoboards and rubber bands
20. Geometric wire forms and patterns
21. Magnetic letters and numbers, magnetic board
22. Math books
23. Measuring devices (spoons, cups, containers, various sizes)
24. Metric step-on scales, metric platform scale, metric plastic measure set (spoons and cups, 1 ml to 250 ml), balance scales with metric weights (1 g to 50 g)
25. Number lines
26. Pegs and pegboard
27. Place value charts
28. Play money
29. Playing cards, checkers and board, chess set and board
30. Rice and sand (for measuring)
31. Rope (for encompassing areas), puzzles, logs
32. Rulers, yardstick, tape measure
33. Scales and objects to weigh
34. Sum stick, adding machine, calculator
35. Thermometers
36. Trundle wheel, compass, measuring rods and containers
37. Unifix cubes

WOODWORKING CENTER

1. Awl
2. Backsaw
3. Band-aids
4. Bath soap, mild
5. Brace and bit
6. Broom, dustpan
7. Broom, dustpan, rags
8. Brush
9. "C" clamps, 4"–6"
10. Cardboard (tri-wall, large posterboard boxes)

11. File, cabinet, half round 8"
12. File card for cleaning file
13. First aid kit
14. Formica, tile, linoleum
15. Glue (Elmer's)
16. Hammers 7 to 10 oz. (claw) with wooden handles
17. Hand drill with several bits
18. Hinges, knobs, nuts, bolts, hooks
19. Hole-punch, center
20. Hooks and screws
21. Large-wood supply (soft pine or spruce, finished or unfinished wood, molding and doweling, plywood)
22. Magnets
23. Miter box
24. Monkey wrench
25. Nails (variety)
26. Nailing block
27. Paint
28. Paintbrushes
29. Paint scraper
30. Paint shirts
31. Paint stain
32. Pencils, scissors, string, wallpaper scraps, tacks, tapes, leather, wire, chicken wire, paper clips, glue
33. Plane
34. Pliers, combination, 6 in.
35. Pulleys, rope
36. Rags
37. Rasp (for smoothing edges)
38. Rulers, yardstick
39. Safety glasses
40. Sandpaper, paint, shellac, brushes
41. Saw, coping (for cutting curves)
42. Saw, hand crosscut, 16 and 11 pt.
43. Saw, keyhole or compass
44. Sawhorse
45. Screwdrivers, slotted and Phillip's head type

46. Shop vacuum
47. Sink
48. "Small"-wood supply (toothpicks, popsicle sticks, tongue depressors, paint stirrers, small branches and sticks, "end grain" scrips, box of assorted scrap wood)
49. Storage shelves
50. Sure-forms
51. Trash can with lids
52. T-square
53. Vice for workbench
54. Wheels, small, styrofoam, bottle caps, pop-tops from cans
55. Wire cutter
56. Wood scraps
57. Workbench
58. Work gloves

SCIENCE CENTER

1. Aquarium, large
2. Batteries
3. Bird-feeding station
4. Bottles
5. Cage for insects, bug house
6. Cages for live animals, animal food
7. Calendars, clocks, hour glass, egg timer, sundial
8. Candles
9. Chart and graph paper
10. Chemicals, assortment from home: vinegar, baking soda, table salt, baking powder, sugar, cream of tartar, rubbing alcohol, epsom salts, iodine, ammonia, hydrogen peroxide
11. Clear plastic containers with labels for "raw materials"
12. Compass
13. Electrical equipment, electrical bell, bulbs, switches, hot plate, flashlight
14. Fibers: nylon, silk, rayon, linen
15. Flower boxes
16. Heat, water
17. Kaleidoscope, color paddles
18. Kite, locks, iron filings, mechanical junk, slinky, strings

19. Low shelving for puzzles, games, displays
20. Machines, simple
21. Magazines (especially farm and science magazines)
22. Magnets (bar, U, horseshoe)
23. Magnifying glass (hand, tripod), microscope, telescope
24. Mirrors and lenses
25. Objects that float and sink
26. Objects to smell, taste, hear, touch, see
27. Paper and pen for labeling
28. Pendulums, pendulum frame, pendulum bobs
29. Plastic tubs for storing materials and supplies
30. Prisms
31. Pulleys, levers, inclined planes, screws, wheels and axles, bolts, gears
32. Resource material, pleasurable nature reading (e.g., *Ranger Rick*)
33. Rock and shell collections
34. Rope, drinking straws, food coloring, stopwatch, stethoscope, sponges, keys
35. Rugs
36. Scales (balance, kitchen, spring), weights, assorted materials for balancing
37. Science kits
38. Seeds to plant and classify
39. Shapes
40. Sink, preferably with hot and cold water
41. Soil, different kinds
42. Tables
43. Tape measures, yardstick, meter stick, rulers, dry and liquid measure containers
44. Terrarium
45. Thermometers (outdoor and indoor, Celsius and Fahrenheit), barometer
46. Things to classify
47. Things to take apart and put together
48. Tuning forks
49. Watering cans, trowel, flower pots, incubators
50. Windows (preferably low enough for the children to see out)
51. Wood, wire, glass

SOCIAL STUDIES CENTER

1. Activity kits (e.g., Community Helpers)
2. Art materials (paints, easels, chalk, crayons, clay, paste)
3. Blocks and transportation toys
4. Cartons and boxes
5. Cartoons
6. Cassette player, cassettes, and headsets
7. Charts of information
8. Class books about social studies topics
9. Clothing for dramatic/role play
10. Cooking equipment and utensils
11. Encyclopedias
12. Equipment such as telephone to take apart
13. Filmstrips relating to social studies
14. Globe (primary)
15. Graphs
16. Magazines and catalogs
17. Maps (city, neighborhood, state, U.S., world)
18. Materials to make a diorama, peep box, models
19. Microcomputer and software
20. Overhead projector and transparencies
21. Paper for writing, construction, chart
22. Pictures and study prints
23. Question and problem cards
24. Radio, television, VCR
25. Real objects (flags, coins, costumes)
26. Record player, headset, and records
27. Scrapbooks
28. Slide projector and color transparency slides
29. Social studies books
30. Teacher-made activity cards
31. Typewriter
32. Works of art (paintings, drawings, scuptures, basketing, pottery, architecture)

HOME LIVING AND CREATIVE DRAMATICS

1. Added objects as needed for special emphasis
2. Artificial fruits, vegetables
3. Books, magazines, newspapers
4. Brooms, mop, dustpan
5. Brushes
6. Chest for dress-up clothes, shoes, hats
7. Child-sized wooden sink, stove, refrigerator, cupboard
8. Clothes rack
9. Cooking supplies (measuring spoons and cups, minute timer, mixing bowls, hot plate, toaster oven, saucepans, wooden spoons, eggbeater, paring knife, cookie cutter, pot holder, aprons or smocks, dishpans, rolling pin, muffin tin, cookie sheets, paper towels, plates, napkins, recipe task cards or chart, spatula, grater, sifter, whisk, blender, aluminum foil, cutting board, electric fry pan, colander, vegetable brush)
10. Curtains for window
11. Dish pan
12. Dishes, silverware
13. Doll bed and other furniture
14. Doll carriage
15. Doll clothes
16. Dolls
17. Flower vase with flowers
18. Ironing board, iron
19. Jewelry, shoes, handbags, hats (including various occupational hats such as fireman, policeman, hardhat, nurse, helmet, cap, etc.), coats, scarves, dresses for play, props for playing doctor, beauty parlor
20. Materials for making puppets (scissors, glue, pens, markers, cloth scraps, paper bags, boxes, costumes, yarn, buttons, trinkets, styrofoam balls, styrofoam cups, handkerchiefs, tongue depressors, string, socks, paper plates, spools, cardboard rolls, pint-sized milk cartons, clay or playdough)
21. Mirror
22. Pails, sponges
23. Puppets/puppet theater
24. Rocking chair
25. Shelves
26. Small rug

27. Small table, chairs, bed
28. Sponges, cloths, potholders, aprons
29. Sufficient space to allow free movement
30. Telephone, classroom telephone book, datebook

FINE ARTS CENTER

Music

1. Autoharp (and cards made out with markings for familiar songs)
2. Carpet or rug
3. Double-headed tom-tom
4. Dowel sticks
5. Earphones
6. Glasses of water and spoons
7. Kalimba (with cards)
8. Manuscript paper for children to write songs
9. Materials for children to make their own instruments (boxes, paper plates, bottle caps, pebbles, stones, beans, cans)
10. Models of staff and notes, separate notes (to match and read), clef signs (traditional and invented)
11. Music books and charts of songs to play
12. Other musical instruments (guitar, ukelele, recorder, etc.)
13. Piano
14. Record player
15. Records
16. Rhythm instruments
17. Rhythm instruments, bought and/or homemade (sticks, bells, cymbals, drums, triangles, tambourines, claves, etc.)
18. Scarves for dancing
19. Shelves
20. Small boxes
21. Songs written on chart
22. Space
23. Tape records and tapes
24. Zim—Gar bells (20 notes)
25. Zither (and cards)

Art

1. Aluminum foil, waxed paper
2. Aprons, old shirts, or smocks
3. Architect's drawing paper
4. Art prints and art objects
5. Art tissue
6. Bags
7. Blankets and sheets
8. Books of crafts, artists, pictures of paintings
9. Box of materials for collages
10. Box of paper scraps and material scraps
11. Boxes of many shapes and sizes
12. Butcher block paper
13. Buttons, different shapes of macaroni, nuts, bottle caps
14. Cake tins for modeling clay
15. Cans: coffee, juice, spice
16. Charcoal
17. Clay boards (9″ × 12″ hot mats), cafeteria trays
18. Cleanup equipment: buckets, sponges, and mops (should be accessible to the children)
19. Coat hangers
20. Colored chalk and pastels
21. Colored toothpicks
22. Compasses
23. Construction paper
24. Containers with lids for mixed paints
25. Cord, yarn, string, and thread
26. Corn starch, laundry starch
27. Corrugated cardboard
28. Crayons
29. Crepe paper
30. Drying rack
31. Electrical wire
32. Fadeless paper
33. Finger paint
34. Fingerpainting paper
35. Florists' wire

36. Flour, salt (for play-dough)
37. Food coloring
38. Glue (Elmer's)
39. Glue sticks
40. Hair spray
41. India ink and stamp pad
42. Inner tubes
43. Instant papier-mâché
44. Iron
45. Jewelry
46. Lace, ribbon, felt
47. Looms
48. Magazines and catalogs, greeting cards, newspapers
49. Magic markers
50. Manila paper
51. Materials for weaving, stitchery
52. Modeling clay
53. Newsprint
54. Paintbrushes
55. Paint (tempera)
56. Paper clips, brads, staples, pins
57. Paper punch
58. Paste
59. Pencils (lead, colored)
60. Pipe cleaners
61. Plaster of paris
62. Plastic garbage can with lid for clay (pottery)
63. Play dough
64. Posterboard
65. Pottery clay
66. Rubber cement
67. Rulers
68. Scissors
69. Shells, seeds, dried flowers
70. Socks
71. Sponges
72. Stapler

73. Sticky tack
74. Straws, needles
75. Styrofoam trays
76. Talcum powder
77. Tape
78. Telephone wire
79. Wallpaper samples
80. Water colors
81. White drawing paper
82. Wood scraps
83. Working space: tables, easels, countertops, floor and outdoor space
84. Yarn

QUIET AREA

1. Pillows
2. Rocking chair
3. Rugs
4. Screen or drape of material to eliminate noise of other classroom activities

This should be a quiet place where a child may go to be alone to think or do what he or she wishes. It should be a comfortable relaxing area but include no specific materials. Children may bring their own materials to this center.

OUTDOOR CENTERS

1. Aluminum or plastic sand utensils
2. Bales of straw
3. Balls (various sizes, 8″ to 24″)
4. Bean bags
5. Building blocks
6. Equipment for crawling and tunneling
7. Heavy wooden benches
8. Jump ropes (long and individual)
9. Jungle gym
10. Ladders (cleats at each end, 3′ × 5′)
11. Large packing boxes
12. Large sewer pipes (set in cement)

13. Low balance beams
14. Low climbing ropes
15. Low horizontal ladders
16. Low turning bars
17. Parent-made equipment and materials (storage unit to build, wooden climbing structure, telephone spools, wooden bridges and structures, cans and barrels, tire construction, rolling slide, trees encircled with brick, nets for climbing)
18. Planks
19. Platforms for climbing and swinging
20. Riding toys (wagons, tricycles, wheelbarrows)
21. Safety climbing tree
22. Sailboat
23. Sand and water play table with top
24. Sandbox
25. Sand toys
26. Sawhorses (various heights)
27. Scrap lumber for large construction
28. Steering wheel and column attached to a heavy box
29. Swings (tire or leather seats)
30. Tires: tractor, automobile, bicycle
31. Tools for gardening (shovels, rakes, hoes)
32. Tools for woodwork
33. Tree trunks
34. Wading pool
35. Walking boards (cleated and of various lengths, 5' to 6' and 8" to 12" wide)
36. Water hose
37. Wooden boxes, packing crates, rope handles, cardboard cartons
38. Wooden steps, wooden ladder

SAND AND WATER CENTER

1. Box of objects of sinking and floating (sponge, nail, rubber eraser, pencil, leaf, nickel, paper clip, rock, cork, crayon, twig, acorn, peanut, rubber band, wooden bead, lengths of sticks, spools, odd pieces of wood, scissors)
2. Brushes of several sizes
3. Bubble pipes, egg beaters, and other mixers (whisks, spoons)

4. Cakes of soap, soap flakes, liquid soap
5. Chart paper, markers
6. Corks, sponges
7. Dump trucks, small cars
8. Flexible plastic tubing (of several diameters)
9. Food coloring
10. Funnels of different sizes
11. A hose and/or pitchers to fill the tub (the teacher can mark the water line with a colored marker so children can fill the tub to the best level)
12. Measuring spoons and containers
13. Meat basters
14. Pieces of wood
15. Plastic aprons for the children
16. Plastic containers and lids
17. Plastic dishes (cups, bowls, mugs, beakers, muffin tins)
18. Plastic eyedroppers
19. Rolling pin, shells, stones
20. Sand and water table and/or a large galvanized (or plastic) tub
21. Scales (balance)
22. Several lengths of pipe and hose
23. Sheets of plastic, and old shower curtain, or an absorbent rug to place under the tub
24. Sieves of all shapes and sizes, sprinkler tops on bottles
25. Small sponges
26. Sponges and a pail, mop for cleanup
27. Storage space for materials
28. Straws
29. Styrofoam cork
30. Tempera paint
31. Weights (ounces, grams)
32. Wheelbarrow, trowels, spoons, shovels, buckets, sticks, rakes, ladles, dump trucks, sand combs, ice cream scoop

Early Childhood Commercial Suppliers

ABC School Supply, Inc.
6500 Peachtree Industrial Boulevard
P.O. Box 4750
Norcross, GA 30071

American Guidance Service
4201 Woodland Road
P.O. Box 99
Circle Pines, MN 55014-1796

American Science and Engineering, Inc.
Education Division
955 Massachusetts Avenue
Cambridge, MA 02139

Carolina School Supply
2619 West Boulevard
P.O. Box RRR
Charlotte, NC 28203

Childcraft Educational Corporation
20 Kilmer Road
Edison, NJ 08818

Community Playthings
Rifton, NY 12471

Constructive Playthings
1277 East 119th Street
Grandview, MO 64030

Creative Publications
5040 West 111th Street
Oak Lawn, IL 60453

Cuisenaire Co. of America, Inc.
P.O. Box 5026
White Plains, NY 10602-5026

Cypress Publishing Corporation
1763 Gardena Avenue, Suite 100
Glendale, CA 91204

Delta Education, Inc.
P.O. Box M
Nashua, NH 03061

Developmental Learning Materials
P.O. Box 4000, One DLM Park
Allen, TX 75002

Didax Educational Resources
6 Doulton Place
Peabody, MA 01960

Educational Teaching Aids
159 West Kinzie Street
Chicago, IL 60610

Good Apple
1204 Buchanan Street
P.O. Box 299
Carthage, IL 62321-0299

Gryphon House
P.O. Box 275
Mt. Rainier, MD 20712

Incentive Publications, Inc.
3835 Cleghorn Avenue
Nashville, TN 37215-2532

Lakeshore Learning Materials
2695 East Dominguez Street
Carson, CA 90749

Leicestershire Learning Systems
Chestnut Street
Lewiston, ME 04240

Listening Library, Inc.
P.O. Box L
Old Greenwich, CT 06870

McGraw-Hill Book Company
Webster Division
1221 Avenue of the Americas
New York, NY 10020

Nienhuis Montessori U.S.A., Inc.
320 Pioneer Way, Department 4
Mountain View, CA 94041

Scholastic Book Services
904 Sylvan Avenue
Englewood Cliffs, NJ 07632

Stones Southern School Supply
3800 Holly Springs Road
Raleigh, NC 27606

Teaching Resources Corporation
50 Pond Park Road
Hingham, MA 02043

Weston Woods
Weston, CT 06883

Reference List

Ackerman, D. B. (1989). Intellectual and practical criteria for successful curriculum integration. In H. H. Jacobs (Ed.), *Interdisciplinary curriculum: Design and implementation* (pp. 25–37). Alexandria, VA: Association for Supervision and Curriculum Development.

Adams, P. (1982). *Children's workshops: Ideas for carpentry centers*. Columbus, GA: Columbus College, School of Education. (ERIC Document Reproduction Service No. ED 242 387).

Adams, R. J. (1967). *Creative woodworking in the kindergarten*. Minneapolis: T. S. Denison.

Adelman, H. S., & Taylor, L. (1993). *Learning problems and learning disabilities*. Pacific Grove, CA: Brooks/Cole.

Allen, J., & Catron, C. E. (1993). *Early childhood curriculum*. New York: Macmillan.

Allen, K. E., & Hart, B. (1984). *The early years: Arrangements for learning*. Englewood Cliffs, NJ: Prentice-Hall.

Anderson, S., & Hoot, L. (1986). Kids, carpentry and pre-school classrooms. *Day Care Early Education, 13,* 12–15.

Aronson, S. S. (1991). *Health and safety in child care*. New York: HarperCollins.

Asher, S. R., Renshaw, P. D., & Hymel, S. (1982). Peer relations and the development of social skills. In S. Moore & C. Cooper (Eds.), *The young child: Reviews of research* (Vol. 3), Washington DC: National Association for the Education of Young Children.

Ashley, B. (1981), May. *Teaching idea file*. Workshop presented at the annual meeting of the International Reading Association, Atlanta, GA. (ERIC Document Reproduction Service No. ED 323 561).

Atkinson, M. L. (1984). Computer assisted instruction: Current state of the art. *Computers in the Schools, 1*(1), 91–99.

Atwood, V. A. (1985). Bubble-good data: Product testing and other sources. *Social Education, 39,* 147–148.

Bangert-Drowns, R., Kulik, J. H., & Kulik, C. C. (1985). Effectiveness of computer-based education in secondary schools, *Journal of Computer-Based Instruction, 12*(3), 59–68.

Banks, J. (1990). *Teaching strategies for the social studies* (4th ed.). White Plains, NY: Longman.

Banks, J., & Clegg, A. (1985). *Teaching strategies for the social studies: Inquiry, valuing and decision-making* (3rd ed.). White Plains, NY: Longman.

Barnett, R. R. (1981). *Let out the sunshine*. Dubuque, IA: William C. Brown.

Beaty, J. (1990). *Observing development of the young child* (2nd ed.). Columbus, OH.: Merrill.

Beaty, J. (1992a). Block center. In *Preschool: Appropriate practices* (pp. 41–63). Orlando, FL: Harcourt Brace Jovanovich.

Beaty, J. (1992b). *Preschool: Appropriate practices.* Orlando, FL: Harcourt Brace Jovanovich.

Beaty, J. (1992c). *Skills for preschool teachers* (4th ed.). New York: Macmillan.

Beaty, J. J., & Tucker, W. H. (1987). *The computer as a paintbrush*. Columbus, OH: Merrill.

Becker, W. C. (1971). *Parents are teachers*. Champaign, IL: Research Press.

Bennett, W. (1986). *First lessons: A report on elementary education in America.* Washington, DC: U.S. Government Printing Office.

Berends, P. B. (1983). *Whole child/whole parent.* New York: Harper & Row.

Bergen, D. (1987). *Play as a medium for learning and development: A handbook of theory and practice.* Portsmouth, NH: Heinemann.

Berger, E. H. (1991). *Parents as partners in education* (3rd ed.). New York: Macmillan.

Bergman, A. (1990). *Learning center: Activities for the full-day kindergarten.* West Nyack, NY: Center for Applied Research in Education.

Berry, C. F., & Mindes, G. (1993). *Planning a theme-based curriculum.* Glenview, IL: Good-Year.

Bloom, B. S. (1956). *Taxonomy of educational objectives: The classification of educational goals: Handbook I, Cognitive domain.* New York: McKay.

Bostley, E. J. (1985). How to teach music as a daily discipline. *The School Administrator, 16* (4). Arlington, VA: American Association of School Administrators.

Bostley, E. J. (1986). *Proceedings of the 1986 Southeastern Music Education Symposium.* Athens: The University of Georgia Center for Continuing Education.

Bracey, G. W. (1987). Measurement-driven instruction: Catchy phrase, dangerous practice. *Phi Delta Kappan, 68,* 683–686.

Brandt, R. (1988). On students' needs and team learning: A conversation with William Glasser. *Educational Leadership, 45*(6), 38–45.

Brannen, N. (1978). *Woodworking: Arizona HSST/DCA competency-based training module #30.* Coolidge, AZ: AZ/NV Child Development Associates. (ERIC Document Reproduction Service No. EDI 180 638).

Braun, S. J., & Edward, E. P. (1972). *History and theory of early childhood education.* Worthington, OH: Charles A. Jones.

Bredekamp, S. (Ed.). (1987). *Developmentally appropriate practice in early childhood programs serving children from birth through age 8* (expanded ed.). Washington, DC: National Association for the Education of Young Children.

Brice, R. (1992, Spring). Developmentally appropriate practice and parent involvement. *Kappa Delta Pi Record,* p. 71.

Brodinsky, B. (1976). Twelve major events that shaped America's schools. *Phi Delta Kappan, 58* (1), 68.

Broman, B. L. (1982). *The early years in childhood education* (2nd ed.). Prospect Heights, IL: Waveland.

Brown, V. S. (1992). Your green pages. *Teaching PreK–8, 21,* 65.

Bruner, J. S. (1966). *Toward a theory of instruction.* Cambridge, MA: Harvard University Press.

Bryant, J. C. (1983). *Why art, how art.* Seattle, WA: Special Child Publications.

Burke, E. M. (1986). *Early childhood literature: For love of child and book.* Boston: Allyn and Bacon.

Burns, P. C., & Broman, B. L. (1983). *The language arts in childhood education* (5th. ed.). Boston: Houghton Mifflin.

Cain, S. E., & Evans, J. M. (1990). *Sciencing: An involvement approach to elementary science methods.* Columbus, OH: Merrill.

Campbell, S., & Frost, J. L. (1985). The effects of playground type on the cognitive and social play behaviors of grade two children. In J. L. Frost & S. Sunderlin (Eds.), *When children play* (pp. 81–87). Wheaton, MD: Association for Childhood Education International.

Carroll, D., & Carini, P. (1991). Tapping teachers' knowledge. In V. Perrone (Ed.), *Expanding students' assessment* (p. 40). Alexandria, VA: Association for Supervision and Curriculum Development.

Carroll, R. (1985). Exploring the history of a neighborhood: A community project. *The Social Studies, 77,* 150–154.

Cartledge, G., & Milburn, J. F. (Eds.). (1986). *Teaching social skills to children* (2nd ed.) New York: Pergamon.

Catron, C. E., & Allen, J. (1993). *Early childhood curriculum.* New York: Macmillan.

Cauley, K., & Tyler, B. (1989). The relationship of self-concept to prosocial behavior in children. *Early Childhood Research Quarterly, 4,* 51–60.

Chambers, J. A., & Sprecher, J. W. (1980). Computer-assisted instruction: Current trends and critical issues. *Communications of the ACM*, *23*(6), 332–342.

Chapin, J., & Messick, R. (1992). *Elementary social studies: A practical guide* (2nd ed.). White Plains, NY: Longman.

Cheek, E. H., Jr., Flippo, R. F., & Lindsay, J. D. (1989). *Reading for success in elementary schools.* Orlando, FL: Holt, Rinehart & Winston.

Chenfeld, M. B. (1983). *Creative activities for young children.* New York: Harcourt Brace Jovanovich.

Chilcoat, G. W. (1985). The literary popular story paper as classroom activity: The role of women in nineteenth century America. *The Social Studies, 76*, 76–79.

Child Care Employee Project. (1989). *Who cares? Child care teachers and the quality of care in America: Report of the National Child Care Staffing Study.* Oakland, CA: Author.

Children's Defense Fund. (1990). *Children 1990: A report card, briefing book and action primer.* Washington, DC: Author.

Chittenden, E. (1991). Authentic assessment, evaluation, and documentation of student performance. In V. Perrone (Ed.), *Expanding student assessment* (p. 22). Alexandria, VA: Association for Supervision and Curriculum Development.

Chosky, L. (1986). *Teaching music in the twentieth century.* Englewood Cliffs, NJ: Prentice-Hall.

Clancy, L. (1991). *Preschool teacher's month-by-month activities program.* West Nyack, NY: Center for Applied Research in Education.

Claycomb, P. (1992). *The busy classroom.* Mt. Rainier, MD: Gryphon House.

Clemens, S. G. (1983). *The sun's not broken, a cloud's just in the way.* Mt. Rainier, MD: Gryphon House.

Clements, D. H. (1989). *Computers in elementary mathematics education.* Englewood Cliffs, NJ: Prentice-Hall.

Clements, D. H., & Battista, M. T. (1987). Testudinal testimony: Why *Logo* for learning mathematics? *Logo*-based geometry. *Logo Exchange, 61*,(20), 20–21.

Clewett, A. S. (1988). Guidance and discipline: Teaching young children appropriate behavior. *Young Children, 43*, 26–31.

Cliatt, M. P., & Shaw, J. M. (1992). *Helping children explore science.* New York: Macmillan.

Cochrane, O., Cochrane, D., Scalenta, S., & Buchanan, E. (1984). *Reading, writing, & caring.* New York: Richard C. Owen.

Cohen, R. (1987). Implementing *Logo* in the grade two classroom: Acquisition of basic programming concepts. *Journal of Computer-Based Instruction, 14* (4), 124–132.

Cohen, S., & Rae, G. (1987). *Growing up with children.* New York: Holt, Rinehart & Winston.

Colbert, C., & Taunton, M. (1992). Developmentally appropriate practices for the visual arts education of young children. [Briefing paper]. Reston, VA: National Art Education Association.

Cole, A., Haas, C., Heller, E., & Weinberger, B. (1976). *A pumpkin in a pear tree.* Boston: Little, Brown.

Coleman, M., & Skeen, P. (1984–1985). Play, games, and sport: Their use and misuse. *Childhood Education, 61*, 192–197.

Coletta, A., & Coletta, K. (1986). *Year 'round activities for four-year-old children.* West Nyack, NY: Center for Applied Research in Education.

Collier, M. J., Forte, I., & MacKenzie, J. (1981). *Kids stuff.* Nashville, TN: Incentive Publications.

Computer Services Section. (1990). *I.L.S./I.M.S. checklist.* Raleigh: Division of Media and Technology, North Carolina Department of Public Instruction.

Conley, P. R., & Akin, B. J. (1991). *Comprehension checkups grades 1–5.* Englewood, CO: Teacher Ideas Press.

Connolly, F. W., & Eisenberg, T. E. (1990). The feedback classroom: Teaching's silent friend. *Technological Horizons in Education Journal, 17*(5), 75–77.

Corbitt, M. K. (Ed.). (1987). The impact of computing technology on school mathematics: Report of a National Council of Teachers of Mathematics conference. In L. W. Barber (Ed.), *Exemplary practice series: Mathematics* (p. 79). Bloomington, IN: Center on Evaluation, Development, and Research, Phi Delta Kappa.

Cory, S. L. (1989). *The effects of two different methods of teaching* Logo *on the problem-solving abili-*

ties of fifth grade students. Unpublished doctoral dissertation, University of North Carolina at Chapel Hill.

Cowe, E. (1982). *Free play: Organization and management in the preschool and kindergarten*. Springfield, IL: Charles C. Thomas.

Creative Associates, Inc. (1979). *Blocks: A creative curriculum for early childhood*. Mount Rainier, MD: Gryphon House.

Creative Associates, Inc. (1979). *House corner: A creative curriculum for early childhood*. Washington, DC: Author.

Criteria for play equipment. (1990). Rifton, NY: Community Playthings.

Criteria for selecting play equipment for early childhood education: A reference book. (1981). Rifton, NY: Community Playthings.

Croft, D. J. (1990). *An activities handbook for teachers of young children* (5th ed.). Boston: Houghton Mifflin.

Crossett, B. (1983). Using both halves of the brain to teach the whole child. *Social Education, 47*, 266–268.

Cunningham, P. (1991). *Phonics they use: Words for reading and writing*. New York: HarperCollins.

Curwin, R. L., & Mendler, A. N. (1988). *Discipline with dignity*. Alexandria, VA: Association for Supervision and Curriculum Development.

David, J., & Mitchell, A. (1992). *Explorations with young children: A curriculum guide from the Bank Street College of Education*. Mt. Rainier, MD: Gryphon House.

Davidson, L., McKernon, P., & Gardner, H. (1981). *Documentary report of the application of psychology to the teaching of music*. Reston, VA: Music Educators National Conference.

Davis, H. G. (1980). Reading pressures in the kindergarten. *Childhood Education, 57*(2), 76–79.

Day, B. (1978). Where children write to read. *Childhood Education, 54*(5), 229–233.

Day, B. (1983). *Early childhood education: Creative learning activities* (2nd ed.). New York: Macmillan.

Day, B. (1988a). *Early childhood education: Creative learning activities* (3rd ed.). New York: Macmillan.

Day, B. (1988b). What's happening in early childhood programs across the United States. In C. Warger (Ed.), *A resource guide to public school early childhood programs* (pp. 3–31). Alexandria, VA: Association for Supervision and Curriculum Development.

Day, B. (1992a). Early childhood education: A developmental perspective. *Kappa Delta Pi Record, 28*(3), 67–70.

Day, B. (Ed.). (1992b). *North Carolina Public School early childhood programs: A call for leadership*. Charlotte: The North Carolina Association for Supervision and Curriculum Development.

Day, B., & Drake, K. N. (1983). *Early childhood education: Curriculum organization and classroom management*. Alexandria, VA: Association for Supervision and Curriculum Development.

Day, B., & Drake, K. N. (1986). Developmental and experiential programs: The key to quality education and care of young children. *Educational Leadership, 44*(3), 24–27.

Day, B., Drake, K. N., & Thomas, T. S. (1991a). *Early childhood education: Classroom management and curriculum organization*. Alexandria, VA: Association for Supervision and Curriculum Development. [Accompanying videotape with same title].

Day, B., Drake, K. N., & Thomas, T. S. (1991b). *Early childhood education: Facilitator's manual*. Alexandria, VA: Association for Supervision and Curriculum Development.

Day, B., Malarz, L., & Terry, M. (1992). *The care and education of young children*. Alexandria, VA: Association for Supervision and Curriculum Development.

Day, M. C., & Parker, R. K. (1977). *The preschool in action* (2nd ed.). Boston: Allyn and Bacon.

Decker, C. A., & Decker, J. R. (1992). *Planning and administering early childhood programs* (5th ed.). Columbus, OH: Merrill.

Dede, C. J. (1987). Empowering environments, hypermedia and microworlds. *The Computing Teacher, 20*(3), 20–24.

Derman-Sparks, L., & A.B.C. Task Force (1989). *Anti-bias curriculum: Tools for empowering young children*. Washington, DC: National Association for the Education of Young Children.

Dickson, W., & Raymond, M. W. (1984). *Language arts computer book*. Reston, VA: Reston Publishing.

D'Ignazio, F. (1988). Bring the 1990's to the classroom of today. *Phi Delta Kappan, 70*(1), 26–27.

Distefano, P., Dole, J. & Marzano, R. (1984). *Elementary Language Arts*. New York: Wiley.

Dodge, D. T. (1988). *The creative curriculum for early childhood*. Washington, DC: Teaching Strategies.

Dodge, D. T. (1991). *The creative curriculum for early childhood* (2nd ed.). Washington, DC: Teaching Strategies.

Dodge, D. T., & Colker, L. J. (1992). *The creative curriculum for early childhood* (3rd ed.). Washington, DC: Teaching Strategies.

Dodge, D. T., Koralek, D. G., & Pizzolongo, P. J. (1989). *Caring for preschool children* (Vol. 2). Washington, DC: Teaching Strategies.

Dooly, N. (1992, Fall). Multimedia expands the classroom. *OIT Review*, pp. 6–7. (Office of Information Technology, University of North Carolina at Chapel Hill).

Drake, K. N., & Sher, K. R. (1992). Developmentally appropriate early childhood education: Theory and practice. In B. Day (Ed.), *North Carolina Public Schools early childhood programs: A call for leadership* (pp. 21–41). Charlotte: North Carolina Association for Supervision and Curriculum Development.

Dunn, K. J., & Dunn, R. S. (1987). Dispelling outmoded beliefs about student learning. *Educational Leadership, 44*(6), 55–62.

Edwards, B. (1979). *Drawing on the right side of the brain*. Los Angeles: Houghton Mifflin.

Eheart, B. K., & Leavitt, R. L. (1985). Supporting toddler play. *Young Children, 3*, 18–22.

Ellis, A. K. (1977). *Teaching and learning elementary social studies*. Boston: Allyn and Bacon.

Essa, E. (1992). *Introduction to early childhood education*. Albany, NY: Delmar.

Evans, E. D. (1975). *Contemporary influences in early childhood education* (2nd ed.). New York: Holt, Rinehart & Winston.

Faddis, B. (1991). *Alternative program evaluation ideas for early childhood education programs*. Portland, OR: Northwest Regional Educational Laboratory.

Feeney, S., Christensen, D., & Moravcik, E. (1991). *Who am I in the lives of children?* (4th ed.). New York: Macmillan.

Fein, G. (1982). Pretend play: New perspectives. In J. F. Brown (Ed.), *Curriculum planning for young children* (p. 23). Washington, DC: National Association for the Education of Young Children.

Fein, G., & Rivkin, M. (1986). *The young child at play: Reviews of research*. (Vol. 4). Washington, DC: National Association for the Education of Young Children.

Feldman, J. R. (1991). *A survival guide for the preschool teacher*. West Nyack, NY: Center for Applied Research in Education.

Feuer, M. J., & Fulton, K. (1993). The many faces of performance assessment. *Phi Delta Kappan, 74*(6), 478.

Fisher, B. (1991). *Joyful learning*. Portsmouth, NH: Heinemann.

Foust, S. J., Vurnakes, C. D., Simpson, R. J., Bremer, L. & Wolf, K. (1984). *Centers galore* (Book 5). Greensboro, NC: Education Center.

Fox, S. E., & Allen, V. G. (1983). *The language arts: An integrated approach*. New York: Holt, Rinehart & Winston.

Frost, J. L. (1986). *Playground maintenance checklist*. Austin: Texas Department of Human Services.

Frost, J. L. (1992). *Play and playscapes*. Albany, NY: Delmar.

Frost, J. L., & Klein, B., L. (1983). *Children's play and playgrounds*. Austin, TX: Playscapes International.

Gardner, H. (1983). *Frames of mind: The theory of multiple intelligences*. New York: Basic Books.

Gartrell, D. (1987). Punishment or Guidance? *Young Children, 42*(3), 55–61.

Gearheart, B., Mullen, R. C., & Gearheart, C. (1993). *Exceptional individuals*. Pacific Grove, CA: Brooks/Cole.

Gibbons, J. H. (Dir.). (1988). Power on! New tools for teaching and learning. *OTA Report Brief*. Washington, DC: U.S. Congress, Office of Technology Assessment.

Gibbons, J. H. (Dir.) (1989). Linking for learning: A new course for education. *OTA Report Brief*.

Washington, DC: U.S. Congress, Office of Technology Assessment.

Gibson, D. (1989). Below the grade. *Triangle Business, 5*(27), 1–6.

Gibson, D. (1989). A state at risk. *Triangle Business, 5*(12), 1–8.

Gilbert, J. G. (1989). A two-week K–6 interdisciplinary unit. In H. H. Jacobs (Ed.), *Interdisciplinary curriculum: Design and implementation* (pp. 46–51). Alexandria, VA: Association for Supervision and Curriculum Development.

Gillings, H., & Griffiths, D. (1989). Problem Solving. In R. Crompton (Ed.), *Computers and the primary curriculum 3–13*. Philadelphia: Falmer Press.

Glasser, W. (1990). *The quality school: Managing students without coercion*. New York: Harper & Row.

Goleman, D., Kaufman, P., & Ray, M. (1992). *The creative spirit*. New York: Dutton.

Gollnick, D. M., & Chinn, P. C. (1990). *Multicultural education in a pluralistic society*. New York: Macmillan.

Gordon, A., & Browne, K. W. (1993). *Beginnings and beyond: Foundations in early childhood education* (3rd ed.). Albany, NY: Delmar.

Grace, C., & Shores, E. (1992). *The portfolio and its use*. Little Rock, AR: Southern Association on Children Under Six.

Grady, E. (1992). *The portfolio approach to assessment*. Bloomington, IN: Phi Delta Kappa Educational Foundation.

Graves, M. (1989). *The teacher's idea book*. Ypsilanti, MI: High/Scope Press.

Graves, R. (1987). *The R.I.F. guide to encouraging young readers*. Garden City, NY: Doubleday.

Greenberg, M. (1979). *Your child needs music*. Englewood Cliffs, NJ: Prentice-Hall.

Gullo, D. (1991). *Use ongoing evaluation for decision making and curriculum development*. Unpublished manuscript.

Guteck, G. L. (1991). *Cultural foundations of education*. New York: Macmillan.

Guy, K. A. (1991). *Welcome the child*. Washington, DC: Children's Defense Fund.

Hall, N. (1989). *Writing with reason*. Portsmouth, NH: Heinemann.

Hamilton, L. (1989). *Child's play*. New York: Crown.

Hardacre, J. (1991). *Increasing teachers' competence in observing, assessing, and reporting children's play in education settings*. Doctoral practicum, Nova University, Fort Lauderdale, FL. (ERIC Document Reproduction Service No. ED 340 464).

Harlan, J. (1988). *Science experiences for the early childhood years* (5th ed.). New York: Macmillan.

Harms, T, Clifford, R. M., & Cryer, D. (1980). Early Childhood Environment Rating Scale. New York: Teachers College Press.

Harry, B. (1992). *Cultural diversity, families, and the special education system*. New York: Teachers College Press.

Hatcher, B. (1983). Putting young cartographers "on the map." *Childhood Education, 59*, 311–315.

Hatcher, B. (1985). Children's homes and neighborhoods: Untapped treasures from the past. *The Social Studies, 75*, 155–159.

Hauser-Cram, P., Pierson, D. E., Walker, D. K., & Tivnan, T. (1991). *Early education in the public schools*. San Francisco: Jossey-Bass.

Head Start nutrition education curriculum. (1989). Upper Montclair, NJ: Montclair State College. (ERIC Document Reproduction Service No. ED 325 238).

Heining-Boynton, Audrey L. (1992, Spring). Early childhood foreign language education: Developmental perspectives and implementation guidelines. *Kappa Delta Pi Record*, p. 74.

Heller, M. F. (1991). *Reading-writing connections: From theory to practice*. White Plains, NY: Longman.

Hendrick, J. (1992). *The whole child* (5th ed.). New York: Macmillan.

Henninger, M. L. (1991). Play revisited: A critical element of kindergarten curriculum. *Early Child Development and Care, 70*, 63–71.

Hennings, D. G. (1990). *Communication in action: Teaching the language arts* (4th ed.). Boston: Houghton Mifflin.

Herman, J. L., Aschbacher, P., & Winters, L. (1992). *A practical guide to alternative assessment*. Alexandria, VA: Association for Supervision and Curriculum Development.

Heron, B., Singer, K. H., Barker, B., & Lunsford, D. G. (1989). *A memorandum of understanding between Triangle J. Council of Governments and Orange County School Board regarding the creation of a model school.* Hillsborough, NC: Orange County Public Schools.

Herr, J., & Libby, Y. (1990). *Designing creative materials for young children.* San Diego, CA: Harcourt Brace Jovanovich.

Hess, R. D., & Croft, D. J. (1981). *Teachers of young children* (3rd ed.). Boston: Houghton Mifflin.

Hildebrand, V. (1980). *Guiding young children* (2nd ed.) New York: Macmillan.

Hildebrand, V. (1981). *Introduction of early childhood education* (3rd ed.). New York: Macmillan.

Hillebrand, V. (1993). *Management of child development centers* (3rd ed.). New York: Macmillan.

Hinitz, B. S. F. (1992). *Teaching social studies to the young child.* New York: Garland.

Hirsch, E. (1984). *The block book.* Washington, DC: National Association for the Education of Young Children.

Hohman, M., Banet, B., & Weikart, D. P. (1979). *Young children in action.* Ypsilanti, MI: High/Scope Educational Research Foundation.

Holtje, A. K., & Szeglin, C. B. (1991). *Creativities! Art activities across the elementary curriculum.* West Nyack, NY: Parker.

Houle, G. B. (1987). *Learning centers for young children.* West Greenwich, RI: Consortium.

Howe, K. R., & Miramontes, O. B. (1992). *The ethics of special education.* New York: Teachers College Press.

Howell, K. W., Fox, S. L., & Morehead, M. K. (1993). *Curriculum-based evaluation* (2nd ed.). Pacific Grove, CA: Brooks/Cole.

Hull, R. H., & Dilka, K. I (Eds.). (1984). *The hearing-impaired child in school.* Orlando, FL: Grune & Stratton.

Hunt, T., & Renfro, N. (1982). *Puppetry in early childhood education.* Austin, TX: Renfro Studios.

Hutt, C., & Bhavnani, R. (1976). Predictions from play. In J. S. Bruner et al. (Eds.), *Play: Its role in development and evolution* (pp. 216–219). New York: Basic Books.

Hymes, J. L., Jr. (1991). *Early childhood education: Twenty years in review—A look at 1971–1990.* Washington, DC: National Association for the Education of Young Children.

Instructional Materials Services. (1989). Chris Held's 4–5 combination classroom, Phanton Lake Elementary School. [Video]. *Model for the future: The self-contained integrated technology classroom.* Bellevue, WA: Bellevue Public Schools.

Instructor Books. (1981). *Instructor's big holiday book.* New York: Instructor.

International Society for Technology in Education (ISTE). (1990, October). Evidence of the effectiveness of educational technology. In L. Braun (Ed.), *Vision TEST: (Technologically enriched schools of tomorrow)* (pp. 7–10). Eugene, OR: Author.

Irving, J., & Currie, R. (1986). *Mudluscious: Stories and activities featuring food for preschool children.* Littleton, CO: Libraries Unlimited.

Irwin, D. M., & Bushnell, M. M. (1980). *Observational strategies for child study.* Fort Worth, TX: Holt, Rinehart & Winston.

Isenberg, J., & Jalongo, M. J. (1993). *Creative expression and play in the early childhood curriculum.* New York: Macmillan.

Jacobs, H. H. (1989a). The growing need for interdisciplinary curriculum content. In H. H. Jacobs (Ed.), *Interdisciplinary curriculum: Design and implementation* (pp. 1–11). Alexandria, VA: Association for Supervision and Curriculum Development.

Jalongo, M. R. (1985). When young children move. *Young Children, 6,* 51–57.

Jantz, R. K., & Klawitter, G. (1985). Inquiry and curriculum change: Perceptions of school and college/university faculty. *Theory and Research in Social Education, 13*(2), 61–72.

Jarolimek, J. (1986). *Social studies in elementary education* (7th ed.). New York: Macmillan.

Jarolimek, J., & Parker, W. (1993). *Social studies in elementary education* (9th ed.). New York: Macmillan.

Jenkins, K. S. (1982). *Kinder-krunchies.* Pleasant Hill, CA: Discovery Toys.

Jewel, M. G., & Zintz, M. V. (1986). *Learning to read naturally.* Dubuque, IA: Kendall/Hunt.

Johnson, B. (1978). *Cup cooking*. Lake Alfred, FL: Early Educators Press.

Johnson, H. (1982). *The act of block building*. New York: Bank Street.

Johnson, J. E., Christie, J. F., & Yawkey, T. D. (1987). *Play and early childhood development*. Glenview, IL: Scott Foresman.

Joint Committee on Standards for Educational Evaluation. (1981). *Standards for evaluations of educational programs, projects, and materials*. New York: McGraw-Hill.

Kalman, B. (1991). *Early schools*. New York: Crabtree.

Kamii, C., & Williams, C. K. (1986). How do children learn by handling objects? *Young Children, 41*(1), 23–26.

Katz, L. (Ed.). (1984). *Current topics in early childhood education*. Norwood, NJ: Ablex.

Katz, L., & Chard, S. (1989). *Engaging children's minds: The project approach*. Norwood, NJ: Ablex.

Khayrallah, M. A., & Van Den Melraher, M. (1987). *Logo* programming and the acquisition of cognitive skills. *Journal of Computer-Based Instruction, 14*(4), 133–137.

Knapp, M. S., & Shields, P. M. (Eds.) (1991). *Better schooling for the children of poverty: Alternatives to conventional wisdom*. Berkeley, CA: McCutchan.

Komoske, P. K. (Dir.). (1990). *The integrated instructional systems report*. Water Mill, NY: Education Products Information Exchange Institute.

Koppelman, P. (1976). *The house that Jack and Jill built*. San Francisco: Rosenburg Foundation. (ERIC Document Reproduction Service No. EDI 149 013).

Kostelnik, M. J., Soderman, A. K., Whiren, A. P. (1993). *Developmentally appropriate programs in early childhood education*. New York: Macmillan.

Kostelnik, M. J., Whiren, A. P., & Stein, L. C. (1986). Living with He-Man. *Young Children, 4*, 3–9.

Krathwohl, D. R., Bloom, B. S., & Masia, B. B. (1964). *Taxonomy of educational objectives: The classification of educational goals: Handbook II, Affective domain*. New York: McKay.

Krogh, S., (1990). *The integrated early childhood curriculum*. New York: McGraw-Hill.

Kulik, J. A., Kulik, C. C., & Cohen, P. A. (1980). Effectiveness of computer-based college teaching: A meta-analysis of findings. *Review of Educational Research, 50*(4), 525–544.

Kulik, J. A., Kulik, C. C., & Shwalb, B. J. (1986). The effectiveness of computer-based adult education: A meta-analysis. *Review of Educational Research, 2*(2), 235–252.

Lansing, K., & Richards, A. E. (1981). *The elementary teacher's art handbook*. New York: Holt, Rinehart & Winston.

Lay-Dopyera, M., & Dopyera, J. (1990a). *Becoming a teacher of young children* (3rd ed.). Lexington, MA: D.C. Heath.

Lay-Dopyera, M., & Dopyera, J. (1990b). *Instructor's manual to accompany becoming a teacher of young children* (4th ed.). New York: McGraw-Hill.

Lay-Dopyera, M., & Dopyera J. (1993). *Becoming a teacher of young children* (5th ed.). New York: McGraw-Hill.

Leeper, S. D., Witherspoon, R. L., & Day, B. (1984). *Good schools for young children* (5th ed.). New York: Macmillan.

Leiblum, M. D. (1982). Factors sometimes overlooked and underestimated in the selection and success of CAL as an instructional medium. *AEDS Journal, 15*, 67–77.

Lillie, D. L., Hannum, W. H., & Stuck, G. B. (1989). Computers and instruction in the schools of tomorrow. In D. L. Lillie (Ed.), *Computers and effective instruction* (p. 73). White Plains, NY: Longman.

Lindberg, L., & Swedlow, R. (1980). *Early childhood education: A guide for observation and participation* (2nd ed.). Boston: Allyn and Bacon.

Lindstrom, M. (1957). *A study of normal development in children's models of visualization*. Berkeley: University of California Press.

Long, J. D., & Frye, V. H. (1989). *Making it til Friday* (4th ed.). Princeton, NJ: Princeton Book Company.

Lowenfeld, V., & Britain, W. (1982). *Creative and mental growth* (7th ed.). New York: Macmillan.

Lynch-Brown, C., & Tomlinson C. M. (1993). *Essentials of children's literature*. Needham Heights, MA: Allyn and Bacon.

Lynch-Fraser, D. (1982). *Dance play: Creative movement for very young children*. New York: Walker.

Madaus, G. F., & Tan, A. G. (1993). The growth of assessment: Challenges and achievements of American education. *1993 ASCD Yearbook* (p. 53). Alexandria, VA: Association for Supervision and Curriculum Development.

Mallet, J. J. (1975). *Classroom reading games activities kit*. West Nyack, NY: Center for Applied Research in Education.

Maness, B. (1992). Assessment in early childhood education. *Kappa Delta Pi Record, 28*(3), 77–80.

Manhattanville Music Curriculum Program. (1970). *MMCP final report*. Washington, DC: U.S. Office of Education. (ERIC Document Reproduction Service No. ED 045 865).

Marion, M. (1991). *Guidance of young children*. (3rd ed.). New York: Macmillan.

Mark, M. L. (1986). *Contemporary music education*. New York: Schirmer.

Marotz, L. R., Cross, M. Z., & Rush, J. M. (1993). *Health, safety & nutrition for the young child* (3rd ed.). Albany, NY: Delmar.

Marshall, H. (1989). The development of self-concept. *Young Children, 44*, 44–49.

Martin, D. S. (1985). Ethnocentrism revisited: Another look at a persistent problem. *Social Education, 49*, 604–609.

Martorella, P. (1985). *Elementary social studies: Developing reflective, competent, and concerned citizens*. Boston: Little, Brown.

Mason, J. M., & Au, K. H. (1986). *Reading instruction for today*. Glenview, IL: Scott Foresman.

Mast, L., Rowland, B., & White, B. (1992). Evaluating teachers of young children. In B. Day (Ed.), *North Carolina Public Schools' early childhood programs: A call for leadership* (pp. 151–172). Charlotte: North Carolina Association for Supervision and Curriculum Development.

Maxim, G. (1983). *Social studies and the elementary school child*. Columbus, OH: Merrill.

Maxim, G. (1985). Creativity: Encouraging the spirit of wonder and magic. In G. Maxim (Ed.), *The very young* (pp. 359–402).

Maxim, G. (1993). *The very young* (4th ed.). New York: Macmillan.

Mayesky, M. (1986). *Creative activities for children in the early primary grades*. Albany, NY: Delmar.

Mayesky, M., Neuman, D., & Wlodkowski, R. J. (1985). *Creative activities for young children* (3rd ed.). Albany, NY: Delmar.

McCarthy, B. (1980). *The 4MAT system*. Oakbrook, IL: Excel.

McCaslin, N. (1990). *Creative drama in the classroom* (5th ed.). White Plains, NY: Longman.

McDonald, D. (1979). *Music in our lives: The early years*. Washington, DC: National Association for the Education of Young Children.

McDonald, D., & Simons, G. (1989). *Musical growth and development: Birth through six*. New York: Schirmer.

McDowell, L. J. (1989). *Microcomputers in education*. Report to Dr. Bob Bridges, Superintendent, Wake County Schools, Raleigh, North Carolina.

McGill-Franzen, A. (1993). *Shaping the preschool agenda*. Albany: State University of New York Press.

McGinnis, E., & Goldstein, A. P. (1984). *Skillstreaming the elementary school child*. Champaign, IL: Research Press.

McGowan, T. M. (1985). *Teaching about elections in Indiana schools*. Unpublished doctoral dissertation, Indiana University. Bloomington. (ERIC Document Reproduction Service No. ED 260 998).

Media Evaluation Services. (1988). *Criteria for evaluating computer courseware*. Raleigh: Division of Media and Technology Services, North Carolina Department of Public Instruction.

Media Evaluation Services. (1992). *Advisory list—Instructional technology*. Raleigh: Division of Media and Technology Services, North Carolina Department of Public Instruction.

Meisels, S. J. (1992). *The work sampling system: An overview*. Ann Arbor: University of Michigan, Center for Human Growth and Development.

Meisels, S. J., & Steele, D. (1991). *The early childhood portfolio collection process.* Ann Arbor: The University of Michigan Center for Human Growth and Development.

Meyen, E. L. (1990). *Exceptional children in today's schools* (2nd ed.). Denver: Love.

Meyen, E. L., Vergason, G. A., & Whelan, R. J. (Eds.). (1988). *Effective instructional strategies for exceptional children.* Denver: Love.

Michaelis, J. U. (1976). *Social studies for children in a democracy* (6th ed.). Englewood Cliffs, NJ: Prentice-Hall.

Miller, J. W. (1985). Teaching map skills: Theory, research, practice. *Social Education, 49,* 30–31.

Mitchell, G. L., Bailey, N.C., & Dewsnap, L. F. (1992). *I am! I can! Keys to quality child care.* Chelsea, MA: TelShare.

Molinhar, A. R. (1990, November). Computers in education: A historical perspective of the unfinished task. *Technological Horizons in Education (THE) Journal, 18*(4), 77–93.

Moore, J. G. (1968). *The many ways of seeing.* Cleveland: World Publishing.

Morris, S. (1990, August). Sand and water table buying guide. *Child-Care-Information-Exchange,* pp. 53–60.

Morrison, G. S. (1988). *Early childhood education today* (4th ed.). Columbus, OH: Merrill.

Morrison, G. S. (1991). *Early childhood education today* (5th ed.). New York: Macmillan.

Morrison, G. S., & McClune, R. (1991). *Instructor's guide to accompany early childhood education today* (5th ed.). New York: Macmillan.

Morrissett, I. (Ed.) (1982). *Social studies in the 1980s: A report of project Span.* Alexandria, VA: Association for Supervision and Curriculum Development.

Morrow, L. M. (1989). Designing the classroom to promote literacy development. In L. M. Morrow (Ed.), *Literacy development in the early years: Helping children read and write.* Englewood Cliffs, NJ: Prentice-Hall.

Morrow, L. M. (1993). *Literacy development in the early years.* (2nd ed.). Needham Heights, MA: Allyn and Bacon.

Murdock, C. V. (1984). *Macmillan early skills program: Writing skills.* New York: Macmillan.

Myers, C. (1991, October). Touch the world with kids-92. *Instructor Magazine,* pp. 34–36.

National Association for the Education of Young Children (NAEYC). (1986, September). Position statement on developmentally appropriate practice in programs for 4- and 5-year-olds. *Young Children,* pp. 20–29.

National Association for the Education of Young Children (NAEYC). (1988, January). NAEYC position statement on developmentally appropriate practice in the primary grades, serving 5- through 8-year-olds. *Young Children,* 64–84.

National Association for the Education of Young Children (NAEYC). (1986a). *Accreditation criteria and procedures.* Washington, DC.

National Association for the Education of Young Children and National Association of Early Childhood Specialists in State Departments of Education. (1991). *Guidelines for appropriate curriculum content and assessment in programs serving children ages 3 through 8.* [#725]. Washington, DC: NAEYC.

National Association of Elementary School Principals (NAESP). (1990). *Early childhood education and the elementary school principal: Standards for quality programs for young children.* Alexandria, VA: Author.

National Commission on Testing and Public Policy (NCTPP). (1990). *From gatekeeper to gateway: Transforming testing in America.* Chestnut Hill, MA: Author, Boston College.

National Goals Panel Resource Group. (1991). *Interim report: Readiness for school.* Washington, DC: National Governors Association.

Natriello, G., McDill, E. L., & Pallas, A. M. (1990). *Schooling disadvantaged children.* New York: Teachers College Press.

Neiderman, B. R., & Kuhn, J. N. (1993). *Star light, star bright.* Menlo Park, CA: Addison-Wesley.

Nelsen, J. (1987). *Positive discipline.* New York: Ballantine.

Neuman, S. B., & Roskos, K. A. (1993). *Language and literacy learning in the early years.* Fort Worth, TX: Harcourt Brace Jovanovich.

Newman, G. (1984). *Teaching children music* (2nd ed.). Dubuque, IA: William C. Brown.

North Carolina Department of Public Instruction. (1985). *North Carolina competency-based curriculum, K–3*. Raleigh, NC: Author.

North Carolina Department of Public Instruction (1992, July). *Computer skills curriculum*. Raleigh: Author.

Norton, D. E. (1985). *The effective teaching of language arts* (2nd ed.) Columbus, OH: Merrill.

Oklahoma State Department of Education. (1983). *Growing: Pre-kindergarten through 2nd grade*. Oklahoma City: Author. (ERIC Document Reproduction Service No. ED 239 711).

Oklahoma State Department of Education. (1985). *Growing: Pre-kindergarten through 2nd grade*. Oklahoma City: Author. (ERIC Document Reproduction Service No. ED 280 576).

Oliver, S. D., & Musgrave, K. O. (1984). *Nutrition: A teacher sourcebook of integrated activities*. Newton, MA: Allyn and Bacon.

Olson-Ness, J. (1992). *Teaching strategies for getting students actively involved*. Alexandria, VA: Association for Supervision and Curriculum Development.

Orange County Schools Model School Technology Committee educational recommendations. (1990). Hillsborough, NC: Orange County Schools.

Orange County Schools Technology for Learning. (1991). Hillsborough, NC: Orange County Schools.

Paine, I. L. (1949). *Art aids* (5th ed.). Minneapolis: Burgess.

Palmer, W. S. (1992, Spring). The writing process of young children: A developmental perspective. *Kappa Delta Pi Record*, p. 80.

Papousek, M. (1982, April). *Musical elements in mother-infant dialogues*. Paper presented at the International Conference on Infant Studies, Austin, Texas.

Pappas, C. C., Kiefer, B. Z., & Levstik, L. S. (1990). *An integrated language perspective in the elementary school. Theory in action*. White Plains, NY: Longman.

Parker, J., & Asher, S. (1987). Peer relations and later personal adjustment: Are low-accepted children at risk? *Psychological Bulletin, 102*, 357–389.

Pasternak, M. G. (1979). *Helping kids learn multicultural concepts*. Champaign, IL: Research Press.

Pattillo, J., & Vaughan, E. (1992). *Learning centers for child-centered classrooms*. [NEA Early Childhood Education Series.] Washington, DC: National Education Association.

Paulsen, M. F. (1987–1988). In search of a virtual school. *Technological Horizons in Education Journal, 32*(4), 71–76.

Paulson, F. L., Paulson, P. R., & Meyer, C. A. (1991). What makes a portfolio a portfolio? *Educational Leadership, 48*, 60–63.

Perrone, V. (Ed.). (1991) *Expanding student assessment*. Alexandria, VA: Association for Supervision and Curriculum Development.

Peters, G. D., & Miller, R. F. (1982). *Music teaching and learning*. White Plains, NY: Longman.

Peters, R. (1981). *Infusing global awareness components of environmental education programs into the kindergarten–grade twelve social studies curriculum for purposes of affecting student attitudes and perspectives*. (ERIC Document Reproduction Service No. ED 205 392).

Piaget, J. (1950). *The psychology of the child*. New York: Basic Books.

Piaget J., & Inhelder, B. (1969). *The psychology of the child*. New York: Basic Books.

Pitcher, E. G., Feinburgh, S. G., & Alexander, D. (1984). *Helping young children learn* (4th ed.). Columbus, OH: Merrill.

Platts, M. E. (1972). *Launch*. Stevensville, MI: Educational Service.

Prillaman, A. R. (1992, Spring). Infant/toddler care: Future considerations in public education. *Kappa Delta Pi Record*, p. 85.

Provenzo, E., Jr., & Brett, A. (1983). *The complete block book*. Syracuse, NY: Syracuse University Press.

Raebeck, L., & Wheeler, L. (1964). *New approaches to music in the elementary school*. Dubuque, IA: William C. Brown.

Rainbow, E. (1981). A final report on the three year investigation of the rhythmic abilities of young children. *Bulletin of the Council for Research in Music Education, 66*, 69–73.

Raines, S. C., & Canady, R. J. (1989). *Story stretchers: Activities to expand children's favorite books*. Mt. Rainier, MD: Gryphon House.

Raines, S. C., & Canady, R. J. (1991). *More story stretchers: More activities to expand children's favorite books*. Mt. Rainier, MD: Gryphon House.

Ramsey, M. E., & Bayless, K. M. (1980). *Kindergarten: Programs and practices*. St. Louis: Mosby.

Read, H. (1945). *Education through art*. New York: Pantheon.

Read, K., Gardner, P., & Mahler, B. C. (1987). *Early childhood programs: Human relationships and learning* (8th ed.). Fort Worth, TX: Holt, Rinehart & Winston.

Read, K., Gardner, P., & Mahler, B. C. (1993). *Early childhood programs, human relationships and learning* (9th ed.). Chicago: Holt, Rinehart & Winston.

Read, K., & Patterson, J. (1980). *The nursery school & kindergarten*. (7th ed.). New York: Holt, Rinehart & Winston.

Roberts, L. (1989, February). *Power on! New tools for teaching and learning*. Presentation on this Congressional Office of Technology Assessment publication to the North Carolina Educational Technology Conference, Greensboro.

Roblyer, M. D., Castine, W. H., & King, F. J. (Eds.). (1988). Assessing the impact of computer-based instruction: A review of recent research. *Computers in the Schools, 5*(2). [Special issue].

Rogers, D. L. (1985). Relationships between block play and social development of young children. *Early Childhood Development and Care, 20*, 245–261.

Rogers, D., & Zimmerman, M. (1990 *Elementary language arts*. Dallas: Houghton Mifflin.

Roopnarine, J. L., & Johnson J. E. (Eds.). (1993) *Approaches to early childhood education* (2nd ed.) New York: Macmillan.

Rousseau, J. J. (1957). *Emile*. New York: Dutton.

Rozmajzl, M., & Boyer-White, R. (1990). *Music fundamentals, methods, and materials for the elementary classroom teacher*. White Plains, NY: Longman.

Rudolph, M., & Cohen, D. H. (1984). *Kindergarten and early school* (2nd ed.). Englewood Cliffs, NJ: Prentice-Hall.

Safford, P. L. (1989). *Integrated teaching in early childhood*. White Plains, NY: Longman.

Sampson, M., Van Allen, R., & Sampson, M. (1991). *Pathways to literacy*. Orlando, FL: Holt, Rinehart & Winston.

Sanford, A. R., Williams, J. M., James, J. C., & Overton, A. K. (1983). *A planning guide to the preschool curriculum* (rev. ed.). Winston-Salem, NC: Kaplan.

Saracho, O. N. (1991). Educational play in early childhood education. *Early Child Development and Care, 66*, 45–64.

Schafer, R. M. (1976). *Creative music education: A handbook for the modern music teacher*. New York: Schirmer.

Schlereth, T. J. (1980). *Artifacts and the American past*. Nashville, TN: American Association for State and Local History.

Schug, M., Todd, R., & Beery, T. (1984). Why kids don't like social studies. *Social Education, 48*, 382–387.

Schultz, T. (1988). *Right from the start: The report of the NASBE Task Force on Early Childhood Education*. Alexandria, VA: National Association of State Boards of Education.

Schweinhart, L. J. (1986). Research findings support child development programs. *Educational Leadership, 44*(3), 16.

Schweinhart, L. J., Weikart, D. P., & Larner, M. B. (1986). Consequences of three curriculum models through age 15. *Early Childhood Research Quarterly, 1*, 15–35.

Seefeldt, C. (1980). *Teaching young children*. Englewood Cliffs, NJ: Prentice-Hall.

Seefeldt, C. (1984). *Social studied for the preschool-primary child* (2nd ed.). Columbus, OH: Merrill.

Seefeldt, C. (1993). *Social studies for the preschool-primary child* (4th ed.). New York: Macmillan.

Seefeldt, C., & Barbour, N. (1990). *Early childhood education: An introduction* (2nd ed.). Columbus, OH: Merrill.

Self, E. (1977). *Teaching significant social studies in the elementary school*. Chicago: Rand McNally.

Selph, A., & Street, B. G. (1975). *Alphabet soup*. Durham, NC: American Printers.

Sherwood, E. A. (1990). *From mudpies to magnets*. Mt. Rainier, MD: Gryphon House.

Shores, E. F. (1992). *Explorers' classrooms*. Little Rock, AR: Southern Association on Children Under Six.

Shultz, T. (1988). *Right from the start: The report of the NASBE Task Force on Early Childhood Education*. Alexandria, VA: National Association of State Boards of Education.

Silverman, R., Welty, W. M., & Lyon, S. (1991). *Instructor's manual to accompany case studies for teacher problem solving*. New York: McGraw-Hill.

Skeen, P., Garner, A., & Cartwright, S. (1984). *Woodworking for young children*. Washington, DC: National Association for the Education of Young Children.

Skelton, S. C., & Hamilton, A. C. (1990). *Using puppets with young children*. Paper presented at the Annual Conference of the Alabama Association for Young Children, Mobile, Alabama. (ERIC Document Reproduction Service No. ED 317 275).

Slavin, R. E., Karwait, N. L., & Madden, N. A. (1989). *Effective programs for students at risk*. Boston: Allyn and Bacon.

Smith, B., & Williams, S. (1983). *Once upon a year*. Houston, TX: Learning Innovations.

Smith, C. A. (1982). *Promoting the social development of young children*. Palo Alto, CA: Mayfield.

Southern Association on Children Under Six (SACUS). (1990). *Developmentally appropriate assessment*. Little Rock, AR: Author.

Spache, G. D., & Spache, E. B. (1986). *Reading in the elementary school* (5th ed.). Boston: Allyn and Bacon.

Spandel, V., & Stiggins, R. J. (1990). *Creating writers: Linking assessment & writing instruction*. White Plains, NY: Longman.

Speas, J., Martelli, L., Graham, A., & Cherryholmes, L. (1983). *Communities*. New York: McGraw-Hill.

Stanley, W. (1985a). *Review of research in social studies education 1976–1983*. [Bulletin 75]. Washington, DC: National Council for Social Studies.

Stanley, W. B. (1985b). *Social studies research: Theory into practice*. Washington, DC: National Institute of Education. (ERIC Document Reproduction Service No. ED 268 064).

Stephens, L. (1983). *Developing thinking skills through real-life activities*. Boston: Allyn and Bacon.

Sullivan, M. (1982). *Feeling strong, feeling free: Movement exploration for young children*. Washington, DC: Association for the Education of Young Children.

Superka, D., Hawke, S., & Morressett, I. (1980). The current and future states of the social studies. *Social Education, 44*, 362–369.

Suzuki, S. (1969). *Nurtured by love*. New York: Exposition Press.

Swift, M.S., & Spivack, G. (1975). *Alternative teaching strategies*. Champaign, IL: Research Press.

Taylor, B. J. (1985). *A child goes forth*. (6th ed.). Minneapolis: Burgess.

Taylor, B. J. (1993a). *Early childhood program management: People and procedures* (2nd ed.). New York: Macmillan.

Taylor, B. J. (1993b). *Science everywhere: Opportunities for very young children*. Fort Worth, TX: Harcourt Brace Jovanovich.

Templeton, S. (1991). *Teaching the integrated language arts*. Dallas: Houghton Mifflin.

Thompson, D. (1981). *Easy woodstuff for kids*. Mt. Rainier, MD: Gryphon House.

Tierney, R. J., Carter, L., & Desai, L. (1991). *Portfolio assessment in the reading-writing classroom*. Norwood, MA: Christopher-Gordon.

Toward the thinking curriculum: Current cognitive research. (1989). Washington, DC: Association for Supervision and Curriculum Development.

Travis, N., & Perreault, J. (1981). *Day care personnel management*. Mt. Rainier, MD: Gryphon House.

Trostle, S. L., & Yawkey, T. D. (19891). *Creative thinking and the education of young children: The fourth basic skill*. (ERIC Document Reproduction Service No. ED 204 105).

Van Cleaf, D. W. (1985). The environment as a data source: Map activities for young children. *Social Education, 50*, 145–146.

Van der Zande, I. (1990). *1, 2, 3 . . . The toddler years*. Santa Cruz, CA: Santa Cruz Toddler Care Center.

Van Hoorn, J., Nourot, P., Scales B., & Alward, K. (1993). *Play at the center of the curriculum.* New York: Macmillan.

Viguers, R. H. et al. (1958). *Illustrators of children's books 1946–1956.* Boston: Horn Book.

Walsh, H. (1980). *Introducing the young child to the social world.* New York: Macmillan.

Warlick, D. (1988). What does research say? *On-Line, 2*(4), 4–6.

Warren, J. (1983). *Language games: Early learning activities.* Palo Alto, CA: Monday Morning Books.

Warren, J. (1984). *Storytime early learning activities.* Palo Alto, CA: Monday Morning Books.

Wasik, B. H. (1992, Spring). At risk young children enter school: What are the developmental implications? *Kappa Delta Pi Record,* p. 87.

Webb, T. B. (1992). Multi-age grouping in the early years: Building upon children's developmental strengths. *Kappa Delta Pi Record, 28*(3), 90–93.

Weikart, D. P., Epstein, I. S., Schweinhart, L. J., & Bond, J. T. (1978). Ypsilanti Preschool Curriculum Demonstration Project: Preschool years and longitudinal results. *Monographs of the High/Scope Educational Research Foundation* (vol. 4). Ypsilanti, MI: High/Score Foundation.

Weis, L., Altbach, P. G., Kelly, G. P., & Petrie, H. G. (Eds.). (1991). *Critical perspectives on early childhood education.* Albany: State University of New York Press.

Westley, J. (1991). *ThemeWorks: Houses.* Sunnyvale, CA: Creative Publications.

Wilkerson, R. (1986). *An evaluation of the effects of the 4MAT system of instruction on academic achievement and retention of learning.* Unpublished doctoral dissertation, University of North Carolina at Chapel Hill.

Wilkerson, R. (1992). Integrated teaching and learning: A developmental perspective. *Kappa Delta Pi Record, 28*(3), 93–96.

Williams, S. R., & Worthington-Roberts, B. S. (1992). *Nutrition throughout the life cycle* (2nd ed.) St. Louis: Mosby-Year Book.

Wilson, B. L. (1983). *Effect of task and authority structures on student task engagement.* Paper presented at the annual meeting of the American Educational Research Association, Montreal, Quebec, Canada. (ERIC Document Reproduction Service No. ED 230 416).

Winner, E. (1982). *Invented worlds: The psychology of the arts.* Cambridge, MA: Harvard University Press.

Wirth, A. G. (1993). Education and work: The choices we face. *Phi Delta Kappan, 74*(5), 361–366.

Wolfgang, C. H., Mackender, B., Wolfgang, M. E. (1981). *Growing and learning through play.* New York: McGraw-Hill.

Wollons, R. (Ed.). (1993). *Children at risk in America.* Albany: State University of New York Press.

Women's Educational Equity Act Program. (1985). *Women as members of communities: Third grade social studies.* Washington, DC: Author. (ERIC Document Reproduction Service No. ED 260 998).

Yawkey, T. D. (1990). The role of adults in children's play. In S. C. Wortham & J. L. Frost, (Eds.), *Playgrounds for young children: National survey and perspectives.* Reston, VA: American Alliance for Health, Physical Education, Recreation, and Dance.

Yeargan, H., & Hatcher, B. (1985). The cupcake factory: Helping elementary students understand economics. *The Social Studies, 76,* 82–84.

Zeitler, W. R., & Barufaldi, J. P. (1988). *Elementary school science: A perspective for teachers.* White Plains, NY: Longman.

Zessoules, R., & Gardner, H. (1991). Authentic assessment: Beyond the buzzword and into the classroom. In V. Perrone (Ed.), *Expanding student assessment* (p. 47). Alexandria, VA: Association for Supervision and Curriculum Development.

Zimmerman, M. (1975). Research in music education with very young children. In J. M. Jennings (Ed.), *Music education for the very young child* (Report of the Fourth International Seminar on Research in Music Education) (p. 11). Wellington: New Zealand Council for Educational Research.

Zion, L., & Raker, B. (1986). *The physical side of thinking.* Springfield, IL: Charles C. Thomas.

Index

About the Author

Dr. Barbara D. Day is Professor and Chair, Curriculum and Instruction, and Director of the Carolina Teaching Fellows Program at the University of North Carolina – Chapel Hill.

Professor Day is a former early childhood teacher, elementary school principal, and assistant superintendent of schools. She has served as chair of Early Childhood Education, Teaching and Learning, and (currently) Curriculum and Instruction at the University of North Carolina at Chapel Hill. Her textbooks are used at major universities and are translated into several foreign languages. She authored *Open Learning in Early Childhood Education, Early Childhood Education: Creative Learning,* 2nd edition, *Early Childhood Education: Creative Learning,* 3rd edition, and, with Leeper and Witherspoon, *Good Schools for Young Children,* 5th edition, published by Macmillan College Publishing Company. In addition, she is the author with Drake of *Early Childhood Education: Curriculum Organization and Classroom Management,* published by the Association for Supervision and Curriculum Development. She served as the national Early Childhood expert on ASCD's 1991 video staff development program, a 40-minute videotape program and Facilitator's Manual which won the CINE Golden Eagle Award. Dr. Day's research studies are numerous and have been published in a variety of educational journals.

Barbara Day is an international lecturer and traveler. She has studied early childhood education in many parts of the world, including Great Britain, the Scandinavian countries, Germany, Switzerland, Russia, China, Korea, Singapore, and Japan. Additionally, she has served at the national and international levels of several professional organizations, including Kappa Delta Pi, the Association for Supervision and Curriculum Development, and the Delta Kappa Gamma Society International, and has won leadership awards from Phi Delta Kappa and ASCD. Dr. Day was invited to become a member of the National Association of State Boards of Education's Early Childhood Education Task Force, which led to the publication of *Right From the Start*, a blueprint for the improvement of early childhood education throughout the United States. She has served as President of the Association for Supervision and Curriculum Development, and from 1988–1992 chaired ASCD's Policy Commission in Early Childhood Education, a commission composed of thirteen school districts from across the United States whose primary mission was the improvement of early childhood education programs. In addition, Professor Day regularly directs and serves as the keynote speaker for professional organizations, honor societies, and national curriculum study institutes throughout the United States and abroad.